Sacred Space and ...

The Politics, Culture and History of Shi`ite Islam

Juan Cole

I.B.Tauris *Publishers*
LONDON • NEW YORK

Published in 2002 by I.B. Tauris & Co Ltd
6 Salem Road, London W2 4BU
175 Fifth Avenue, New York, NY 10010
www.ibtauris.com

In the United States of America and in Canada distributed by
Palgrave Macmillan a division of St Martin's Press
175 Fifth Avenue, New York NY 10010

ISBN 186064 736 7 paperback
ISBN 186064 761 8 hardback

A full CIP record for this book is available from the British Library
A full CIP record for this book is available from the Library of Congress

Library of Congress catalog card: available

Printed and bound in Great Britain by MPG Books Ltd, Bodmin
Text prepared by the author as CRC

Dedication

To Nikki Keddie: teacher, mentor, pir.

Contents

1. Introduction   1

Early Modern Arab Shi`ites and Iran

2. The Shi`ites as an Ottoman Minority   16

3. Rival Empires of Trade and Shi`ism in Eastern Arabia   31

4. Jurisprudence: The Akhbari-Usuli Struggle   58

5. Indian Money and the Shi`ite Shrine Cities   78

6. Mafia, Mob and Shi`ism in Iraq (co-author: Moojan Momen)   99

India and the British Empire

7. The Shi`ite Discovery of the West   123

8. Women and the Making of Shi`ism   138

9. Sacred Space and Holy War: The Issue of Jihad   161

The Twentieth Century

10. Shi`ites as National Minorities   173

11. The Modernity of Theocracy   189

Notes   212

Suggestions for Further Reading   248

Index   251

Acknowledgements

I am grateful to many colleagues and friends for sharing their insights with me as I wrote this book. I owe an enormous debt to Nikki Keddie, to whom I dedicate it. Sohrab Behdad has always been willing to react to my thoughts on modern Iran, and especially its economic dimensions. I have learned a great deal from conversations and joint panel appearances with Abbas Amanat and Said Amir Arjomand. Roy Mottahedeh's encyclopedic knowledge of Iran and Shi`ism is matched only by his generosity in sharing it. Farhad Kazemi and Ali Banuaziz have always been supportive, as has Mohamad Tavakkoli-Targhi. Barbara Metcalf has been especially helpful over the years with regard to South Asian Islam. Werner Ende and Rainer Brunner kindly invited me to a conference in Freiburg in 1998 where I met for the first time some of the authors cited in the notes, below. I am grateful to Moojan Momen for graciously permitting me to reprint in this collection our co-authored article, "Mafia Mob and Shi`ism in Iraq." None of these scholars, of course, bears any guilt for the imperfections remaining in the present work.

I wish to thank the University of Michigan Office of the Vice Provost for Research and to the School of Letters, Sciences and the Arts and my own History Department for a subvention of the paperback version of this book.

My explorations in the modern history of Shi`ite Islam have progressed crabwise over the past 15 years. Much of the writing in this book has never before been published. I have attempted to bring the chapters that previously appeared as journal articles up to date where I thought it necessary, and to indicate in the notes the latest scholarship on the subject.

Chapter 3 was first published as "Rival Empires of Trade and Imami Shi`ism in Eastern Arabia 1300-1800," *International Journal of Middle East Studies* 19, 2 (1987):177-204 and appears here by the kind permission of Cambridge University Press. An earlier version of chapter 4 appeared as "Shi'i Clerics in Iraq and Iran 1722-1780: The Akhbari-Usuli Controversy Reconsidered," *Iranian Studies* 18, 1 (1985):3-34. A prior incarnation of chapter 5 was "'Indian Money' and the Shi'i Shrine Cities of Iraq 1786-1850," *Middle Eastern Studies* 22, 4 (1986):461-80. Chapter 6, co-authored with Moojan Momen, was published as "Mafia, Mob and Shi`ism in Iraq: The Rebellion of Ottoman Karbala 1824-1843," *Past and Present* 112 (August 1986):112-43, and we are grateful to the

Past and Present Society for permission to reprint it. Chapter 7 was published as "Invisible Occidentalism: 18th-Century Indo-Persian Constructions of the West," *Iranian Studies*, 25, nos. 3-4 (1992 [1993]): 3-16. A small portion of chapter 8 was published in a different form as "Shi'ite Noblewomen and Religious Innovation in Awadh," in Violette Graf, ed., *Lucknow through the Ages* (New Delhi: Oxford University Press, 1997). Harvard University Press has allowed "Sacred Space and Holy War in India," in Khalid Masud, Brinkley Messick and David Powers, eds., *Fatwa: Muftis and Interpretation in Muslim Societies* (Cambridge, Mass.: Harvard University Press, 1996), pp. 173-183, to appear as chapter 9.

1

Introduction

The rise of nation-states during the past two centuries has had a profound effect on the writing of history, which has increasingly been tied to artificial "national" frameworks. Stories that cannot be fit into the narrative of the rise of the nation have often been neglected by contemporary historians. Worse, some movements with an international aspect have been reconfigured as national or written about mainly as an element in the formation of particular nations. Thus, most writing about the Twelver branch of Shi`ite Islam after about 1500, when it became the official religion of Iran, has focused on Iranian Shi`ism. The history of Shi`ite minorities in Eastern Arabia, and in what is now Pakistan and Lebanon, was relatively neglected by historians until recently, and of all non-Iranian Twelver communities only those of India and Iraq have been treated at length in contemporary English-language scholarship (and this only during the past decade and a half). Yet, recovering the history of this important branch of Islam in these particular nations is only part of the task that historians must set themselves. Looking at Shi`ite Islam (and other major Islamic movements) outside the box of a national framework, at its international networks and the profound interactions they entail, is among the prime tasks of historians of religion. One historian has spoken of rescuing Chinese history from the nation.[1] I propose that we need to rescue Shi`ite Islam from the nation. Accordingly, this book has no national focus. It is concerned with intellectual and social developments among Arabic-speaking, Persian-speaking, and Urdu-speaking Shi`ites. It examines three arenas of Shi`ite activity, the Arab world, Iran and South Asia (India and later Pakistan) synoptically. That is, I try to keep the interactions between the three consistently in view. One of my readers once spoke of the "vertigo" induced by my alternation between Najaf in what is now Iraq and Lucknow in India, between Manama in Bahrain and Shiraz in Iran. I would argue in reply that this vertigo is a feeling induced by our habit of thinking within "national" categories, categories that are anachronistic if imported into the Middle East and South Asia before the twentieth century, and which obscure important developments even later on.

The interaction of early modern and modern Iranian Shi`ism with its neighbors and even further afield has been much greater than is usually recognized. It was a commonplace of an earlier generation of historians that when Iran's rulers promulgated the Shi`ite branch of Islam in the sixteenth century, it threw up a barrier to communication and trade between the Sunni east and west of the Islamic world. This thesis has the disadvantage of being untrue. It has the additional disadvantage of obscuring the ways in which Iran - throughout the Safavid (1501-1722), Qajar (1785-1925), Pahlevi (1926-1979) and Khomeinist eras - has continued to export and influence religious movements far beyond its borders. Shi`ite Iran was not a bulkhead but a fluid field of interaction, subject to outside influences but also sending tributaries abroad. Iranian Shi`ism exercised a profound influence in these centuries on many regions of the Arab East, South Asia, and Central Asia. This book looks at developments from 1500 to the present, though most chapters deal with the less-studied period before the twentieth century, and with the relatively little-studied Indian and Arab communities and their interactions with Iranian currents. What were the dynamics that allowed newly Shi`ite Iran under the Safavids to exercise religious influence over Iran's neighbors? What were the international implications of the turmoil in Iran of the eighteenth century, and then the restoration of state support for Shi`ism under the Qajars? What was the impact on the religion of the age of colonialism from the eighteenth to the early twentieth centuries? How did the "high modernist" state-building project of the Pahlevis affect the "Shi`ite International?" Finally, how have political Shi`ism and the Khomeinist revolution affected other Shi`ite communities? How did the state structures, political economies and communications networks of each of these eras affect the influences Iranians could bring to bear?

I want to underline that I do not see adherence to Shi`ism as a primordial identity, but rather as a socially constructed one into which individuals are mobilized in every generation or which they adopt for their own reasons. Shi`ites born into the faith have converted out of it to Sunnism, Christianity, the Baha'i faith, secularism, and Marxism. Converts hailing from Sunnism, Hinduism, Judaism, and Christianity have adopted it. Observers once tended to see Twelver Shi`ism as a stagnant tradition mired in rigidity, but the surprise of the new academic literature on it is that Shi`ism has arguably been growing significantly not only in the past five hundred years but in the past two hundred. The Shi`ite majority of Iraq (where they are estimated to be 55 percent of the population) results in large part from the conversion of Arab tribes in the south to this branch of Islam in the course of the nineteenth century. The

Punjabi Shi`ites of Pakistan probably also in the main derive from a conversion movement of the nineteenth century, from the Suhravardi Sufi order to Twelver Shi`ism. Because of demographic movements rather than conversion, Twelver Shi`ites are now a plurality (probably 40 percent or so) of the population of Lebanon, whereas in the nineteenth century they may have accounted for as little as six percent of the population of Mount Lebanon. Nor does Shi`ite Islam have a single essential essence. It is a diverse tradition. As a religion, it has been very different when practiced in pre-modern, semi-feudal societies, in capitalist dictatorships or democracies, and in the current Iranian theocracy. In every generation, the choice has had to be made, of whether to be Shi`ite and of what that might mean. The interaction of the Iranian community with its neighbors has been an important dynamic in those choices.

Who have the Shi`ites been in history? The split in Islam between Shi`ites and others goes back to the crisis of succession that followed the Prophet Muhammad's death. The partisans (*shi`a*) of the Prophet's son-in-law and cousin, `Ali ibn Abi Talib, supported his accession to power. A permanent constituency grew up for `Ali and his descendants, the House of the Prophet, which sought to transform hereditary charisma into political power. The Twelver line ended in exoteric history with Hasan al-`Askari, alleged to have a young son (Muhammad al-Mahdi) who disappeared into a supernatural realm and would return eventually to fill the world with justice. The Twelver branch afterwards developed as a scripturalist religion with ulama that often studied with Sunni scholars and used similar techniques to elucidate texts. The rest of the Muslims, rejecting the hereditary claims of the `Alid lines, recognized the prior rights of four early elected caliphs (only the last being `Ali himself), and then acknowledged the subsequent sultan-caliphs. Twelvers remained a minority most places, though various sects of Shi`ism gathered great numerical strength in medieval Syria, southern Iraq, and eastern Arabia, as well as some towns in Iran. In the eleventh century Isma'ili Shi`ites ruled Fatimid Egypt and Twelver Buyids ruled Iran and Iraq. But this interlude of Shi`ite power ended with the Turkish Saljuq invasions and the victory of the Sunni Ayyubids over the Crusaders and Fatimids.

The establishment of the Safavid dynasty in Iran from 1501 and the conversion of a majority of those who lived on the Iranian plateau to Twelver Shi`ism over the succeeding two centuries constituted among the more important religious developments in early modern Islam. The world historian William McNeill compared this development to the Protestant Reformation in Europe. Safavid Iran was a large country, more than three times the size of modern France, but it had a tiny population, at probably 5 million or so, compared to most of its powerful neighbors. Iran was nevertheless a relatively wealthy and influential state, able to fend off the

Ottomans, the Uzbeks, and the Mughals and even sometimes to grow at their expense. Its tribal army, made up of Turkmen cavalrymen who worshipped the Shi`ite Imams and wore read headgear (thus acquiring the name Qizilbash or redheads) was later supplemented by Georgian slave soldiers. Its lucrative silk trade, along with a powerful military, lent it importance in world affairs. Along with tribal armies and silk, however, its other most important impact was religious. Iran, like most of the Muslim world, had been a majority Sunni society until the Safavids made Shi`ism the state religion and promoted it for most of the succeeding two centuries.

If we think of Shi`ite Iran as like the body of a bird and the Shi`ite communities of India as its right wing, those of the Arab East constitute its left. The Safavid revolution had an immediate impact on the older, Arabic-speaking Twelver communities. However, this impact was probably not as politically or intellectually deep as in India, because of the dominance in the Arabic-speaking regions of the Sunni Ottoman empire and because Persian learning was less central to Arab Shi`ite identity than to Indian.

The isles of Bahrain escaped Ottoman domination, and their many Shi`ites were instead affected by the rise of Iranian Shi`ism. The Shi`ites of Bahrain were under Portuguese rule 1521-1602, and then fell to the Safavids until 1717. It is my thesis that Ismailis predominated there from Carmathian times (the ninth and tenth centuries of the Common Era), but that after the Safavid revolution they gradually became Twelvers, in part because their intellectuals tended to study in Iran or in Iran-influenced centers of learning in what is now Iraq. The more than a century of direct Safavid rule strongly molded local clerical institutions and thought. After 1717, however, Bahrainis were ruled first by Oman, and then by the Sunni local Al-Khalifa dynasty, suffering subordination and occasional persecution at the hands of a Sunni dynasty. Iranian influence on Bahrain was further limited because that island adhered from the eighteenth century to the conservative Akhbari School of jurisprudence, whereas in Iran the Usuli school largely won out by the early nineteenth century.

The Ottoman-ruled Arabophone Shi`ite communities included the Twelvers of Jabal `Amil near Tyre and Sidon, of Baghdad and Basra in what is now Iraq, and of al-Hasa further down the Persian Gulf littoral. The Ottomans made a major distinction among Twelvers, reserving harshest treatment for those who adhered to the esoteric sect of Safavid followers known as Qizilbash. Clearly, they feared the Qizilbash Twelvers more for their political support of the Safavid leaders than for their doctrines, and their jurists declared them apostates who should be killed and against whom holy war was necessary. The Ottoman-Safavid international political struggle often had unfortunate repercussions for

Arab Twelvers, whom the Ottomans feared as a pro-Safavid fifth column behind their own lines. The very aggressiveness of Safavid Shi`ism toward Sunnis caused a backlash against Arab minorities. Twelvers suffered disadvantages in Iraq, which the Ottomans took from the Iranians in 1534 and held thereafter, with a hiatus of Safavid reconquest 1623-1638. This region constituted a frontline in the two powers' tug of war, and the loyalties of the Twelvers in Baghdad, the shrine cities, and Basra were always suspect. Once they had conquered territories beyond Basra on the coast of the Persian Gulf, the Ottomans treated the Shi`ites in the area known as al-Hasa (eastern Arabia) harshly. The Twelvers who lived in what is now Lebanon were not the objects of as much Ottoman suspicion, probably because they were far from the border with Shi`ite Iran, and some of their clans were incorporated into the Ottoman military and administrative apparatus.

The eighteenth century was a disastrous one for Twelver Shi`ism. Sunni Afghan tribal cavalries overthrew the Shi`ite Safavids in 1722, initiated a long period of political chaos in Iran and of Sunni rule or of the rule of chieftains not particularly sympathetic to the Shi`ite clergy. In the first six decades of the century the conservative, literalist Akhbari school of jurisprudence appears to have become dominant in many Shi`ite centers, especially outside Iran. But in the last quarter of the eighteenth century the more scholastic, clericalist Usuli school witnessed a resurgence in the shrine cities near Baghdad, allowing its partisans to train the next generation of Shi`ite clergymen in Iran and even places like India, and ensuring its eventual victory nearly everywhere save Bahrain.

This development was important because the Usuli school gives a special place to the clergy, valuing their scholastic reasoning in the law, and insisting that all lay believers follow and emulate their rulings and example. The Ottoman Shi`ites probably benefited from the political decentralization that the empire underwent in the eighteenth and early nineteenth centuries, allowing local Shi`ite Arab notable families more space to maneuver. But the Tanzimat ("reorganization") reforms that began in 1826 led to a gradual tightening of the Ottoman grip. Thus, the province of Baghdad was restored to direct Ottoman rule in the early 1830s, and in the 1840s strong measures were taken to end the semi-autonomy of the Shi`ite shrine cities.

Let us now turn to developments in India. The rise of a Shi`ite dynasty in Iran coincided with the establishment of several new Muslim dynasties in India, the rulers of which looked to Iran as the model for imperial style in the sixteenth century. Iran's preeminence in this regard had several roots. First, Persian was widely viewed in the early modern Muslim world anywhere east of the Tigris as the ideal court language, and was preferred for this purpose even by Turkic-speaking monarchs in Central and South Asia. Iran was often called "*vilayat*," literally "authority," but here apparently in the sense of "the metropole," among South Asian Muslims. The Safavids thus assumed not only the throne of Iran but also the position of role models for other dynasties. Of course, the Uzbeks, the Mughals, and the Ottomans committed themselves to Sunni Islam, but most were generally rooted in claims legitimacy having to do with Turco-Mongol descent and they based their power on a Sunni Turkic tribal cavalry. Other rulers, lacking this strong source of legitimacy, were more open to establishing it by modeling themselves loosely on the Safavid court, even to the extent of adopting Shi`ism. Further, Shi`ite Iranian émigrés at regional courts often played a key role, both in founding new dynasties in South Asia and in encouraging the conversion of newly-established regional rulers. In this regard, the trade routes between Iran and India became an important conduit of religious ideas, bringing the latter along with silk, grain, horses, raisins and wine from Shiraz and Bandar Abbas to Indian cities such as Surat, Bijapur, Golconda and Hooghli. The early modern states in South Asia that emulated Iran's Safavid court tended to be in the non-Mughal South, and included Ahmednagar, Bijapur and Golconda. These were gradually incorporated into the Sunni Mughal empire in the course of the seventeenth century, however.

During the eighteenth century, the Mughal Empire radically decentralized, relinquishing power from the capital of Delhi to its major provinces, which emerged as royal courts in their own right. The western Deccan and central India fell to the Hindu Marathas, the eastern Deccan was devolved on the Sunni Nizam of Hyderabad, Punjab fell to the Sikhs, Kabul and Peshawar to the Sunni Durrani dynasty. Bengal, Sindh and Awadh each developed local Shi`ite dynasties that began as regional Mughal governorships. Especially after about 1725, these regional courts increasingly became post-Mughal successor states. Shi`ism in Bengal flourished in the eighteenth century, with the state providing ample government patronage for Shi`ite practices and institutions such as seminaries. Many Iranians immigrated to the nawabate, as merchants and Muslim learned men. Shi`ism lost this privileged position, however, when the British conquered the province in 1757.

The most important and long-lived Shi`ite successor state to the Mughals was Awadh (which the British called Oudh), ruled by the Nishapuri dynasty 1722-1856. It is the scene for a number of the chapters in this book. Situated between Bengal and Delhi at the foot of the Nepalese Himalayas, it was founded by Mir Muhammad Amin Nishapuri (d. 1739), known as Burhan al-Mulk, the first nawab of Awadh. He came to the Mughal Empire from eastern Iran in 1708 and rose rapidly in government service. He became governor of Awadh in 1722, and quickly formed an alliance with local Sunni townsmen and rural Hindu rajas, the local intermediate elites. He resisted the Mughal emperor's one attempt to transfer him to another province, which was a sign of the increasing autonomy of the province, and he later collaborated with the Iranian invader Nadir Shah, who rewarded him by conferring Awadh on him and his descendants as a hereditary nawabate. He also left behind a substantial contingent of Shi`ite Qizilbash cavalrymen, who joined the Awadh military. The nawabs gradually consolidated their hold on Awadh, and began in a minor way to build up local Shi`ite constituencies and institutions. Shi`ites never became more than a very small minority in the province. Some ninety percent of the population was Hindu, and only three percent of the Muslims were Shi`ites. Shi`ism as the royal religion, however, had a vastly disproportionate impact on politics and culture throughout the nineteenth century. Since Awadh at its height comprised a population of 10 million, moreover, the Shi`ites could have been as many as 300,000, a significant community in pre-modern times. In contrast, Iran's population in 1800 has been estimated at only 5 million, though some 80 to 90 percent of these were Shi`ites. What is now Iraq in 1800 probably only had a population of one million, and since this was before the large-scale conversions of the tribes, its Shi`ite community at that point may have been no bigger than that of Awadh.

Awadh was gradually surrounded by the British, being among the forces defeated at Baksar in Bihar by British forces in 1764. The indemnities and other payments levied by the British on Awadh forced it into debt to them. The British demanded the concession of some Awadh territory in the north later in the century, and then annexed over half the province in 1801 to pay for the claimed arrears in Awadh tribute. The rulers of the province were thus deprived of the opportunity for expansion, and instead lost substantial territory, after which they were surrounded by the British on three sides. It is not surprising that they should have invested their wealth in culture rather than in the military, and, of course, that culture had a strong Shi`ite coloration.

Thousands of immigrants came into Awadh from Iran over the decades, serving as physicians, bureaucrats, military men, poets, chroniclers, and clerics or ulama. They remained a small minority over-all, but they were a noticeable component of the urban population. Persian could be heard spoken by some common people in the streets of the capital, Lucknow, in the late eighteenth century, as well as at court and among literary figures. Enormous numbers of Persian words entered local speech, contributing to the further development of Urdu, which began enjoying an important place in Awadh culture. Urdu was a mixture of what we would now call Hindi grammar with Arabic, Persian and Turkish vocabulary and idioms, spoken by both the Muslim and some elements of the Hindu elite in much of the subcontinent. Ironically, the nawabs of Awadh, despite their Persian ancestry, became the foremost patrons of Urdu poets in the late eighteenth and early nineteenth centuries, leading to a flourishing of the language there. The Awadh court contributed significantly to the development of Urdu, which had begun supplanting Persian even in late Mughal Delhi. The foundational texts of Urdu literature often have a strongly Shi`ite tinge because they were written in Lucknow, and *marthiyya* or traditional elegies in commemoration of the martyred Shi`ite Imams constituted a major genre.

The Awadh nawabs supported the creation and growth of a Shi`ite clerical corps, made up both of local Shi`ite ulama and of immigrant Iranians. Indeed, a rather lively set of debates were conducted about whether the local clerics or the Iranians were better Shi`ites. Because of their knowledge of local court protocol and customs, the Indian Shi`ite ulama tended to become ensconced in positions of influence such as Friday prayer leader and seminary teacher, and to receive the patronage of the Shi`ite nawabs (later kings) of Awadh. Iranian clerics sometimes preferred to settle among Shi`ite communities ruled by the British, where they were free from the demands made on them by the Awadh state. The Awadh nawabs did respect the great Shi`ite jurisprudents of the Iraqi shrine cities, and bestowed on them enormous amounts in patronage and put them in charge of large-scale philanthropic works such as canal building. The Shi`ites in Awadh remained a tiny minority of the population, and the religion functioned more as a symbol of royal distinctiveness and prerogatives than as a missionary faith aimed at converting the masses. The chroniclers do maintain, however, that in the 1840s hundreds of Hindus and thousands of Sunnis became Shi`ites. I show below that a distinctive set of South Asian Shi`ite practices grew up in Awadh that was significantly shaped by Muslim noblewomen, demonstrating the centrality of gender to the tradition, though this point is seldom recognized in the existing literature.

Increasing conflicts in the 1850s between Sunni revivalists and Hindus drew the Shi`ite state of Awadh into the fray, so that it put down the Sunni militants, partially at British insistence, in 1855. The conflict that developed in Ayodhya near Faizabad, over a Hindu temple to the monkey-god Hanuman that Sunnis maintained had once been a mosque that was usurped, bears an uncanny resemblance to that in precisely the same town in the early 1990s. In the contemporary struggle, Hindu revivalists insisted that the Baburi mosque had been built above the temple marking the birthplace of the god Rama, and in 1992 they tore down the mosque, initiating a wave of violence against Muslims. The trope of illicit squatting on sacred space appears to have long-term appeal in North India, and to be an element in the imaginary of communal violence. The Shi`ite establishment in Awadh was much reduced in power and influence in 1856 when the British annexed the province, after which the decline of Shi`ite patronage led to a great slackening if not a total halting of Iranian immigration into the area (unlike the situation in Bombay). Shi`ites in British India often went to Iran for seminary study or to master Persian poetry, and a small number of them could afford the pilgrimage to the shrines of the Imams in Iraq, so that contacts between Iran and South Asian Shi`ites continued. They were not as extensive as before, however, and the gradual decline in knowledge of Persian among most Muslims in the century after the annexation further limited Iran's influence. The rise, first of Urdu, and then of Hindi-English medium schools after independence, along with the new projects of Indian and Pakistani nationalism, helped foster among South Asian Shi`ites a certain amount of independence and a turn inward to local traditions that was not interrupted in a major sort of way until the Islamic Revolution of 1978-79.

In chapter 10, I come back to consider the impact of twentieth-century developments on what Lebanese scholar Chibli Mallat called the "Shi`ite international," the international networks of Shi`ite activists coming out of local communities from Tyre in Lebanon to Lucknow in India.[2] The Pahlevi period in Iran, 1925-1979, is usually seen as a time of secularization in that country, and it is almost certainly true that the sort of patronage given by the Qajar court and courtiers to Shi`ite institutions abroad was much curtailed during these decades. Reza Shah, who crowned himself in 1926, gradually adopted Western commercial codes and established national educational institutions, pushing the Shi`ite clergy out of realms on which they had earlier exercised great influence. During the early 1950s, when clerics formed part of an alliance of nationalists, leftists and religious groups to support Prime Minister Mohammad Musaddiq, they regained some influence. When Musaddiq was overthrown by a CIA-backed coup in 1953 and the young Muhammad Reza Shah (r. 1941-1979) was put back on the throne, the Shi`ite activists fell into disfavor with the state. The shah castigated the Shi`ite clergy as "black reactionaries," and further weakened their power base with a number of measures, including land reform. The drying up of Iranian and Indian patronage and the turn to nationalism in Iraq led to a drastic decline in the wealth, power and numbers of the Shi`ite clergy teaching at Najaf and Karbala, and to a substantial reduction in the student body. Still, even during this unusual period of secular emphases, contacts among Shi`ite thinkers continued to be extensive. Even the Pahlevis did bestow some patronage on religious edifices, such as the shrine to Zaynab near Damascus or the Shi`ite mosque at Tyre. Some Iranian money flowed to the Lebanese Shi`ite community through the good offices of Musa Sadr, an Iranian of Arab extraction who became the leader of the Lebanese community in the 1960s and 1970s. Talks continued between Iranian representatives and the Sunni clergy of al-Azhar on Muslim ecumenism and the possibilities for lessening or healing the Sunni-Shi`ite rift. The most important links among Shi`ites of various nationalities in the twentieth century, however, were not established on the governmental level. The intellectual impact of the Iraqi scholastic Baqir al-Sadr was enormous, and that of Ayatollah Ruhollah Khomeini became so after his exile from Iran to Turkey in 1964 and his subsequent resettlement in Iraq. Even if in reduced numbers, Shi`ites from all over the world still did come to the Iraqi shrine cities for a seminary education in the 1960s and 1970s, where they often fell under the spell of clerical revivalists like al-Sadr and Khomeini.

Khomeini began putting forth a vision of Shi`ite theocracy in the late 1960s, which immediately became influential among Shi`ite Islamists opposed to Pahlevi secularism. The central problem for classical Shi`ism had been that of legitimate authority. Shi`ites had placed all authority in the hands of the immaculate Imam. So when the Imamate ended as an institution with the disappearance of the Twelfth Imam as a child in 280 A.H., Shi`ites experienced a crisis of authority. It was the Imam who authorized Friday prayers and appointed the Friday prayer-leaders? Now that he was gone, could such congregational prayers even be held? It was the Imam who authorized the collection of religious taxes, whether alms, the "fifth," or the agricultural tithe. Without an Imam, could such taxes even be paid? To whom would they go? Shi`ite thinkers put forward two major responses to this crisis. The literalist Akhbaris had often been willing to see some central Muslim practices lapse in the absence of the Imam. Some advised that one should just tax oneself the amount that should have gone to alms, and bury it in the ground so that it could be spewed forth from the earth at the Resurrection. They held that Friday congregational prayers should be cancelled during the Occultation of the Imam. The rationalist Usulis on contrary believed that the collectivity of the Shi`ite learned men could stand general proxy for the Imam in his absence, and could authorize the common-law Muslim states that grew up during the Occultation to appoint prayer leaders, collect taxes, and lead defensive holy war or jihad to protect the community.

Khomeini took the Usuli logic one step further. If the Usuli jurisprudents could authorize a civil monarchy or state to undertake these religious obligations in the absence of the Imam, then was it not more fitting that they should in fact erect a state themselves and rule on behalf of the Imam in accordance with Shi`ite law? Khomeini pointed to the appointment by early Imams of mediators among the learned men to resolve the community's disputes, as proof of the standing of the clerics to establish a state. He cleverly played on the resemblance of the early Arabic word for mediator with that of "ruler" in later Arabic.

The "modernization" policies of Muhammad Reza Shah have often been blamed for the revolution in Iran. Yet many scholars, especially Nikki Keddie, have argued that it was not modernization per se that provoked the discontents but rather the skewed, uneven, emphases of the shah's government. The rural areas were disadvantaged by the loan policies of government agencies, which favored urban enterprises. Big business was treated more favorably than small businesses. Some think that the emphasis on urban industry over agriculture in government policy accelerated the emigration to the cities of large numbers of peasants seeking jobs as day laborers, who erected for housing tin shanties without sewerage and other amenities.

The burgeoning of population growth, along with the substantial expansion of the university system and of opportunities to study abroad, produced a large class of first-generation intellectuals. More were produced than could get good jobs, and in any case often feared that their Western-style education would rob them of their authenticity and leave them adrift in an alienating modernity. In addition, the shah's autocracy had produced a police state in which much of the populace was spying on their compatriots for the state, and in which discourse critical of the regime could result in imprisonment and torture. At a time, in the early 1970s, when the Soviet government probably only had about 1,000 prisoners of conscience, the shah's government had an estimated 10,000. Many students and intellectuals turned to a radical vision of Shi`ite Islam or to Marxism. The oil shock of the 1970s, when after the 1973 Arab-Israeli War the price of petroleum quadrupled in four years, brought a windfall to Iran that was difficult to digest. It produced enormous spending on imports, creating frustrating bottlenecks. It also produced high inflation, which the shah unwisely attempted to blame on shopkeepers, thus alienating an important component of the bazaar. The vast oil wealth presented the shah's technocrats with very difficult choices, since if they suddenly invested too much of it in the country's economy they risked producing hyper-inflation, but if they did not, the masses would complain about not sharing in the windfall. Unable to find a happy medium, they produced both results. These problems were exacerbated by an economic downturn and lower petroleum prices 1977-78, putting sudden strains on a system that had been retooled to expect continued high rents on oil. Most other Middle Eastern countries that produced significant amounts of petroleum had small populations and a lack of what economists call "absorptive capacity" (the ability of the economy to put to work large inputs of capital). Iran was unique among major oil states in having, in the late 1970s, a population of about 37 million. This absorptive capacity, ironically enough, made it much more vulnerable to massive dislocation from the oil boom than were much smaller countries in the Gulf. The populations of the sheikhdoms could easily be bought off with health and education benefits and good incomes, and the bulk of their oil income willy-nilly had to be plowed back into investments, often in the West. Because the Iranian government could plausibly invest in Iran, it was faced with discontents that its peers were spared. Because of the shah's rigid dictatorship, censorship of the press, curbing of political expression (he moved to a one-party state in 1976), imprisonment of intellectuals and others for expression of conscience, political discontent in Iran had no legitimate outlet. Because there were few civil intermediate institutions between the state and the people, the public began turning to the mosques as the only safe place to express any sort of dissidence.

Khomeini's strong rhetorical skills and his bright vision of a righteous, clerically-ruled state that would supplant the den of corruption that was Pahlevi government captured the imagination of millions of Shi`ites around the world, especially in Iran. The revolution against the Shah in 1978-1979 was exceedingly complex, and a majority of revolutionaries were not Khomeinists. They consisted of clerics, bazaar artisans and shopkeepers, and recent immigrants to the cities from villages, but also of middle class intellectuals and teachers and left-leaning workers. The clerical networks and their lower middle class supporters did, however, play an important role in the revolution, and they were the ones with the organizational skills and ideological vision to capture it after the beginning of February, 1979, when Khomeini returned to Tehran from Paris. The Khomeinist state is treated in chapter 11, below.

In the first eight months after the revolution, the clerics made an alliance with lay religious nationalists and retained many technocrats in the cabinet. Prime Minister Mehdi Bazargan, an engineer and the owner of a small factory, had supported Musaddiq in the 1950s oil nationalization crisis. In this period a new constitution was enacted that made the head of state the "supreme jurisprudent" and subordinated the army and the elected government to him in many ways. The first incumbent of the new office, of course, was Khomeini. A twelve-member Guardianship Council was also established, with wide powers of legislative review. Early in the revolution, Khomeini confronted the Bazargan government over its tendency to favor the interests of the nationalist middle class, insisting that free electricity and housing be given to the very poor or "barefoot." A parallel government grew up, of vigilante revolutionary guards and other zealous supporters of Khomeini and of hard-line Shi`ite radicalism, often shunting aside the government police and municipal officials. When in October of 1979 the deposed shah went to the U.S. for cancer treatment, radicals in Iran feared this move was a cover for a planned coup aimed at restoring the monarchy. They invaded the U.S. embassy in Tehran and took its staff hostages for the succeeding 444 days. Khomeini tested the wind, and when he saw how popular the hostage-taking was, he supported it. Prime Minister Bazargan, who did not, resigned.

French-trained, left-leaning economist Abolhassan Bani Sadr, who was favored by Khomeini, then won the presidential elections early in 1980. For the next year and a half, Muslim leftist intellectuals like Bani Sadr struggled with conservative clerics for the fate of the nation. Bani Sadr, however, lacked grass roots support and declined to organize a political party. He did attract the allegiance of many in the Mujahidin-i Khalq, a leftist Muslim organization with a well-organized guerila wing. Leftist and rightist activists began actively clashing with one another at rallies, forcing Khomeini to make a choice. Despite his earlier rhetoric in favor of the barefoot, he increasingly moved to the right. Bani Sadr was impeached in June, 1981, and had to flee the country for Paris. In 1981-1983, Iran was plunged deeply into social conflict. Mujahidin-i Khalq terrorist bombings and shootings were met with mass arrests and summary executions not only of its members but of sympathizers and other dissidents. Often, fifty prisoners were executed each day. Despite their apolitical character, nearly two hundred members of the Baha'i religious minority, considered heretical by the Shi`ite clergy were killed, and several thousand jailed. This bloody period has been called by some historians "the Great Terror." Even after the terror subsided, repression continued. The universities were purged of thousands of professors who did not toe the "line of the Imam" (i.e. Khomeinism), and Khomeini called upon children to inform on their parents to the state.

From 1983 through 1989, clerical rule was established on a regular footing. In October, 1981, cleric `Ali Khamenei was elected president. `Ali Akbar Hashimi Rafsanjani emerged as a popular speaker of the parliament, most of whose members belonged to the Islamic Republican Party (not so much a party as a loose grouping of the politically like-minded). Law was Islamized. A bloody and fruitless war with Iraq was pursued long after Saddam Hussein (who began it with his invasion of Iran in 1980) began suing for peace.

Khomeini died in 1989. Khamenei was chosen as his successor as supreme jurisprudent, and Rafsanjani was elected president. Although Iran's state remained a politically repressive, these two leaders moved away from some of the worst excesses of the Khomeini years. The number of political prisoners executed, or at least those that could be known about, fell dramatically. Rafsanjani chose to sit out the Gulf War.

The attention of the revolutionary state to education and rural development began bearing fruit, as rates of literacy rose substantially, even among women. Rafsanjani by the mid-1990s was even seeking reintegration with some Bretton Woods international institutions, since he wanted a World Bank development loan. Successive parliamentary elections produced sessions with increasing numbers of lay members, and fewer and fewer clerics.

The 1997 elections produced a surprise, when a dark horse named Muhammad Khatami garnered some 70 percent of the vote. Khatami, a cleric, had lived in Germany and written on civil society in the tradition of the left-liberal sociologist, Jürgen Habermas. He had been minister of culture briefly in the early 1990s, but was dismissed because hardliners thought him too liberal. He appears to have been elected primarily by the votes of youth and women, who chafed under the strictures of the hard-line Khomeinists. Khatami gained further support in the parliamentary elections of 1999, and was elected to a second term in 2001. His attempt to liberalize Khomeinism has largely failed, meeting concerted opposition from Supreme Jurisprudent `Ali Khamenei and from the Guardianship Council, which struck down many liberalizing measures enacted by parliament and forestalled others. After a brief flowering of a freer press after 1997, dozens of newspapers have been closed by the clerics. The Guardianship Council also vets those who can run for office, and has attempted to exclude known liberals from running. The mild-mannered and cautious Khatami has seemed unwilling or unable to use his substantial public mandate effectively to challenge the hardliners. Among the more controversial initiatives launched by Khatami was a dialogue between the American and Iranian peoples rather than at the level of the government.

Iranian and American relations improved in the wake of the September 11, 2001 attacks on the World Trade Center and the Pentagon by al-Qaida, a secret terrorist organization made up of an estimated 5,000 cultists. Al-Qaida's membership is fanatically hyper-Sunni, and its allies among the Afghan Taliban and the Pakistani Lashkar-i Tayyiba and Sipah-i Sahaba had been responsible for the massacres of thousands of Shi`ites in Afghanistan and hundreds in Pakistan.  Iran backed the Afghan Northern Alliance, which included the Shi`ite Hizb-i Vahdat representing the Hazaras, and so became willy-nilly allied with the U.S., which supported the same group against the Taliban. Despite continued hard-line rhetoric from Khamenei and some other clerics, the Khatami government agreed to help find and return to the U.S. any servicemen who strayed into Iranian territory in the course of the bombing raids and special operations maneuvers in Afghanistan. From a government that had held U.S. embassy staffers hostage only two decades before, this commitment was nothing short of astonishing. When he came to the U.S. for a meeting of the United Nations in fall, 2001, President Khatami gave an interview with Cable News Network reporter Christiane Amanpour. He expressed heartfelt sympathy for the trauma inflicted on the American people by the terrorists of 9/11 that was unmistakeably sincere, and struck some observers as going further than some putative allies of the U.S. such as Saudi Arabia's Crown Prince `Abdu'llah. Even as Iran appeared to be warming to the U.S., at least for the moment, the clerical regime faced new challenges. In soccer riots that same fall of 2001, angry young men for the first time openly chanted the name of Reza Shah II, the secularist pretender to the Iranian throne resident in the United States, as a sign of their deep dissatisfaction with Iran's Shi`ite government. They also chanted pro-U.S. slogans. With the fall of the Taliban, the only other modern Muslim experiment in theocracy had ended ignominiously. The future of Iran's clerically-ruled government almost certainly depends on whether it can find a way to satisfy the increasingly democratic aspirations of Iran's new generation.

2

The Shi`ites as an Ottoman Minority

The salient attribute of Arab-speaking Twelver Shi`ites has been their minority status. This status has caused them much hardship and certainly contributed to the mobilization of large numbers of them out of Shi`ism and into Sunnism at some points in time (as in Mamluk Syria of the fourteenth and fifteenth centuries). But for those in every generation who accepted Shi`ism, either as an inheritance or through conversion, their minority status also helped maintain their identity. Their celebration of the martyrdom of the Prophet's grandson, Husayn, on the battlefield of Karbala in A. D. 680 gave them a highly emotive and resilient mythos from which to draw strength. As a prominent observer of nationalism notes, "Battle myths are even more crucial for maintaining ethnic sentiments in later generations than the initial events, and . . . a community's geo-political location, its relationship with other communities and polities, and especially the nexus of states in which it finds itself, helps to feed and keep alive the members' sense of their common destiny."[1] One focus of this survey will therefore be Ottoman and post-Ottoman policy toward the Twelver minorities. Six varieties of majority policy have been common in history: assimilation, pluralism, legal protection of minorities, population transfer, continued subjugation, and extermination.[2] In each period and area investigated, I will ask about the state's treatment of the Imamis. This survey will not deal with Bahrain, yet another Arabic-speaking Twelver community, insofar as it was not Ottoman territory. The history of that community is taken up in Chapter 3, below.

A second focus will be the results of the policies followed by the majority toward the minorities. Several important social consequences have been suggested for discrimination against a minority in society: residential segregation, social segregation, stereotype reinforcement and constriction of opportunities, conflict, the economic exploitation of the minority by the majority, reduction of the minority group's power, and status deprivation.[3] It is safe to say that Twelvers in Sunni societies have at one time or another suffered all these effects of discrimination, but the historical question has to do with the specifics of time and place. How has their relationship to the state, and then the nation-state, changed over time or varied by region? In what ways have they participated in nation-building even with, or because of, the constraints of social closure?

I

For the Arab Twelver minority communities, four of the past five centuries have been ones of Ottoman Sunni dominance. Because of their status as a minority looked upon as heretical, however, their history has an altogether different rhythm from that of the Sunni elite at the imperial center. Twelvers often benefited from times of Ottoman weakness and decentralization and felt greater restrictions during times of renewed Ottoman strength. A brief sketch of the history of the Ottoman-ruled Twelver Arab minority communities is best organized into three distinct historical periods, in which political and economic forces acted so as to have broad, general effects. The first period, 1516-1750, witnessed often harsh Sunni Ottoman rule over most Arab Twelvers, with Ottoman repression often exacerbated by the Twelver chauvinism of the Safavid rulers of Iran. The second, from 1750 until the mid-nineteenth century, saw Twelver local elites come to the fore at a time of decentralization in the great Sunni empires.

The Ottoman armies that rolled over western Asia and North Africa early in the sixteenth century conquered peoples highly diverse in their religious traditions, though the majority adhered to some form of Sunni Islam. Especially in the Fertile Crescent, however, Muslims of various creeds dwelt.   The mountains of what is now Lebanon sheltered esotericist Shi'ites of several stripes, from the Druze to the Ismailis. Moreover, Jabal 'Amil near Tyre and Sidon formed a major base for Twelver Shi'ism.   Syria contained large numbers of Nusayris, Shi'ites who accepted Twelve Imams but held beliefs Twelver ulama considered heretical.   The provinces of Baghdad and Basra in what is now Iraq encompassed numerous Twelvers, and the shrine cities of Najaf, Karbala, Samarra' and Kazimayn attracted Twelver pilgrims from all over Asia. Twelvers also dwelt in Ottoman al-Hasa further down the Persian Gulf littoral and on the isles of nearby Bahrain.

What policies did the Ottomans adopt toward these Arab Twelver communities?   First, the Ottomans made a major distinction among Twelvers, reserving harshest treatment for those who adhered to the esoteric sect of Safavid followers known as *Qizilbash* (wearers of red headgear) for their distinctive crimson hats. These were typically Turkic pastoral nomads, many of whom idolized the Safavid monarchs as divine. Clearly, they feared the Qizilbash Twelvers more for their political support of the Safavid leaders than for their doctrines. In the condemnation of this group issued at the request of Sultan Selim I, Ottoman jurisconsult Ibn Kemal Pashazade referred to them as a "sect (*ta'ife*) of the Shi`a" and declared them apostates whose men must be killed, whose wealth and women are allowed to any Sunnis who wish to usurp them, and against whom holy war is incumbent.[4] Against the Qizilbash Twelvers, the Ottomans showed a willingness to resort to extreme measures such as population transfer and extermination. After an Anatolian rebellion in 1501 Bayezid relocated some 30,000 extremist Shi`ites to Morea in Europe, and in 1514 Selim I ordered a massacre of 40,000 Anatolian Qizilbash.[5] The Ottoman attitude toward quietist Twelver Shi`ites in the Arabic-speaking provinces was often quite different, but Shi`ites of any sort always risked be conflated with Qizilbash, especially on the Ottoman-Safavid frontiers.

Thus, an important cause for continued Ottoman hostility towards Twelvers was the rise of the Twelver Safavid state in Iran during the sixteenth century, and its fierce enmity with Istanbul. This international political struggle often had unfortunate repercussions, not only for Anatolian Qizilbash, but also for Arab Twelvers, whom the Ottomans sometimes feared as a pro-Safavid fifth column behind their own lines. The very aggressiveness of Safavid Shi`ism toward Sunnis caused a backlash against Arab minorities. Prominent Twelvers dwelling in the Hijaz wrote to Safavid religious authorities protesting that Iranian attacks on Sunnis and public cursing of the caliphs whom Sunnis revered had provoked hostility toward Shi`ites in the holy cities.[6]

Twelvers also suffered disadvantages in Iraq, which the Ottomans took from the Iranians in 1534 and held thereafter, with a hiatus of Safavid reconquest 1623-1638. This region constituted a frontline in the two powers' tug of war, and the loyalties of the Twelvers in southern Iraq were always suspect. Ottoman administrators in sixteenth century Baghdad lamented that there was "no end to the heretics and misbelievers."[7] Ottoman policy toward Twelvers in Iraq varied with political circumstances. In the early 1570s Istanbul ordered the execution of men who secretly took a stipend from Shah Tahmasp to recite the Qur'an at shrines for the Iranian monarch, forbade the granting of fiefs to locals, whom it ordered watched for signs of heresy, and in Mosul forbade `Ashura' ceremonies mourning the martyred grandson of the Prophet, Imam Husayn. But in this period the Ottomans sought to avoid acts so grave that they might provoke hostilities with Iran. Witch-hunts for Qizilbash sympathizers of the Safavids turned up fief-holders, local notables in the cities, and even the administrator of a sanjak, some of whom were accused of being in league with Bedouin and Turkoman tribespeople.[8]   During the Safavid reconquest of Iraq Sunnis were massively persecuted and the shrine of `Abd al-Qadar Gilani in Baghdad damaged; on the Ottoman retaking of Baghdad in 1638 Hasan Pasha ordered the Sunni shrine repaired, largely with receipts from confiscated Twelver lands, and a general slaughter of all persons of known Persian descent took place.[9]

The Ottomans, once they had extended their lines down to the western littoral of the Persian Gulf to conquer al-Hasa in 1550, expropriated lands of Twelvers and closed off the trans-Arabian pilgrimage route so as to deny Twelvers access to Mecca and Medina. Even after 1590, when they once more allowed trade and pilgrimage from al-Hasa to the Hijaz, they forbade Twelvers to pursue it and so hurt merchants of this community. Despite the Arab ethnicity of the area's Imamis, the Ottoman authorities saw them as Iranians (*acem*).[10]

The Twelvers in the Levant, less exposed to the frontiers of Ottoman-Safavid warfare, had a less precarious position. Although one magnate from the prominent Twelver Harfush clan in Baalbek took part in a local rebellion against the Ottomans in 1520, other members of the Harfush family later served in the Ottoman military and remained important local notables and even officials. In 1534 a member of the Harfush clan was made governor of Baalbek, and his son `Ali al-Harfush succeeded him. But `Ali was executed by the Ottomans late in the sixteenth century, possibly because they suspected him of leaning toward the Safavids. The family regained the office of governor and remained prominent until after 1625, when their regions came into the orbit of the Druze Ma`nid notables.[11]

The Shi`ites in the Levant therefore had quite a different position than those in what is now Iraq.  Twelver alliances with Druze magnates could sometimes thwart Sunni pashas.  The Ottomans counted the Twelvers in Baalbek and Jabal `Amil as Muslims in their censuses without referring to their legal rite. Shi`ites in Damascus, a small minority were said to practice pious dissimulation *(taqiyya)*, denying their Shi`ite sympathies because they felt their lives would otherwise be in danger because of Ottoman intolerance. Only in rare cases did Istanbul persecute the Twelvers in this region on ideological grounds, as when they crushed a messianic movement begun by the Sufi Uways al-Qaramani (d. 1544) that spread an expectation of the imminent advent of the Mahdi (Muslim messiah) among the area's Twelvers.[12] In the Levant, clan rivalries and alliances, and economic interchange, could generate a whole range of relationships wherein sectarian identity played only a small part. Yet disabilities remained for Imamis, and the dangers of a Twelver scholar or notable becoming too prominent in Ottoman Syria are demonstrated by the fate of the great Twelver jurist Shaykh Zayn al-Din al-`Amili (the "Second Martyr"), whom, Shi`ite hagiographers charge, the Ottomans executed for heresy.[13]

Leaving aside the highly politicized Shi`ism of the Qizilbash, then, at the level of day-to-day administration it seems often not to have mattered a great deal to Ottoman tax collectors what religion the tax-payers followed, as long as receipts were good. In fact, therefore, the Ottomans followed a policy toward most Twelver Arab peasants of continued subjugation. Since the Ottomans declined to acknowledge the Ja`fari rite of the Twelvers, however, their legal status remained problematic. All non-Sunni Muslims in the Ottoman empire, not only the Twelvers but also the Druze and `Alawis, suffered from their lack of recognition as legitimate religious communities. Ironically, the Ottomans actually favored Jews (though still as second-class subjects) and encouraged their immigration into their empire during the sixteenth century, whereas they often persecuted Shi`ite Muslims.[14] In regard to the Twelver Qizilbash sect the Ottomans pursued even more drastic policies such as population transfer, execution, and even attempted extermination.

Twelvers' spiritual, ritual and legal life nevertheless went on under the Ottomans. Their ulama traveled from Ottoman Sidon to Ottoman Najaf for studies. Indeed, such travel for study played so important a role in the cross-fertilization of ideas that the Second Martyr's own sons from Jabal `Amil learned much that they did not know from their father's old students in Iraq.[15] The network of students, teachers, and pilgrims crisscrossed imperial borders as well as provincial ones, so that many Twelvers from Jabal `Amil went to make their fortunes in newly Shi`ite Iran, where `Amilis became almost a clerical caste, or in the Twelver-ruled state of Golconda in southern India.[16]

Because of the importance of foreign patronage to Twelver ulama and notables, the fall of Safavid Iran to Sunni Afghan invaders toward the end of this period, in 1722, and the decades-long disestablishment of Shi`ism as a state religion can only have had a dramatic impact on Twelver morale in Jabal `Amil, Iraq, and al-Hasa. The Iraqi shrine cities, already under Sunni Ottoman rule, had at least looked to the Safavids for infusions of wealth, gilding of shrines, and contributions to the ulama. Now the proud Isfahani clerical families themselves crowded into Najaf and Karbala as refugees, ironically seeking the protection of Ottoman law and order from the Afghan Ghilzai marauders.

In the period 1500-1750, then, the Ottomans engaged in a rhetoric of forced assimilation (or in the case of the "Qizilbash" even extermination) toward the Twelvers, while in fact practicing in most Arab regions a policy of simple subjugation. The consequences of this subjugation varied by social class. Twelver magnates and intermediate strata certainly suffered by being denied opportunities of advancement and patronage (*intisap*) in Istanbul, or even in provincial capitals like Damascus and Baghdad, (though some, especially in the Levant, attained local power as emirs and a subordinate feudal position in the Ottoman military). Social segregation and constriction of opportunities therefore did follow from Ottoman prejudices. Conflict, economic exploitation, reduction in minority power and status deprivation all also characterized relations of the Sunni majority with the Twelver minority before 1750.

Twelvers kept a strong sense of demotic identity, despite their marginal condition, through several rituals. First, they frequently mourned the martyred Imams or scions of the Prophet's House, especially Husayn. In Nabatiya, these rituals came to be especially bloody, involving public self-flagellation.[17] Such rituals included not only the self-affirmation of pledging fealty to the Twelve Imams, but also the cursing of the early Caliphs, whom they saw as usurpers. Sunnis felt that the Twelvers, in insisting on such cursing, kept a dirty little secret. Their ceremonies, in this view, had at their core a mysterious blasphemy. For Twelvers, however, the ritual mourning of Imam Husayn carried with it a dual message, of patient perseverance in the truth even unto martyrdom, and of courageous battle with steel against tyranny. At various times, either of these Janus heads might be emphasized.

Second, where the social conditions threatened believers with death, Twelver jurists required pious dissimulation (*taqiyya*) or the denial that they were Shi`ites. This verbal self-negation was designed to substitute for physical annihilation. Some Twelvers argued against holding communal Friday prayers in the absence of the Imam, for fear it would provoke violence among Sunnis. Others insisted on the prayers despite their provocative nature. The sense of danger, the need to conceal, informed all religious observances performed by Twelver Shi`ites in places where they formed a minority. For Sunnis, the Hijazi holy cities of Mecca and Medina constitute places where one may be a complete Muslim - indeed, where one never sees a non-Muslim. We learn, however, that even great Twelver scholars from the Iraqi shrine cities dissimulated about their convictions when they went to Ottoman-ruled Mecca. When the major Usuli scholar and later head of the Imami establishment in the shrine cities of Iraq, Sayyid Mihdi Tabataba'i (d. *circa* 1797), left Karbala to go on pilgrimage in the 1770s he assiduously dodged questions from Sunnis about his rite.[18] The existential ambiguity of such daily misrepresentation of one's innermost self cannot easily be understood by outsiders. Third, Twelvers generally considered most outsiders ritually impure, and favored endogamy, though exceptions clearly occurred.[19]

We can see here at the outset several elements in the Twelver Arabs' ethnic survival.[20] Jabal `Amil, southern Iraq, and eastern Arabia all constituted fairly compact and defensible territories that proved relatively difficult of access for outsiders. Their highly organized clan lineages threw up paramount chiefs who demanded respect from neighbors and from the imperial center on the basis of their command of armed force. When force failed, Twelvers could legitimately dissimulate to escape persecution. Both a highly trained corps of clergy or ulama, and a subaltern stratum of cantors of mourning poetry, helped preserve, transmit, and spread knowledge of the texts and central beliefs and practices of Twelver Shi`ism among townsmen and peasants. A strong belief in the ritual pollution of outsiders, much different from the attitude among Sunnis, also helped isolate the Twelver communities and reinforced tendencies to endogamy.

II

The second period saw more autonomy for the Twelvers, and brought up the question of whether they had sufficient resources to take advantage of it. The Ottomans, increasingly preoccupied with eastern Europe and the growing Russian threat, and suffering from the eroding effects of high inflation in Anatolia, willy-nilly allowed greater autonomy to their Arab provinces from the middle of the eighteenth century. Ottoman slave-soldier (*kullar*) regimes became virtually autonomous in Egypt, the Levant, and Iraq. Even these rulers depended for provincial support on local elites, and Albert Hourani characterized this period as one of "the politics of the notables."[21] It seems indisputable that Twelvers on the whole benefited from this decentralization. The virtual eclipse of Twelver Shi`ism during the previous century as a political force in Asia thus proved a short-term phenomenon.  At the same time as local notables promoted rising Twelver power in the Ottoman Arab lands, the Zands and then Qajars restored Twelver power in Iran, and Awadh or Oudh emerged as a substantial Shi`ite-ruled state in post-Mughal India.

Just as local Sunni notables, merchants and ulama played a more active role in this period because of the weakness at the Ottoman center, so Imami notables came to the fore in their regions. In Jabal `Amil Twelver feudal bosses, and in Iraq Twelver tribal leaders, urban-based date plantation owners, Sayyids, and ulama in the shrine cities asserted at times an unprecedented autonomy. Still, Sunni governors ruled over the Iraqi Imamis from 1750 to 1831, and even revered Twelver shrines like that of Imam `Ali had Sunni caretakers appointed over them for most of this period. Sunni officials in the shrine cities, however much they detested Shi`ism, tolerated it and the pilgrimage trade associated with it for the wealth it brought southern Iraq.[22]

As will be discussed at greater length in Chapter Six below, in the 1820s the shrine city of Karbala began to evolve into a virtual city-state, ruled by a coalition of local notables, urban gangs, and ulama with little reference to the slave-soldiers in Baghdad, much less to Istanbul. Karbala Twelvers began publicly saying Friday congregational prayers in their own manner, whereas previously they had either said them only in private or had refrained from gathering for them at all. Twelver ulama and institutions received large amounts of money from believers in Iran, from the Iranian government and its officials, and from the Twelver government of Awadh in north India, wealth that also helped Imamis assert their independence of the Baghdad governors, and, later, Ottomans.[23]

The Ottomans lost their grip on the Levant even before they did so on Iraq, and Twelver Shi`ite feudal chieftains in Jabal `Amil, formerly co-opted by the governing Druze Ma'ns, asserted greater local control in the middle of the eighteenth century. They benefited from the cotton-driven commercial revival of southern Syria, especially after they acquired the *iltizam* (fief-like land grant) of Tyre in 1759.[24] Later in the century, Twelver feudal bosses at first allied themselves with Ahmad Pasha al-Jazzar, the potentate of `Akka, in his struggles with other local notables in Damascus and the Levantine coast. The Pasha later expanded into Twelver territory itself, however, coming into conflict with powerful Twelver clan chieftains. Al-Jazzar and his successor preferred to have their own officials in charge of the Imami areas, but from the 1820s the Twelver clan chiefs were given control once more over Jabal `Amil provided they acted as tax farmers and vassals for `Akka.[25] In this period local elites and their shifting political alliances most directly affected the lives of Twelvers, rather than the directives of the sultan and his religious establishment in Istanbul.

Ironically, genuine Ottoman reassertion came decades later in the Levant than in Iraq, despite the former's greater proximity to Istanbul. Sultan Mahmud's plans for increased centralization were at first delayed by the Ottoman civil war of the 1830s, in which the insurgent Egyptians (subjects of the sultan before and after this war) occupied Greater Syria for almost a decade. The Shihabis, a local vassal dynasty who collaborated with the Egyptians, had important allies among the Twelvers, though rival Twelver leaders and disgruntled peasantry did at times challenge Egyptian-Shihabi rule, especially in the late 1830s.[26] The reestablishment of light Ottoman sovereignty over the Levant with European help in 1840 actually initiated a generation of Twelver near-autonomy in Jabal `Amil under Hamd Bey and `Ali al-As`ad. Imami authors have seen a cultural efflorescence in Jabal `Amil in the first six decades of the nineteenth century, partially fueled by the patronage of Twelver magnates such as Hamd Bey.[27] In Baalbek during the 1840s and 1850s the Ottoman authorities were forced to appoint members of the Twelver notable clan, the Harfush, as almost autonomous local governors, though they sporadically attempted to weaken them by playing one family off against another.[28]

In the Persian Gulf, sedentary Twelver populations faced raiding and domination by Sunni and Wahhabi pastoralists. Periodic Wahhabi occupations of al-Hasa, and Sunni Utubi dominance of Bahrain, subjected Shi`ites to various sorts of discrimination. In Iraq and the Levant the shifting alliances of relatively weak local Sunni notables required a willingness to play with all the pieces on the board and a consequent de-emphasis on the Sunni triumphalist ideology of the old Ottoman variety, leaving Twelvers wider interstices for cultural and political self-assertion. In the Gulf, however, puritan Wahhabi ideology subjected traditional or esoteric Twelvers to even harsher persecution than they had suffered under the Ottomans, and the new tribal bases of power in the region left their villagers and townsmen with few options other than political submission or flight.

From 1750 to the middle of the nineteenth century, then, Twelvers in the decentralizing Ottoman empire rallied. Greater local power led to the retention of more resources at home, and therefore to a mitigation of the worst disabilities Twelvers normally suffered under Ottoman rule. With the exceptions of al-Jazzar's rule in Palestine in the late eighteenth century, and Sunni and Wahhabi tribal incursions in Eastern Arabia, less conflict, economic exploitation, and detraction from minority power took place at a local level. This improvement was owed, however, to Ottoman weakness rather than to any change in Ottoman policy. In this phase, ethnic identity among Twelvers came to the fore partially because of their relative distance from Istanbul at a time of weakness in the imperial center. They could under these circumstances bring more effectively into play some of their natural advantages as an ethnic community: their political clout in the Iraqi shrine cities, their tribal control over trade routes between Iran and Iraq, and their often dominant position at the Mediterranean port of Tyre.[29]

III

The rest of the nineteenth century saw the strengthening of imperial control over the provinces and the increasing impact of the capitalist world market, centered in industrializing Europe, on the Ottoman empire. The net result of these changes for most Twelvers was probably negative.

They lost much of the semi-autonomy they had gained in southern Iraq and Jabal `Amil. One of the two Twelver states remaining in the world (Awadh) was absorbed into the British Indian empire, and Twelvers were on the whole badly placed to take advantage of the new commercial opportunities opening up.

From the late eighteenth century and throughout the nineteenth, the Shi`ite shrine cities of Najaf, Karbala and later Samarra emerged as key trainers of Shi`ite clergy for the whole world and as places where Iranian and Indian dissidents could go into exile. Their ulama were successful, from the eighteenth century, in proselytizing the Arab tribes of southern Iraq, bringing many of them over to Shi`ism. (This mass conversion may have in part been a reproof from the tribespeople to their Sunni Ottoman overlords, and a protest of their treatment by the latter). Ethnically Iranian Shi`ites formed a substantial minority in Najaf, Karbala, and Baghdad. Shi`ite clergymen from Iran such as Sayyid Murtada Ansari were often prominent in the leadership of the religion from the shrine cities, and helped train both Arabic-speaking speaking and Persian-speaking students. Meir Litvak has argued that the Shi`ite clergy of Ottoman Iraq were most often in a weak position, disliked and even despised by their Sunni rulers, and so they needed to curry favor with both the British and the Qajar dynasty of Iran. This need for foreign assistance led them to be relatively quietist with regard to Iranian politics, with only a few major exceptions, throughout the nineteenth century. At the same time, he feels that the shahs in Iran paid far more attention to cultivating Iranian ulama in Qum, Isfahan, and elsewhere, because they felt them more influential. The Qajars did bestow stipends on ulama in Iraq, and donated funds to gild shrines.[30]

Sometimes the Iranians felt strongly about the treatment of Iraqi Shi`ites, and there was pressure on Muhammad Shah to go to war with the Ottomans when the latter invaded Karbala and massacred rebellious Shi`ites in 1843 (see Chapter 6 below). It is worth noting, however, that he did not succumb to this pressure. Perhaps it is precisely because monies coming from the Indian Shi`ite courts were so much less politicized on the surface that the Ottomans allowed them in and the Shi`ite clergy sought them. Too close an association with the shah of Iran could make one look too much like a traitor to Istanbul. The violent Ottoman occupation of Karbala in 1843, Yitzhak Nakash has argued, had two major consequences. One was that most of the great Shi`ite scholars moved instead to neighboring Najaf, which gained a preeminent position as a Shi`ite center. The other was that the Iranian government, alarmed at the violence in Karbala against Iranian subjects, succeeded in pressuring the Ottomans to grant Iranian subjects certain immunities, giving them thereafter a favorable position in Iraq. Iranian officials dominated posts like the mayor of Najaf and the custodian of the shrine of Imam Husayn in Karbala until 1917.[31]

Although an ideal has long been articulated in Twelver jurisprudence of the dominant Usuli school that there should be one central Shi`ite jurisprudent to whom all Shi`ites should look for guidance, this ideal was seldom put into practice before the communications revolutions of the twentieth century. Despite the prominence of Iranian cleric Murtada Ansari in Iraq during the 1850s, for instance, his major institutional role appears to have been to supervise the funds coming into the shrine cities as religious taxes and donations. For the most part regional Shi`ites put their ultimate faith in the most prominent of their local clergymen. Even in the twentieth century, the Arab Shi`ites often looked to the leading jurisprudent in Iraq for their guidance rather than to an Iranian.

As noted, from 1826 the Ottoman Sultan Mahmud II began an effective centralization of the empire. In 1831 direct Ottoman rule was reestablished over Iraq and the slave-soldiers ousted. The sultan's modernization of his armed forces, however, could not alone have rescued him from the ambitious viceroy of Egypt, Muhammad `Ali, who made a bid to take over the empire in the 1830s. Only European intervention saved the sultan from losing this Ottoman civil war. After the 1840 Treaty of London, however, the process of centralization continued apace outside Egypt. It met opposition from the Twelvers of southern Iraq, who, especially in their shrine cities, had attained a sort of autonomy. When the city of Karbala unanimously refused to accept a Turkish garrison, hard line Ottoman governor Najib Pasha ordered an invasion that crushed the Imamis' opposition in January of 1843 and left some five thousand dead. The cruelty of Ottoman troops toward the civilian population, which had wholeheartedly supported the rebellion, carried with it the emotional baggage of Sunni hostility toward Twelvers. So too did the Ottoman policy of making Imami shrines into barracks for rowdy infantrymen. The Ottomans continued thereafter aggressively to face down the Twelvers, whether in the shrine cities or in the hinterland where tribespeople roamed, and once again to collect from them taxes and tribute.[32]

Some disabilities of Twelvers in nineteenth century Ottoman Iraq derived more from their social position than their perceived heterodoxy. Thus, the Twelver Khaza`il tribespeople often participated in revolts against Baghdad's attempts to extract more money from them or to manipulate their politics, and it would be difficult to prove that such conflicts differed substantially from those between the Ottomans and the Sunni Kurdish clans. In the south, tribal coalitions formed easily across sectarian lines in the face of imperial encroachments. The Ottomans launched campaigns against the tribes and marsh Arabs and even went so far as to drain swamps in order to control them. As the century wore on, the modernizing Ottomans increasingly gained the military advantage over the Khaza`il and other Shi`ite tribes.[33]

Twelver peasants, tribespeople, and marsh Arabs in southern Iraq suffered from the economic changes in the second half of the nineteenth century, as well. Ottoman land-registration practices and enforced sedentarization reduced many proud Twelver pastoralists to landless peasants laboring for their chief, who became a large landlord. The opening of the Suez canal in 1869 favored the cultivation of cash crops and the Sunni urban brokers. The economic gap between urban Sunnis and the Twelver marsh Arabs widened considerably.[34]

The rise of Ottoman reformism and the promotion of an ideology of Ottoman nationalism that would offer all subjects of the sultan equal rights should on the face of it have benefited the empire's Twelvers. But even the application of greater rationalism in government can prove invidious. The career of reformer Midhat Pasha provides several anecdotes that demonstrate how differently the "reformers" might look to a Shi`ite. On becoming governor of Baghdad province in 1869, Midhat's first task was to subdue the largely Twelver tribes to the south in order to increase state revenues. He initiated the Ottoman reconquest of the Twelver region of al-Hasa in 1871, with an eye both to military strategy and to tax income (Twelvers in the Gulf may have preferred Ottoman rule to that of the Wahhabis, but they did complain of mistreatment and over-taxation at the hands of the Ottomans). Midhat then had the treasures and offerings stored at Shi`ite shrines in Najaf appraised at TL 300,000, and proposed an auction so that the proceeds could be used for public works like a railway line. Midhat's son sadly reported that "this reasonable proposal, however, was vetoed by the Persian Ulemas." In the 1890s the government of Sultan Abdülhamid II (r. 1876-1909) attempted to curb Shi`ism and to proselytize Twelvers, hoping to convert them to Sunnism. The central government dared not go too far in this direction, however, lest it provoke rebellion in the Iraqi south.[35]

Later in the century urban Twelvers in Iraq became involved in secret societies, opposition to the tobacco monopoly granted by Iran's shah to a Britisher, and the ferment that preceded the Iranian Constitutional Revolution of 1905-1911. The involvement of Iraqi Shi`ites with the call for a constitution in Iran sensitized them also to the increasing dissatisfaction within the Ottoman empire with Abdulhamid II's absolutism. With the Young Turk revolution of 1908 and the introduction of parliamentary party politics, many of Iraq's Twelvers showed renewed interest in Ottoman public affairs. They, however, along with many other Arab Ottomans, shared in the subsequent disillusionment produced by the

Young Turks' turn toward despotism and exaltation of Turkish ethnicity within the empire.[36]

As noted, the Ottoman recovery in the Levant came later than that in Iraq. By the 1850s and 1860s the rural feuding and peasant revolt that disrupted Palestine, Mt. Lebanon and the Shouf mountains had raised the real danger of European intervention, especially with the Christian-Druze violence of 1859-60 in which some 10,000-15,000 Christians died. Shi`ite notables had long been clients of either Druze or Maronite magnates, and were often caught in the middle. The Ottomans finally reacted by garrisoning more troops and more actively ensuring order. They also accepted legal changes that gave more equality to non-Muslim religious minorities and protected commerce. Just as Maronite and Druze feudal bosses lost some autonomy through this Ottoman reassertion, so too did the Imami landlords in Jabal `Amil. In 1864 `Ali Bey al-As`ad and another Twelver large landlord were imprisoned by the Ottoman authorities, probably on charges of withholding tax monies from Istanbul. Thereafter the center tightened administration and tax collecting in Jabal `Amil. As of 1859, as well, the Twelver Harfush family was deprived of its power in Baalbek, and the area came under direct Ottoman rule. On the other hand, the new judicial regime established for the Mutasarrifate of Mount Lebanon, a separate administrative unit with a Maronite Christian majority, did extend an unusual recognition to the Twelver Shi`ites on the part of the Ottomans. An administrative council was established in 1864 with 12 members from the various religious communities, and one of them was to be a Shi`ite. The central court was also directed to have six official counsels, representing the major religious communities, including one for the Shi`ites.[37]

Twelver peasants, lacking the Maronites' links to Europe, remained largely uninvolved in the silk industry and other production for the world market in the nineteenth century, thereby falling behind other confessional communities in income and sophistication. The greatest oppression of Twelvers in the Levant derived from the system of subsistence peasant farming and quasi-feudal bosses and landlords, from which they did not even begin to escape in the nineteenth century. The abjectness of their economic niche affected the Twelvers' political position as well, relegating them to relative unimportance in the eyes of Ottoman governors, whereas Maronites and Druze gained the virtual partition of the vilayet of Beirut as it was gerrymandered to fit their competing interests. If the reforms of 1856 and the establishment of a Christian-dominated Mutasarrifate in Mount Lebanon challenged Sunni and Druze elites by giving more equality to Christians, they virtually pushed the Twelvers to the bottom of the Levantine social ladder.

Twelvers in al-Hasa continued to suffer tribal rule, witnessing several Wahhabi incursions and contests with mainly Sunni tribes, and direct Saudi rule 1792-1818 and 1843-71. These contests were punctuated by attempts of imperial centers to assert themselves, as with the Egyptian expeditions of 1819 and 1839 and the Ottoman reconquest of 1871. Shi`ites suffered from the opprobrium in which their branch of Islam was held by `Utubis, Wahhabis or Ottomans. In the first Saudi state, the Wahhabis made a concerted effort to assimilate the Twelvers forcibly to Wahhabism. The second state was somewhat less oppressive religiously, partially because of its weakness.[38] Some Twelver ulama in the area so resented the disestablishment that they attempted, unsuccessfully, to intrigue at Nasir al-Din Shah's court for the Qajar annexation of Eastern Arabia. The Ottoman reconquest of the area in 1871 made little difference to the lives of local people, since the empire remained very weak in the area, with only small garrisons. Complaints about excessive taxation were lodged, though the Ottomans were certainly far more religiously tolerant than had been the Wahhabis.[39]

In the Ottoman Empire, vigorous demotic Shi`ite communities had existed long before the advent of the Safavids in Iran, in Jabal `Amil, al-Hasa, and some cities of Iraq. As most of these came under Ottoman rule, the political rivalries between Iran and the Ottomans made them suspect as a fifth column in the eyes of Istanbul. These Arabic-speaking Shi`ites had no local courts to receive gifts, favors or support from the Safavids and their successors. Most of them could benefit from Shi`ite ascendency in Iran only indirectly, by studying there or developing contacts with its nobles.

From the mid-nineteenth century, Twelver minorities lost whatever previous semi-autonomy they had gained during the age of the politics of the notables. They were forced to submit once again to more direct Ottoman rule in Iraq, al-Hasa and the Levant. In the first phases of Ottoman reassertion, rebellious Twelvers in Iraq were dealt with harshly by their Sunni vanquishers, their institutions disrupted, shrines desecrated, populations sometimes displaced, local leaders deposed. That is, after a period during which Ottoman weakness had led to greater de facto toleration of Shi`ites, the Tanzimat reforms involved a policy toward them of renewed subjugation. The Ottomans subjugated the Levant with less violence, whereas in Karbala, which was resisted, the Ottomans showed themselves entirely capable of massacring the recalcitrant Shi`ites. Especially from 1856, changes occurred in the ideology of the empire. The Tanzimat decrees of equality for all Ottoman subjects marked a move toward a majority policy of pluralism, where cultural variability is permitted as long as it does not threaten national unity and security. The new ideologies of Ottomanism and, later in the century, pan-Islam, did seem to promise an improvement in the status of Shi`ite subjects of the sultan. In the event, the Tanzimat reforms benefited the Christians more than the Twelvers, and pan-Islam had strong Sunni commitments behind the scenes.

Late in the nineteenth century Sultan Abdulhamid pursued two contradictory policies toward the Shi`ites of Iraq. On the one hand, he sought to cultivate their support for his Pan-Islamic project, which aimed to unite all Muslims against European colonialism. On the other, he acceded to the requests of his strongly Sunni administrators to allow them to attempt to missionize the Shi`ites on behalf of Sunnism. In fact, neither Pan-Islam nor Sunni missions to the Shi`ites had any observable success. Constriction of Imami opportunities continued, however. Moreover, the Imamis' relative economic position deteriorated. Twelver peasants in Jabal `Amil, and Twelver tribespeople, marsh Arabs and peasants in Iraq, continued to live a largely subsistence economy, and landlordism increased as a social phenomenon and problem in the Twelver Arab areas. Whereas Maronite and Sunni merchants in Beirut, and Jewish and Sunni brokers in Baghdad began to participate in the world economy, at least as compradors, the Ottoman Shi`ites occupied the more backward sectors of the empire's economy.

3

Rival Empires of Trade and Shi`ism in Eastern Arabia

The history of the Shi`ite Muslims in the isles of Bahrain and the oases of Qatif and al-Hasa has been little studied despite the economic and political importance lent them by the large petroleum deposits in their region. The significance of this community has been further magnified by the rise in the Gulf region of Shi`ite radicalism, as in the Iranian Revolution of 1978-1979, the failed 1981 Shi`ite coup attempt in Bahrain, and the continued struggle of some Bahraini Shi`ite oppositionists against policies of the ruling emirs in the past few years. The study of Shi`ism in the Gulf has advanced so little that even a basic chronology and overview of institutional developments are lacking for all but the most recent decades. A full history of Twelver Shi`ism in the Gulf would require archival research in Portuguese, Iranian, Ottoman, Dutch, French, and British repositories, in addition to extensive manuscript work in eastern Arabia itself. Until this daunting task is tackled in a thoroughgoing manner, it may be useful to make a preliminary survey of Twelver Shi`ite history in the Gulf in its formative pre-modern period of 1300-1800 on the basis of more accessible sources, such as published travel accounts and Twelver Shi`ite biographical dictionaries.

The following overview has the limited ambition of showing shift from Ismaili Shi`ism to the Usuli school of Twelver Shi`ism; and finally to the Akhbari school of Twelver Shi`ism, as the major ideological orientation of Bahrain Twelvers. In addition to tracing institutional and ideological developments, this study has several analytical concerns. These questions include the relationship of dynastic, social, and economic changes to Shi`ism, the shifting economic bases of religious institutions, and the specific social origins of the Twelver clerical corps (ulama).

Eastern Arabia has been an arena of contention between Sunni Muslims, partisans of the orthodox caliphs, and Shi`is, partisans of the Prophet's cousin and son-in-law, `Ali. We are concerned with two major branches of Shi`ism here.  The Ismailis follow one of several still-existing lines of `Ali's descendants through Isma`il b. Ja`far al-Sadiq. The Twelvers followed Isma`il's brother Kazim and his descendants, holding that the later eleventh Imam had a small son who went into supernatural occultation and would return in the future.

The geographical isolation and economic richness of eastern Arabia help explain why it sometimes threw up regional states. But that wealth, combined with its relatively small population, also accounts for the many attempts that nearby great powers made to incorporate this region into their territories. Its proximity to undersea pearl fields enriched its merchants and notables while also attracting conquerors; divers and peasants seldom shared much, however, in Bahrain's fabled prosperity. The area benefited from the trade in spices between Asia and Europe, some of which passed through the Gulf. The Baharina or indigenous Arab Shi`ite inhabitants of eastern Arabia are still a majority on the isles of Bahrain and once constituted an even greater proportion of the population.[1]  Other areas of Shi`ite settlement include the port city and oasis of Qatif, and the oases of al-Hasa, both now in Saudi Arabia.[2] Al-Hasa consists of a group of oases in a 180 sq. km "L" shape southeast of Qatif, which take their collective name from pools of water (*hisy*) collecting above a stony substratum in sandy soil. The region has traditionally produced dates, horses, and fine textiles.

The wealth of this region often gave it an autonomy from surrounding powers expressed in a local ideology of Shi`ism. The Shi`ite pastoralists, peasants and pearl divers were dominated by their own elite of clan elders, urban merchants, and landholders. But Sunni Bedouins and distant naval powers often conquered the Shi`ite triangle. Eastern Arabia formed part of the medieval Islamic empires. From the late ninth century AD, however, a local branch of the Ismaili movement, the Carmathian (Qarmati) sect, set up a polity there. A radical religious group encompassing pastoralists, peasants and townsmen, it established a more egalitarian social system than was normal in the 10th century Middle East.[3] The Carmathian state controlled for a while the Arabian peninsula's overland trade and pilgrimage routes, but from the middle of the 11th century they lost political control to local Sunni tribes loyal to the Sunni Saljuqs. A succession of tribal dynasties and Gulf naval powers thereafter exercised varying degrees of control. In 1330, the forces of Hurmuz, ruled in the early 14th century by Qutb al-Din Tahamtam, conquered Bahrain.[4]

The Baharina gradually traded the radical, egalitarian Ismailism of the ninth through 11th century Carmathian movement for a more quietist version of Shi`ism the Twelver or Imami branch which Sunni rulers considered less objectionable.[5] This change is now difficult to trace.

Carmathian tribes remained politically important at least into the 15th century. But from the 13th century Twelver biographical dictionaries begin mentioning ulama from Bahrain and al-Hasa. For instance, Maytham b. `Ali al-Bahrani (d. 1280 AD) wrote on Twelver doctrine, affirming free will, the infallibility of prophets and imams, the appointed imamate of `Ali, and the occultation of the Twelfth Imam.[6] By tracing the history of Twelver Shi`ism through biographical dictionaries, we can gain some picture of indigenous cultural and religious developments.

Jarwanid Bahrain and the Imami Ulama

Sunni rule in the Shi`ite regions of eastern Arabia remained tenuous, and by the end of the 13th century had greatly declined, allowing Shi`ite tribal forces to assert their autonomy. Among these Ismaili populations some Twelver Shi`ites also existed, and Twelver clerical expertise proved useful to the reigning Ismaili chiefs. Twelver experts in Shi`ite law (mujtahids) trained in Iraq were recruited to staff judicial and administrative posts. Twelver and Ismaili law was similar enough to allow this symbiosis, and the Ismaili tribespeople appear to have lacked the seminaries and clerical traditions to produce enough of their own judges and clerical administrators.

At the opening of the 14th century the local Carmathian chieftain, Sa'id b. Mughamis dominated eastern Arabia, probably as a vassal of the Tibi merchant princes of the isle of Qays, tributaries of the Il-Khanid Mongols. In 1305-1306 AD (705 A.H.) Sa'id the Carmathian was defeated in Qatif by Bedouin forces led by Jarwan al-Maliki, of the Quraysh tribe. The Banu Jarwan ruled "the lands of Bahrain" (Qatif, al-Hasa, and the Bahrain isles) for nearly a century and a half, renewing Shi`ite power there. Jarwan was followed by his son Nasir, then by his grandson Ibrahim (still alive in 1417). Al-Sakhawi called the Jarwanids "remnants of the Carmathians," suggesting that they were an Ismaili tribe.[7]

From the 1330s the Banu Jarwan began paying tribute to the Sunni kings of Hurmuz. Local Shi`ite rule gave a certain freedom to the Imami ulama, though Imamis were probably still a minority. The North African traveler Ibn Battuta visited Qatif around 1331, finding it inhabited by Arab tribes whom he described as "extremist Shi`is" (*rafidiyya ghulat*). This is how a Sunni would describe Ismailis. He noted that in Qatif the mosques called to prayer in an openly Shi`ite manner, including phrases about `Ali. Ibn Batutta described the great wealth of the area, writing that the Jarwanid ruler took one fifth of the pearl revenues in taxes, and saying that al-Hasa grew more dates than any place else in the world.[8]

The major Imami Shi`ite figure in Bahrain during this era was Shaykh Ahmad b. `Abd Allah Ibn al-Mutawwaj al-Bahrani called by one early source "the leader of the Imamis in his time."[9] A mujtahid, his legal rulings were renowned in the east and the west. Shaykh Ahmad Ibn al-Mutawwaj studied in Iraq at al-Hilla with `Allama Fakhr al-Din Muhammad al-Hilli (d. 1369), the son of the celebrated Usuli innovator `Allama al-Hilli, receiving diplomas from him and other Iraqi scholars. Shaykh Ahmad adopted the new Usuli school from his teacher, but he had differences with some Usulis, debating Shams al-Din Muhammad b. Makki, the Imami "First Martyr" (d. 1384), several times. In Bahrain, the local Ismaili rulers, the Banu Jarwan, put Shaykh Ahmad Ibn al-Mutawwaj in charge of policing market prices (*hisba*) and deciding legal questions.

As an Usuli, Shaykh Ahmad believed that legal rulings could be derived from the Qur'an and the Imami oral sayings, not simply through finding a scriptural source and interpreting it literally, but through the independent exercise (*ijtihad*) of legal reasoning (*`aql*, based on Greek rationalism). Here, as elsewhere, the willingness of Usuli clerics to cooperate with and legitimate the state under which they lived, performing judicial and administrative functions, made them more useful to the state than were the conservative Akhbaris. Akhbaris insisted on a literal interpretation of the Qur'an and oral reports, and often disallowed the central functions of the Islamic state in the absence of the Twelfth Imam.

The 1300s witnessed important advances in institutionalizing the position of at least some Imami ulama, which would have helped men like Shaykh Ahmad Ibn al-Mutawwaj bring many into the Twelver branch. Indeed, at least one member of the Banu Jarwan became a Twelver cleric - Shaykh Jamal al-Din Hasan al-Matbu` al-Jarwan of Al-Hasa.[10] Another Imami figure who attained high posts under the Jarwanids, Shaykh Nasir al-Din Ibrahim b. Nizar al-Ahsa'i, served as chief judge (*qadi al-qudat*) and became an important teacher.[11] Perhaps nowhere else in the Islamic world of the 14th century did Imami Shi`ites have the kind of freedom and institutional position they possessed in Jarwanid Bahrain and East Arabia.

During the 15th century east Arabian Shi`ites maintained their strong links with Iraq. The direction of the trade routes may have facilitated travel from eastern Arabia to the Shi`ite shrine cities. Already in the 1420s Venice was the destination for some spices brought by merchants from further East through the Gulf and thence to Basra for transshipment via Syria.[12] Twelver Shi`ite merchant-ulama could combine study and pilgrimage with trade, and some became teachers. Shaykh Nasir Ibn al-Mutawwaj of Bahrain taught the Sufi Shi`ite Ahmad b. Fahd al-Hilli (d.

1437), which indicates that the Shi`ite scholars of Bahrain were considered to have preserved Imami oral reports that made it worthwhile to study with them. Ahmad b. Fahd al-Hilli in turn taught another Sufi Shi`i, Sayyid Muhammad Nurbakhsh (d. 1463), whose father was from the Qatif region.[13]   Nurbakhsh rose to become the leader of the Kubrawiyya Sufi order in Iran, and claims were put forward that he was a mahdi or messiah. His esoteric ideas may owe something to an undercurrent of folk Shi`ism in East Arabia that maintained Ismaili traditions.

Ahmad b. Fahd al-Hilli trained more orthodox scholars as well, and one of his students helped to promote Imami orthodoxy in Bahrain. Shaykh Muflih b. Hasan came originally from near Basra but emigrated to Bahrain, settling in Salmabad during Jarwanid times.[14] He wrote a commentary on `Allama al-Hilli's *Shara'i` al-Islam* and a work aimed at Sunnis on `Ali's right to the caliphate. In Bahrain, he excommunicated Ibn Qarqur, a notable whom he accused of playing with the Law of Islam. This anathema suggests the continued existence of heterodox ideas among influential Shi`ites in Bahrain, and the role of Iraqi-trained Imami ulama in spreading more scripturalist Twelver notions. Shaykh Muflih's commentary on the work of `Allama al-Hilli indicates that he was an Usuli, apparently the major Imami legal school under the Jarwanids. At least, several other 14th century scholars from the region wrote commentaries on Usuli works.[15]

The century and a half of local Ismaili rule by the Jarwanids as vassals of the Sunni Hurmuz empire allowed the extensive development of Twelver thought and institutions. Twelver clerics became court judges, took control of the market police, and served as jurisconsults. They had to make compromises with their Ismaili patrons. Yet they certainly enjoyed more freedom, and, indeed, privilege, than Sunni rulers would have granted.

Banu Jabr

The middle of the 15th century witnessed a revival of tribal and dynastic struggles over markets in the region as the Banu Jabr, a Sunni Bedouin tribe originally from Najd but settled in Al-Hasa, came into conflict with Banu Jarwan. Sayf b. Zamil al-Jabri rose up against and killed the last Jarwanid ruler, taking over his lands. With this economic and territorial base, the Banu Jabr became a major force in east Arabia, intermarrying with the ruling family of Hurmuz.[16] A leader of the Banu Jabr obtained the cession of Bahrain and Qatif from the king of Hurmuz, the titular sovereign of those areas, except for some gardens the monarch reserved to himself. But later Salghur Shah of Hurmuz changed his mind about this arrangement, which deprived him of the extensive pearl and date revenues of Bahrain and Qatif, and he made war on Banu Jabr until they, in 1485, agreed to pay him tribute after all. This agreement lasted until 1507. Thereafter the Hurmuzis made several inconclusive attempts to wrest Bahrain from the delinquent Banu Jabr.[17]

The 1460s marked the first time for a century and a half that east Arabian Shi`ites labored for a prolonged period under a local Sunni government, and this change produced traumatic readjustments. For two centuries, the Shi`ite Baharina were to endure the governance of non-Shi`ites. The Jabrids appointed Maliki Sunni judges instead of Shi`ite ones, initiated Sunni Friday prayers, and greatly encouraged the pilgrimage to Mecca. They forced some Shi`ite judges to become Sunnis.[18] Shi`ite ulama, though disadvantaged were not wholly quiescent. Shaykh Muflih's son, Shaykh Husayn (d. 1526), continued to help spread a concern with Imami law and theological orthodoxy in Bahrain.[19] He went on pilgrimage to Mecca or visitation to the shrine cities of Iraq nearly every year, which attests, not only to his piety, but also to his wealth. The sources do not indicate the provenance of that wealth, but it seems likely that these early Imami scholars were involved in the pearl trade, just as were those of the 17th and 18th centuries. Even under the Sunni Jabrids, some Shi`ites became wealthy and prominent.

Banu Jabr ended the appointment of Shi`ite scholars to head the judiciary and the market police, and persecuted Shi`ism. But they clearly did not extirpate it, and a few Shi`ite ulama, some of them local men of substance, continued to study, teach, and write in the lands of Bahrain. Jabrid hostility to Shi`ism may have been one reason Shaykh Muhammad Ibn Abi Jumhur al-Ahsa'i (b. 1434), one of the region's great minds in that era, spent most of his intellectual life abroad.[20] He had the misfortune to complete his education just as the Jabrids came to power. He began his studies in al-Hasa with his father, but went on to Najaf in Iraq. The 1480s and l490s found him teaching in Iraq and Iran, though he visited Al-Hasa in 1488. His theological works were informed by illuminationism in the school of Suhrawardi, Sufi metaphysics after Ibn `Arabi, and scholastic metaphysics in the style of Avicenna. A profound knowledge of Avicenna was common among Imami scholars of eastern Arabia, but the Sufi emphases were rarer, because Sufi leaders were seen as competitors of the Imams. Scholastic metaphysics characterized the work of Maytham b. `Ali, noted above, and Nasir al-Din Tusi, popularized it in the 13th century. Ibn Abi Jumhur was not the first or only Imami Sufi. One earlier Twelver with similar proclivities was the Iranian Sayyid Haydar Amuli (b. 1320), an adherent of the school of Ibn `Arabi.[21]

Ibn Abi Jumhur's interest in esoteric styles of thought might have derived from currents in his homeland (Ismailism and Sufism were both present there in his youth). He sought to synthesize his Usuli beliefs with other traditions, and this departure from narrow orthodoxy might have been in part made possible by the fall of the Shi`ite establishment in eastern Arabia. The Imami community in the late 1400s had few sanctions or mechanisms of social control at its command.

Jabrid rule displaced Shi`ites from their positions of privilege under Banu Jarwan, depriving ulama of judicial and other official posts and sources of income. Some were even forced to embrace the Malik rite of Sunnism. But the Shi`ite peasants, divers, and weavers had less reason to desert their partisanship for `Ali, and those Imami ulama with independent incomes as pearl traders could likewise weather the storm.

Religious changes were not the only ones they faced. The Shi`ites of Bahrain, Qatif, and Al-Hasa dwelled along the renowned spice route from South and East Asia to Europe. Their geographical position and their own coveted economic resources, ensured that the rise of new global empires would have an immediate impact upon them.

RIVAL EMPIRES OF TRADE AND THE SHI`ITE TRIANGLE

The Portuguese and the Ottomans in the Gulf

The Gulf Shi`ites directly felt the changes brought about by Portuguese mercantile expansion on the seas of the Old World and Sunni Ottoman imperial conquest of the Arab lands of southwest Asia and North Africa. Shaykh Hasan b. Muflih would have witnessed from Bahrain, no doubt with horror, the rise of Portuguese power and the reduction of the island kingdom of Hormuz to a proxy for the Europeans. The Portuguese, having discovered the route to the Indian Ocean from the Atlantic by the Cape of Good Hope, swiftly began setting up a maritime empire based at Goa in India, into which they integrated the Persian Gulf entrepot port of Hurmuz, along with its political and economic dependencies, such as Bahrain.

Portuguese commander Albuquerque quickly realized the riches to be had by controlling the Hurmuz spice trade and the Bahrain pearl fisheries. The Portuguese finally took Hurmuz in 1515, after fighting a fierce naval battle against the island's navy. The Europeans, having made the Hurmuz shahs of the Qutb al-Din dynasty their vassals, wished to penetrate further into the Gulf itself. They faced the obstacle of the politically powerful Banu Jabr, led by three brothers who controlled Oman, the Persian Gulf coast west of Oman, and the Bahrain-Qatif area. Muqrin, the Jabrid ruler of Bahrain, refused to render tribute to the Portuguese-Hurmuzi condominium. In 1521 a joint Portuguese-Hurmuzi force undertook an expedition against Bahrain which subdued it and left Portuguese garrisons. Thus began three quarters of a century of European rule over the Shi`ites of Bahrain, though these Europeans exercised their authority over the islands through Hurmuzi governors, sometimes of doubtful loyalty.[22]

The Ottomans extended their empire into Syria (1516) and Egypt (1517), then marched on Iraq (1534). Their armies, backed by artillery, took the southern Iraqi port of Basra in 1536. They proceeded down the southern littoral of the Gulf, reaching al-Hasa in 1550, from which the Portuguese attempted, and failed, to dislodge them by sacking Qatif in 1552. Although the Portuguese could not expel the Ottomans from Al-Hasa and Basra, neither could the Turks push the Europeans out of the southern Gulf in their counterattacks on Hurmuz and Musqat later in 1552. Thereafter, the Portuguese decimated the Ottoman Basra fleet as it attempted to move to the Red Sea. In their contest with the Sunni Ottomans, the Portuguese looked to another new power in the region, the Twelver Shi`ite Safavids of Iran, as allies, guaranteeing the Iranians passage over the Gulf to Bahrain and Qatif (the starting point of the inner-Arabian trade route to Mecca and the Red Sea).[23]

Portuguese Bahrain suffered economically from high Portuguese duties and tribute, from the disruption of trade routes by naval battles, and from Portuguese economic policies. These policies included their attempt to divert the spice trade away from the Gulf-Mediterranean route to the Atlantic and shipping Bahrain pearls to Portugal on their own vessels. Formerly, Bahrain's merchants had traded the pearls themselves to Hurmuz and India.[24]

Ottoman rule also had unfortunate effects on the Shi`ites of Qatif and Al-Hasa. Many local Shi`ite landlords, whom the Ottomans saw as Iranians (*acem*) likely to support their Safavid enemies, had their land expropriated. The Ottomans closed off the trans-Arabian trade and pilgrimage route from Qatif to Mecca from the 1550s until at least 1591, which hurt local merchants who used to trade to Mecca in Indian goods. Istanbul feared that al-Hasa Shi`ites might spread Safavid propaganda in the Hijaz, and even when they reopened the route they barred Shi`ites from using it.[25]

Some positive economic developments did occur in the second half of the 16th century that may have benefited some Baharina. The Ottomans promoted a revival of the pepper trade from the Indian Ocean over their Arab possessions and thence to Europe. The Portuguese ceased their attempt to divert all of that trade to the Atlantic, and the spice route did indeed revive in what Braudel called the "Mediterranean revenge."[26]

Gulf Shi`ites suffered many vicissitudes during the Portuguese-Ottoman rivalry of the 16th century. They felt harsh European rule and watched their cities looted. In the first half of the century Portuguese economic policies caused some decline in the trans-Fertile Crescent trade with Europe. The Shi`is, under the local rule of Sunni vassals of the Portuguese and Ottomans, suffered religious disadvantages. The second half of the century saw an economic upturn, as the spice route revived and military encounters between the Ottomans and Portuguese grew less frequent. A status quo emerged, with the Ottomans in control of the mainland from Basra to al-Hasa and of the overland spice route to the Mediterranean, while the Portuguese, with their naval superiority, dominated the southern Gulf from Bahrain to Hurmuz, as well as the Indian Ocean trade.

Safavid Shi`ism and Portuguese Bahrain

Religious developments in the Iranian north had cultural implications for the Shi`ites of Bahrain as great as the hegemony of the Portuguese and the Ottomans. With the rise of a Shi`ite state in Iran, the eastern Arabian Shi`ites had an ideological ally in the region for the first time since the pro-Shi`ite Buyids last ruled Iraq in the middle of the 11th century. Still, Portuguese rule in the Gulf prevented its Arab Shi`ites from feeling the full impact of Safavid religious developments for another century.

In 1501, Shah Isma`il, leader of the militant Safavi Shi`ite Sufi order, became Shah of Iran with the help of Turkoman Shi`ite tribesmen from Anatolia. The new state imposed Shi`ism on Iran, ritually cursing Sunni holy figures, burning mosques, and expropriating the land of Sunnis. But the Safavids' preoccupation with their Ottoman foes in the northwest and in Iraq left them no opportunity to conquer the Persian Gulf. The Safavids in any case lacked a navy. Thus, they first accepted the nominal allegiance of the Sunni Hurmuzi dynasty, which at least in theory ruled most of the Gulf, then after 1514 accepted the Portuguese Hurmuzi condominium.

Under the Safavids, Imami Shi`ism in Iran changed greatly, with Usulism coming to the fore as a formal religious establishment and state religion. Especially in the reign of Shah Tahmasp (1533-1576), a corps of Shi`ite ulama attracted from Jabal `Amil and Iraq began making vast changes in the way Twelver Shi`ism was practiced. Prominent among these innovators was Shaykh `Ali b. `Abd al-`Ali al-Karaki (d. 1534), from what is now southern Lebanon.[27] In the first year of Shah Tahmasp's reign al-Karaki ordered that in every town a Shi`ite prayer leader be appointed. Since many Shi`ite ulama held Friday congregational prayers invalid in the Occultation, this move dismayed conservatives, especially Arab Shi`ites still under Sunni rule. But al-Karaki clearly intended to build up an ulama structure under his own authority and to make himself useful to the new regime by having his prayer leaders pronounce blessings on the Safavids in the Friday afternoon sermon. He allowed the collection of land tax (*kharaj*) in the Occultation, another controversial opinion, and wrote rules for Safavid tax collectors. He ordered that Shi`ites cease practicing pious dissimulation (*taqiyya*) out of fear of Sunnis, since they now had Safavid protection, and instituted the public cursing of the first two Sunni Caliphs.

By allowing the central functions of the state to be undertaken by someone other than a divinely appointed Imam, al-Karaki and his cohorts from Jabal `Amil made themselves general proxies for the Hidden Imam and legitimized the Shi`ite Safavid regime. They also began creating a Shi`ite religious hierarchy, staffed lin part by Arabs, based mostly on the newly created offices of Shi`ite prayer leader and Shaykh al-Islam. Safavid Usulism emerged as the ideology of Arab immigrant ulama within Iran, who sought upward mobility and the implementation of a new vision of Shi`ism through their alliance with the Safavid state. These innovations provoked opposition from two quarters. First, as Arjomand has shown, in Iran the old indigenous families in charge of religious institutions such as judgeships and pious endowment supervision, many of whom now embraced Shi`ism, resented the upstart Lebanese.[28] Second, many Shi`ites of the Arab world found al-Karaki's innovations inappropriate to their own situation, given their status as minorities under Sunni rule.

Arab Shi`ite ulama living in Mecca wrote to the immigrant Arab prayer leaders of Isfahan, complaining that their policy of publicly cursing the first caliphs revered by the Sunnis was causing a Sunni backlash against Shi`ites outside Iran.[29] An Arab figure from eastern Arabia, Ibrahim al-Qatifi, helped combat al-Karaki's establishmentarian form of Usuli Shi`ism.[30] Although he studied with al-Karaki when he first arrived in the shrine cities from Qatif in 1507, he later developed a bitter personal enmity for him. Al-Qatifi cautiously accepted the necessity of independent legal reasoning, and so could be categorized as an Usuli.[31] But, deriving from Sunni-ruled Jabrid Qatif, he advocated a conservative Usulism that would not exacerbate Sunni persecution of Shi`ites. Clinging to the conservative political culture of minority Shi`ism, he rejected the legitimacy of holding Friday prayers during the Occultation, of collecting kharaj land taxes, and of associating with rulers.

Al-Qatifi, based in Iraq, refused to take money offered him by Shah Tahmasp, for which al-Karaki publicly rebuked him. Shaykh `Ali invoked the example of Imam Hasan, who took a stipend from the Umayyad ruler Mu`awiya, pointing out acerbically that Shah Tahmasp was not as bad as Mu`awiya, nor was al-Qatifi better than Hasan. Al-Qatifi's reply to this argument was that taking money from an unjust (*zalim*, i.e., not divinely appointed) ruler was reprehensible, citing Shams al-Din Muhammad b.

Makki the First Martyr's argument that Hasan, as Imam, had a legal right to the money from Mu`awiya. Ulama, the argument implies, have no such right. Al-Qatifi resented al-Karaki's rise to the top of the Shi`ite establishment in Iran from 1533, saying he claimed to have a monopoly on learning and he intrigued against Shaykh `Ali with one of the latter's former students. Al-Qatifi lived to see the Ottoman conquest of Iraq in the 1530s, after which, aside from a hiatus during the reign of Shah `Abbas the Great, Iraqi Shi`ites labored under Sunni rule. Perhaps for this reason, the shrine cities remained centers of a more cautious, conservative type of Shi`ism than the liberal, establishmentarian Usulism of al-Karaki and his like.

In Safavid Iran, particularly in the capital, al-Karaki's version of Usulism became well entrenched. The major opposition to this school came from Akhbari jurisprudence. Akhbarism rejected the legitimacy of independent legal reasoning and denied the need of the laity to emulate mujtahids or professional jurisprudents. A major intellectual figure in the revival of this strict constructionist approach to Shi`ism, Muhammad Amin Astarabadi (d. 1624), attacked the mujtahids from Mecca, in the Arab world.[32] Astarabadi's restatement of conservative Shi`ite thinking found great acclaim in the shrine cities of Iraq, and, Arjomand has argued, in Iran among Iranian religious officials in competition with the `Amili mujtahids.[33]

Although the ulama based in Bahrain and eastern Arabia were under European rule while the Safavids were elaborating a new form of Twelver Shi`ism, they were not wholly isolated from these developments. Several Shi`ite ulama from Bahrain studied with al-Karaki, so that his activist Usuli ideas were known on the islands. But the domination of the Sunni Banu Jabr and then of the Portuguese made a more formal Shi`ite establishment on the Safavid model impossible to develop on Bahrain. The scholars living in Bahrain under the Portuguese in the 1500s are given for the most part short notices in the biographical dictionaries. The times were unpropitious for great Shi`ite scholarship. The Shaykh al-Islam of Safavid Isfahan, Muhammad Baqir Majlisi (d. 1699), wrote a century later that the Portuguese appointed Sunni governors of Bahrain who attempted with some brutality to convert the populace from Shi`ism to Sunnism.[34]

Some Shi`ite scholars of Bahrain are mentioned in the sources for this period. Sayyid Husayn b. Hasan al-Ghurayfi al-Bahrani (d. 1593), an Akhbari from a village in the south of the main island of Bahrain, wrote a work forbidding the emulation of mujtahids (*al-Ghunya fi muhimmat al-din `an taqlid al-mujtahidin*).[35] But rationalist approaches to thought also continued to exist. Shaykh Da'ud b. Abu Shafiz, a theologian, litterateur, philosopher, and polymath, wrote on logic in the school of al-Farabi. Also a great but humble debater, he often took on al-Ghurayfi. Likewise, when the father of the important 17th century Safavid thinker Baha' al-Din `Amili passed through in Bahrain, Shaykh Da'ud debated him.[36]

Usuli thought penetrated the island. Shaykh Husayn b. `Ali of the Abu Sirdal clan also studied with Shaykh `Ali al-Karaki.[37] Shaykh `Abd Allah, the grandson of Muflih mentioned above, received a diploma (*ijaza*) in 1548 that said his grandfather was instructed by the mujtahids, who in turn went back to the Imams, and thence to the Prophet himself. Thus, the old link some Bahraini clans had with the Usuli family of the `Allama in Hilla was a source of price to these local Usulis.

Twelver Shi` ism in Portuguese Bahrain continued to show intellectual vigor, with both strict constructionists of an Akhbari orientation and rationalists of the Safavid Usuli variety represented on the island. The rise of Imami Iran under the Safavids may have lent that branch more prestige and perhaps led some in Bahrain still clinging to Ismailism to become Twelvers. Portuguese domination interfered with easy travel to Iran and prevented Bahraini Imami scholars from helping spread Shi`ism in Safavid Iran, a role left to the clerics of Jabal `Amil and the urban centers of Iraq. In Bahrain, the Shi`ites remained a persecuted group under local Sunni Arab rule with no major religious institutions or offices under their control. In Al-Hasa the Shi`ites fell under Sunni Ottoman control, as did their brethren in Iraq and Jabal `Amil, though in fact the Ahsa'is remained largely under the domination of local Arab Sunni tribesmen owing loose fealty to the Ottomans.

Safavid Bahrain, 1602-1717

The 17th century witnessed the Safavid conquest of Bahrain and the growth of Bahraini religious institutions in a manner similar to that in Iran the previous century. Usuli Shi`ism, with its posts of Friday prayer leaders and mujtahid-judges and its syllabus in formal seminaries, became the reigning orthodoxy. Shi`ite scholars from Bahrain trekked to Isfahan for studies with Usuli luminaries like Baha' al-Din `Amili and some of them settled in the capital and in southwestern Iran, cross-fertilizing Iranian religious culture with ideas from the Arab Gulf. The economic and political integration of Bahrain into the Safavid empire facilitated emigration from Bahrain to Iran on a larger scale than in the past.

In 1602, the Safavid military occupied Bahrain.[38] Teixera described the isles around 1610 as inhabited by Arabs with an Iranian minister and garrison. He estimated the official value of the yearly pearl trade of

Bahrain at 500,000 ducats, with another 100,000 smuggled on the black market. The tax-farm of the islands itself was worth 4,000 ducats annually. The governors sent from Iran appear from their names mostly to have been Qizilbash notables and al-Nabhan wrote that one was removed by the shah after the Baharina complained of extortion.[39]

With the rise of Dutch and British mercantile and naval power in the first decades of the 17th century, the Safavids saw an opportunity to dislodge the Portuguese from the Gulf altogether. The Portuguese protection system, requiring that Asian merchants pay high tariffs and bribes to Portuguese officials in return for safety from Portuguese attacks, had grown so onerous to Indian merchants that they began reviving the overland route to Iran from Lahore through Qandahar. At the same time, new Dutch naval technology and trade routes allowed the Dutch to bypass the Portuguese factories. Gulf trade probably fell in the first decades of the 17th century which weakened the Portuguese at Hurmuz. In a joint 1622 Anglo-Iranian campaign against Hurmuz, the Iranians expelled the Portuguese, who retired to Goa.[40]

With Hurmuz now an Iranian dependency, the Safavids briefly reverted to the practice of administering Bahrain from that island. Later, Bahrain fell under the administrative jurisdiction of the Beglarbegi of Kuhgilu centered at Bihbahan in southern Iran. But the governor of Bahrain always exercised a great deal of autonomy. With Iranian dominance of Bahrain, the marketing entrepot for its pearls shifted to the Iranian Persian Gulf port of Congoun near the administrative center of Lar.[41]

The Dutch and British East India Companies, new economic institutions that by their control of the sea, their lower protection costs, and their knowledge of world prices represented an advance on the protection racket that constituted the Portuguese empire, began carrying Iranian and Indian merchants for a transport fee. The Companies traded with the local merchants, as well as competing with them, setting up a system of European-staffed Asian trade alongside their trade to Europe. The 17th century witnessed Dutch supremacy, as well as a gradual shift after 1650 from pepper to cotton textiles as the major European import from the East though pepper imports did not decline in absolute terms. The Gulf trade overland to the Levant continued, despite the decline of Venice, to remain important along with the Red Sea route, especially for the French. The Gulf also witnessed expanded commerce between the East and Iran and Iraq. The Dutch, for instance, brought Indonesian pepper and Bengal sugar into the Gulf.[42]

Ulama and Religious Institutions in Safavid Bahrain

In the 16th century, Portuguese-Hurmuzi rule had restricted Imami Shi`ites in Bahrain and denied their scholars the patronage and positions that would promote scholarship. In the 17th century Safavid financial and administrative support in the islands allowed a great increase in the number of trained ulama and the sophistication of their work. The nature of the transformation of religious life among Twelver Baharina under the Safavids has never been sketched. We have not had a picture of how the Safavids founded institutions such as Friday prayers or how they built up an ulama corps. The social origins of the ulama, their relations with the secular notables and with the laboring orders, and their internal disputes all merit discussion. Such an inquiry bears, not only on the history of eastern Arabia, but on that of Iran as well, given the great immigration of ulama from Bahrain to that country late in the Safavid period and their wide intellectual influence.

At this point, discussion of the Shi`ites will narrow to the islands of Bahrain. In contrast to the many illustrious scholars on the islands, few ulama are noted in the biographical dictionaries for this period from Ottoman Al-Hasa and Qatif, and they often emigrated to Bahrain or Iran. The 1670 expulsion of the Ottomans from Al-Hasa by the Banu Khalid tribe may have shifted the local balance against the sedentary population, and without an Ottoman garrison the sort of local order may not have existed that would have encouraged a flourishing urban intellectual life. On Bahrain, new religious institutions evolved. The Safavids faced the problem of ruling a relatively distant island, bordering the Ottomans, and warding off Portuguese attacks. As they did within 16th century Iran, they met this strategic and logistical problem, in part, with an ideological solution. By favoring the Imami Shi`ite ulama and firmly implanting Shi`ism, they hoped to secure the islands of Bahrain, with their centrality to trade routes and their fabulous pearl wealth.

The 1602 incorporation of Bahrain into the Shi`ite Safavid empire opened its Arab Shi`ites to Iranian religious influences, as well as making it easier for its ulama to emigrate to Iran. Sayyid Majid al-Sadiqi al-Jidd-Hafsi of Bahrain (d. 1619), for instance, gained the reputation of spreading the study of Imami oral traditions in Shiraz, holding salons for its ulama and giving Friday afternoon sermons in Shiraz. He met the Imam-Jum`a of Isfahan, Baha' al-Din `Amili and in Shiraz wrote the endowment deed for Fars Governor Imam Quli Khan's seminary.[43]

From this point on, many Bahrani ulama are mentioned as emigrating to Iran, where they often held high religious posts. For instance, Majid Al-Abu Shabana al-Bahrani served as religious court judge in Shiraz and Isfahan.[44] Likewise, later in the century Shah Sulayman made Shaykh Salih al-Karzakani religious court judge in Shiraz.[45] Al-Karzakani's friend Shaykh Ja`far b. Kamal al-Din (d. 1677) left Bahrain with him because they fell upon hard times, but went on to Hyderabad in Shi`ite-ruled Golconda, South India. He and al-Karzakani had made a pact that whichever of them first struck it rich through patronage abroad would help the other.[46] The old Gulf connection with South India thus did not die out, though emigration to Iran became far more frequent. As noted, ulama from Ottoman Al-Hasa and Qatif also traveled to Iran. Shaykh Ja`far of Qatif (d. 1619) was forced to leave his village of al-Tuba because of heavy debts, going to Bahrain and then accompanying Sayyid Majid al-Sadiqi to Iran. He studied religious sciences, receiving a diploma from Baha' al-Din al-`Amili in 1607, but he primarily became known as a poet.[47] The flow of scholars from Bahrain to Iran grew steadily throughout the 17th century. In his study of Safavid ulama, Arjomand found "a shift from the clear predominance of Jabal `Amil over the other Arab regions in the first 140 years of our period to an equally clear predominance of Bahrain in the last fifty."[48]

In Bahrain itself, the Safavids promoted religious institutions, firmly establishing Imami Shi`ism as the dominant orthodoxy. They arranged for Friday prayers to be said in the name of the Safavid shah and offered patronage to ulama and mosques. The status group of the Imami ulama became more differentiated from notable literati and took on the aspect of a profession. As always in the formation of a profession, the question of its members' social origins and control of resources arises. In Safavid Bahrain the ulama were drawn from a range of backgrounds among the propertied classes.

The Safavids created a set of religious institutions in Bahrain, both from pious and from ideological motives. One of the first was Friday congregational prayers, first led in the early 1600s by Shaykh Muhammad al-Ruwaysi.[49] He believed such prayers to be an absolute obligation (*wujub `ayni*), a stance taken also by most high Safavid religious officials, but disputed by many 16th century conservatives and Akhbaris. At the end of the Friday prayers the religious officials pronounced blessings on Safavid rule, and the Safavids were eager to institute them. Early Imami opinion tended against the validity of these prayers in the Occultation, and only with the rise of the Safavids and the development of a new sort of Usulism did they become widespread. Under Banu Jabr and Hurmuz, of course, such Shi`ite institutions had in any case been forbidden.

The second important institution created by the Safavids was an Imami chief religious judgeship. Al-Ruwaysi, an unrivaled expert in the law and in Imami oral reports, assumed this post as well. His successor as chief religious official, Sayyid `Abd al-Ra'uf al-Musawi (1604-1650), was appointed to the post of Shaykh al-Islam through Hurmuz. `Ali al-Bahrani glosses "Shaykh al-Islam" as chief judge, suggesting that in Bahrain this post primarily involved supervision of the judicial system.[50] The succession of Safavid Shaykh al-Islam in Bahrain is seen in Figure 1.

The quite considerable wealth of the Shi`ite learned men in Safavid Bahrain derived both from public and from private sources. The government generously funded the new religious institutions it created. In addition, most high ulama had been born into notable families or entered the ranks of the wealthy through trade. We have one European witness to the mechanisms of government funding for Imami ulama. The French traveler Jean de Thévenot wrote from Basra in 1665 of Bahrain's pearl-derived riches. Basing himself on reports from a Portuguese official, Manuel Mendez Henriquez, who had firsthand experience with Safavid Bahrain, Thévenot put the number of pearling boats based on the island at two to three thousand, each of which paid a toll to the governor for permission to go pearling. In addition, they paid a yearly tax. Thévenot goes on to make the remarkable assertion that the shah of Iran never touched most of this revenue, because it belonged to the mosques, and the monarch owned only the heavier pearls.[51] In interpreting this passage, it is hard for the historian not to conclude that the vast extension in Shi`ite religious institutions, the building of mosques and training of a Safavid-style ulama corps, was subvented by religious taxes on pearl wealth. A doctrinal basis may lie behind this governmental munificence. According to Usuli doctrine, believers must pay one fifth (*al-khums*) of certain kinds of revenues, including wealth gained on treasures from the sea, to the mujtahids, to be used for religious institutions and for philanthropy to the poor. If Thévenot's informant is to be believed, the Safavids actually ear-marked the *khums* on pearls for the ulama. Of course, many rich wealthy private individuals also donated money on similar grounds to the ulama.[52] Other funds came into the hands of the ulama as perquisites of office. Al-Musawi, for instance, controlled pious endowments (*wilayat al-awqaf*) and oversaw the market police. Supervision of newly founded Twelver pious endowments, also proved an increasingly important source of wealth for the clerics in Iran during this period.[53]

Immense riches were given into the control of the ulama for public purposes, but most high ulama were also personally wealthy. It would be anachronistic to suppose that any great distinction between private and public monies was consistently maintained. Not all high ulama in Bahrain were born with wealth and status. but most were. Sayyid `Abd al-Ra'uf al-Musawi derived from a notable clan called Banan, who said they went back to the seventh Imam through the renowned al-Radi family. Shaykh Muhammad b. Sulayman al-Maqabi (d. 1674), on the other hand, rose from a relatively indigent background [54] He began studying with Shaykh `Ali b. Sulayman al-Qadami, the chief religious dignitary in Bilad, and

Shi`ite Shaykh al-Islams in Safavid Bahrain

Muhammad ar-Ruwaysi

Sayyid `Abd al-Ra'uf al-Musawi
(1604-1650)

`Ali b. Sulayman al-Qadami
(d. 1654)

Salah al-Din al-Qadami

Muhammad b. Sulayman al-Maqabi
(d. 1674)

`Ali b. Ja`far al-Qadami (deposed)

(d. 1719)

Sulayman b. Salih al-Dirazi

Muhammad b. Majid al-Mahuzi
(d. 1693)

Sayyid Hashim al-Tubli
(d. Ca. 1695)

Sulayman b. `Abdullah al-Mahuzi
(1664-1709)

Ahmad b. `Abdullah al-Biladi
(d. 1725)

entered the pearl trade as a wholesaler. He later became Friday prayer
leader at a mosque in the village of his mentor, al-Qadam.

During the pearling season when the ships from al-Qadam came back
from diving, al-Maqabi went down and bought their entire catch of pearls
and the cloth in which they had traded. Then pearl retailers from all over
Bahrain would come to his house to buy. The people of the village had
made an agreement to sell only to him, forcing retailers to buy from a

single dealer. Al-Maqabi, in turn, gave advances on profits (*murabiha*) to the villagers and shared out money among them such that, his biographer says, no one went away disappointed. Yusuf al-Bahrani gives an idealized picture of the relationship between the mujtahid-wholesalers and their village congregation of divers. He tells the story that once a man from the village of Bani Jamra near Diraz came to al-Maqabi with a large pearl of unknown quality. Al-Maqabi bought it for a small price, then gave it to a jeweler who worked it into a fine gem, so that it sold for 50 tumans. The next time al-Maqabi saw the diver, he explained to him that the pearl had turned out to be worth far more than he originally paid for it, and the Shaykh wanted to share some of the subsequent huge profits with the diver. The man refused, saying he had sold it fairly, and that had the pearl proven defective al-Maqabi would have taken the loss. Al-Maqabi insisted, and finally they found a mediator who apportioned the profits between them.

Village families seeking wealth through pearling did not always have such happy endings, as one of al-Maqabi's students found. Shaykh Sulayman b. Salih al-Dirazi came from a family involved in pearl diving and trading.[55] He was in the house of his older brother Ahmad, who maintained pearling ships. When Ahmad sent young Sulayman out to dive for pearls, the younger brother was struck with an illness. Sulayman felt sorry for him and took him out of pearling work, leaving him in the house with instructions to study. He hired al-Maqabi to tutor him, and Shaykh Sulayman eventually rose to become chief source of emulation in Diraz.

Safavid donations to religious institutions helped assure ulama support for the government. The differences in the values of the ulama and those of the notables, however, did on occasion lead to friction between the religious institution and the state. When the Shah called Salih al-Karzakani, to Shiraz as court judge, he invested him with a robe of honor. Al-Karzakani was at first inclined to decline it, out of Imami reluctance to be associated with imperfect rulers, but friends and notables successfully implored him not to incur the Shah's wrath. In distant Bahrain, relations between the ulama and local notables took on great importance, since these magnates and the Qizilbash governors often had influence in the court at Isfahan.

Shaykh `Ali b. Ja`far al-Qadami (d. 1719) ran into trouble with the authorities. The Imami ulama of Bahrain had so quickly built up their institutions that they began to compete for certain kinds of influence on society with government officials. Shaykh `Ali b. Ja`far haughtily refused to flatter the Safavid governor and provoked the hostility of many in the notable class in the capital city of Bilad al-Qadim. They sent reports to Shah Sulayman (1667-1694) accusing him of improprieties and the Shah had him arrested and brought in chains from Bahrain to Iran. In Kazirun, near Shiraz, Shaykh `Ali made contacts with notables that could influence the court. They cleared his name with the Shah, and he settled in Kazirun as a Friday prayer leader.[56] On the other hand, the local notables lobbied the Shah to put Shaykh Muhammad al-Maqabi in charge of the market police and religious courts. The power of local notables was such that their discontent even led to the dismissal of one of the Qizilbash governors. Still, the more scrupulous ulama would stand up to them when a matter of principle was at stake. The mujtahid Shaykh Muhammad b. Majid al-Mahuzi (d. 1693) had ambivalent relations with the local deputy governor Muhammad Al-Majid al-Biladi, who helped rule on behalf of the Safavids. Once he intervened for Sunni pearl merchants from Qatar from whom al-Biladi had bought pearls without ever paying and employed verse to prick his conscience.[57]

The main lines of ulama ideology in Safavid Bahrain can be discerned from the biographical dictionaries. A majority clearly supported the legitimacy of Friday prayers even during the occultation and it likewise upheld the permissibility of taking employment with a secular government. Usuli ideas were certainly important and even seem to have been dominant during the 17th century. Shaykh `Ali b. Sulayman al-Qadami (d. 1654), religious head of the Shi`ites in Bahrain, received a diploma from the Usuli Baha' al-Din al-`Amili in Isfahan. He wrote a book allowing the emulation of mujtahids, an Usuli position, and considered Friday congregational prayers an individual obligation (the strongest possible stance on the issue). He also promoted the transmitted sciences, that is, spreading the lore of Imami oral reports in Bahrain. Yusuf al-Bahrani says he removed the "numerous heresies" (bida` `adida) that had darkened Bahrain which implies the imposition of Imami scripturalist orthodoxy on the folk religion of the Baharina.[58]

Shaykh Sulayman b. `Abd Allah al-Mahuzi (1664-1709), another Shi`ite religious head, likewise wrote many works on the principles of jurisprudence from an Usuli point of view though Yusuf al-Bahrani wrote that one later work seemed to indicate that he moved toward Akhbarism. He compiled a book of Imami oral reports for Shah Sultan Husayn Safavi (r. 1693-1722), for which he received 2,000 ashrafis. He therefore associated with rulers and took money from them. He wrote a book on the duty of performing Friday congregational prayer (refuting contemporaries who forbade it), and accepted rational sciences, including metaphysics. Most Akhbaris, on the other hand, forbade the study of rationalist theology and philosophy. The last Safavid Shaykh al-Islam, Ahmad b. `Abd Allah al-Biladi (d. 1725), kept alive the tradition of rational sciences.[59] This rationalist, Usuli tenor to Safavid Bahrain's intellectual life comes as a surprise in view of the islands' later reputation as an Akhbari stronghold. But even the 18th century Akhbari revivalist, Yusuf al-Bahrani, was brought up in a traditionally Usuli family, as will be seen below.

The Safavid Shaykh al-Islam in Bahrain possessed great religious authority. If a newly appointed Shaykh al-Islam normally lived outside the capital city of Bilad al-Qadim, he was called upon to take up residence in this seat of government and center for merchants and ulama upon accepting the post. The chief religious dignitary often attempted to continue his teaching activities which created a large circle of students and influencing the capital's vigorous intellectual culture.

The islands were hardly free of doctrinal dispute. Even the Shaykh al-Islams sometimes took unusual positions. Sayyid Hashim al-Tubli, chief religious dignitary 1693-95 and known for his compilation approach to studies of the oral reports from the Imams, wrote a treatise demonstrating the excellence of the Twelve Imams over any of the prophets save Muhammad. Such a stance is redolent of Ismaili influence.[60] Nor had all Twelvers, even all Usulis, accepted the transformation of Bahraini religion into a Safavid-style religious establishment. The mujtahid Shaykh Sulayman al-Isba`i (d. 1690), settled in the provincial town of Shakhura, wrote against the holding of congregational prayers in the Occultation.[61] Despite his conservatism, he also attacked the Akhbaris.

A dispute occurred during `Ali al-Qadami's brief tenure as clerical head of Bahrain that sheds light on the nature and handling of religious conflicts among the growing clerical class. He appointed Shaykh Ahmad b. Muhammad al-Isba`i, an Usuli jurisprudent, religious court judge for Bahrain. Al-Isba`i, from the village of Abu Isba`, became known for taking unusual stances in law. For instance, he held it an obligation upon the non-clerical notable class (al-a`yan) to practice independent legal judgment (ijtihad) in Islamic law and denied the validity of acting according to oral reports (khabar al-ahad) from the Imams that had only been transmitted by one individual in each early Islamic generation. Al-Isba`i's stance on ijtihad may have made some sense in a small Shi`ite community of only a few tens of thousands like Bahrain, given that the tiny literate notable class of landowners and big merchants also produced most of the ulama. But it threatened clerical privileges and cannot have made him popular among his colleagues. In the case of a woman who remarried during her husband's absence, al-Isba`i ruled she belonged to the first husband. Shaykh `Ali b. Sulayman, as Shaykh al-Islam, called the decision into question. They submitted the dispute to the judges of Shiraz and Isfahan, who upheld al-Isba`i. The incident caused al-Qadami to feel enmity for al-Isba`i, whom he eventually dismissed.[62]

Yusuf al-Bahrani's biographical dictionary illuminates a great deal about Shi`ism in Bahrain during the 17th century. One notes the strong Usuli influence in the capital, Bilad al-Qadim, as well as among many chief religious dignitaries appointed by the Safavids. Safavid notables and ulama cooperated in promulgating Friday congregational prayers, not only in the capital but in the provincial towns to the south and west, with their latent functions of legitimating the Safavid state and providing clerics with a way of influencing the public. They founded seminaries (madrasas) to train ulama. Clerics received ultimate control over Islamic courts and over policing prices in the market. The chief religious dignitary (ra'is) appointed by the state presided over all of these activities from Bilad, so that some degree of centralization existed in the islands. Ulama suppressed religious ideas conflicting with those of Safavid Shi`ism. In return for their services to the state, the ulama received benefices, and, if Thévenot is to be believed, the profits of a good deal of the pearl revenue. In promoting Imami Shi`ite ideology through the religious institution, the Safavids helped make their rule in this distant island outpost more secure.

This program of institution-building and religious socialization, which coincided with the perceived welfare both of the state and of the rising clerical elite, met some opposition. Yusuf al-Bahrani wrote nothing about the fate of the Sunnis, though many must have resisted, fled, or become Shi`ites. Even Usuli ulama of provincial towns like Abu Isba adhered to beliefs such as extending the privilege of ijtihad to non-ulama notables, or the illegitimacy of Friday congregational prayers, which brought them into conflict with the new religious hierarchy. Akhbarism remained a minority school of jurisprudence, though Shaykh Yusuf knew little about its history; few of his chains of transmission led through 18th century Akhbaris, since his father and teachers were Usulis. Over the century, tensions developed between the notables ruling Bahrain for the Iranians and the ulama corps. Notables sought power and authority through their connection with the Safavid court, whereas the high ulama made their own play for authority on the basis of their scriptural values and styles of life. These tensions erupted in the case of Shaykh `Ali b. Ja`far al-Qadami whom the local notables had deposed by manipulating their contacts at the Shah's court which demonstrated that the power of the notables remained more effective than the authority of the ulama.

The ulama came from the landed and merchant classes, as numerous remarks in the biographical dictionaries show, and many of them derived from old notable families. Some, however, originated in poorer families of less status. Shaykh Sulayman b. Salih al-Dirazi labored as a common pearl diver in his youth, though his family did own ships rather than being propertyless workers. Shaykh Muhammad b. Sulayman al-Maqabi parlayed his religious prestige as Friday prayer leader in al-Qadam into a monopoly in wholesaling local pearls and imported cloth that earned him a fortune. The divers and small ship owners no doubt agreed to such an arrangement to avoid underbidding one another and driving down prices on an open market. Still, the ulama-merchants profited by skimming off a substantial surplus as middlemen in the pearl trade. In Safavid Bahrain, pearl trading, landholding, and religious office often went hand in hand.

Although earned as well as inherited wealth could serve as a passport into the ulama elite, achieving the highest religious posts and the confidence of the notables who influenced those appointments required both learning and wealth. Often a thin line demarcated notables from their clerical cousins, since many appear to have gained some seminary training and writing religious poetry about the Imams was a national pastime. Public recitation of religious poetry probably served, along with congregational prayers, to link the ruling class vertically with the Shi`ite divers and peasants whose labor the ruling class exploited. Unfortunately, the Shi`ite folk culture of this period remains inaccessible.

The Eighteenth Century

In 1717, Bahrain and Qatif fell to invading Omanis of the `Ibadite branch of Islam. The Safavids failed to recoup, and met their own end five years later in 1722 with the Afghan invasion; the 1730s witnessed the rise in Iran of Nadir Shah, with his Sunni-Shi`ite ecumenism. The political and socioeconomic events of the age also caused changes in culture. Powerful challenges, in which ulama from Bahrain and Al-Hasa played major roles, grew up in the 18th century to Safavid-style Usulism. These included the Akhbari revival after 1722 in Bahrain, the shrine cities of Iraq, and the small towns of southwestern Iran (all of which had continued to have important Akhbari populations even in Safavid times). Also important was the esoteric Shaykhi movement of Shaykh Ahmad b. Zayn al-Din al-Ahsa'i (1753-1826), so unlike anything in mainstream Imami Iran or the shrine cities that it probably reflected underground religious currents still running among ordinary Shi`ites and others in eastern Arabia and southern Iraq.

The Omani invasions of Qatif and Bahrain, conducted with the help of some Sunni tribes in the area, disrupted the institutional life of Shi`ites. The Omani rulers imposed high taxes on the merchant-ulama which caused many to flee to southwestern Iran or to Najaf and Karbala in Iraq. The European Hamilton wrote that extensive desertion of the islands by Arab Shi`ite pearl fishers made Bahrain unprofitable for the Omanis. The invasion began a long period of political insecurity in the Gulf, as `Utubi Sunni tribes wrestled for supremacy over its islands and littoral with the Omanis and then with the Iranians under Nadir Shah and Karim Khan Zand. Carsten Niebuhr found in 1763 that Bahrain's 360 towns and villages had, through warfare and economic distress, been reduced to only 60. Though Bahrain still yielded 300,000 French livres in duties on pearls and dates every year, little of it went any longer to Shi`ite ulama. Meanwhile, the British East India Company gradually established commercial hegemony over the Gulf. Toward the end of the 18th century a new contender for domination appeared in the form of the Saudi-Wahhabi alliance based in Najd, which conquered regions along the Gulf in the name of their tribal Islamic reformism.[63]

A generational shift from Usulism to Akhbarism among some families can be witnessed in the available biographies. Shaykh `Abd Allah al-Samahiji (1675-1723), was born in a village on a small island next to Awal and raised in the town of Abu Isba on the larger island. His father, a pure Usuli who detested Akhbaris, trained him as a mujtahid. Shaykh `Abd Allah fled the Omani invasion for Isfahan, where he pleaded with Shah Sultan Husayn and the Shaykh al-Islam to repulse the attackers, but was refused help. Al-Samahiji then settled in the southwestern Iranian town of Bihbahan. Becoming an Akhbari, he wrote a treatise denying the validity of independent legal reasoning (*ijtihad*) on the grounds that it did not exist in the time of the Imams. Still, Shaykh `Abd Allah affirmed the validity of Friday congregational prayers during the Imam's Occultation. The neo-Akhbaris of his generation were not as conservative as the Akhbaris of the 15th century had been.[64] Al-Samahiji was joined in Bihbahan by Sayyid `Abd Allah al-Biladi (d. 1767), who likewise fled the Omani conquest of Bahrain and studied with the old man, deserting his ancestral Usulism for Akhbarism. Al-Biladi rose to become the leader of Friday congregational prayers in Bihbahan.[65]

Younger members of the Al-`Asfur family of Diraz likewise adopted Akhbarism, even though this clan of pearl merchants and ulama had been staunch Usulis during the Safavid period. The most famous neo-Akhbari of this family, Shaykh Yusuf al-Bahrani (1695-1722), forsook Bahrain because the Oman, invaders' exactions bankrupted his pearl business. Attempting to begin life again in Shiraz, he suffered through the 1724 Afghan siege and sack of that city, finally settling in Karbala in Ottoman Iraq. There he became his generation's major exponent of the neo-Akhbari creed.[66]

Al-Bahrani's neo-Akhbarism accepted only two sources for Imami jurisprudence, the Qur'an and the oral reports from the Imams. He did not, however, go so far as to say that no verse in the Qur'an could be understood without the interpretation of the Imams, a position held by the Safavid-era Akhbari revivalist Astarabadi which Shaykh Yusuf denounced as extremist. He rejected the Usuli principles of consensus (*ijma*) and independent reasoning (*`aql, ijtihad*). Indeed, he questioned rationalist approaches to religion in general, quoting with approval a condemnation of reading philosophy and theosophy. But Shaykh Yusuf accepted the validity of Friday prayers in the Occultation and did not completely reject Usuli positions on other issues. His Bahrani neo-Akhbarism sought to be an intermediate path between extremist Usulism and extremist Akhbarism.[67]

Yet the trend to Akhbarism was not followed by all in Bahrain. Some, especially in the old Safavid provincial capital of Bilad, clung to Usulism. Shaykh Muhammad b. `Ali al-Maqabi who flourished in the middle of the 18th century, became prayer leader and chief of the ulama in Bilad, writing works on jurisprudence in which he expounded the classical Usuli stance of al-Shahid al-Thani.[68]   Indeed, most inhabitants of Bilad remained Usulis through the 18th century and opposed the Akhbari leaders of the rival city of Diraz. In the late 18th century, Shaykh `Abd Allah al-Biladi, a mujtahid, engaged in a rivalry with the Akhbari leader Shaykh Husayn Al-`Asfur (d. 1802) of Diraz. Shaykh Husayn's Akhbari followers considered him a spiritual renewer (*mujaddid*) such as many Muslims believe appear at the beginning of every Islamic century.[69]

Aside from the renewed Usuli-Akhbari struggle, a new movement was introduced into the area by Shaykh Ahmad b. Zayn al-Din al-Ahsa'i. Although his fame spread and a new school of Imami Shi`ism became attached to his name only after his 1806 emigration to Iran, he spent the first 50 years of his life in al-Hasa, Bahrain, and southern Iraq. New scholarship has been produced on this Shaykh Ahmad concentrating on his later career in Iran. A full understanding of this visionary and enigmatic figure, however, must eventually come to terms with his eastern Arabian heritage and context.[70]

He came of a branch of the Sunni Mahashir tribe that several generations previously had settled in the town of al-Mutayrafi in Al-Hasa, adopting Twelver Shi`ism. He described mid-18th century al-Hasa as a provincial land of villages wherein the rural inhabitants practiced a folk Islam at variance with urban, Shari`a-based codes. As a youth, he enjoyed the tribal festivals they held, with music, drums, and singing. But a strong meditative sense led him to study Arabic grammar, religious sciences, and poetry. His account of his early years in Al-Hasa makes clear the importance of visions of the Imams for his adolescent religious development, and even for his mature development as a scholar. His brief autobiography suggests that the political instability of his times encouraged him as a young man to see the things of this world as ephemeral and to concentrate his energies on otherworldly meditation. Like many contemporary Akhbaris in the area, he said his ideas opposed those of the philosophers and theologians but agreed with the oral reports of the Imams. He also disagreed with Sufism and attacked the doctrine of existential monism (*wahdat al-wujud*). Unlike the Akhbaris, however, who criticized philosophers and theologians from a literalist, scripturalist stance, al-Ahsa'i criticized them from a theosophical and esoteric point of view. Indeed, in his qualified approval of reason (`aql`) and in his defense of the jurisprudential principle of consensus, he came closer to the Usuli position than to the Akhbari.[71]

Shaykh Ahmad studied with Shaykh Husayn Al-`Asfur, nephew of Shaykh Yusuf al-Bahrani, an Akhbari who had many students in Bahrain despite the turbulence of the era, and received a diploma from Shaykh Ahmad b. Hasan al-Dumastani. Shaykh Ahmad engaged in a long debate with Sayyid `Abd al-Samad al-Zinji a landed cleric in Bahrain, and copied out books produced by 18th century Bahraini scholars.[72]   Only in the 1790s, in the wake of the Wahhabi attack, did he leave al-Hasa again and succeed in studying with the great Usuli teachers in the Iraqi shrine cities. His later doctrines included the importance of mystical illumination (*ishraq*) for Shi`ite thinkers and jurisprudents, and the positing of ethereal bodies (made up of elements from Hurqalya, a realm between the physical and the divine) which all men possess. His application of his theory of ethereal bodies to the Muslim doctrines of the Prophet's ascension to heaven from Jerusalem and the bodily resurrection of the dead at the judgment day infuriated many literalist ulama. Both his visions of the Imams as a basis for his scholarly knowledge and his doctrine of Hurqalya derived from his local context. In the 17th century Sayyid Hashim al-Ahsa'i got in touch with early hadith sources through visions; Sayyid Hashim al-Tubli thought the Imams superior to most prophets; and Shaykh Ahmad's doctrine of Hurqalya derived from his contact in southern Iraq with Mandaeans. Moreover, Shaykh Ahmad received some of his esoteric ideas from the 15th century mystic Ibn Abi Jumhur al-Ahsa'i (whom he cites) and possibly from folk Shi`ism still influenced by Ismaili esotericism.[73]     Shaykh Ahmad's structural position resembled that of Ibn Abi Jumhur, in that he wrote at a time when Sunni tribal invasions had crippled the Shi`ite establishment which allowed individual speculation to flourish. His doctrines took root especially in Hufuf and al-Mubarraz in al-Hasa.

The main trend in 18th century Bahrain, however, was toward Akhbarism. Three immediate factors in the frequent adoption of Akhbarism are suggested by the biographical accounts available. The first is political; Akhbarism seems to have been embraced by many after the fall of Bahrain and of the Safavids to Sunni invaders. After 1717, with only short intervals, non-Shi`ites ruled Bahrain locally, even though some Sunni tribal chiefs owed fealty to Iran for a while. This pattern suggests, here as elsewhere, a link between Usulism and the Shi`ite state. Akhbarism as an ideology suited most out-of-power Imamis better, as it required a less activist role and fewer ulama links with the Establishment.

Second, a generational gap seems apparent. Sons both around the turn of the century into strict Usuli families, disappointed by the failure of the

Shi`ite establishment to meet the Omani and Afghan challenges, rebelled against their upbringing and adopted Akhbarism. Many Shi`ites from Bahrain were displaced by the Omani invasion to southwestern Iran and to the shrine cities of Iraq, centers of more conservative jurisprudence. There, as refugees, they tended to adopt the Akhbarism of their hosts.

Third, within Bahrain geographical divisions emerged. The eminence of Shaykh Yusuf al-Bahrani in Karbala helped swing his brothers and cousins of Al-`Asfur to Akhbarism, and ultimately the whole town of Diraz. The old Safavid Usuli center of al-Bilad clung to the rationalist school much longer, its mujtahids remembering a time when the Safavids appointed them to head the entire Shi`ite religious establishment in Bahrain and to administer as a religious tax a portion of the islands' rich pearl revenues. Qatif also remained an Usuli stronghold.

Conclusion

The rich interplay of local social structures and economic conditions with regional dynastic rhythms and the rise of European mercantile empires made a dramatic impact on Shi`ism in Bahrain from the 14th through the 18th centuries. A trend toward the adoption of Twelver Shi`ism began after the defeat of the Carmathians, since the Twelver branch was considered less radical and less objectionable by Sunni leaders. From 1300, local Carmathian tribal chiefs allowed scope for the growth of early Imami institutions and of the Usuli school. This relative freedom for Imamis ended with the rise of Banu Jabr and the conquest by the Portuguese-Hurmuzi condominium. The post-1501 Twelver Shi`ite state in formerly Sunni Iran under the Safavids had little immediate impact on Shi`ites in Bahrain and Eastern Arabia, though some scholars from that region did study with Safavid Usulis in Iran.

The 1602 incorporation of the Bahrain islands into Shah `Abbas's Iranian empire, along with Dutch and British mercantile but not political hegemony, gave Bahrain prosperity and allowed local Twelver Shi`ites to dominate the political and religious life of their islands. Subvented by huge pearl revenues, the ulama set up a whole range of institutions to administer and spread Imami Shi`ism, including seminaries, Friday prayer leaderships, religious judgeships, and market police. Informal salons also played a major role in helping spread Shi`ite culture among the elite. Shi`ite ulama, drawn from notable landholding and merchant families, had a paternalistic attitude toward their peasants and divers and attempted to eradicate what they saw as extremist folk beliefs. The relationship of the ulama with laymen, always complex, was further complicated when the clergy also acted as wholesalers for pearls brought them by divers in their congregations. Given the trust laymen often reposed in them, the ulama in this situation could be accused of conflict of interest and exploiting their position for gain.

The Omani invasion of 1717 and the fall of the Safavids five years later dealt a lethal blow to the Usuli religious establishment on Bahrain. Many disillusioned scholars of the younger generation adopted the conservative Akhbari school, with its disallowal of many functions of the state during the Occultation of the Imam. No Shi'ite state, after all, existed from 1722 to 1763 when the Zands consolidated their power. Akhbarism, although it had long existed on the islands, came to dominate them. The political and institutional chaos of the 18th century also allowed some Shi'ite thinkers to express individualist views, and such as those of Shaykh Ahmad al-Ahsa'i. Shi'ite ulama, formerly rich, often declined into poverty or found themselves forced to emigrate to Iran or Iraq. Shi'ite culture continued on the islands, however, even in the face of repeated Sunni tribal invasions, and the peasants and divers retained their partisanship for the family of the Prophet. Even in the 1860s, out of a population of 70,000, all the subsistence peasants, and five sixths of the inhabitants of Manama, were Shi'ites.[74] Dynasties and clerical wealth from the pearl or spice trade sometimes created Shi'ite religious establishments, but the often exploited common folk kept alive faith in the Imams in times of Sunni domination.

4

Jurisprudence: The Akhbari-Usuli Struggle

It has long been held that the eighteenth century was pivotal in the history of Imami Shi`ite thought and jurisprudence in Iraq and Iran. At the beginning of this era, it is said, the previously dominant Usuli School declined, and the conservative Akhbari school came to the fore. This intellectual revolution coincided with the fall of the Safavid dynasty in Iran and the disestablishment of Shi`ism under the Afghans and then Nadir Shah. Standard accounts would have us believe that Akhbarism became dominant. Then late in the century, as the Qajars came to power, the Usuli School staged a comeback in the shrine cities of Iraq and subsequently in Iran.[1]

This version of events, deriving from published nineteenth-century Usuli works, contains elements of truth. But an examination of manuscript sources from the period and of later biographical dictionaries suggests that the standard view needs revision. In particular, the periodization needs to be made more precise and the biographies of the major intellectual leaders need to be rewritten with more detail and greater accuracy.

Moreover, most treatments of the period adopt an approach depicting the struggle between conflicting schools of thought in terms of great men and of abstract ideas. A more fruitful approach would treat the corps of religious scholars, or ulama, as a group in society, influenced by social and economic developments as well as political ones. Schools of thought should be seen as ideologies supporting the position or aspirations of differing groups of ulama. Family histories written in the eighteenth century are an essential but as yet unused resource in this endeavor of revision.

Several critical questions need to he asked about the period: Is there good evidence that Akhbari religious and legal doctrines dominated the religious establishment in Iran during the eighteenth century? What do we really know about intellectual currents in Iran's major cities at that time, or for that matter about the less populous but still important small towns (*qasabihs*)? Did Akhbarism really only come to the fore in the Iraqi shrine cities in the eighteenth century, or had it been dominant there earlier? When exactly did the Usuli revival take place in Iraq? Was it as late as the Qajar period? The following examination of manuscript sources and re-examination of some printed ones seek to clarify the history of Shi`ism in this crucial century.

During the eighteenth century in Iran and Iraq the established central political institutions of the preceding two centuries were weakened or destroyed, with major demographic and cultural shifts taking place. It began with nearly a quarter century of Shah Sultan Husayn Safavi's weak rule (1694-1722) in Iran and Ottoman Governor Hasan Pasha's firmer administration (1702-1724) in Iraq. There followed in Iran 25 years of more or less Sunni rule, beginning with the conquest of Isfahan by Ghalzai Afghans, followed by the Islamic ecumenist Nadir Shah (1736-47), who employed the Sunni Afghan tribes as allies in his bid to create an empire.

After a long interregnum in which political chaos dominated the center, the Shiraz-based Shi`ite ruler Karim Khan Zand (1763-79) consolidated his position, emerging as the major force in Iran west of Khurasan. Upon his death, the Qajar tribe gained political pre-eminence, creating a new Shi`ite state that ruled throughout the nineteenth century and into the twentieth. In Ottoman Iraq, which suffered Iranian incursions under Nadir Shah during Ahmad Pasha's governorship Sulayman Abu Layla Pasha (1750-62) created a new, regionally-based slave-soldier state that continued under his successors until the reassertion of direct Ottoman rule in 1831.[2]

These political trends made a major impact upon the Shi`ite ulama.[3] Under Shah Sultan Husayn and his predecessor, Shah Sulayman, the high ulama in Iran won great influence, position, and wealth. Arjomand has shown that in so doing the foreign religious scholars from Syria, Bahrain, and Iraq displaced, to some extent, the indigenous "clerical estate" of landed notables who had held official religious office.[4] The Safavid capital, Isfahan, became the cynosure of the Shi`ite clerisy, a center of learning with 48 colleges and 162 mosques, and a place where important career contacts could be made.[5] The clergy waxed so powerful that some openly preached the necessity for the ruler to be, not only a Sayyid, but a mujtahid or senior jurisprudent trained in Ja`fari law This disputed the claim of the Safavis, who, though they asserted their descent from the Prophet, were laymen given often to loose morals. The dominant view supported the legitimacy of Safavid rule against clerical pretenders.[6] Not everyone trusted the ulama, as a seventeenth-century folk saying from

Isfahan testifies "Keep a wary eye in front of you for a woman, behind you for a mule, and from every direction for a mullah."[7] Most of the clergy were neither independently wealthy nor too proud to associate with the government, as they held this was permissible whenever they would otherwise fear for their lives or whenever they felt they could thereby help the Shi`ite community.[8]

The Afghan conquest of Isfahan in 1722 displaced hundreds of scholarly families and delivered a mortal blow to the dynasty that had assured their fortunes. The Sunni Ghalzais and Nadir Shah expropriated the endowments supporting the clergy, leading to a relative impoverishment and a decline in the influence of this group. During the second quarter of the eighteenth century great numbers of Shi`ite clergymen and merchants fled Iran for the shrine cities of Ottoman Iraq, adding a new ethnic component to the Arab quarters of these cities. Under the Safavids the high ulama establishment in the center had favored the Usuli School of jurisprudence, which legitimated an activist role for the clergy as legal scholars in society. The Iraqi shrine cities, laboring under Sunni Ottoman rule, had remained centers of the more conservative Akhbari School. With the collapse of Shi`ite rule in Iran and the anticlericalism of the new rulers, the ulama in any case lost much of their previous opportunity for an active social role. The congregation of hundreds of Iranian clerical families in the Akhbari strongholds brought them under the conservative influence of that school. Isfahan itself, while weakened, remained a center of rationalism, mysticism, and Usulism throughout this period, exercising a countervailing influence in those areas. Other Iranian centers of Usulism also remained. The rise of Akhbarism in the eighteenth century largely occurred in the consciousness of Isfahani immigrants to Iraq.

The Majlisi Family

One way to determine the import of the eighteenth century for the Imami clergy is to examine the fate of prominent families. We are fortunate in having a family history from the pen of Aqa Ahmad Bihbahani, scion of two ulama dynasties, the Majlisis of Isfahan and the Bihbahanis of Karbala.[9] Mulla Muhammad Taqi Majlisi (d. 1656), from a Syrian family that emigrated to Iran during early Safavid rule, led Friday congregational prayers in Isfahan, the capital. An extremely significant figure with Sufi and Akhbari leanings, his works wielded great influence for centuries, while his position in Isfahan lent him religious and political power.[10] Mulla Muhammad Taqi had three sons and four

daughters. All three sons became ulama and the daughters married clergymen as well. One son, Mulla `Aziz Allah, renowned as an author on
religious sciences and belles-lettres composition, grew so wealthy that he
rivaled the very rich merchant Mirza Muhammad Taqi `Abbasabadi. The
second son, Mulla `Abd Allah, emigrated to India. A network of Iranian
and Indian long-distance merchants carried information on the overseas
job market to Isfahan, whose intellectuals were prized at the Mughal
court.[11]

The youngest brother, Muhammad Baqir Majlisi (d. 1699), had no
reason to emigrate. He succeeded his father as prayer leader
(Imam-Jum`a) for the capital, and under Shah Sultan Husayn rose to the
rank of Shaykh al-Islam. As a representative of the increasingly
influential ulama class, Mulla Muhammad Baqir waged a deadly
campaign against its competitors for state patronage, such as the Sufis. He
further initiated a short-sighted persecution of Sunnis, as well as of the
20,000 Hindu merchants and money-lenders in Isfahan who competed
successfully with local concerns.[12] He adopted a strong commitment to
the practice of independent legal reasoning (ijtihad), in contrast to his
father.[13]   His high social position allowed him to marry into the notable
class, one of his three wives being the sister of Abu Talib Khan
Nihavandi.

Of Mulla Muhammad Taqi Majlisi's four sons-in-law, two were from
Mazandaran, one from Shirvan north of Azerbaijan, and one was a Fasa'i
from Fars province in the south. Of the last, Aqa Ahmad Bihbahani knew
nothing. Mulla Muhammad Salih Mazandarani (d. 1670) came to Isfahan
as a youth to escape poverty in his home province, eking out a living as a
student on a stipend in the capital. His brilliance so impressed Majlisi I
that he gave him his daughter Amina Begum in marriage. The girl, highly
literate and trained in the religious sciences, gained a reputation as a
mujtahida, or legal scholar, in her own right.[14]   Despite having married
well, Mazandarani never became wealthy, living out his days in Isfahan as
a mujtahid or religious jurisprudent.

Among the second generation of Majlisi's descendants one can count
at least nine who became or married mullas, links being established with
prestigious Sayyid families. Muhammad Baqir Majlisi's daughters
married mullas, some cousins. One of his sons married into the Sayyids of
Ardistan. A daughter wedded a Sayyid clergyman, Amir Muhammad
Salih Khatunabadi.[15]   He succeeded his father-in-law as official prayer
leader in Isfahan at the beginning of the eighteenth century, the post
eventually becoming hereditary in his line. That this branch of the family
remained in Isfahan throughout the period of that city's tribulations,
retaining an important clerical post, further suggests that even after 1722
it did not entirely decline as a center for the ulama. It indicates, moreover,

that clerical elites maintained continuity in spite of turbulence at the center, just as central and provincial administrators often retained posts even when the regime changed.[16]

Of Muhammad Salih Mazandarani's sons, two emigrated to Awrangzib's India. Aqa Muhammad Sa'id Mazandarani emerged as a favored court poet in Delhi, with the pen name "Ashraf."[17] His brother, Aqa Hasan `Ali, followed in his footsteps. For sons of Shi`ite ulama to succeed socially in the strongly Sunni atmosphere of the Mughal court it was necessary for them to concentrate on literary or medical pursuits, which they did With some success. In Iran, Muhammad Salih's daughter married into a clerical Sayyid family, wedding the Shaykh al-Islam Mir Abu al-Ma`ali, a union that produced several leading ulama based in the shrine cities in the middle of the eighteenth century.

Many members of the third generation lived through the terrible siege and sack of Isfahan, some of them scattering elsewhere. Among those who remained, two important ulama emerged at this point. In 1714 Mir Muhammad Salih Khatunabadi, the prayer leader, passed away and was succeeded by his son, Mir Muhammad Husayn. He held the post through the Afghan period and until his death in 1738 in Nadir Shah's base of operations, Mashhad. During the Nadir Shah era the position of Imam-Jum`a was held by Mir Muhammad Husayn's distant cousin and aunt's husband, Muhammad Taqi Almasi (d. 1746).[18] He was forced to adopt the shah's Sunni-Shi`ite ecumenism. After one successor from outside the family, the post of Imam-Jum`a thereafter reverted to the Khatunabadis on a permanent basis early in the Qajar period.

The third generation intermarried with other clerical elites in Najafabad (near Isfahan), Mashhad, and Isfahan itself. There was some settlement in Najaf and Karbala. Although Bihbahani appears deliberately to have included in his family history only those lines that remained ulama, even some of their daughters began marrying artisans. This may have been simply a natural effect, downward mobility being the fate of most descendants of any wealthy family. Given the prior exclusion of so many from the genealogy, however, it might reflect the impoverishment even of the ulama. A grandson of Muhammad Salih Mazandarani continued a family tradition in following his father to India. Unlike Muhammad Ashraf, however, Muhammad `Ali "Daman" settled in Murshidabad, Bengal, rather than in Delhi. In the first half of the eighteenth century the Mughal court underwent serious decline, leading poets to seek patronage elsewhere.

The two rising Shi`ite-ruled provinces of Bengal and Awadh might have offered particularly congenial settings for Shi`ite scholars from Iran. It was only in the last quarter of the century, however, that the nawabs of Awadh settled down to a provincial court of their own, being until then based largely in declining Delhi. Thus, Shi`ite-ruled Bengal began to attract the Majlisis who wanted to peddle their literary talents in India. As the nawab's capital after 1704, flourishing Murshidabad, a major commercial center and producer of silk goods, offered immigrants great opportunities.[19] Moreover, in the late seventeenth- and early-eighteenth centuries the Bengal port of Hughli had become an important trading center for Iranian long-distance merchants. Indeed, they amassed more capital than any other group in the city. Such a congregation of Iranians ensured the growth of Shi`ite institutions and patronage for Shi`ite scholars.[20] The existence of a convenient transportation network based on trade between the ports of Iran and Hughli also may have encouraged scholars to land there rather than risk the increasingly insecure land route through Afghanistan and the Punjab to Delhi.

The fourth generation continued to produce scholars in Isfahan such as Taqi Almasi's son Mirza `Aziz Allah (d. 1750/1163), a historian as well as a theologian. The turbulence of the times is indicated in the death of some while traveling to Mashhad, and the passing away of others far from home in Najaf. Of those who stayed in Isfahan several deserted the pulpit for the bazaar, producing a dyer (*sabbagh*), a fuller (*gadhar*), and daughters that married a hat maker (*kulah-duz*) and a copper smelter (*rikhtihgar*).

In the Mazandarani line, one sees ulama tying themselves to the richer classes of the bazaar, seeking new forms of economic security when their links to the courts were so disrupted from 1722 to the rise of the Zands. Their bazaar links and the relative political independence this fostered were to prove crucial to the growth of ulama power in the nineteenth and twentieth centuries.[21] Of Mulla Muhammad Akmal's two wives, one was a granddaughter of Muhammad Salih Mazandarani. The children of the other wife did not become mullas, working in Isfahan and Tehran as money changers (*sarraf*) or in Zand Shiraz as money coiners (*zarrabi*). The children of the Majlisi wife, however, did become mullas, among them Aqa Muhammad Baqir Bihbahani.

Aqa Muhammad Baqir first married the daughter of Aqa Sayyid Muhammad Tabataba'i, congregational prayer leader for the small town of Burujird in Luristan, whom he met in Karbala after the Afghan invasion. Aqa Muhammad Baqir later settled in the small Iranian town of Bihbahan, which in this period served as the stronghold of the Kuhgilu tribe. There he married the daughter of a merchant, Hajji Sharafa. Bihbahan was increasingly integrated into Fars province, serving as a hinterland town to the Persian Gulf port of Bandar Rig, which in 1750 was so prosperous as to rival Bushehr.[22] Like his father, then, Bihbahani developed marital links both with high status ulama families and with wealthy bazaaris, a step even more necessary for him as he had the tragedy to come of age just as the Safavid dynasty fell and Iran was thrown into political turmoil.

Likewise, a female cousin in Najafabad married a jeweler whose relatives monopolized high religious posts in their town.

Another Mazandarani line in the fourth generation did not take up religious occupations at all. Mulla Muhammad Salih (named for his grandfather) had a daughter who married a merchant, Mirza Amin Tajir, and a son who emigrated to Bengal as a civil servant for Viceroy `Ali-Vardi Khan Mahabat Jang (1740-56).[23] `Ali-Vardi Khan's brother had come to Iraq and Iran as part of his visitation of the Imams in Najaf and Karbala. In Isfahan he struck up a friendship with Mulla Muhammad Salih, then returned to the court in Delhi. When, in 1740, his brother was appointed viceroy of Bengal, he wrote to Mulla Muhammad Salih informing him that he needed good men to staff his upper bureaucracy. The latter dispatched his son, `Ala' al-Din Muhammad, from Isfahan forthwith. As this ruling family was Shi`ite and Iranian, they favored the importation of other Iranians for such posts. The networks of pilgrimage and visitation in which the ulama were involved enabled them to make contacts crucial for career changes and at that point steamy but rich Bengal might have looked more appealing than Isfahan, with its decaying mosques. Sometimes the change of career and life style was very great. The descendants of the Majlisi court poets Ashraf and Daman in Murshidabad were so debauched that Aqa Ahmad Bihbahani refused to include their names in his genealogy.

On the other hand, the Sayyid descendants of Mazandarani through Mir Abu al-Ma`ali, a Shaykh al-Islam, determinedly remained mullas. They established links with high status Sayyid families in small centers like Burujird, and Aqa Muhammad Baqir was able to take advantage of these bonds. The descendants of daughters who had married into a mujtahid family in Mashhad became notables (addressed as nawabs) in Yazd, where they lived in palaces. Their children in turn attained the high religious offices of Sadr and Shaykh al-Islam in Yazd.

The fifth generation, many of whom were born under Nadir's rule and lived to see the advent of the Qajars, continued to establish bazaar ties. Imam-Jum`a Muhammad Taqi Almasi's grandson, `Allama Mirza Haydar `Ali became a mullah. But his sister married a polisher of precious stones (*hakkak*) whose grandsons congregated in the Qajar capital of Tehran. The family produced other mullas and married into the Khatunabadis. Almasi's grand-niece married twice, first Mirza Muhammad Mihdi Tajir-i `Abbasabadi, of a prominent Isfahani commercial dynasty, and then a Sayyid whose descendants became mullas and merchants. This generation produced more skilled artisans in Isfahan, a silk weaver (*tikmih-duz*) and a confectioner (*qannad*), and a good number of extended family members lived in the shrine cities of Iraq, not all of them as mullas (they included a copper smelter).

Among the heirs of Muhammad Salih Mazandarani one finds a weaver of fine cloth (*nassaj*), and a druggist in Kazimayn. But most members of the family were either mullahs or Bengali civil servants. Some, like Hajji Muhammad Isma'il, had one wife in Murshidabad and another in Karbala, where he retired. A sister of the wealthy Bengali branch of the family married into the Bihbihani mujtahid dynasty in Karbala. Among the family's mullas, especially in the Bihbahani and Tabataba'i lines, one notes in this period a resurgence of power and patronage. The Zands, while not as generous to the ulama as the Safavids had been, did provide some sinecures. In the shrine cities themselves huge amounts of money were placed in the hands of the leading ulama by Nawab Asaf al-Dawla of Awadh and other patrons in India and Iran. The slave-soldier government in Iraq continued to allow Karbala and Najaf a good deal of autonomy.

Aqa Ahmad provides little information on the sixth generation, many of whom lived into the nineteenth century. Numbers perished in the Iraqi plague of 1773-74 or the Wahhabi invasion of Karbala in 1801, the devastation wrought by these events encouraging many survivors to emigrate. In 1801, for instance, a man moved to Murshidahad and two brothers in the Mazandarani line to Faizabad in Awadh. A new wave of Iranian emigration to India from 1790 also coincided with a significant expansion of trade, particularly the Iranian import of Indian cotton goods.[24]

From 1764 Bengal was decisively under British control, while Awadh continued to flourish under Shi'ite rule in the north. Murshidabad was no longer an administrative center, and its silk and other industries were dealt a blow by the famine of 1769-70, from which the city never recovered. In the early 1800s Aqa Ahmad found the area's Muslim notables and learned tradition impoverished, the British in control, and whatever wealth still existed in the hands of Hindus.[25] In addition, the Iranian-dominated port of Hughli rapidly declined in favor of British Calcutta. In the latter part of the eighteenth century scholarly families emigrating from Iran and the shrine cities began to settle in the flourishing cities of Awadh. One Murshidabadi branch of the Majlisi clan moved to Lucknow and intermarried with the family of Asaf al-Dawlah's chief minister in the 1790s, Raja Jhao Lal, a convert to Shi'ite Islam.[26] Aqa Ahmad Bihbahani himself left Kermanshah for India because of financial difficulties, settling in Patna as the congregational prayer leader after failing to find patronage in Awadh.

The prestigious clerical dynasty of the Majlisis adopted varying strategies to deal with the problems they faced in the eighteenth century. These included emigration to the Iraqi shrine cities where a constant stream of pilgrims and long-distance merchants provided them with a livelihood as legal advisers and supervisors of charitable contributions and pious endowments. Some managed to retain religious office in a declining Isfahan, while others intermarried with rich merchants or well-off artisans, when possible. With the decline of court patronage for scholars and the expropriation of endowments, more were probably forced into low status trades - cotton or silk weavers, smiths, dyers, bleachers, and hat makers - than would normally have been the case. Many settled in Iran's small towns and large villages, where local tribal leaders came into prominence with the decline of central government. The smaller centers were less likely to attract marauding invaders, prospering as local trade depots, even as some large cities declined. Members of the Majlisi family colonized high religious office in Najafabad, Ardistan, Kazirun, Bihbahan, and Yazd. Finally, numbers sought employment in India as literary men, civil servants, and physicians.

Neo-Akhbari Dominance 1722-1763 in Iraq

Against this backdrop of geographical and class dislocation, the ulama of the eighteenth century fought out a decisive battle on the interpretation of Shi`ism.[27] The conflict between strict constructionist Akhbari and rationalist Usuli jurisprudents centered on two sets of issues. The first concerned the sources of law, with the Akhbaris restricting them to the Qur'an and the oral reports of the Prophet and the Imams. The rationalists insisted that the consensus of the jurisprudents could also serve as a source of legal judgment, as could the independent reasoning (*ijtihad*) of the jurist. The Usulis Shi`ites divided all Shi`ites into formally trained jurisprudents (*mujtahids*) and laymen, stipulating that the ordinary believers must emulate the mujtahids in matters of subsidiary religious laws.

The rationalists asserted that the mujtahids, as general representatives of the Hidden Imam, could substitute for him in performing such tasks as rendering legal judgments, implementing rulings, collecting and distributing alms (*zakat* and *khums*), mandating defensive holy war and leading Friday congregational prayers. While Akhbaris accepted that the relater (*muhaddith*) of oral reports from the Imams could perform the functions of judges, they often disallowed some or all of the others in the absence of an infallible Imam. Akhbaris further rejected any division of believers into laymen and mujtahid-exemplars, holding that all Shi`ites must emulate the Twelve Imams. In practice, Akhbaris also made interpretations.

During the Safavid period the Usuli school, associated with the ruling establishment, gained in influence. From the time of Shaykh Abd al-`Ali al-Karaki (d. 1533), Isfahan's Imam-Jum`as were for the most part Usulis. Late in the period, Muhammad Baqir Majlisi exemplified the Usuli ethos. The situation outside Isfahan in the late seventeenth century is harder to gauge. In some provincial centers Akhbaris remained influential. The Imam-Jum`a and Shaykh al-Islam of Qum under Sulayman Shah (1667-94), Muhammad Tahir, a bigoted Akhbari brought up in Najaf, caused a row with the court by censuring the monarch's morals.[28] Al-Hurr al-`Amili (d. 1708 or 1709) immigrated to Mashhad from Syria, becoming Shaykh al-Islam. A staunch Akhbari, he disallowed the use of reason and wrote against rationalist theology.[29] The family of the Akhbari Ni`mat Allah Jaza'iri (d. 1701) settled in the small Iranian town of Shushtar, in Khuzistan, as Akhbari prayer leaders.[30] As noted, the Akhbari school had found favor with some of the ulama in the shrine cities of Iraq, as well.

Shaykh Yusuf al-Bahrani (1695-1772), a key figure in the intellectual development of Shi`ism in Karbala, grew up in the village of Diraz on the isle of Bahrain.[31] His grandfather, a pearl merchant, helped bring him up. His father, Shaykh Ahmad, a student of Shaykh Sulayman al-Mahuzi in Bahrain, adhered to the Usuli School, detesting Akhbaris. Usuli jurisprudence was an important current in Safavid-ruled Bahrain. In 1717 al-Bahrani's family fled an invasion from Masqat, settling on the mainland at Qatif for a while.[32] After his father's death Yusuf commuted to Bahrain to keep up the family pearl business, pursuing his studies in his spare time. Financial difficulties, partly owing to the high taxes charged by the invaders, led him to emigrate to Iran soon after the Afghan conquest of 1722. He lived in Kerman, then moved to Shiraz where he gained the patronage of the governor. He invested in agriculture, which his patron allowed him to pursue tax-free, and he began his famed work on law, *al-Hada'iq al-nadira*. He fled the city after the Afghan army had reduced it in 1724 by mass slaughter and looting, and settled in Karbala in Iraq. There his financial situation improved, perhaps through trade.

Al-Bahrani adopted the Akhbari school, rejecting his early schooling in Bahrain. As a refugee from Iran in Karbala, he may well have been dependent on the largesse of Akhbari religious dignitaries. Moreover, the same political instability that propelled him from his homeland and deposed the Safavids apparently made an establishment-oriented school of jurisprudence like Usulism less appealing. As time went on, al-Bahrani moved away from a strict Akhbarism to a neo-Akhbari position which had Usuli elements. Nevertheless, he rejected Usuli principles of legal reasoning, the syllogistic logic Usulis allowed in interpreting the law, and the legitimacy of holy war during the occultation of the Imam.[33]

When the influx of Iranians came into Karbala from Isfahan and other Iranian cities, especially during the interregnums of 1722-36 and 1747-63, the Akhbari teachers in the shrine cities had the opportunity to expose many young Iranians to their ideas. Al-Bahrani's many students included not only other Arabs but in later years such Iranian scholars as Sayyid Muhammad Mihdi Tabataba'i of Burujird, Mirza Muhammad Mihdi Shahristani, and Mulla Muhammad Mihdi Niraqi.[34]

The trend to Akhbarism after 1722 may be witnessed in another major eighteenth-century figure, Aqa Muhammad Baqir b. Muhammad Akmal (1705-90), born in Isfahan and descended on his mother's side from Muhammad Taqi Majlisi. Since the chronology of his career has remained confused, a reinterpretation is offered here. Aqa Muhammad Baqir departed from his home town for Najaf after the death of his father and the 1722 Afghan invasion. In Iraq he studied the rational sciences with Sayyid Muhammad Tabataba'i of Burujird and the oral reports of the Imams with Sayyid Sadr al-Din Qummi.[35]   The latter had trained in Isfahan, returning to Qum as a teacher. He was forced to flee the Afghans, first to Hamadan and Kermanshah, and finally to Najaf. Under the influence of Qummi, an Akhbari, the young Aqa Muhammad Baqir likewise came to adhere to this school.[36] While in Najaf in the late 1720s Aqa Muhammad Baqir married the daughter of his teacher, Sayyid Muhammad Tabataba'i (other marriage alliances existed between the two families). In 1732 (1144) his first son, Muhammad 'Ali, was born in Karbala.

In 1732-33 Nadir invaded Iraq, his troops occupying the Shi'ite holy places of Samarra, Hilla, Najaf, and Karbala, over which he appointed Iranian governors. Ottoman reinforcements soon arrived, forcing Nadir to make a peace treaty and withdraw after he visited the shrine cities.[37] These military engagements created insecurity even in the holy cities of Iraq, and there may at this time have been some exodus of anxious refugees to still more secure sites.

Whatever the reasons, Aqa Muhammad Baqir traveled early in the 1730s to Bihbahan on the border of the Iranian provinces of Khuzistan and Fars. Many Isfahani scholarly families scattered to such small towns (qasabih) in southern Iran, which were relatively near to the shrine cities and offered greater security in this period than large cities; moreover, Aqa Muhammad Baqir had a cousin there teaching in the local seminary.[38] At that point the town served as a stronghold for the semi-autonomous Kuhgilu tribe and the headquarters of its Beglarbegi. The latter had allied himself with Nadir Shah against Muhammad Khan Baluch in a bid to maintain his local control over the area.[39] In the 1730s the town, lying on a north-south trade route from the port of Daylam, was in decline.[40]

Aqa Muhammad Baqir found the religious institutions dominated by Akhbaris from Bahrain.[41] Although he may at first have gotten along with them, at some point he reverted to his Isfahani Usulism, engaging in bitter polemics with the Akhbaris. His son, Aqa Muhammad `Ali, boasted that he never emulated any jurisprudent, being already a mujtahid when he came of age at 15 (in 1747).[42] This statement suggests that his father was an Usuli again by the late 1730s. Aqa Muhammad Baqir established firm links to the elite in Bihbahan and its suburb of Qanavat, marrying the daughter of the headman in the latter and the daughter of Hajji Sharafa the merchant in Bihbahan.[43] He emerged as a popular prayer leader and teacher, remaining for 30 years.

Sunni-Shi`ite Ecumenism in Iran 1736-1751

While Aqa Muhammad Baqir found refuge in Bihbahan, the ulama in most parts of Iran suffered the assaults of Nadir Afshar. In 1736 he gave up the fiction of being merely the agent of the young Safavid heir, having himself declared shah upon the plain of Mughan and abolishing the Safavid state altogether. He made it one of the cornerstones of his policy that Iranians should renounce the Shi`ite practice of cursing the first two caliphs of Sunni Islam and tried to have Shi`ism incorporated into Sunnism as a fifth legal rite. Much of Shi`ite law was based on the precepts of the sixth Imam, Ja`far al-Sadiq, whom Nadir proposed to place on par with the founders of Sunni legal rites such as Abu Hanifa and ash-Shafi`i. Nadir attempted to negotiate with the Sunni Ottomans an acceptance of this theological compromise, but never proved successful. More important, the policy did allow him to keep the loyalty of both his Afghan troops and his Qizilbash cavalry, the former fierce Sunnis and the latter extremist Shi`ites. Nadir Shah forced the Shi`ite ulama to agree to this compromise, executing one cleric for opposing him.[44] Wherever they felt it necessary they went along, but the assent of many surely represented no more than pious dissimulation (*taqiyya*), as Nadir's proposal contradicted their most cherished dogmas.

Still, many clerical officials were incorporated into Nadir's state and had to represent his policies. For instance, Mirza Ibrahim, qadi of Isfahan, became Nadir's military judge (*qadi-`askar*).[45] The shah sent Abu al-Qasim Kashani, the Shaykh al-Islam, and Mulla `Ali Akbar, Mullabashi, to Istanbul to negotiate with the Ottoman ulama. In addition, Nadir sought to weaken the clergy, and to guard against any potential clerical opposition to his policies, he confiscated the rich endowments that had supported the seminaries and mosques of Isfahan.[46]

On his return from India, Nadir Shah once again prepared for conflict with the Ottomans in Iraq. He coordinated a two-pronged attack, through Kirkuk and Shahrizur in the north and from Arabistan to Basra in the south, dispatching troops to occupy, once more, the Shi`ite shrine cities in

the summer of 1743.   In November, 1743, Nadir Shah convened a
congress of ulama from Iran, Afghanistan, and Transoxiana, as well as
from the shrine cities, in order finally to resolve the differences between
Sunni and Shi`ite. He attempted to propitiate the Shi`ite ulama of Najaf by
ordering the gilding of Imam `Ali's shrine.

The conference, after much debate and haggling, produced a document
that rejected the past Shi`ite practice of cursing the first two caliphs,
stipulating that Shi`ites should abandon it on pain of death; that
recognized the legitimacy of the rule of the first three Sunni caliphs; and
that granted the Iranians the right to follow the legal rite of Imam Ja`far
al-Sadiq and yet remain within the Muslim community. The list of
participants reveals that most of the Iranian ulama were Imam-Jum`as and
qadis of Iran's chief cities. No mention appears in the biographical
dictionaries of the role the Akhbari establishment at the shrine cities
played in these negotiations, nor did al-Suwaydi refer to them, but they
were almost certainly involved. The Iranians took the lead in the
negotiations on the Shi`ite side, particularly Nadir Shah's compliant
Mulla-Bashi. The Ottomans rejected the document that emerged.[47] Some
Shi`ite officials genuinely committed themselves to Nadir's ecumenical
stance. The Imam-Jum`a of Isfahan from 1746 to 1787, Shaykh Zayn al-
Din `Ali, wrote a refutation of a treatise by Mulla Haydar `Ali in 1751,
who opposed the policy. Haydar `Ali had insisted that all sects other than
the Imami were ritually impure and outside Islam. Shaykh Zayn al-Din
replied that Sunnis were also Muslims.[48]

One long-lasting effect of Nadir Shah's Iraq campaign of the 1740s
was the provisions in the peace treaty he finally concluded with the
Ottomans that concerned Iranian pilgrims to the Iraqi shrine cities. While
the shah ceded these cities once more to the Turks in September 1746, he
stipulated that Iranian pilgrims be able to visit the shrines and that "so
long as these pilgrims carried no merchandise, the Governor and officials
of Baghdad were not to levy any tax upon them."[49] The unimpeded access
for Iranians to Karbala and Najaf guaranteed by the Treaty of Kurdan
meant prosperity for merchants, shopkeepers, and clerics who lived off
the pilgrim trade. Moreover, in the eighteenth century the shrine cities
paid no tribute to the government in Bagdad.[50]

The Usuli Revival in the Zand Period

In Bihbahan, Aqa Muhammad Baqir escaped from what the communalist
Imami ulama perceived to be the indignities of Nadir's ecumenism, and
for some time remained unaffected by the turbulent twelve-year
interregnum in central government that Iran experienced in the wake of
the Afsharid's bloody demise. But the growing power of the Zands

disturbed the tranquility of Bihbahan in 1757-58, when Karim Khan first attempted to subdue the tribespeople in its vicinity. In July of 1757 the Zands took Bihbahan, imprisoning the old beglarbegi and replacing him with one of their supporters, and levied an annual tribute of 7,000 tumans. The Zands decisively pacified the area in 1765.[51] It may have been these military campaigns and the disruptions they brought to local power and patronage structures that encouraged Aqa Muhammad Baqir to return to Iraq sometime in the early 1760s.

Bihbahani, as he was now known, found the shrine cities an extremely hostile environment for an Usuli. Shaykh Yusuf al- Bahrani, in his late 60s and ten years senior to the newcomer, presided over the religious establishment in Karbala as the prestigious dean of Shi`ite scholarship. Al-Bahrani's neo-Akhbaris considered Usulis to be ritually impure, touching Usuli works with handkerchiefs to shield their fingers from any polluting effects.[52] More serious, anyone walking in the street with Usuli literature beneath his arm risked violent assault.[53] The power structure in the shrine cities consisted of an Arab landholding elite, a number of mafia-type gangs, and the leading clerics. Most important figures among the ulama probably had had to make alliances with the Sayyid landholders and with the chief gangsters who ran protection rackets in the bazaars. At this point, the Akhbaris appear to have had the important gangster or luti contacts, and could employ these to intimidate Usuli rivals.

Bihbahani at first faced so many difficulties in Karbala that he seriously considered returning to Iran. His eldest son, Aqa Muhammad `Ali, had even greater difficulties adjusting to the new intellectual milieu. He joined Yusuf al-Bahrani's classes, receiving a diploma (*ijaza*) from him. But he did not pursue further studies with him because he kept wishing to contradict the old man's neo-Akhbari teachings, which would have been highly improper (and perhaps even dangerous). Aqa Muhammad `Ali therefore went on pilgrimage to Mecca, settling in Kazimayn until 1772.[54]

Aqa Muhammad Baqir began teaching Usuli texts secretly in his basement to a select and trusted number of students, many of them former pupils of al-Bahrani. These included his young grand- nephew on his first wife's side of the family, Sayyid Muhammad Mihdi Tabataba'i (1742-96), who had settled in Najaf in 1755 but now returned to study with his great-uncle.[55] Also involved was Bihbahani's sister's son, Sayyid `Ali Tabataba'i (1748-1801), a mere teenager at the time. When the Iranians had originally come to the shrine cities in the 1720s, many of them penniless refugees, they had been integrated into the Akhbari ideology of their Arab hosts and benefactors. Forty years later, the founding of an Usuli cell in Karbala led by members of the Majlisi aristocracy may well have signaled the increasing financial and social independence of the ethnically Iranian quarters in the shrine cities.[56] While the Iranian scholarly families originally depended heavily on government land grants and emoluments in Iran, which many of them lost after 1722, the history of the Majlisi family sketched above suggests that they increasingly forged links with merchants and skilled artisans in the bazaars, giving them a new financial base. Though fallen from their semi-feudal notable status and dispossessed of their lands around Isfahan, many Iranian expatriates could increasingly compete with the wealth of merchant-ulama, like al-Bahrani, on his own terms. The partial upturn in ulama fortunes in the Zand period, moreover, coincided with the economic rebound of the artisan and merchant classes with whom they were intricately linked.[57]

Aqa Muhammad Baqir had strong merchant contacts through his in-laws in Bihbahan and his half-brothers in Isfahan and Shiraz, important insofar as they might encourage merchants who came through Karbala to put charitable contributions in his hands and seek his rulings on commercial disputes. It is also possible that his sister-in-law's brothers in Bengal might have channeled charitable contributions from Indian notables to the shrine cities through him. Wealth was essential to the success of a great teacher, as he attracted students by providing them with stipends to live on. It was also indispensable in insuring that the gangster bosses were on his side.

At some point Bihbahani began to feel that he had enough students, monetary support, and security to challenge al-Bahrani openly, an event that led to the polarization of the scholarly community in Karbala during the 1760s. In 1772, when al-Bahrani died, Bihbahani had attained such a prestigious position that he read the funeral prayers for his late nemesis. Shaykh Yusuf's demise removed the most vigorous Akhbari leader from the field, allowing Aqa Muhammad Baqir, then 67, to spend his last clear-minded decade in consolidating his position. In this he was aided not only by his nephews, the young Tabataba'is, but by a number of other former students of al Bahrani who now adopted the Usuli jurisprudent as their leader, including the Iranians Muhammad Mihdi Niraqi and Mirza Muhammad Mihdi Shahristani and the Arabs Shaykh Ja`far al-Najafi and Sayyid Muhsin Baghdadi.[58] These in turn helped their aging mentor to train a whole new generation of youthful mujtahids who came from Iran to the shrine cities in the last years of Zand dominance and the opening years of Qajar rule.

The Usuli revival in Iraq began to exert influence on Iran, where Usuli currents had always run strong, with a wave of ulama reimmigration from the shrine cities in the 1770s. Political tensions between Iraq and Iran arose in the early 1770s, when the slave-soldier ruler `Umar Pasha levied a frontier toll on Iranian pilgrims in contravention of the 1746 Treaty of Kurdan.[59] The new policy adversely affected the economy of the pilgrim-dependent shrine towns. In 1772, the same year that Shaykh

Yusuf passed away, a catastrophic plague epidemic raced through Iraq, claiming hundreds of thousands of lives, perhaps a quarter of a million in Baghdad alone.[60] The existence of the shrines of the Imams as pilgrimage sites contributed to frequent epidemics in Iraq, especially as Shi`ites often transported corpses to them for reburial.[61] Towns that became depopulated immediately attracted Bedouin raids and further destruction. `Umar Pasha therefore attempted to keep people in the cities during the plague, which lasted for some eighteen months.[62]

How to respond to the epidemic became an issue among the Shi`ite clergy as well, since many of them were morally and financially attached to their shrines and convinced of the divine protection they offered. Bihbahani and his chief disciples did their utmost to clear people from the festering urban centers, in defiance of 'Umar Pasha. Aqa Muhammad Baqir strictly enjoined his son Aqa Muhammad `Ali to flee Kazimayn for Iran. The latter only reluctantly complied, settling for the rest of his life in Kermanshah, near the Iraqi border.[63] Sayyid `Ali Tabataba'i supported his mentor's stance with the hadith report, "Greet not oblivion with your own hands."[64] Sayyid Muhammad Mihdi Tabataba'i took his family out of Najaf through Isfahan to Mashhad during the plague, teaching and giving diplomas in Isfahan and Khurasan until his return in 1779.[65]

This firm commitment to fleeing the plague preserved the lives of many in Bihbahani's circle, and it had the secondary effect of spreading his ideas to urban centers in Iran as his relatives and students scattered there. The loss of life in Iraq in 1772-73 was monumental. The Sunni cleric al-Suwaydi taught a class of a thousand students at a mosque in Basra before the plague reached there, then fled to Kuwait. On his return a few months later, when the epidemic had subsided, he found that everyone who had attended his class was dead. The toll in the shrine cities was equally high.[66] The Akhbari Arab natives of Karbala and Najaf could not easily escape the writ of `Umar Pasha forbidding them to leave the cities, since unlike the Iranian Usulis they did not necessarily have family or second homes in Iran. They may well therefore have been exposed to heavier casualties from the disease. Moreover, the former social order of the shrine cities could not help but be disrupted by so immense a catastrophe, allowing Bihbahani's young Usuli cadres to move into the power and culture vacuum upon their return.

The impact Bihbahani's movement had in Iran in the Zand period may be witnessed in the careers of such clerics as Mulla Muhammad Mihdi Niraqi and Mulla Muhammad Reza Tabrizi. Niraqi (d. 1794) was born near Kashan and studied in Isfahan with the theologian Isma`il Khaju'i (d. 1759). He then went to Karbala, probably during the governmental interregnum of the 1750s, studying with Shaykh Yusuf al-Bahrani. When Bihbahani returned to Karbala Niraqi began studying with the Usuli teacher. He then settled in Kashan, where he was writing on commercial law for merchants and in defense of Usuli jurisprudence in the years 1766-72.[67]

Tabrizi (d. 1793) also stayed for a long while in Iraq, studying with Muhammad Mihdi al-Fatuni and Aqa Muhammad Baqir Hizarjaribi. He, like so many others, attached himself to Bihbahani in the 1760s. He thereafter returned to Tabriz, where he led prayers and gave sermons. After a visit to the shrine at Mashhad, he made his way to the Zand capital of Shiraz in the south. He became close to Karim Khan Zand, who appointed him military judge (*qadi-'askar*). The ruling Zand dynasty, though ungenerous to the lower ranks of clerics and religious mendicants, was open-handed with the high ulama, for whom it built mosques and living quarters in Shiraz.[68] When the Zand state declined after 1779 Tabrizi returned to Iraq.[69] In Kermanshah during the Zand period Bihbahani's son Aqa Muhammad 'Ali - another product of the Usuli revival - became extremely influential, intermarrying with the notable class there.[70]

The new mood in the shrine cities was epitomized by Bihbahani's student Shaykh Ja'far b. Khidr al-Najafi (d. 1812), who later authored the *Kashf al-ghita'* in refutation of Akhbarism:

The hair of his head and beard was already white in his youth. He was a big man of high aspirations and sublime courage, with great strength of intellect and insight. He had a strong appetite for licit sex (*al-ankihah*) and food, and for establishing links with kings and rulers for the sake of the religious benefits he believed to lie therein.[71]

The Usuli revival was, in Iranian terms, a largely Zand-period phenomenon which the Qajars came to support later on. In the shrine cities themselves the Usuli victory coincided with the rise of local Shi'ite power and the decline of central Ottoman control, such that Usuli principles like the holding of Shi'ite congregational prayers could be implemented, something the Ottomans had not tolerated when their hand in Iraq was firmer.

The First North Indian Usuli Disciples

The degree to which the Usuli school dominated the shrine cities at the end of the 1770s is demonstrated by the memoirs of an Indian student and pilgrim, Sayyid Dildar 'Ali Nasirabadi (1753-1820). Nasirabadi brought with him from the Shi'ite-ruled nawabate of Awadh a copy of Muhammad Amin Astarabadi's *al-Fawa'id al-madaniyya*, a work hugely popular among Shi'ite thinkers in North India. Written nearly two centuries earlier, this major statement of the Akhbari creed attacked such classical Usuli writers as Hasan ibn al-Mutahhar al-Hilli.

Sayyid Dildar 'Ali and his companion landed at plague and war-devastated Basra, proceeding up the Euphrates by boat.[72] During this long boat journey Nasirabadi made friends with an Arab Shi'ite, also en route to Najaf, where he had just begun his studies with Shaykh Ja'far al-Najafi. Their discussions came around to the principles of jurisprudence. Nasirabadi supported the Akhbari position, while his Arab friend took the side of the Usulis. The Indian criticized Usuli acceptance of consensus among scholars as an independent source of Shi'ite law, asking why something should be true simply because large numbers of persons believed it. He also attacked Usulis for believing in the exercise of independent judgment (ra'y) by the jurisprudent. In this discussion Sayyid Dildar 'Ali first encountered the now largely Usuli atmosphere of the shrine cities, finding it disturbing.[73]

After performing visitation to the shrine of Imam 'Ali, Sayyid Dildar 'Ali met with the scholar Sayyid Muhsin Baghdadi (d. 1810s/1230s), who wrote on the principles of jurisprudence and became the prayer leader in Kazimayn.[74] Nasirabadi remarked on the fact that most North Indian Shi'ite ulama, including himself, were Akhbaris. The Iraqi replied that this was owing to their unfamiliarity with Usuli works. He then gave him a refutation of Astarabadi's opus. Sayyid Dildar 'Ali read it, but the book left his doubts unresolved. He next met with Shaykh Ja'far al-Najafi, discussing whether scholarly consensus can constitute a proof in jurisprudence. Nasirabadi left dissatisfied. Later, he again brought up this matter with Baghdadi, who upheld the Usuli view that consensus does indeed constitute a source of law. Sayyid Dildar 'Ali listened and grew quiet, deciding that if he insisted on arguing these points with his teachers it would he impossible to learn anything. The important scholars in Iraq at that time were apparently Usulis, and he had little choice hut to attempt to benefit from them.

Nasirabadi shifted north to Karbala, studying the oral reports from the Imams with Aqa Muhammad Baqir Bihbahani, then 75, and law with Sayyid 'Ali Tabataba'i and Mirza Mihdi Shahristani (the latter having himself been to India). In spite of his silence on the issue, his reputation as an Akhbari followed him to Karbala, where Sayyid 'Ali once embarrassed him in front of an Indian nobleman by stressing his debt to the mujtahids. Sayyid Dildar 'Ali determined to throw himself into an intensive study of Usuli works, since they were the ones difficult to find in India. He began survey reading on the issue of the validity of those oral reports that were related by only a single transmitter in each early generation (khabar al-ahad).[75] After much study of the classical writers

Sayyid Dildar `Ali began to feel that Astarabadi's position on this issue was indefensible. Within a few months of his arrival in Iraq, he adopted the Usuli school, one factor surely being that this ideology was in vogue at the prestigious centers of Shi`ite scholarship. He later attributed his change of views to his proximity at that point to the holy tombs of the Imams.[76]

When Sayyid Muhammad Mihdi Tabataba'i returned to Iraq, Nasirabadi, who had heard him praised as virtually sinless (ma`sum), sought him out and studied with him briefly. He pointed out to his teacher that in the Usuli system a believer must either be a mujtahid himself, or he must emulate a living mujtahid. But, he continued, the Shi`ites of India were deprived of any opportunity for either, so that they might land in perdition. Tabataba'i replied that this was not at all the case. The Shi`ites in India, he maintained, must simply practice caution (ihtiyat), following the strictest of the major positions on any matter of law. Nasirabadi riposted that Majlisi I once said that the most cautious position was not always the correct one. Sayyid Muhammad Mihdi answered that such instances were rare.[77] Sayyid Dildar `Ali's dissatisfaction with the practice of caution as a solution to the dilemma of Indian Usulis suggests that even then he saw the need for religious leadership that would result from the spread of Usulism in Awadh.

Nasirabadi had great difficulty being taken seriously as a scholar because of his Indian background, some Iranian students insisting that there simply were no ulama in India. They found the very thought of an Indian mujtahid absurd, given that only three scholars at the shrine cities were recognized exemplars.

After about a year and a half, Sayyid Dildar `Ali returned to India overland via Kazimayn, Tehran, and Mashhad, wintering in Khurasan and studying with Mirza Muhammad Mihdi Mashhadi. On arriving in Lucknow he met with Awadh First Minister Hasan Riza Khan and had an interview with Nawab Asaf al-Dawla. In 1781 he began teaching and writing in Lucknow, producing a wide-ranging attack on Akhbari ideas and beginning the task of training a new generation of Shi`ite scholars in Usuli sciences.

Sayyid Dildar `Ali's experiences demonstrate that in 1779 Usuli jurisprudence already dominated most intellectual circles in Iraq. His adoption of that school and his transmission of it to North India paralleled a similar process among other Shi`ite pilgrim-students from Iran, Afghanistan, and elsewhere in Iraq. By virtue of their centrality to Shi`ite pilgrimage and higher education, the shrine cities exercised extraordinary influence on intellectual currents elsewhere in the Shi`ite world.

The questions asked at the beginning of this chapter can now be answered, if not with complete satisfaction, then at least provisionally. The evidence does not support the belief that Akhbari religious and legal doctrines dominated the religious establishment in Iran during the eighteenth century; they certainly did not prevail in major centers like Isfahan. Akhbarism, or at least conservative jurisprudence based closely on the Imami oral reports, was popular in the Iraqi shrine cities long before the eighteenth century. Iranian immigrants to Iraq during the turbulent period 1722-1763, adhering to Usulism, may have come to resent this situation more than had previously been the case. But the real change was not a sudden Akhbari dominance in Iraq; rather, it was an influx of Usuli-inclined Iranians into the shrine cities. These Iranians temporarily adopted the Akhbarism of their Iraqi hosts, but reverted to Usulism in the 1760s. The Usuli dominance of the shrine cities came, not at the end of the century with the rise of the Qajars, but in the 1760s and 1770s during the Zand era in Iran.

Given Usuli dominance in Iran, the fall of the shrine cities of Iraq to this clerical ideology meant the elimination of one of Akhbarism's last strongholds. From the shrine cities, with their complex network of pilgrimage and study that linked them to the rest of the Shi`ite world, Usuli ideas then spread to distant areas like North India.

Usulism emerged as the favored ideology of the shrine cities at a time when the central Ottoman empire had declined and even the local vassal state grew extremely weak and little able to control the Shi`ite cities firmly. Local elites came to prominence in these city-states, composed of Arab landowners, Arab and Iranian ulama, and gangster bosses. Usulism, with its emphasis on the leading role of the religious scholars in generally representing the absent Imam and serving as exemplars for lay believers, resonated with the increasing local power possessed by the Imami ulama in the shrine cities.

These developments appear also to be related to state formation in Qajar Iran and in Nawabi Awadh: the ruling classes in both regimes favored Usulism. Usulism, with its doctrine that the ulama can legitimate Friday prayers (said, in fact, in the name of the secular ruler) and its position on state-related functions such as defensive holy war, proved more amenable to the needs of the rising rulers in Iran and North India. Conservative Akhbarism, in which most state-related functions of Islamic government were considered lapsed in the absence of the Imam, could not fulfill state needs for legitimation nearly as well. In the nineteenth century, Akhbarism virtually disappeared as a major school of Shi`ism, and only Usulis were left to write the history of what had happened.

5

`Indian Money' and the Shi`ite Shrine Cities

As we have seen, adherents of the Shi`ite branch of Islam held the cities of Najaf, Karbala and Kazimayn holy, making them theological and pilgrimage centers. The towns grew up around the tombs of Imams, early Islamic figures who Imami Shi`ites believed should have been the political and spiritual heads of the Islamic community. In this chapter, I wish to examine issues having to do with their political economy. The economic position of Shi`ite clerics at the shrine cities was clearly an element in their great power. Much remains to be discovered, however, about the precise roots of that economic position and the impact of phenomena such as the rise of modern capitalism.[1] Below, I explore the economic importance for the leading Iraqi clerics of funds donated by the Shi`ite rulers of Awadh in North India, in order to illuminate the influence on clerical institutions of foreign donations and projects.

Even during early Islamic times, the shrine cities in what is now Iraq were important Shi`ite centers. As noted above, for most of the Safavid period (1501-1722), the shrine cities in Iraq remained under the rule of the Sunni Ottoman Empire, and Shi`ites in Iraq remained a minority. Still, the existence of a neighboring Shi`ite state greatly changed the position of the shrine cities. The Safavid kings bestowed great patronage on the shrines and religious scholars in Iraq. Pilgrims went from Iran to the shrines when political and other considerations allowed, and they often combined pilgrimage with trade, so that the shrine cities began to serve as desert ports. Najaf and Karbala, despite the occasional attention given them by rulers, suffered from inadequate and irregular water supply. Canal works could give them life, as with the Husayniyya canal built for Karbala by Ottoman Sultan Suleiman the Magnificent in the sixteenth century. These canals tended to silt up over time, however, causing the towns to decline for long stretches of time. In the eighteenth century Karbala rose to prominence on the strength of dam work and road building carried out by

Baghdad governor Hasan Pasha. In the nineteenth century Karbala was eclipsed by Najaf, in part because of the Hindiyya canal, the story of which I tell below.[2] Given the expensive gifts proffered by newly Shi`ite Iranian notables, the pilgrim traffic, and increased commerce, cities like Najaf and Karbala could in some eras become centers of wealth as well as of law and theology. They also grew in political importance. Iranian clerics critical of the Iranian state could flee to the shrine cities, where they could subsist in a Shi`ite atmosphere and yet escape the wrath of their rulers. The sixteenth century also witnessed the establishment of Shi`ite-ruled states in South India, the rulers of which often sent contributions to the shrine cities. Indeed, even Sunni rulers in the subcontinent, who had a special regard for the prophet's grandson Imam Husayn, sent substantial gifts to his shrine at Karbala

In the course of the eighteenth-century, a slave-soldier dynasty arose in Iraq, owing only loose fealty to the Istanbul-based Ottoman Empire.[3] The Sunni slave-soldiers ruled the shrine cities with a light hand, allowing local urban notables to come to the fore. These included Sayyid Arab landholders, city-based mafiosi who practiced extortion on shopkeepers and pilgrims, and the religious scholars, with their control of shrines, pious endowments, and lands. The relative autonomy of the shrine cities gave the Shi`ite clerics a power that could be better justified by the activist Usuli than by the conservative Akhbari school.

In the late eighteenth century two new Shi`ite states emerged. One, the Qajar (1785-1925), subdued Iran.[4] The other, the Nishapuri, presided over a post-Mughal successor state in North India called Awadh, 1722-1856.[5] In both Qajar Iran and nawabi Awadh the Usuli school came to be the dominant approach to jurisprudence. In Awadh, there is good reason to think this was because local Akhbaris, then the majority, opposed Friday congregational prayers, while Usulis allowed them. The Nishapuri nawabs, involved in a process of state formation, needed Friday prayers and the Friday prayer mosque as legitimating symbols of their Shi`ite rule.[6]

One channel of Usuli influence into North India was pilgrimage to Iraq. As we have seen, the young Shi`ite scholar Sayyid Dildar `Ali Nasirabadi set out from the Awadh capital of Lucknow in 1779 for a two-year trip to the shrine cities during the time of Nawab Asaf al-Dawla (r. 1774-97) and his Chief Minister Hasan Riza Khan. Initially an Akhbari, he found the atmosphere of Najaf and Karbala to be overwhelmingly Usuli at that time. He pursued a brief course of studies with Aqa Muhammad Baqir Bihbahani and his leading disciples. After much struggle and study he embraced Usulism before returning to Lucknow. On his return he became the Friday prayer leader and served as a conduit for

Usuli ideas in the region.[7] He also spread respect for Bihbahani and the
Usuli mujtahids among Awadh's growing class of Shi`ite high notables.

This Indian connection proved highly lucrative for the Usuli clerics in
the shrine cities. In the late 1780s Awadh Chief Minister Hasan Riza Khan
remitted Rs. 500,000 to Najaf through the Iranian firm of Hajji Karbala'i
Muhammad Tihrani for the construction of a canal in the middle
Euphrates that would bring water to perpetually dry Najaf. The project,
aimed at sparing inhabitants and pilgrims inconvenience, was completed
in 1793. It became known as the Asafiyya or Hindiyya canal, after its
patron. The Awadh government also had a Shi`ite mosque at Kufa rebuilt
in 1786 and endowed a hostel for Indian pilgrims and a library in Najaf
with 700 autograph manuscripts. Later Nawab Asaf al-Dawla sent another
Rs.200,000 to the mujtahids in Iraq. Nakash sees the Hindiyya canal
works, which were renewed in the 1840s, as among the factors that helped
establish Najaf as the preeminent Shi`ite city of pilgrimage and learning
in the nineteenth century.[8] The nawab's channeling of such large sums to
the chief Usuli ulama in the shrine cities, on the advice of Sayyid Dildar
`Ali, strengthened them and further contributed to Usuli dominance. Nor
was Najaf the only beneficiary of Awadh largesse. While he was chief
minister 1795-98, Tafazzul Husayn Khan Kashmiri remitted a great deal
of money to Bihbahani's successor Aqa Sayyid `Ali Tabataba'i for the
poor and the ulama in Karbala.[9]

The financial intermediaries for these transactions were Shi`ite long-
distance trading houses with outlets in Lucknow and in the shrine cities.
However, their willingness to transfer and loan funds to notables engaged
in ostensibly pious projects left them exposed to great risks. An example
was the case of Mirza Riza, the son of Hajji Karbala'i Muhammad
Tihrani, versus the heirs of Hasan Riza Khan, the former chief minister of
Awadh. In the late 1780s Hajji Karbala'i lent Chief Minister Hasan Riza
Khan Rs.228,436 as part of the Rs.700,000 Awadh government donation
for the building of the canal to Najaf

Mirza Riza presented letters in court appearing to be from the chief
minister promising to repay the loan in November of 1792. On 8
September 1798 he allegedly again undertook to settle his account,
writing to his creditor, 'The accounts of the stoppage of your mercantile
concerns, the importunity of the schroffs and others, and your pecuniary
embarrassments have, God is my witness, distressed me . . .[10] Both
debtor and creditor died before any further transaction could take place,
so Mirza Riza attempted to recoup the loss from the late chief minister's
estate through the government courts of Nawab Sa`adat `Ali Khan (r.
1798-1814) in 1806. He asked the Iranian ruler Fath-Ali Shah to intervene
with Awadh's nawab on his behalf, and the Qajar monarch wrote to his
fellow Shi`ite ruler supporting Mirza Riza's claims.[11]

In India, Nawab Sa'adat 'Ali Khan turned the case over to the mufti of the religious court, probably the Sunni Mawlavi Zuhur Allah (d. 1840).[12] Mirza Riza claimed the principal of Rs.228, 436, plus Rs. 150,010 interest. The mufti of the court rejected the claim on several grounds. First, he said, the dates of the copies of the letters and the replies presented as evidence were confused and therefore they were of suspect authenticity. Second, the precise kind of money loaned was not specified in the suit, making it difficult to appraise the value of any damages. Third, the taking of interest on loans was prohibited according to Islamic law.[13]

The episode demonstrates the importance at this point of Iranian long distance merchants in the transfer of huge sums from Awadh to Iraq. That they were able to handle the transmission of several hundred thousand rupees with no apparent difficulty, and even to sustain substantial losses of principal, attests to the mercantile importance of these Shi'ite Iranian mediators between India and Mesopotamia. That the firm of Hajji Karbala'i even considered suing in a Muslim court for interest and interest penalties speaks clearly of Iranian business practice of the time.[14]

The other philanthropic concerns of Awadh's rulers continued to make the Indian connection important to the Usuli mujtahids in Iraq. Nawab Sa'adat 'Ali Khan sent large sums to the shrine cities after Karbala was sacked in 1801 by Arabian tribesmen of the fundamentalist Sunni Wahhabi sect, fierce enemies of the Shi'ites.[15] He also had a silver and velvet canopy for the shrine of Imam Husayn at Karbala made in Lucknow and sent via Bombay to Iraq under British auspices. To the dismay of the outraged British, ulama in Karbala demanded a Rs. 8,000 offering in cash before they would agree to accept the canopy.[16] This sort of demand demonstrates one source of clerical wealth. The pious rich could not deposit gifts in the form of immovable wealth at the shrines unless they also contributed some liquid wealth to the clerics in control of the shrines.

In addition to strengthening the position of the Usuli mujtahids against remaining Akhbari rivals by putting huge sums of money in their hands for patronage, the Asafiyya canal at first had a dramatic effect on the tribal power balance within Iraq, since it unexpectedly caused the Shatt-al-Hilla to dry up, hurting the Khaza'il tribe and its dependencies. The area near Najaf grew more productive agriculturally, attracting new tribes that clashed with the cultivators already established there.[17]

The new canal was not properly kept in repair, gradually silting up, so that from 1816 the Nawab Ghazi al-Din Haydar of Awadh considered attempting to have it dug out. But Da'ud Pasha, by now aware of the possible political and ecological effects of the undertaking, attached too many conditions. Da'ud Pasha was willing to have the canal revived only if it could be so routed as to benefit groups other than Shi'ites. This demand aroused the suspicions of the Awadh nawab, who was primarily concerned with succoring the Shi`ites. Another difficulty facing the project was that neither Awadh nor the British could arrange for the continued upkeep of the canal, something that the Baghdad pashas would have to undertake. Ghazi al-Din Haydar envisaged endowing lands for this purpose in Iraq, but the Iraqi government was unlikely to allow large amounts of land to be alienated in a foreign endowment.[18]

Capitalism and Religious Donations to Iraq

The remission of substantial sums of money to the shrine cities of Karbala by the rulers and notables of Awadh established a long-term tie between them and the leading Shi`ite ulama in Iraq. The brokers in this relationship, Awadh's own clerics, often went to Iraq on visitation and grew personally acquainted with the chief mujtahids of Karbala and Najaf. Because Sayyid Dildar `Ali Nasirabadi had studied briefly under Bihbahani and his major disciples a special tie of sentiment existed between the clergy of Awadh and the Usuli heirs of Bihbahani in Iraq. While between 1786 and 1815 very large sums flowed from Awadh to the Iraqi shrine cities, thereafter the amounts declined, partly because of the pressure huge loans to the British East India Company [EIC] placed on the Lucknow treasury.

In December, 1815, Ghazi al-Din Haydar sent Rs. 100,000 to Najaf and Karbala through the British government. The increasingly powerful EIC supplanted the Iranian long-distance merchants as the banker of choice in such transactions.[19] Nawab Ghazi al-Din's grandmother, Bahu Begam, left Rs.90,000 in her British-guaranteed will to the shrines in Iraq, specifying that the EIC transmit the sum to Sayyid Muhammad, the son of Sayyid `Ali, and to Mirza Muhammad Husayn Shahristani, the son of Muhammad Mihdi Shahristani, both of Karbala.[20] Mirza Muhammad Mihdi had visited India himself and Sayyid Dildar `Ali held a diploma from him gained in Karbala 1779-80, so that the Shahristani family had strong ties with the pious Shi`ites of Awadh.

Grants from Awadh not only demonstrated a recognition of the position of leadership attained by the individual named, it further strengthened that leadership by putting enormous sums at his disposal. While Ghazi al-Din Haydar's hopes for rebuilding the Asafiyya canal to Najaf never materialized, and his son Nasir al-Din Haydar put the money into a local hospital instead, some wealth, in the form of contributions and lapsed stipends, continued to be sent to the shrine cities in the 1820s and 1830s.

In the period 1815-30 developments occurred among the landed Shi`ites in Awadh that impelled them to accept interest on loans to

Europeans. These developments were also to structure Awadh contributions to the Shi`ite clerics of Iraq. The changes in the relationship between the British economy and that of India brought about by the Industrial Revolution, creating a world-dominating textile industry, strengthened the hand of the EIC. The Company, formerly merely a government-backed enterprise of circulating merchant capital, evolved into an instrument in the expansion of industrial imperialism. The terms of the game radically changed. Awadh's landed classes, sensitive to this evolution, began to perceive the insecurity of their traditional landholding forms of wealth in the new environment.

At the same time, the EIC began its costly war in Nepal, 1814-16. The Nawab Ghazi al-Din Haydar succeeded his father, Sa`adat `Ali, acquiescing in November of the same year to the Company's request for a loan of ten million rupees to help defray the expenses of the war. Ten individuals or families, mostly relations of the nawab, received the Rs.600,000 in interest payments each year. Four months later Ghazi al-Din Haydar agreed to a second loan of ten million rupees, on similar terms. In 1825 the same ruler responded favorably to the governor-general's request for yet another loan of ten million rupees at the low rate of five per cent interest, again payable by the resident to notables and relatives of the court.[21]

These arrangements began the creation of a class of rentiers depending on payments from interest to supplement the income from their less stable landed wealth (which took the form of land grants or *jagir*s that could be expropriated at will by later Awadh rulers). The British government guaranteed the stipends to the recipients and their descendants. The creditors hardly demonstrated much business sense by the low, fixed interest rates they charged. The recipients, transformed into a strange mixture of Mughal-style nobility and new bourgeoisie, passively subsisted on the periphery of the growing world market.

While Ghazi al-Din Haydar earlier showed no scruples about making the loans, when his treasury got low he suddenly evinced pangs of conscience. In May 1826, Lord Amherst informed the resident in Lucknow that yet another five million rupees would be needed to wind up the Nepal war. Rickett's talks proved successful, but Amherst felt he was doing the nawab a favor in any case.[22] Ricketts wrote on 25 July, "Your remark that the money has been drawn from unproductive coffers is strictly correct, and so far His Majesty in point of fact is a gainer by the transaction; but the Sacrifice of his Religious tenets, which forbid interest being received, throws this advantage completely into the Shade in His eyes . . ."[23]

Both the move of the Awadh ruling class into the role of banker for the EIC and the involvement of some notables in the British-ruled Ceded

Provinces in capitalist agriculture created a new economic atmosphere, presenting difficulties for the Shi`ite ulama who served these classes in transition. Sayyid Dildar `Ali, writing before most of these developments, had cautioned against taking interest on loans to Europeans.[24]

But in the early 1830s his son Sayyid Muhammad Nasirabadi, the chief mujtahid in Lucknow, resolved the issue by reversing his father's ruling. Asked if interest might be taken from Jews, Christians, Hindus and Sufi Muslims, Sayyid Muhammad replied that interest could be taken from polytheists by consensus and that Sufis could be considered ritually polluted and polytheists. As to Jews and Christians, he added, there were differences of opinion, but the clearest view in his opinion was that they could be charged interest.[25] Since most Sunnis were Sufis in Awadh, according to this ruling wealthy Shi`ites could loan on interest to almost the entire population of the country, excluding only a small minority of other Shi`ites. Like Christianity in Europe's own age of commercial expansion, Imami Shi`ism demonstrated an ability to adapt itself to modern capitalism. As the patrons of the jurisprudents became more bourgeois, so too did the social ideology proclaimed by the clerical establishment.[26]

These developments directly affected the Indian finances of the Iraqi Shi`ite mujtahids. The deeds bestowing guaranteed stipends on Ghazi al-Din Haydar's dependents often provided funds for Najaf and Karbala where the recipient died without heirs. The deed of 17 August 1825 for one of the king's wives, Mubarak Mahall, gave her an allowance of Rs. 120,000 per year from interest on the loan to the EIC.[27] It stipulated that upon her demise one-third of the allowance would be paid to whomever she appointed in her will, the remaining two-thirds being split between the chief mujtahids in Najaf and Karbala. In case of intestacy, the mujtahids in Iraq received the whole stipend of Rs. 120,000 per year.

As Awadh's guaranteed pensioners began dying off, such stipends began to provide high incomes for the two chief mujtahids in the pre-eminent holy cities, becoming known in Iraq as a prize worth contending for by the rivals for religious authority. Ironically, leading Shi`ite clerics were receiving funds gained from loaning on interest, involving them directly in an important overseas institution in the growth of British capitalism. Even before the "Oudh Bequest" began paying out on the death of the two wives of Ghazi al-Din Haydar in 1849, other major funding was bestowed on the shrine cities by the Awadh court. All such funds became known as the "Indian money" (*pul-i Hindi*).

One example of rivalry involving the "Indian Money" concerned the leaders of the Usuli and Shaykhi schools in Karbala. Although Usulism had generally won out against Akhbarism in the early nineteenth century, another Shi`ite school had appeared. Founded by Shaykh Ahmad al-

Ahsa'i (1753-1826), who studied with the Usuli greats at the shrine cities in the late eighteenth century, Shaykhism emphasized the importance of esoteric, intuitive knowledge and denied the resurrection of the physical body.

Al-Ahsa'i's chief disciple, Sayyid Kazim Rashti (d. 1844), succeeded him in Karbala upon his death, and developed his teacher's doctrines into a new school of Imami Shi`ism that differed somewhat from Usulism. Usulis began virulently attacking Shaykhism. In 1828 Sayyid Kazim Rashti met twice with a group of Usulis who attempted to clarify Shaykhi doctrine and to force Rashti to renounce some of his teachings. Shi`ites in Karbala became polarized between the minority Shaykhis and the majority Usulis (led by Sayyid Ibrahim Qazvini.) In the 1830s several attempts were made on Sayyid Kazim's life, but the school and its leader doggedly survived.[28]

Because of the links of pilgrimage and study that bound the shrine cities to the rest of the Shi`ite world, Shaykhism had an impact on North India as well. The most vigorous advocate of Shaykhism in Awadh, Mirza Hasan `Azimabadi (d. 1844), came of a Delhi family settled in Patna.[29] He pursued his study of Shi`ite sciences as a young man with one of Sayyid Dildar `Ali's eminent sons, Sayyid Husayn Nasirabadi, in Lucknow.

Mirza Hasan went on pilgrimage to Mecca and then on visitation to the shrine cities of Iraq. He elected to reside in Karbala, where he gradually became a close follower of Sayyid Kazim Rashti. In 1836 `Azimabadi returned to Lucknow, where he worked as a preacher, promulgating the doctrines of Shaykh Ahmad al-Ahsa'i and Sayyid Kazim Rashti. He translated one of al-Ahsa'i's doctrinal works from Arabic into Persian and wrote an original composition on Shaykhi theology. When `Azimabadi succeeded in gathering a sizable following, his former teacher Sayyid Husayn Nasirabadi felt compelled to refute him and to attack his positions.

In the 1830s Sayyid Kazim Rashti, the Shaykhi leader, was in charge of the Indian money for a while.[30] But after his student, Hasan `Azimabadi, came into conflict with Sayyid Husayn Nasirabadi in Lucknow it began being given to Rashti's nemesis Sayyid Ibrahim Qazvini. The Shaykhis' loss of this resource, which the Usulis instead captured, injured the Shaykhi cause. At that time the other possible source of royal patronage, the Iranian monarch Muhammad Shah Qajar (1834-48), was bestowing his largesse on Sufis rather than mujtahids. The wealth pouring in from Awadh may have taken on exaggerated importance.

Public Works in Iraq

With the accession in Lucknow of Muhammad `Ali Shah, who took a keen interest in religious public works, the treasury of Awadh once again began providing substantial funds to the mujtahids in Najaf and Karbala. In a letter dated 1839 (1255) the North Indian clerics informed the ulama in Iraq that the new Awadh monarch, having a great love for the holy shrines and all who dwelt in their vicinity, had heard that the Asafiyya canal was dry and wished to have it repaired. He ordered that Rs. 150,000 be sent to each of the two cities through the British resident via the Political Agent in Turkish Arabia. The letter instructed the ulama to let Lucknow know the money arrived and to ensure it they spent it for the purpose stipulated.[31]

British records show that in June 1839, the Awadh government remitted Rs. 30,000 to Iraq for the repairs to the canal, and the following summer sent another Rs.250,000 to complete the work. In November 1841, the king of Awadh sent Rs.26,000 to Karbala for religious purposes, the total coming to just over Rs.300,000 split two ways.[32] The ulama grew so comfortable in using the British diplomatic pouches to communicate between Lucknow and the shrine cities that they began sending religious manuscripts and letters by British post. This process was facilitated, not only by EIC power in India, but by the growing power and influence of the British political agent in Iraq in the 1830s and 1840s.[33]

In the summer of 1841 Sayyid Ibrahim Qazvini, the leading Usuli mujtahid of Karbala, wrote to Muhammad `Ali Shah, signing himself the agent (*vakil*) of the "just king" (*al-sultan al-`adil*) and mentioning that Rs. 150,000 had arrived through the British agent in Baghdad. The phrase "just king" meant the Twelfth Imam in Shi`ite law books but in political discourse the ulama often used it for temporal monarchs. Noting that work had already begun, Qazvini said that the water was badly needed, as the gardens and fields where pilgrims pitched their tents were entirely desiccated. He boldly suggested further projects to the Awadh ruler, writing that the tombs of Imam Husayn and of `Abbas needed Rs.50,000 worth of gilding.[34]

The project to bring more water to the Shi`ite shrine cities was not without its opponents in the Ottoman government. In 1831 the Ottomans had reasserted direct rule over Iraq, and Ali Riza Pasha, the new governor who supplanted the slave-soldiers, had already once come into conflict with the semi-autonomous Shi`ite city-states. The new governor was not as conscious as had been the old that more water for irrigation would strengthen the peasant cultivators and Shi`ite tribesmen in the vicinity of the rebellious holy cities, but there were those around him who worried about these things. Ali Riza Pasha also faced great pressure from the

British, who wished to maintain themselves as the sole means for the Awadh government to communicate with the outside world. British Agent Robert Taylor reported from Baghdad early in 1842:

I also found it necessary to request his [the Pasha's] permission to complete two canals to the holy towns of Kerbalah and Najaf, now under repair and improvement for the purpose of conducting the water of the Euphrates to those places, the expences of which were borne by the King of Oude, and the Ameer Naseer Khan of Sind, to which request he has assented, though under considerable opposition from interested persons about him.[35]

On 17 May 1842 Muhammad `Ali Shah died and was succeeded by his more pro-clerical son Amjad `Ali. Sayyid Ibrahim Qazvini sent his condolences, stating he needed more money for the canal and other projects and wanted to know if, with the change of administration, he still had a mandate for his work. He said Kazimayn needed a dam and Rs. 5,000 was required for the shrine of Salman Farsi near Baghdad. As for work already commissioned, the canal had been sufficiently dug out in the Karbala vicinity that water was plentiful for both farmers and pilgrims. In addition, he was undertaking repairs to the tomb of `Abbas and gilding the ante-room of Imam Husayn's shrine.[36]

The Lucknow mujtahids informed the chief cleric in Imam `Ali's shrine city, Shaykh Muhammad Hasan al-Najafi, that Amjad `Ali Shah had mounted the throne, praying God would render his sovereignty eternal.[37] They explained that the new king was much less generous than his father, and that the ulama in Iraq should account more conscientiously for sums remitted. The Nasirabadis' secretary, Sayyid Muhammad `Abbas Shushtari, admonished Shaykh Muhammad Hasan at one point, saying he had sent Rs. 100,000 for Najaf through the British agent (al-balyuz al-kabir), but no receipt had been returned. Finally a receipt for only Rs. 46,000 arrived from al-Najafi. He wondered if the Iraqi was being cautious, pondering whether to accept the donation. The young secretary added sharply, "but it is hoped of you (al-ma'mul minkum) that you will make haste in informing us of its receipt in full, insofar as we assumed you had decided to proceed."[38] The imperious tone, bracketed with flowery expressions of admiration, reveals something of the superiority the Lucknow mujtahids felt as the paymasters of their more prestigious colleagues in Iraq.

From October 1842 to January 1843, Karbala was under siege by Ottoman forces at the command of the new, hard-line governor, Najib Pasha, who was determined to reduce the defiant city. In January 1843, Ottoman troops entered the town in a bloody occupation that left at least

5,000 persons dead and wrought extensive damage to buildings and shrines.[39] The new political climate brought the Awadh-sponsored building works to a grinding halt. Al-Najafi wrote to Lucknow, explained that the Ottoman military maneuvers had delayed repairs to the canal but that he was now preparing to resume work.[40] Sayyid Husayn Nasirabadi replied with sympathy for the victims of the Karbala disaster but grumbled that he still had no receipt for the Rs. 150,000 he had remitted to Najaf, and he wanted a detailed report on the progress of work on the Asafiyya canal.[41]

Shaykh Muhammad Hasan replied that he had received the entire amount for the canal repairs and had prepared the groundwork, but that the Ottoman military action in the canal vicinity had resulted in a postponement (apparently Shi`ite laborers living near the canal had fled). He said that three farsakhs needed to be dug out, but that the sum received allowed completion of only half the project since the Ottoman rulers were now charging imposts that drove the cost up to Rs. 100,000 per farsakh. In view of the mujtahids' statements that Amjad `Ali Shah declined to send more funds, he had not thought it wise to embark on a project that might be impossible of accomplishment.

He optimistically suggested that if any money were left over when the canal was finished, there were many mosques and shrines that needed to be repaired, to which it could profitably be applied. Al-Najafi clearly did not believe that the money had dried up and attempted to force more remittances by claiming the job could not be done with the amount already sent. He also reminded Nasirabadi of the multitudes of poor and refugees from devastated Karbala thronging Najaf, seeking the succor of the ulama.[42]

Sayyid Husayn Nasirabadi posted a letter to al-Najafi stating that he was pleased at the state of the various construction projects, but that Amjad `Ali refused to send another Rs. 5,000 to complete the building of the shrine of Muslim. He did, however, remit that amount for the relief of the poor and stricken who survived the Karbala ordeal.[43] Shaykh Muhammad Hasan later corresponded again with Lucknow, addressing Sayyids Muhammad and Husayn Nasirabadi with their court titles of Sultan al-`Ulama' and Sayyid al-`Ulama'. He said their last missive mentioned that the Just King was now inclined to provide funds for the completion of the canal but noted that no money had yet arrived. He admonished them to fulfill their pledge, informing them that he had placed his son, Shaykh `Abd al-Husayn; in charge of the project, as he was his heir apparent in expounding the Law of Islam.[44]

Charitable Contributions to Iraq and Charges of Corruption

The river of Indian rupees flooding into the Iraqi shrine cities included a small but steady branching stream fed by direct philanthropy. Muhammad `Ali Shah in 1841 assigned promissory notes worth Rs. 300,000 as an endowment originally separate from local building funds, dedicating the interest of Rs. 12,000 per year to the support of 200 indigent Indian Shi`ites in Iraq at Rs.5 per month each.[45] As with the other Awadh monies, the charity was paid out to the two leading mujtahids, of Karbala and Najaf, by the British Political Agent in Baghdad.[46]

In a missive to Sayyid Ibrahim Qazvini probably written in the middle of 1843 the Awadh clerics noted that although the king had put aside a certain amount of the money sent for food for the poor, Qazvini was his general agent and it all depended on his judgment. They nevertheless suggested that the money should be divided three ways, one-third for the poor, one-third for disaster relief, and one-third for needy ulama and students in the shrine cities.[47]

While the "Oudh bequest" later became a political tool in the hands of British administrators in the quest to influence the ulama, in the 1830s and 1840s they seemed more interested in proving they could be honest brokers. Sometimes they were more scrupulous than the Shi`ites themselves. Mirza Khalil, the Iranian ambassador to Bombay killed in an affray in 1832, had asked the British government to donate Rs. 10,000 per year to the mujtahids and poor of Karbala. When his heirs claimed the stipend for themselves the British government insisted on giving it to the shrines in accordance with the dead man's will.[48]

In the 1840s the British role in the remission of charities to the shrine cities became an embarrassment for them. Rawlinson wrote to the governor-general in 1844 to express his growing concern:

I have been repeatedly solicited by the heads of the Sheeah population of this Pashalic to bring to the notice of the right Hon'ble the Govr. Gen'l of India, with a view to its being communicated to H.M. the King of Oude, through the British Envoy at his Court, the gross misapplication to which are subjected his Majesty's munificent donations to the Holy Shrines in the vicinity of Bagdad. Nearly four lakhs of Rupees have been remitted by H.M. through the Bagdad treasury within the last few years, with a view of providing for the comfort and security of the Sheeah pilgrims at Nejjef, Kerbela & Samarra, but it is stated and generally believed, that owing to the total want of surveillance in the distribution of the funds, but a very small portion only of the bequest has been appropriated to the purposes of charity.

In the event therefore of His Majesty making any similar donation in future, it would seem almost indispensable, in order to give effect to his wishes, that a trustworthy agent should be deputed by him from India to superintend the disbursements in the country. It may indeed, I think, be questionable whether, if this precaution be neglected the sums should be remitted through a British Treasury; for I perceive that, so notorious has been the peculation the part of the Chief Priests of Kerbelah & Nejjeff in whose favour the money has been remitted from India that our own credit has suffered from having been in any way connected with the transaction.[49]

The governor-general acted upon Rawlinson's advice, incurring the subsequent displeasure of the Court of Directors, who instructed him to abstain from entering into any communication with the Awadh ruler on such matters. The political agent in Baghdad remained anxious, protesting in 1846 that a bill arrived for Rs. 18,000 endorsed by an Awadh government official in favor of Sayyid Ibrahim Qazvini rather than the Political Agent, which he said was irregular and might subject him to embarrassment.[50] Qazvini's behavior as the agent for Awadh philanthropies in Karbala grew so unsatisfactory that he was finally replaced. A decade after the 1856 British annexation of Awadh, Iqbal al-Dawla, a member of the Nishapuri former ruling family with extensive contacts in London, endeavoured to have the funds put in the hands of a resident Indian mujtahid in 1866-67. But the British government balked because the wording of the bequest excluded this step.[51]

Letters from the ulama in Lucknow give some credence to British complaints, in that the Iraqi mujtahids were suspiciously slow in returning receipts for the hundreds of thousands of rupees received, they reported cost overruns of 100 per cent in three years, and Indian pilgrims had difficulty sharing in the Awadh cornucopia. On one occasion Sayyid Muhammad Nasirabadi sent Rs. 4,211 to Shaykh Muhammad Hasan al-Najafi for distribution to the believers and Sayyids, noting that he had heard from several sources, including Mirza Hasan `Azimabadi, that Sayyid Musa Hindi was not getting any relief funds.[52] That some information on the maldistribution of funds by Usuli mujtahids at the shrine cities derived from Shaykhi sources points to the way factional disputes helped unearth such practices.

Even had the high ulama spent the funds from Lucknow in an entirely efficient and upright manner, the very delivery into their hands of Rs.400,000 from 1839 to 1844 would have greatly strengthened their local political position. They could use the money to mobilize major urban social groups, endowment supervisors, merchants, builders' guilds, and gangsters providing protection, behind programs of urban renewal that vastly extended the range of their patronage. Large numbers of stipends could be offered as scholarships to students, creating a huge following and helping undermine support for rivals like the Shaykhis and Babis.[53]

Relationships among the Major Players

The major actors in the gargantuan philanthropic donations of the 1840s, the Awadh notables and their clergy, the British, the Ottomans and the Shi'ite ulama of the shrine cities were linked by the transactions in a network of relationships. Often the letters from that period reveal with startling frankness the attitudes of the clergy to the other actors.

The clerics held conflicting and contradictory views of their patrons among the Shi'ite nobles. We have seen that the ulama often referred to the Awadh monarch as a just king, implicitly accepting the legitimacy of his government. Both Sayyid Ibrahim Qazvini and Sayyid Husayn Nasirabadi referred to Amjad 'Ali Shah as the "helper of the ulama." The Indian scholars were more given to flattering the monarchs, however, and strove constantly to persuade their counterparts in Iraq to write in flowery Persian thanking the kings in Lucknow and their notables for the contributions. The mujtahids in Iraq, however, tended to write in incomprehensible Arabic in a straightforward manner that offended Indian protocol.[55] The 1840s, a decade of power and wealth for the Shi'ite ulama, ended with ominous signs of declining court patronage for them. Amjad 'Ali Shah died in 1847, and while his son Vajid 'Ali continued many clericalist policies for a while he was far less generous. Shushtari lamented in 1848, "gone are the grandees who donated philanthropy, and the kings who aided the ulama and the Sayyids."[56]

The respect that the clerics offered to their noble and notable patrons was often tinged with an unspoken contempt. Shi'ite status groups (clerics, Sayyids, notables and nobles) engaged in a lively competition for honor. Clerics saw themselves as the true, principled Shi'ites, and their ambivalence toward the worldly, wine-bibbing nobles surfaced during stressful times. Sayyid 'Ali Naqi Tabataba'i (1809-81), a grandson of Bahr al-'Ulum, wrote a letter to Sayyid Husayn Nasirabadi about the 1843 Ottoman sack of Karbala (discussed at length in the next chapter).[57] Sayyid Husayn in reply expressed grief over the happenings in Karbala. He did not blame the incident on the Sunnis as one might have expected, but remarked that one seldom found notables (*umara'*) or magnates (*'ama'id*) with hearing ears.[58] Sayyid Husayn Nasirabadi saw the Karbala disaster as an indictment of the ruling classes, both Sunni and Shi'i, whom he excoriated as corrupt.[59] Clearly, when the clerics felt the Shi'ite notables had failed them they were willing to class them together with

Sunni noblemen as godless.   Likewise, the minor Usuli scholar
Muhammad Yusuf Astarabadi at Karbala in the spring of 1843 to Sayyids
Muhammad and Husayn Nasirabadi in Lucknow.[59]   Astarabadi barely
survived the sack of Karbala by the Ottomans in January 1843. He was
wounded in the head, made to carry booty for his captors, lost his eldest
son and saw his entire library and lifework burned. As he sat amidst the
debris in the shell of a house in the martyred city of Husayn, he penned an
anguished cry of radical purport: "Would that there were no king ruling
over us, and none over Iran!'" If there had to be a king, he declared, he
should be a pious defender of Shi`ites from their enemies. He implicitly
blamed the Ottoman sultan for ordering the invasion and the Iranian
monarch for not coming to the aid of his fellow Shi`ites.   While the
statement might on the surface appear to be an expression of republican
sentiments, in fact it simply demonstrated the low esteem with which
some clerics actually viewed rich and powerful Muslims.

How did the clerics who were collaborating in funding the
improvements at the shrine cities view one another? The relationship of
the high ulama in North India to the mujtahids in the shrine cities
remained a complex one. They all addressed each other as the "best of the
mujtahids," the "exemplar of the people," the "heir of the prophets,"
indiscriminately and in a manner calculated to debase the coin of the
superlatives, rendering them no more than pleasantries. A story from
Sayyid Husayn Nasirabadi's biography illuminates the relationship.
Shushtari wrote that Sayyid Husayn allowed the deputation of judicial
authority (al-istinaba fi'l-qada), considered a very minority opinion that
seemed to contradict Shi`ite consensus. After Muhammad Hasan al-Najafi
took the same stance in his *Jawahir al-kalam* others in Awadh changed
their views, agreeing that such deputation was permissible. Sayyid
Husayn, on the other hand, not once changed his mind on a major
position.[60] The story demonstrates that al-Najafi's authority as a mujtahid
and source for emulation (marja` al-taqlid) carried weight with many
North Indian ulama in the 1840s, but that the Nasirabadis maintained a
degree of pride and independence.

While mujtahids were forbidden from practicing emulation of other
jurisprudents, the Usuli emphasis on the greater authority of the most
learned (al-a`lam) jurisprudent led to the emergence of a small number of
pace-setters whose judicial opinions widely commanded respect and
around whom a new consensus often formed. In the mid-nineteenth
. century each of the major centers of Shi`ite learning possessed one or two
leading mujtahids who, through their reputation for erudition and their
control of pious endowments and charitable contributions, dominated the
religious establishment. Shaykh Muhammad Hasan in Najaf, Sayyid
Ibrahim Qazvini in Karbala, Sayyid Muhammad Baqir Shafti in Isfahan

and Sayyid Muhammad Nasirabadi in Lucknow, among others, formed a select group of exemplars whose rulings were not only emulated by large numbers among the laity but were often deferred to by other mujtahids.

In the 1840s a convention existed that of all the great centers Najaf was preeminent, so that the head of the religious establishment in that city was considered the leader (*ra'is*) of all the Shi`ites, especially by virtue of his control of religious donations. In a biographical notice of Shayh Muhammad Hasan al-Najafi, one of his students wrote in 1846 (1262), "upon him devolved the leadership of the Imamis, both Arabs and non-Arabs, in this, our own time."[61] The anecdote from the life of Sayyid Husayn recounted above, however, indicates that while many ulama in India accepted even al-Najafi's controversial rulings as authoritative, the top mujtahids in Awadh never changed their views on someone else's authority. Deference to Shaykh Muhammad Hasan as the most learned exemplar may have been more common among the lower ranks of mujtahids everywhere than at the very top. It is unlikely that Sayyid Muhammad Nasirabadi in Lucknow or Sayyid Muhammad Baqir Shafti in Isfahan considered al-Najafi more learned than themselves or more authoritative in his rulings. Nasirabadi maintained that he was esoterically taught his knowledge by the Twelfth Imam himself.

In 1849 or 1850 (1266), Shaykh Muhammad Hasan convened a gathering of mujtahids at Najaf where he named as his successor one of his close students, Shaykh Murtada Ansari (d. 1864). He reportedly introduced his nominee to the other jurisprudents, saying "This is your exemplar (*Hadha marja`ukum*)."[62] Ansari, who controlled 200,000 tumans per year in charitable donations, emerged as the most widely recognized jurisprudential source for emulation in the Shi`ite world. Later in the nineteenth century Muhammad Mihdi Kashmiri of Lucknow wrote of Ansari, "His cause attained renown throughout all horizons, and he was mentioned in the pulpits in a manner unparalleled before him. He was an exemplar to the Shi`ites in their entirety, in their religion and in their worldly affairs."[63] Again, while such sentiments in favor of Ansari clearly existed in Awadh, it is unlikely that any of the leading members of the Nasirabadi family acknowledged anyone else as more learned than themselves.

For their part the jurisprudents in the shrine cities did not simply dismiss the Indian mujtahids as rustic bumpkins, at least to their faces. Shaykh Muhammad Hasan al-Najafi constantly asked the Lucknow mujtahids to send copies of their compositions to Najaf, where they were read and circulated, early Awadh use of the printing press making Shi`ite authors there accessible to readers in the Middle East. When he read Sayyid Muhammad Nasirabadi's *ad-Darba al-Haydariyya* in defense of temporary marriage, he called it the "crown of Shi`ism," referring to the

author's father, Sayyid Dildar `Ali, as "the seal of the mujtahids."[64]
Elsewhere he noted that Sayyid Dildar `Ali's long work on the principles
of religion entitled "Mirrors for Minds" had arrived, upon which he
lavished effusive praise, attributing the brilliance of the family's
compositions to their descent from the Imams.[65]

The British Government and the Shi`ites

The other partner in the endowment transactions was the British,
whose ability to transfer large amounts of money safely to the Middle
East the ulama appreciated. The alliance between the British Government
of India and Awadh, and the role of the Political Agent in Baghdad as
paymaster for the Iraq mujtahids, suggested to some Shi`ites that they
ought to pursue a British policy.

In 1849 the Imam-Jum'a of Tehran wrote to the governor-general of
India, Dalhousie, urging that he extend the special protection of his
government to the Shi`ites in India:

It is evident that no one can in that Country do anything illegal, but, at the
same time as it frequently happens during the ten days of Mohurrum,
fights and disputes arise among the young and ignorant low people of the
Sheeah and Soonee persuasions, this servant of the holy law hopes that an
order will be given by that illustrious Government to the Governor-
General of India that numerous instructions shall be given by him for the
protection of the Sheeah wherever they may be, and more particularly
with regard to the people of Lucknow, and in a more especial manner, His
excellency the Chief Priest of the time, Seid Mohamed Sahib [Nasirabadi]
and the Sheeahs of Moorshedabad and Calcutta and Madras and
Hyderabad and Bombay and that the learned people of that sect should be
treated with respect and consideration. This will not only be an obligation
granted to this servant of the holy law but also a cause of rejoicing to the
great and the whole people of Persia . . .[66]

Dalhousie, who coveted Awadh for the British Empire, was an unlikely
protector for the partisans of Imam `Ali. While the British on the ground
may have been willing to promote themselves with Iran as representatives
of a partially Shi`ite power, the policies of the governor-general and the
Lucknow resident brought them into ever more bitter conflict with the
mujtahids of Awadh in the 1850s.

From 1850 the "Oudh Bequest" set up by Ghazi al-Din Haydar Shah
with the third Oudh (Awadh) loan, began being paid out by the British.

Initially, in hopes of avoiding direct entanglement in the affairs of Baghdad, it was drawn from an account in Bombay by agents of the two recipient Shi`ite clerics, one the leading jurisprudent in Karbala, the other his counterpart in Najaf. The British Resident in Baghdad, Rawlinson, however, worried about the money being completely outside his control, and from 1852 he convinced the British government to have the bequest funds paid directly from the Baghdad consulate to the two clergymen. In Najaf the recipient in the 1850s was Murtada al-Ansari, considered by many to be the supreme exemplar or most authoritative of the Shi`ite jurists of the time. He was said at this time to receive in voluntary religious taxes, primarily from Shi`ites in Iran, some £9,000 sterling per year (200,000 tumans). The £5,000 a year he received from the Oudh Bequest thus constituted an enormous sum, and represented an extremely important influx of wealth into the Shi`ite clerical institutions in Ottoman Iraq, especially since Sayyid `Ali Naqi Tabataba'i in Karbala also collected £5,000 a year from the bequest.[67]

From 1867 the British stipulated that a third of the funds were to be spent on indigent Indian pilgrims and residents in the shrine cities. They put distribution of these funds in the hands of the Indian nobleman Iqbal al-Dawla (d. 1887), a member of the deposed Awadh royal family who had supported the British during the 1857 Great Rebellion ("Mutiny"). This funneling of monies to the Indians contradicted the stipulations of the 1825 deed, but it was apparently felt to be good politics for the British Government of India to attempt to gain the gratitude of its own Shi`ite subjects. In 1860 Murtada al-Ansari ceased agreeing to receive monies from the bequest, citing health considerations. Known as a cautious and upright man he may simply have desired, however, to avoid even giving the appearance that he had fallen under British influence. Thereafter the Najaf share went to the Bahr al-`Ulum family of clerics. In Karbala it continued to go to the Tabataba'i family. This arrangement lasted until 1903. The distribution of the funds was plagued by controversy and they sometimes proved a mixed blessing. Local mafia attempted to extort some of the money from Sayyid `Ali Bahr al-`Ulum (d. 1881), and he resorted to calling upon the Ottomans to arrest the gangsters, which they did. This incident suggests that the funds did not necessarily imply independence of the state for the clergy. The recipients were often charged by rivals with neglecting to spend much of the bequest money on the poor, instead distributing it to family members and hangers-on. In 1875 a group of indigent Arab Shi`ites even went so far as to lodge a complaint with the Ottoman government against their own co-religionists and jurisprudents, saying it was being misused. The Bahr al-`Ulum family was tempted into going deeply into debt to money-lenders, using the Oudh bequest payments due them as collateral. By 1902 the moneychanger at the British Residency, through whom the funds flowed, had given so much in the way of loans to the mujtahids that he was withholding half the sums paid out to service their debts to him.[68] Even thus encumbered, the funds were highly significant. The annual Iranian government budget was a little less than £200,000 in the 1850s. If it is true, as Floor has estimated, that the entire religious establishment of Iran disposed of a little over 2 million tumans (£100,000 sterling) per year in the 1850s and 1860s, then the Oudh Bequest alone provided funds to the Iraqi clerical establishment equal to a tenth that total.[69] For the much smaller Shi`ite population of southern Iraq, this was an enormous sum. That the religious institutions were funded at a level that compared so favorably to the budget of the civil government helps explain their enormous power and influence in nineteenth-century Iran and Iraq.

Despite our inability to quantify the proportion of the religious economy of the shrine cities constituted by the Indian money in the nineteenth century, there can be little doubt, that it was extremely important. The canal building involved expenditures of hundreds of thousands of rupees. From 1850, the Oudh Bequest channeled £10,000 sterling annually into the hands of the leading Shi`ite clerics of Ottoman Iraq, among their more significant sources of income. There is a sense in which Indian money was key throughout the nineteenth century to making Najaf and Karbala major centers of Shi`ite learning and cultural power despite their location in the Sunni-dominated Ottoman Empire and the competition of Iranian cities such as Qom and Mashhad. The British complained periodically of "corruption" in the distribution of the money, but Litvak has argued that they simply did not understand the workings of the patronage system among the clerics. Great Muslim jurisprudents needed to build up funds in order to support their students and attract followers.

In designating certain individuals its recipients, the Awadh notables and ulama helped shore up the leadership positions of Usuli mujtahids against Akhbari and Shaykhi rivals from the late eighteenth century on. Moreover, projects like the Asafiyya canal had a discernible impact on the ecology of Iraq in the area around the shrine cities, on population movements and agriculture. Ironically, the water may have enabled some pastoralists to settle in the vicinity of the shrine cities as farmers, a move the Ottomans encouraged and sometimes enforced, opening them to the proselytizing of the Shi`ite clergy and their supporters. In the course of the nineteenth century large numbers of tribespeople converted to Shi`ism.

Beyond these considerations, however, the case of the Indian money illustrates in part the importance of monetary contributions made to the clerical establishment by Shi`ite governments and high notables. One conclusion that can be suggested on the basis of the evidence presented here is that the mujtahids were far more closely tied to governments than has generally been recognized. The Usuli clerics in the nineteenth century are often seen as highly independent of the Iranian government, in contrast to the Sunni ulama in the Ottoman Empire. But money is influence, and to the extent that Shi`ite mujtahids received gifts, stipends, and other wealth from governments and high officials, they were beholden to them. Of course, Awadh was too far away to demand much in return from the clerics in Najaf and Karbala. The Ottoman and Iranian states were much closer.

Because India was one of the first areas to take the full brunt of European industrial imperialism, modern capitalism affected Shi`ite finances first there. Substantial sums deriving from interest on loans to the East India Company were disbursed to the Iraqi mujtahids by the British Agent in Baghdad on behalf of the Awadh government. The principal, originally extorted from Hindu peasants by Awadh's Shi`ite tax-collectors, financed further British imperial expansion in the subcontinent, while the interest supported both the Awadh ruling class and its clients, the Shi`ite ulama in India and Iraq. Shi`ite jurisprudents in Lucknow, and presumably in Iraq as well, quickly reinterpreted Imami law so as to allow the charging of interest on loans to Christians. Armed with this ideological justification, the mujtahids entered the ranks of the capitalist rentiers.

It has long been recognized that religious leadership in the Shi`ite world grew somewhat more centralized in the course of the nineteenth century. The magnitude of the sums involved in the Indian money and in the charitable contributions forwarded from Iran suggests that the emergence of the supreme exemplar in mid-nineteenth-century Najaf may have been facilitated by an expanded economic base.

The British played a conspicuous role in helping transfer funds and in providing the mechanism for interest-bearing loans. The increasing British presence at first provoked some conciliatory moves on behalf the prominent ulama. The British were allies of the Shi`ite kingdom of Awadh (Oudh), and their agent in Baghdad had become the distributor of Awadh largesse to the chief mujtahids in Najaf and Karbala. The prayer leader of Tehran apparently wished to strengthen the British-Shi`ite alliance as a means of furthering Shi`ite interests and the interests of the ulama. The 1856 annexation of Awadh and the resultant revolt ("mutiny"), along with increasing British presence in south Iran soured relations for a time. From the 1860s, however, the British disbursement of the Oudh Bequest helped repair their relations with the clerics in the shrine cities and allowed them to play the role of benefactor to Indian

Shi`ite pilgrims.   They gained influence, but its limits were severe, as twentieth-century crises were to demonstrate.

6

*Mafia, Mob and Shi`ism in Iraq**

A virtual rebellion of the Iraqi city of Karbala against central government rule brought about a catastrophic invasion by Baghdad-based Ottoman Turkish forces in January 1843. Because the urban social history of the nineteenth-century Ottoman empire remains comparatively little known, the forms of social organization and local culture that led to the revolt deserve detailed treatment.

The following analysis examines the role of urban gangs in leading the rebellion, in coalition with other social groups. Neighborhood vigilante bands had long existed in Islamic cities. But in the first decades of the nineteenth century, paralleling a decline in government control, "mafia" - gangs that ran protection rackets and acted as a parallel government - grew up in Karbala. Even in this "antisocial" form, it will be shown, the urban gangs could make alliances within the city to emerge as popular leaders against an alien threat, therefore acting as more than mere exploiters.

The toughs had several allies in the fighting. They were employed by the city's indigenous landed notables as bodyguards and hit men. They forged links with Shi`ite Arab nomads outside the town walls. Another group, the "mob" - small artisans and shop-keepers participated in the revolt under the rhetoric of (Shi`ite) religion and (Iranian) ethnicity versus the Turkish Sunni outsiders who sought to subdue them. Finally, the Muslim religious scholars ('ulama') occupied a special position in the shrine city, and also allied themselves to the urban gangs.[1]

This study will employ several techniques to evoke the meaning of gang rule and popular revolt in Shi`ite Karbala. First, a synchronic analysis of the city's various social groups and their relationships to one another will be undertaken. Secondly, a diachronic historical narrative of the processes whereby the town became virtually autonomous, and how it resisted conquest, will be presented to demonstrate how those sociological groups acted towards one another over time. Attention will be paid to the *mentalité* of the major social actors and, as noted, to the crucial role of religion and the religious scholars.

The cleavages among the rebellious groups in Karbala were bridged in an important manner by Imami Shi`ite Islam, a branch of the religion that believed the Prophet Muhammad's son-in-law `Ali and his eleven lineal descendants (termed "Imamns") should have held power in the nascent Islamic empire after his passing. Imamis hold that until the supernatural reappearance of the Twelfth Imam (who went into occultation in the ninth century) all government is less than perfect. Most did, however, accept the interim legitimacy of Shi`ite monarchies such as the Safavids and Qajars in Iran. Shi`ism in Karbala encompassed both the wealthy and the indigent, both Arab and Iranian.

The ruling elite in Ottoman Iraq adhered to Sunnism (the majority branch of Islam except in post-sixteenth-century Iran and contemporary Iraq), which held that after the Prophet's passing political leadership fell to an oligarchically elected caliph. After four early "rightly guided" caliphs, the last being `Ali, political power passed to less revered hereditary monarchies, such as the Umayyad and Abbasid caliphates. Sunnis in the Ottoman empire owed allegiance to the Turkish emperor, but Shi`ites execrated the Ottoman ruler as a heretic and a usurper of an office that should by right belong only to the Twelfth Imam.

Social Structure: Religion, State and the Crowd

As Hanna Batatu pointed out, the ethnic and religious cleavages in what is now Iraq produced three demographic zones. South of Baghdad, Shi`ite Arabs largely made up the population. Sunni Arabs populated most of Baghdad and its northern hinterland. Finally, northeast of Baghdad Kurds predominated, adhering to a form of Sunnism heavily influenced by Sufi mysticism.[2] Strong social and economic cleavages also divided the people. Town dwellers often came into conflict with pastoral nomads. Of an estimated population of 1,290,000 in 1850, fully 35 per cent consisted of pastoral nomads. Another 41 per cent was rural and only 24 per cent was urban.[3] Circassian and Turkish Sunnis filled the upper echelons of the government. Most of the local controllers of large rural estates were Sunni Arabs. Sunni notables often predominated even in the largely Shi`ite south, except in the vicinity of the shrine cities.[4]

For nearly a century, from 1750 to 1831, the weak Ottoman government in Istanbul allowed a corps of slave-soldier (*kullar*) vassals to rule from Baghdad.[5] Even this local government often had difficulty asserting its authority over the factious population. From 1831 the

Ottomans again ruled directly, attempting to impose progressively greater control through their standing army and the bureaucracy in Baghdad. Slave-soldiers and Ottomans engaged in perpetual conflict with the Shi`ite Arab pastoral nomads of the south as refractory taxpayers and frequent raiders of sedentary settlements for booty. Nestled in the territory dominated by Shi`ite tribespeople were the shrine cities of Karbala and Najaf, burial sites of Imams whose remains were sacred to adherents of that branch of Islam.

The city of Karbala lies about 45 miles south-west of Baghdad. It owes its inception and continued prosperity to its possession of the shrine of the Imam Husayn, a grandson of the Prophet Muhammad, who died in a revolt against the Umayyad state in 680. Religious visits to its shrines (often combined with trade) and the influx into the city of wealth in the form of pious offerings and endowments combined to lend it economic, religious and political importance. It also served in a secular capacity as a desert port for long-distance trade.[6] The shrine of the Imam Husayn particularly attracted pilgrims of the Shi`ite branch of Islam. After 1501, the Shi`ite rulers of the Safavid dynasty in Iran bestowed lavish gifts on the city's shrines. Although the Safavids and their Sunni Ottoman foes contested much of Iraq, Karbala remained mostly under the rule of Istanbul.

The city's population, partly drawn from the Shi`ite Arab tribes of southern Iraq, often chafed under Ottoman rule. The political turmoil of eighteenth-century Iran, with its Afghan invasions and the fall of the Safavids, also encouraged large numbers of Iranian refugees to settle in Najaf and Karbala. In the nineteenth century Iranian merchants and noblemen resided there out of a pious wish to be near the shrines or because Iran turned politically dangerous for them. Although Iranian immigrants over time assimilated to Iraq, many maintained their distinctive national costume, knowledge of Persian and underground allegiance to Iran. Because of its prevailing Shi`ism. and the large Iranian ethnic element, Ottoman officials saw Karbala as a potential fifth column.

In the eighteenth and early nineteenth centuries the city government, staffed at the top by Sunnis appointed from Baghdad, controlled many of Karbala's sources of wealth, including the shrines and rights to tax. But this Sunni structure was superimposed over a local Shi`ite Arab 61ite of property-holders. Prominent Arab families owed their local power to control over great economic resources. For instance, one local magnate, the chief of the city's powerful Sayyid families (asserting their descent from the Prophet Muhammad), owned one-third of the cultivated lands and gardens in the vicinity of Karbala. In the 1820s and 1830s local notables, by processes to be discussed below, moved into actual rulership of the town as a virtual city-state. Sayyid `Abd al-Wahhab, head of

Karbala's elite families, became governor of the city in the late 1830s by order of the Ottoman viceroy Ali Riza Pasha .[7]

The majority of Karbala's inhabitants consisted of laborers, semiskilled tradesmen, peddlers and small-time shopkeepers. Many of them ethnic Iranians, they resembled in culture and social situation their Iranian counterparts, called *pishih-varan* or tradespeople.[8] The equivalent of the European "little people" *(menu peuple),* the tradespeople of Karbala, like the great merchants and the city government, exploited the pilgrim trade. They expected the city's governor to assure them of a livelihood by encouraging the pilgrims and by ensuring safety for Iranian visitors coming to Karbala. Largely Shi`ites, they took pride in living in Imam Husayn's city and in having easy access to his shrine. Lavish gifts to the shrines by the Iranian monarchs and the nawabs of Awadh in India tent a certain splendor to the shrine city, in which the little people basked.[9]

They frequently gathered in public assembly to celebrate holy days associated with the Imams and particularly to commemorate the martyrdom of Husayn. The social networks they developed for organizing religious processions could also be called into play at times of political crisis. Karbala's little people were easily stirred to defend the city from Baghdad's attempts to bring it under firmer control - as they did in 824, 1835 and 1842-3. Such disturbances resembled European "Church and king" riots, for the Shi`ite tradespeople held an allegiance to the shah of Iran and would sacrifice a great deal to exclude alien Sunni troops.[10]

The Karbala Mafia

The 1820s and 1830s saw a growth in Karbala of the power of local elites in relation to the center. As will be shown below, urban gang leaders running protection rackets displaced or co-opted the old landholding and merchant families and formed links with nearby Arab tribes. They also allied themselves with the city's leading religious scholars. In this manner they created a coalition of groups interested in autonomy, whether for financial or religious reasons, from the Ottomans. Groups of young men, motivated by chivalric ideas and banding together to defend their quarter of the city, commonly appeared in medieval Iraq. These youths, called `ayyarun, probably derived from families of tradespeople and laborers, rather than from elite families. Sometimes they gained great power in their quarter and engaged in fights with the youths of other quarters. At the margins of urban society these groups sometimes elided into the genuine underworld of vagabonds and thieves.[11]

While the gangs that came to dominate Karbala in the first half of the nineteenth century had a similar historical background, they became more than merely lower-class neighborhood youth clubs. The Karbala gangs were often headed by outsiders and included in their numbers fugitives and deserters from the military. They grew far more powerful than medieval chivalric organizations, coming to rule the city in alliance with local nobles. In short, they underwent a peculiarly early modern transformation, and, refracted in this modern tens, begin to took familiar to the comparative historian. They begin to look like "mafia".

All the elements of mafia, as defined by Hobsbawm, Hess and others, appear in Karbala.[12] These include avoidance of invoking state law and a preference for settling grudges through toughness and a code of manly honor; a patronage system with bosses and retainers; and control of the community's life by an officially unrecognized system of gangs. Such mafia must be clearly distinguished from random urban criminals on the one hand, and from rural peasant bandits on the other. The mafioso lacks complete legitimacy, but erects a quasi-governmental structure with the help of notable-class bosses. Unlike gangsters in a region with a strong state, mafiosi existed in a vacuum of state power, and therefore performed a real service in providing protection, albeit coercive and violent. Mafia-like groups, commonplace in Iraqi and Iranian cities, went by the generic name of *luti* or *awbash*.[13] In the Levant they were called *qabadayat*. The Karbala mafiosi, though differing from their Sicilian contemporaries in being urban rather than village-based, also erected a parallel structure of authority based on extortion rackets and the private use of force, and led by the wealthy. The main factors in Hobsbawm's typology of the Sicilian mafia - the need to defend an entire society from threats to its way of life, the aspirations of the various classes it encompassed and the personal ambitions of vigorous leaders - all played a part in Karbala's mafia as well.

Mafias remain comparatively little known, aside from that in Sicily, but Hobsbawm and Hess have described the early modern historical conditions under which they arise. First, they come into power in a frontier situation of weak state authority - in rural, remote areas like the island of Sicily. Karbala fits this suggestion as a Shi`ite, partly Iranian, enclave. Both Sicily and southern Iraq had for centuries been colonially ruled by distant and shifting centers, so that in neither area did the people invest the formal government with much legitimacy.

The emergence of a new elite where the previously powerful classes have less access to traditional sources of authority also contributes to mafia formation. In Sicily mafias appeared in the wake of the abolition of feudalism and the rise of new rural middle classes. As Hess suggested, the mafia arose as a parallel government after the old feudal order broke down, but before a modern state emerged and pressed its claims to Weberian monopoly over the use of force. When the modern state asserts itself the status of the mafioso changes from subcultural folk-hero to criminal.

Karbala's foreign, government-appointed Sunni elite was expelled from the city as the capital's authority grew weak in the 1820s. The indigenous Shi`ite Arab notables attempted to take their place in monopolizing the city's resources, but lacked a disciplined armed force and had no tradition of legitimate rule. Karbala's sources of wealth - pilgrimage and trade - required security. The Shi`ite notables therefore depended on retainers recruited from among brigands. Unexpectedly the neighborhood ruffians and desperate fugitives that the notables hired emerged as powers in their own right. Ibrahim Za`farani provided protection and gathered tribute for the magnate Sayyid `Abd al-Wahhab. He grew wealthy enough through extortion, fraud and intimidation to enter the propertied elite himself. The sons of petty shopkeepers and minor clergy began to rival old landed Sayyid families in wealth and influence by virtue of their command of armed force. In the 1830s and 1840s the old Shi`ite elites made common cause with the rising gang leaders to resist Ottoman reforms. The city's gangs split into a minority Iranian faction and a majority Arab grouping. The Iranians were led by Mirza Salih, son of an Iranian father from Shiraz and an Arab mother from a family of Shi`ite jurisprudents based in Karbala. Mirza Salih's major ally commanded his own gang of 60-150 Baluchis from Fars province in Iran.[14]

Sayyid Ibrahim Za`farani headed the far larger Arab faction of gang members. His father, an Iranian from Baku, married an Arab woman in Karbala, settling there to sell his saffron. European industrially-made stuffs in the 1830s devastated Iraqi textile manufacturing.[15] It remains unknown whether Za`farani's family suffered business losses because of European competition. Sayyid Ibrahim grew up to indigence, hung about with toughs and finally joined the gangs. He came to prominence by killing one of their leaders. He then formed a policy of liberally distributing booty from criminal activities to his followers, which made him more popular with the rank and file than other gang leaders. He also exhibited a daring that elicited the admiration of his men, mastering the sort of intrigue that could remove dangerous foes and putting together a loose coalition of Arab gangs within the city. Both major gang bosses, Za`farani and Salih, "men of the people", derived from lower-middle-class backgrounds. Through a code of "honor" based on courage, cunning and violence, they gained the respect and fear of the little people from whom they sprang by rising to a position of wealth and power.

The fourteen major gangs, including those grouped around Mirza Salih, ranged in size from 50 or 60 men to 400. Some specialized in particular kinds of extortion; one gang, for instance, farmed the city market or bazaar. Many gangsters came as fugitives from outside Karbala. In addition to the gangs, Za'farani employed his Arab relatives on his mother's side to build an alliance with the neighboring Arab pastoral nomads. He brought the leader of one tribe into the city with 300 men to bolster his own position. Five other Arab tribal leaders outside the city allied themselves with Za'farani. All Shi'ites, they had frequently come into conflict with the Ottoman government.

Although it lay well within Iraq's borders, Karbala had the air of a frontier town. The population showed hostility to the Sunni government in Baghdad, which could seldom station its Sunni troops there without endless trouble. The city became an ideal hide-out for all the murderers, thieves, embezzlers and army deserters in Iran and Iraq. These underworld elements (mostly Arab) mingled with the often Iranian laborers, small-time peddlers and shopkeepers of Karbala's markets, and built up protection rackets aimed at milking the retailers, merchants and pilgrims. The rough, desperate and well-armed toughs organized themselves into large gangs, so that in the absence of a strong central government pilgrims and inhabitants had little choice but to pay a "godfather" for his protection.

Gang chiefs accumulated enough capital in this manner to begin buying land, the most important asset in the nineteenth-century Middle East, and to live in the best houses in the city. A group of about 2,500 *lutis* ruled and inspired dread in the city whose population averaged 20,000, for even though the inhabitants greased gang members' palm s well, they often stole or raped anyway.[16] Members of the old elite, like 'Abd al-Wahhab, helped create the corrupt system by acting as patrons of the thugs, gladly paying off one gang to protect themselves from the others.

The Shi'ite Establishment and the Mafia

The various groups within Karbala were united by a religious consciousness of being Shi'ites and by a perception of the Ottomans as the same Sunni enemy that had persecuted the Imam s and all their partisans down the ages. The gang leaders offered these diverse elements an alternative to Sunni Ottoman control of the town.

The Shi'ite scholars viewed the Hidden Imam as the only ultimately just ruler, although most of them in this period accepted, as the best they could achieve, a temporal power that established order and allowed them to enforce their version of the holy law.[17] While the religious scholars (and indeed many other sectors of the town's population) no doubt deplored the uglier aspects of gang rule, they probably considered it no more evil or illegitimate than they did the prospect of Sunni control.

The Shi`ite religious scholars saw major advantages in keeping the city out of Ottoman control. If the latter re-established their hold on the town, they would put the lucrative shrine endowments and income under the charge of Ottoman officials. They would refer cases to the Ottoman-appointed religious court judge (qadi) rather than to the Shi`ite jurisprudents, and would prescribe the mention of the Ottoman emperor's name in the Friday prayer sermons. Finally, they would impose restrictions on the open performance of the Shi`ite form of Islamic rituals.[18]

Moreover the Shi`ite establishment itself suffered deep and bitter divisions and therefore the leading scholars themselves became embroiled in the factious turbulence of Karbala's gang-dominated politics. This conflict ranged the rationalist Usuli jurisprudents against the more intuitional Shaykhis, followers of Shaykh Ahmad al-Ahsa'i (d. 1826).[19]

The struggle between the two parties, which led many Usuli scholars to excommunicate the Shaykh and his followers, centered on al-Ahsa'i's metaphorical explanations of key doctrines such as the Resurrection, the ascension of Muhammad and the continued life of the Twelfth Imam. The Usuli scholars further feared that Shaykh Ahmad's preference for intuitive knowledge (which he said he obtained by inspiration directly from the Imams) would seriously undermine the authority of their position, based on technical legal knowledge derived from the principle of reasoned endeavor.

The Shaykhis of Karbala were led by Sayyid Kazim Rashti, Shaykh Ahmad's successor, and the Usulis by the jurisprudent Sayyid Ibraham Qazvini. This division of the Shi`ite religious establishment played directly into the hands of the gang leaders. Once one of the leading clergy had offered patronage to a gang leader, his rival had to seek the protection of one of the other gangs or risk violence and intimidation. Major religious scholars traditionally established links with gangs in most Iranian cities. This mutually beneficial relationship provided the cleric with a force that could enforce his decisions, collect his religious taxes and agitate in his favor, often in opposition to the local governor. The gangs, on the other hand, had a protector with whom they could take refuge if the governor moved against them.

In Karbala Za`farani robbed Qazvini of 4,000 *qirans*. Qazvini sought the protection of Mirza Salih and his faction, and Za`farani announced himself a disciple of Rashti. Mirza Salih even appears listed among Qazvini's students, showing that more than one sort of bond linked the two.[20] It appears that Rashti did not relish being protected by Za`farani, for as soon as the Shaykhi leader sensed the Ottoman determination to reassert control, he broke his links with the gang leader in order to assume a mediatory role.

The Re-Establishment of Ottoman Rule in Iraq

Now let us turn to the temporal dimension. In the course of the eighteenth century the Ottoman empire lost control over many of its outlying provinces, accepting vassal states of sometimes dubious loyalty. The most successful such states were headed by adventurous members of the Ottoman or slave-soldier military classes - as in Egypt, Palestine and Iraq. The weakened empire also faced tribal revolts in Arabia and Kurdistan. The valley-lords of Anatolia, who had much more organic roots in the local power structure than did the Baghdad slave-soldiers, likewise made a bid for more autonomy. Karbala in the 1820s was twice-removed from Istanbul's grasp, a city-state in a vassal realm of tenuous allegiance. The gang leaders of Karbala, though urban rather than rural, most resembled the valley-lords, who also often came as close to banditry as to government.[21]

In the late eighteenth century and the first decade of the nineteenth the Marnluks kept a quite strong hold over Karbala. Relations between the town and Baghdad were at least correct. Moreover the city desperately needed the central government. In April 1801 12,000 tribesmen from Najd in Arabia, adherents of the puritanical Sunni reformist sect founded by ibn 'Abd al-Wahhab, pillaged Karbala for booty and as an act of iconociasm.[22] In 1801 the governor of the city fled before the Wahhabi advance, later being executed for not having defended Karbala. This act of retribution aimed at emphasizing the solidarity of the urban-based government with the citizens. It may also have been a sop to Iran, which threatened to annex the shrine cities if Baghdad could not protect them.[23]

While Karbala's merchants left the city temporarily after the attack, and one Indian traveler found it failing into decay in 1803, no major problems then existed between the Sunni administration and the Shi'ite population. The traveler said the considerable revenue yielded to the state by pilgrims led Sunni officials to tolerate Shi'ites in the shrine cities, even though they spat on them elsewhere.[24] With the Egyptians' assertion of control over much of Arabia, and their quelling of Wahhabi revivalism, Karbala's security on its Arabian flank improved.

Relations between Baghdad and Karbala deteriorated after 1820, partly because of poorer political relations between Iran and Iraq. In 1821 war broke out between the two and the Qajar governor of Kirmanshah led Iranian troops into Iraqi territory, reaching almost to Baghdad before a plague outbreak forced him to make peace and withdraw. The war set the stage for Da'ud Pasha's 1824 siege of Karbala. The government acted out of a desire to reassert central control over the town in the wake of conflict with the city's foreign patron, Iran. But the siege was made necessary partly because Karbala had become dangerously autonomous, failing into the hands of local notables and their hired protectors, unruly gangs. The siege, which forced many of the inhabitants to flee to Kazimayn, ended in stalemate rather than in occupation.[25]

From 1826 the reforming Sultan Mahmud II determined to reintegrate these provinces into the centralized empire. In 1830 he sent an envoy to Baghdad with the aim of replacing Da'ud Pasha, who executed Istanbul's man. In retaliation the emperor sent an Ottoman army against Baghdad in 1831 that subdued and destroyed the slave-soldiers, replacing them with a Turkish governor (Ali Riza Pasha) responsible directly to the central government.[26] While reforms proceeded in Turkey, weakening tax-farmers as well as the power of intermediary social groups like military lords and religious scholars, the task of centralizing power in Iraq began.

Just as the independence of the Kurdish and Arab tribespeople stood in the way of this process, so did the semi-autonomy of Karbala. Ottoman viceroy Ali Riza Pasha, a member of the Shi'ite-influenced Bektashi order who mourned for the Imam Husayn annually, sympathized with the Shi'ites.[27] But he came into conflict with them when he attempted to appoint a governor for Karbala, for the powerful gangs murdered or drove away the government's man when he proved a threat to their interests. Such effrontery led the Pasha to demand the right to perform a pilgrimage to the shrine of Husayn, thus reasserting the prerogatives of the center. In this period, too, some members of the powerful propertied-class groups like Sayyids and the clergy were demanding that the government intervene against the gangs.[28]

In the summer of 1835 a show-down occurred between the Ottoman governor and the people of Karbala. The British political agent in Baghdad wrote that the Pasha was planning to attack the town with 3,000 regulars.[29] As reports from 1843 demonstrate, the Ottoman viceroy found himself too weak to occupy the town and struck a deal with the gangs.[30] He considered a long-term occupation of the city to be unfeasible and after a show of strength indicated a willingness to compromise.

The Ottoman viceroy broke with tradition by appointing as governor someone neither Sunni nor from Baghdad, tacitly recognizing the power of the new coalition of local gangs and their patrons. He put 'Abd al-Wahhab, scion of an Arab landed family with strong links with the Arab gangs led by Za'farani, in charge of the city. In return for this appointment 'Abd al-Wahhab pledged to increase payments to Baghdad to 70,000 *qirans*. The new governor appropriated a large portion of municipal revenues to himself and robbed the city's two major shrines of some of their treasures. He used part of the money to pay Za'farani for protection against his foe, Mirza Salih, and gained influence over personages like the Iranian consul by lending him large sums of money. He cultivated the nearby Arab chiefs, allowing them to store their booty in the city.[31] The government of Karbala came directly into the hands of the gangs, which encouraged further immigration of toughs into the city.

Given the reports that reached British ears in the 1830s that many of the city's elite members wanted the Ottomans to overthrow gang rule, we must ask how the citizens were able to muster enough solidarity to face down the Ottoman viceroy. The answer is surely that, in addition to the armed gangs, Karbala's tradespeople also played a crucial role in ensuring the relative independence of their city. Indeed the issue of autonomy aroused them more than any other. The famous incidents of Karbala mob action are not food riots like the market strikes of northern Iran, but political ones.[32] As with crowds elsewhere, the Karbala little people rioted to achieve a specific aim: they wished to prove by their violence that to take the city street by street would cost government troops too dearly. They sought to keep the troops of the "foreign" central government, whether slave-soldier or Ottoman, outside the city walls as much as possible. They often supported local families of wealth and power against generals sent from Baghdad.[33]

The crowd sought to preserve their ways of life and city rights in the face of modern Ottoman centralization. Ottoman reforms, in turn, constituted a response to the economic and political power of industrializing Europe. The Turkish reformers made an assault on tax-farming and other pre-modern institutions and sought to centralize power. Both at the Ottoman center, Istanbul, and in the peripheries of the empire such reforms provoked resistance from social groups whose interests they threatened, including skilled artisans, tax-farming military men and the religious scholars' In the Karbala riots of the 1830s and 1840s we witness a crowd defending itself from rapid social change.[34]

Meanwhile the prospects of the Ottoman Empire for the reassertion of central control were improving. The 1840 Treaty of London, backed by four European powers, put an end to the Egyptian viceroy's bid to take over the empire. The Ottoman emperor, having regained Syria, hoped also to take direct control of the Hijaz. Ali Riza Pasha watched these events closely from Baghdad, aware of their regional implications .35 But just as the proclamation of reforms helped spark a revolt in Rumelia in 1841 by Christian peasants eager for improvement in their situation, so the centralizing tendencies of the empire provoked a backlash from the Shi`ites of southern Iraq .[36]

In September 1842 a new viceroy of Iraq arrived in Baghdad, Muhammad Najib (Mehmet Necip) Pasha. This official - former minister of justice, a staunch conservative and Ottoman chauvinist with intimate ties to the new emperor, Abdulmecid - had opposed the reforms for giving too much away to minorities. The reformers therefore sent him away from Istanbul to serve as viceroy of the Damascus province in January

1841. In Syria Najib Pasha became convinced of the need for greater centralized control. He attempted to subdue the Bedouins, treated the Christian minority severely, and succeeded in excluding British military advisers from the province. Indeed he so antagonized the western powers while in Syria that Istanbul finally transferred him to Baghdad, though he retained the emperor's confidence.[37]

Najib Pasha also wanted strong control of Iraq, which meant facing down the Arab tribes and the urban gangs in the Shi`ite south. Only about forty days after his arrival in Baghdad the Pasha set off on 23 October for Musayyib on the Euphrates, where Serasker Sadullah Pasha had preceded him with some troops, and pitched camp. He gave it out that he intended to oversee repairs to the Hindiyya canal, for which money had recently been donated by the government of Awadh. The canal would help drain marsh land in which refractory Arab tribes took refuge, and would help get water to restive peasants in Hilla.[38]

Rumors began to circulate that Najib Pasha intended to march on Karbala. The Shaykhi leader Rashti wrote to the Iranian consul in Karbala "that many Persians were daily. coming to him for advice, and begged him to go to the Pacha's camp, or to write him to know his intentions".[39] The consul wrote to the Pasha during this period, but his letters concerned injuries done to Iranian citizens by the gangs rather than any possible advance on the shrine city. Iranian families panicked and began leaving for Baghdad.

The Decision to Invade

Meanwhile Najib Pasha sent to Karbala for provisions and sent word that he intended to visit the shrine of Imam Husayn. Municipal authorities replied coldly, offering him only a token amount of provisions and telling him that he could come into the city for the visit only if he left his main force outside and retained only four or five bodyguards. The Pasha, livid on receiving this reply, threatened to take the city by force. Before he began his advance, on 18 November, he wrote to the embassies of Britain, France and Iran, detailing his reasons for contemplating military action. The previous year Ali Riza Pasha had made the same request and also received a reply from city leaders that they would allow him in with only ten or fifteen persons as a retinue. He finally returned to Baghdad without performing the visit. Najib Pasha considered his predecessor to have erred in appointing citizens of Karbala tax farmers and allowing the city to become a refuge for criminal elements. He believed that excluding the Pasha from his own territory constituted "a final demonstration of the revolt of the town "[40] The omission of the Ottoman emperor's name from the concluding sermons at Friday congregational prayers - a mention made elsewhere in Iraq - further symbolized Karbala's independence.[41] Here the city's religious scholars again demonstrated their opposition to Sunni Ottoman rule.

Najib Pasha said that the violence of the gangs in Karbala alarmed him, accusing Za`farani and his men of murdering and robbing at will. The Pasha reported that the gang chief had robbed even eminent Shi`ite scholars and had raped and murdered a lady of reputation.[42] But the strategic implications of Karbala's status disturbed him even more. He saw it as an Iranian-dominated stronghold, complaining that ten thousand Iranian subjects had congregated in the shrine city, but no such concentration of Turks existed in Iran. He insisted that all Muslims revered the shrines in Karbala, that the place belonged to the Ottoman empire and that Iranians only had the right to visit there once a year.[43] Such an Iranian population center, controlled by gangs, lying in his rear with powerful Arab tribes in the vicinity, represented a Trojan horse for his government were hostilities with Iran to break out.[44]

The city responded to the Pasha's threats in mid-November by holding meetings and closing ranks. The elite at first reached a consensus that they should refuse entry to Najib Pasha's troops and defend the town, proposing to buy him off with a sum of money. Gang leaders showed particular determination to keep the Turks out, because they would threaten their control over the city. The flight of wealthy and influential Iranian families to Baghdad alarmed the toughs, who put pressure on them to stay, with all their extensive resources.[45] The gangs argued that the former governor's siege of 1824 had proved unsuccessful. Moreover they emphasized the need of Shi`ites to defend the holy city from Sunni Turkish incursions. Artisans and shopkeepers had no choice but to stay because they feared they would lose what (largely immovable) property they owned should they depart. That eminent members of the Qajar royal family, like the Zill al-Sultan (then in political exile), elected to remain gave heart to the poor and middle-class Iranians.[46]

The Iranian consul in Baghdad attempted to negotiate with Najib Pasha, requesting six months of grace to allow Iranians to leave the town. He later said he wrote the Shaykhi leader Rashti two letters warning that the new Ottoman viceroy was deadly serious in his threat to occupy the city, but Rashti said he never received the missives.[47] Najib Pasha rejected any suggestion that he delay six months in entering the town.

Several city leaders, not including the gang leaders, attempted to negotiate directly with the Ottoman viceroy. The exiled Iranian prince Zill al-Sultan, Rashti, `Abd al-Wahhab and other members of the elite went together to the Pasha's camp at Musayyib. Najib demanded the right to station 300-500 troops inside the city, insisting that the gangs stop operating their rackets and that Za`farani come to him for an audience.

`Abd al-Wahhab replied that some troops might be stationed in Karbala, but that the gangs would never agree to the other terms. The city's governor offered to have Za`farani murdered if only he were given enough time, and Rashti also showed a willingness to abandon Za`farani. In the alliance of nobles and bosses that underpins any mafia, the nobles generally consider the mafiosi expendable. This and several further attempts at negotiation foundered on the intransigence of the gangs and of Najib Pasha, though Rashti and Zill al-Sultan fought hard for a compromise that would allow Turkish troops into the city.[48]

On 11 December 1842 Najib Pasha wrote to Zill al-Sultan and Rashti, asking them to warn the Iranians to separate themselves from the gangs and to leave the town or take refuge in the shrines of Husayn or `Abbas. He cautioned the two leaders that he intended to use force against the gangs should they oppose him, but offered protection to neutral civilians. He said, "whoever of all the people of the Town takes refuge with you, assure and satisfy him of safety".[49] Najib Pasha thus recognized that they had negotiated in good faith, but he also attempted by safety pledges to drive a wedge between the members of the Karbala coalition. He failed to separate the Iranian tradespeople from the gangs, however, because they could not afford the suddenly astronomical price of carriage out of the city for their families and so had to stay and make a stand.

The Advance on Karbala

Gang leaders made feverish preparations to defend the city, arranging for their allies from the Arab tribes to come there in force. The Ottoman viceroy, alarmed, dispatched Serasker Sadullah Pasha with three regiments of infantry, one of cavalry and twenty guns. About 19 December 1842 he arrived at Imam-Nuk, a mile and a half southeast of Karbala. They received sporadic sniper fire but did not return it. Their arrival provoked another attempt at negotiation, again led by Rashti and Zill al-Sultan, which involved the giving of gang hostages in exchange for the Turkish withdrawal of all but 500 men. This effort met failure when Najib Pasha rejected its terms even after Sadullah Pasha had accepted it.[50]

The day after the viceroy's negative message arrived, around 22 December, Sadullah Pasha sent his soldiers out to occupy some favorable positions. Observers on the city walls informed Arab tribespeople and Karbala's laborers and artisans of these strategic troop movements. Fearing an attack, a mob gathered and went out to assault the soldiers, whom they drove back. The crowd captured several artillery pieces and overturned others, retiring at sunset. While the attack by the crowd appears to have had an element of spontaneity in it, the people had hardly acted randomly. It served as a further indication of the militancy of the little people and their distrust of the Ottomans.[51]

The unyielding mood of the crowd may have been reinforced by religious rivalries. Had Rashti succeeded in his negotiations with the Ottomans, his position within the city would have been much strengthened. Rivals like the gang leader Mirza Salih and the Usuli scholars did not wish to see this happen. One of Rashti's disciples later wrote: "However much the noble Sayyid endeavored to dampen the fire of this rebellion through conciliation and forbearance, his opponents declared that they would rather see their women and children prisoners in the hands of the Turks than to have this dispute settled by him".[52] A pro-Shaykhi source written in 1888 indicates that Usuli scholars helped incite tradespeople to attack the Ottoman forces, partly to thwart Rashti. A rumor spread that one of the clergy had seen a dream of `Abbas, the brother of Imam Husayn, who asked him to promulgate holy war against the Turks and promised him ultimate success.[53] In a shrine city such rumors of supernatural aid contributed to a feeling that the holy places were impregnable, and shaped the militant popular mentality of the citizens. But on the practical plane the laborers and tradespeople had no choice but to stay and fight. Their action without doubt helped dishearten the Ottomans, as it aimed to do. It also demonstrated that "the crowd" acted in the revolt independently of the gangs.

The Siege of Karbala

After the mob riot against the Turkish troops, the gangs made extensive preparations to withstand a siege, drawing on the military and technological knowledge of the army deserters among their ranks. They prevented anyone from leaving the city, though carriage was anyway unavailable by then. For the rest of December the Turks fired on or over the town to frighten the inhabitants. Towards the end of December Zill al-Sultan wrote from the Serasker's camp to Qazvini, then in Baghdad, that the thousands of shots fired into the city had damaged tens of buildings, including shrines. He estimated forty inhabitants of Karbala dead in the shelling and put Turkish casualties at a thousand. He said of the Ottomans, who were commandeering muleteers for their logistics, that: "Their camp too is in great distress almost approaching to a famine, but in Karbala food is abundant and cheap".[54] On about 1 January 1843 Qazvini and the Iranian consul, representing the Iranian faction within the city, left Baghdad to begin another round of negotiations with Najib Pasha. But, out of touch with the determined mood of Karbala, they reached terms rejected by city leaders. Rashti wrote to the Iranian consul urging him to come to Karbala, but he retired instead to the safety of

Baghdad. Tragically, those within the besieged town took his action as a sign that no attack was imminent.[55]

Karbala's citizenry during the siege showed a die-hard commitment across a range of social classes to maintaining local autonomy. The roots of this stance lay in the popular mentality that prevailed during the revolt. Although quixotic given the fire-power ranged against them, their underlying attitude had some basis in local experience. First, the coalition of urban gangs, mob and tribesmen had already averted two occupations in the previous twenty years, one as recently as 1835. The inhabitants of Karbala had grown used to a weak and corrupt government in Baghdad which they could bribe or face down. They remained ignorant of the sea change the reforms had wrought in Ottoman lands, and as yet unreconciled to the greater centralization these entailed. Secondly, poor communications among the Karbala leaders in and outside the city led to an underestimation of the danger. Thirdly, rumors were planted that the shah of Iran would dispatch an army of 20,000 men to aid the beleaguered city, and Arab tribal leaders promised another 12,000 reinforcements.[56] The myth that outside assistance was on the way shored up morale and made the people less willing to compromise.

Finally, religious feelings affected the judgment of the crowd, with gang and other city leaders stirring up hate for Sunnis. Tradesmen and laborers lined the city walls to hurl down invective on the Turks and on Sunni holy figures. The clergy contributed to the sectarian rancor, and though they did not join in actual fighting they did help repair damaged walls. The religious official in charge of the shrine of `Abbas (who therefore stood to lose a great deal should the Turks come in) thwarted one set of talks by standing up in the assembly, dashing his turban to the ground and excommunicating anyone who spoke of giving up the town and their wives to the "infidel" Turks. Some preachers boldly proclaimed that the city was engaged in a holy war. While classical Shi`ite thought held that during the Twelfth Imam's absence believers could wage no holy war against Sunni Muslims, the clerics put such legal niceties aside during the siege.[57] Classical doctrine was one thing, the impassioned rhetoric of desperate clergymen another.

The major dissenting view from the popular mentality just described originated with the Shaykhi leader Sayyid Kazim Rashti. Lt.-Col. Farrant reported that he "did all in his power to prevent hostilities, he preached against their proceedings, he was abused and threatened, they would not listen to him".[58] Although Za`farani had announced himself Rashti's follower, the Shaykhi leader's actions demonstrate that he much preferred a conventional government of the Sunnis to the semi-anarchy of even pro-Shaykhi gang rule.

The gang-led coalition in Karbala based itself primarily on violence and coercion, though yearning for regional autonomy played a part. It therefore exhibited weaknesses and could fall apart in the face of stronger forces. The old landed elite also demonstrated a certain ambivalence in choosing between the gangs and the Ottomans, though they lacked the courage to speak out as had Rashti.

The Shaykhis' minority view of events also involved millennialist ideas. Rashti traditionally devoted the fasting month of Ramadan to discussing the characteristics of the promised Mahdi, who would restore justice to the world. The fasting month fell in October 1842, when it increasingly looked as if Najib Pasha might invade. An eyewitness writing six or seven years later said that Rashti elucidated the coming of this messianic figure with particular detail that year.[59] The siege took place in the closing months of A.H. 1258, and the Shi`ite world in the nineteenth century was pervaded by apocalyptic speculations that the promised one (Mahdi) would appear in 1260/ 1844, a little over a year later.[60] In Shaykhi circles, where these speculations received particular emphasis, political quietism and eschewing of holy war against the Sunnis may have been linked with expectations of the imminent advent of a supernatural deliverer.

The five days after the breakdown of the fourth set of negotiations witnessed frantic activity on both sides of the struggle. The gang leaders in Karbala faced increasing difficulties in provisioning and garrisoning the 5,000 Arab tribesmen that had assembled within its walls to aid the defense effort. Ammunition grew so scarce that people tore out the rails around the shrine of `Abbas and melted them down for shot.[61] The Turkish troops also faced great hardship, because the high Euphrates prevented provisions from reaching them from Baghdad, and they suffered from the cold. Using Arab labor and artillery blasts, they cut through the date grove protecting the city walls and finally had to fight a fierce battle with gang forces in order to take up a new position at a tomb just outside the city.[62]

The Occupation

Logistical problems and a high desertion rate forced Sadullah Pasha to decide whether to act or withdraw altogether, and around 10 January a meeting of the officers decided to take the city by force. On 12 January Turkish artillery blasted a breach in the wall between the Najaf and Khan gates large enough to allow an assault. One more round of peace talks opened at this point and city leaders were on the verge of accepting the Serasker's terms when the chief of the Iranian gangs, Mirza Salih, made an impassioned plea that they trust in God and the Prophet and defy the Turks to the end. The Iranians had emerged as the hard-liners, perhaps because they most fervently believed the shah's forces were on the way to aid them.

The Ottoman envoy returned empty-handed to this camp, from which artillery barrages began again and went on till sunset, when both sides settled down for a freezing night. The Arab tribesmen, now 8,000 strong, threatened to leave because of poor meals and cold nights watching the city gates. The gangs therefore billeted them on the civilian population, with whom they celebrated the Muslim festival of sacrifice until late. As all Muslims observed this holy day, they assumed the Turks would do the same, and remained in homes rather than returning to their posts. The gangsters, distrusting the Arabs' steadfastness, nailed the gates Shut.[63]

The Ottoman officers planned out their assault. Three divisions commanded by the leader of the Mosul brigade were to lead the attack. The first would hold the breach, the second would enter the town and open the Najaf gate and the third would commandeer the bastions nearest them, turning the big guns on the city. As an incentive to the disheartened troops, one officer promised to allow them to do whatever they pleased once inside and pledged 150 *piasters* for every luti head.[64]

Before dawn on 13 January 1843 the advance divisions set out, with heavy covering fire from the Ottoman artillery. They had almost reached the breach unopposed when the alarm went out that the Turks were approaching. Both Arabs and citizens rushed to the defense, commanded by an Arab gang leader, but they could not prevent the Ottomans from gaining the breach. The Turks lost 200 men in the assault. The gang forces ran low on powder and were forced to retreat to the cover of neighboring houses, where they kept up fire. One Ottoman division sneaked along the inside of the wall to the Najaf gate, killing the sentinels and swinging it open. Sadullah Pasha immediately moved the main force into the town, while another officer dispatched divisions along the walls to secure other gates, and one through the center of the town that attracted sniper fire from roof-tops. Many men detached themselves from the main body to raid houses for booty.

The force advancing along the wall drove a crowd of mixed civilians and Arab tribesmen before it as they frantically sought egress from the sealed or jammed city gates. At one partially open gate the Ottomans fired into the crowd with devastating effect. Za`farani and 200 of his gangsters fled from the al-Hurr gate, to which they had the key. The Iranian gangs, led by Mirza Salih, remained for the fight, as did the governor, `Abd al-Wahhab. Most of the gang leaders had already sent

away their families.   Several thousand Arabs followed Za'farani in his
flight through the al-Hurr gate.   An Ottoman officer sent 3,000 troops in
pursuit of them and the fleeing Arabs were attacked on another flank by
the Turkish cavalry camped outside the city.   Arab casualties ran
extremely high.

The crush at the narrow al-Hurr gate and the troops' indiscriminate
firing on the people massed there impelled hundreds of citizens to flee
back into the town to seek shelter in the shrines or in the houses of Zill al-
Sultan and Rashti, the refuges designated by Najib Pasha.   Rashti's home
was so full that people spilled into his courtyard, where some sixty-six
persons were crushed by the panicky crowd.   By this time the greater
body of tribesmen and gangs had fled the city.   Nevertheless, the Turkish
division advancing through the center of the town suffered heavy sniper
fire, the intensity of which indicates that many tradespeople joined the
fray on their own.   Many of these were sighted in their ethnic Iranian
dress in the opposition forces.   When the power elite had fled, the little
people remained to defend their bazaar, their holy city.   This opposition
from the crowd infuriated the Turkish soldiers.[65]

Turkish troops chased retreating Arabs to the shrine of 'Abbas, where
snipers fired upon them from a minaret.   The berserk Ottomans let loose a
fearful volley into the crowd seeking sanctuary there, which panicked,
causing more deaths by trampling.   The imperial troops took the
offensive, robbing women of jewelry, sometimes chopping off a limb to
get it.   Fighting even reached the precincts of the holy tomb, where the
Ottomans killed several persons they declared were *lutis*.   The streets
adjoining 'Abbas's shrine were filled with cadavers that the Ottomans set
ablaze with naphtha and covered with blankets to help them burn.   Nearly
250 persons probably perished in the incident.   Nearly 200 more civilians
were slaughtered at the shrine of Imam Husayn before Sadullah Pasha
entered the city at about 10:30 a.m. and forbade further butchery.

The troops then fanned out to plunder the city's residences, raping and
killing.   Often the troops pressed the owners into service as bearers to
transport the stolen goods to camp.   Mulla Yusuf Astarabadi reported that
although he suffered a head wound he was made to carry loot to the camp.
He wrote:

The dead were lying on top of one another to the extent that I could not
cross the street except by walking over the corpses.   It was as if I walked
about invisibly, so many had perished . . . At the foundation of the
mausoleum of our lord Abu al-Fadl 'Abbas ... I descried all about the
illumined sepulcher murdered souls clinging to it, beseeching, seeking
shelter and refuge within it.   I saw most of the dead in the lanes and
bazaars.[66]

Only towards sunset did the Ottoman commander, who had stopped paying for *luti* ears, begin reining in his plundering minions. After careful inquiries Farrant estimated the loss of life inside the city at some 3,000 dead that day, with another 2,000 Arabs killed outside the walls.[67] The number of dead within the city represented 15 per cent of its normal population. The Ottomans lost 400 men.

The Repression of Shi`ism

The religious element in the struggle again surfaced when the Turkish troops turned the court of the shrine of `Abbas into a barrack yard, where animals were stabled and uncouth soldiers sang loose songs, horrifying the dispirited Shi`ites. On 15 January the Serasker received word that Najib Pasha would shortly visit the conquered city. Shi`ite jurisprudents and other notables were put in charge of overseeing the burial of the often burnt, dog-eaten cadavers in mass graves. On 16 and 17 January further plundering occurred as troops searched homes for arms.

On 18 January Najib Pasha arrived in the city and was greeted by a party of notables that included Rashti. The viceroy said his prayers at the shrine of Imam Husayn and paid respect to the holy tombs, but he soon revealed a new administrative order that ended Shi`ite autonomy in the town. Najib Pasha appointed a Sunni governor of Karbala, and announced that with the concurrence of the Sunni *qadi* in Baghdad, an assistant Sunni judge would be appointed in Karbala. Sunni judges would hear all court cases, even where they involved two Shi`ite parties from Karbala. Likewise, the government appointed a Sunni preacher to deliver sermons after Friday prayers and to pronounce blessings on the Ottoman emperor.[68] Thousands of Shi`ites fled Iraq for Iran.

The Shi`ite clergy, alarmed by the disaster and the new, hard-line Ottoman government, began practicing dissimulation *(taqiyyah)* of their faith and canceled further performance of Friday congregational prayers. Shi`ites ceased to pray with their arms held straight down, pretending to be Sunnis from the ritual point of view. Observances of the month of mourning, Muharram, which began on 1 February, were extremely subdued and private, and news of the attack disheartened other Shi`ites in Iraq.[69]

Reactions to the Disaster

Reactions to the calamity within Karbala varied greatly. By late April a semblance of normality had returned to the town and Farrant reported that respectable residents rejoiced that the gangs had been expelled, complaining that "no place could have exceeded Karbellah in debauchery of every sort". He noted that many religious officials considered the calamity a judgment on the place.[70] Wealthy survivors of the occupation were happier with strong state control.

The leaders of the revolt from old landed families, such as `Abd al-Wahhab, fled to sanctuary with friendly tribes and Najib Pasha subsequently pardoned them. Mirza Salih suffered imprisonment in Kirkuk until pardoned. The Arab gangs sought refuge in the Hindiyya, but their leader Za`farani was apprehended and taken to Baghdad, where he fell ill with hectic fever (tuberculosis) and died. The major Arab tribal leaders escaped safely with their men. Najib Pasha's costly military adventure made little long-term change in the social structure of Karbala and the gang organizations, although weakened, continued. Better administration returned prosperity to the city within three years, though Iranian merchants were thenceforth subject to heavy customs duties in the city and within Turkish territory.[71]

The minor Usuli scholar Yusuf Astarabadi reacted with rage against the ruling classes.[72] In a candid letter Astarabadi gave full vent to his grief and outrage, angrily exclaiming, "Would that there were no king *(sultan)* ruling over us, and none over Iran!" [73] Astarabadi clearly blamed the Ottoman emperor Abdulmecid for ordering the attack, and Muhammad Shah of Iran for failing to come to the aid of the beleaguered Shi`ites. He went on to say that if there had to be a monarch, he should at least uphold the Qur'an and defend the Imam `Ali. Astarabadi's antipathy towards monarchy and desire for the enthronement of Shi`ite values represent a rudimentary republicanism, providing evidence of strong, if vague, anti-monarchical feelings among some religious scholars in the shrine cities in the mid-nineteenth century. Solid evidence for such views is otherwise rare.[74]

The Shaykhi leader Rashti interpreted the cataclysm as divine retribution for the failure of the inhabitants to accept his millenarian teachings. The following year, September-October 1843, he refused to expand on the subject of the coming promised one. He feared that were he to repeat his discourse a similar disaster would befall the town, as the people were still unprepared to embrace his views about the Mahdi. [75]

Iran met the news of the bloody capture of Karbala with grief and rage, then with clamor for war. The leading jurisprudent of Isfahan, Sayyid Muhammad Baqir Shafti, attempted to pressure Muhammad Shah into declaring war on the Ottomans by threatening to lead an independent army of 20,000 men into Iraq.[76] Muhammad Shah mobilized, his troops, but in the end took no belligerent steps.[77]

Given the widespread millennial speculations about the coming of the promised Mahdi in 1260/1844, the Sunni enemy's unavenged sacking of so holy a Shi`ite shrine surely heightened expectations that the Hidden

Imam would soon appear to succor the Shi`ites. In May 1844 Sayyid `Ali Muhammad, a young merchant of Shiraz, who had associated briefly with the Shaykhis in Karbala, put forward his claim to be the Bab or gate of the Twelfth Imam and caused a considerable stir in the shrine cities of Iraq.[78]

A large number of Shaykhis responded favorably to the Bab. They had been strengthened in their millenarian fervor, as we noted above, by the teachings of Sayyid Kazim Rashti. The initial excitement caused by the Bab and the following he gained in both Iran and Iraq derived, at least in part, from the millennial expectations caused by the anger and frustration the Karbala episode provoked among devout Shi`ites. The Babi movement spread with lightning swiftness in Iran, especially attracting lower-ranking religious scholars, urban merchants and the bazaar classes. The Bab's message, aside from his own messianic claims, included the abrogation of the Islamic prohibition of interest on loans and the amelioration of the condition of women. The opposition the new religion provoked from the government and the Usuli religious scholars led to its persecution and in turn sparked clashes and uprisings in several Iranian towns in 1848-52.[79]

Conclusion

The data gleaned from archival and manuscript sources and presented above not only give us a detailed picture of gang organization and activities in Karbala, they also help clarify the general role of the urban gangs active in many cities in south Iraq and throughout Iran during the nineteenth century. Although stronger governments could suppress the toughs, when state power waned in the first half of the nineteenth century the gangs took control of entire towns. Wars with modernizing European states like the Russian empire enervated the Ottomans and the Qajars in the late eighteenth and early nineteenth centuries, and at first they had fewer resources to devote to controlling their own remoter provinces.

In response, the Ottomans from 1826 sought to increase resources through the abolition of tax-farming and privileges and through a rationalized and centralized bureaucracy. The manner in which the government initially grew weaker, then attempted to impose greater centralization through new, European-influenced techniques, helped provoke regional clashes in Iraq, with urban violence and gang-led revolts growing common. Outside Karbala the struggle between the Shumurd and Zuqurt factions in Najaf, representing wealthier and poorer quarters of the city, racked that town with violence throughout the nineteenth century.[80]

In Iran, as well, the Haydari and Ni'mati quarters (originally named for mystical Sufi brotherhoods) into which many towns were divided often staged street battles. Gangs dominated Yazd for most of the 1840s and for a time a gang leader effectively ruled the city.[81] Shiraz was, for much of the 1830s and early 1840s, torn by factional rivalries in which allied groups of notables and gang bosses clashed with such ferocity that the local governor often lost control.[82]

From the Euphrates to the Oxus nineteenth-century gangs emerged briefly as popular leaders with great power in a town for several reasons. First, both the slave-soldier and Qajar states lacked the ability to project force quickly and effectively throughout their territories, owing in part to their small standing armies. These states therefore had to depend heavily on appointed local governors, themselves often weak or lacking full central government support. Large pastoral nomadic populations, relatively large urban concentrations, rugged terrain and lack of made roads and transportation technology, made the provinces more difficult to control than was the case in contemporary Europe.

Secondly, the local notables, artisans, shopkeepers and laborers in Iraqi and Iranian towns had little or no allegiance to the central government, and so they sometimes perceived gang rule as no more illegitimate than rule by the state. This especially held true for the Shi`ite towns in Iraq, and often applied in Iran as well. Where- the government taxed the tradespeople without providing services like security, it often drove them to an alliance with their local extortionists. In short, nineteenth-century urban gangs had a common interest with local elites and the local tradespeople in keeping the central government out. Finally, factional divisions among local elites such as landed notables and religious scholars, and among city quarters, often so detracted from urban corporate solidarity as to allow the gangs to divide and rule.

Under these circumstances, gangs in mid-nineteenth-century Iraq and Iran used their armed force in the service of revolts by local notables or by tradespeople against the centrally appointed governor. They often became popular local leaders, transcending (at least for a time) their extortionist background.

In Karbala their provision of makeshift and arbitrary security had the virtue, at least, of allowing more wealth to remain in the city than the Ottomans would have, while assuring the uninterrupted flow of pilgrims and merchants. The city's inhabitants paid the price of a state of rough semi-anarchy. Nevertheless, the evidence indicates that the little people and many Shi`ite religious scholars preferred even gang rule and protection rackets to imperial Ottoman control. (Indeed the Ottoman attack served only to fuel anti-monarchical feelings among some Shi`ite clerics.) Without the active support of the crowd, Karbala could not have warded off central government troops for two decades. The tradespeople, caught between two unpleasant alternatives, chose to be exploited by their local leadership. The prospect of more centralized, bureaucratic Ottoman rule in the 1830s and 1840s, itself a response to the rise of European industrial and political might, provoked the little people to defend their local autonomy.

The role of "mafias" in defending a provincial area against a distant government has long been recognized. But the specifically urban character of the Karbala lutis does raise questions. The urban gang leadership of these popular uprisings must strike anyone familiar with the historiography of early modern Europe as anomalous. The gangsters in Paris, it has often been observed, saw the French Revolution as no more than an opportunity for plunder. Hobsbawm argued that although peasant bandits are "social", in tune with the needs and aspirations of the oppressed peasantry from which they spring, urban bandits are asocial.[83] The widespread involvement of gangs in urban movements of social protest in nineteenth-century Iraq and Iran challenges this paradigm. Indeed it should provoke thought as to whether there is really any such thing as an asocial gang, urban or otherwise. As Anton Blok has pointed out, all banditry is "social" in so far as it occurs in a social context.[84]

Bandits emerge from particular classes and, when successful, their wealth and means of procuring it give them broader interests and alliances. Bandits, rural or urban, engage in anti-social behavior, exploiting the poor as well as the rich, and will join in social revolts when they perceive it in their interests to do.

But luti rule, based on a tenuous coalition of anarchical gangs and upon a vacuum of more legitimate power, exhibited instability and proved a transitional phenomenon. It burgeoned when the old tax farming government declined in the first third of the nineteenth century, but before modern, centralized states arose to impose strict security. Najib Pasha's attack was a harbinger of things to come; but they would come very gradually over the succeeding century.

7

The Shi`ite Discovery of the West

> *Kublai Khan does not necessarily believe everything Marco Polo says*
> *when he describes the cities visited on his expeditions, but the emperor of*
> *the Tartars does continue listening to the young Venetian with greater*
> *attention and curiosity than he shows any other messenger or explorer of*
> *his. In the lives of emperors there is a moment which follows pride in the*
> *boundless extension of the territories we have conquered, and the*
> *melancholy and relief of knowing we shall soon give up any thought of*
> *knowing and understanding them.*
> *- Italo Calvino, Invisible*
> *Cities*

Marco Polo's encounter with Kublai Khan, which Italo Calvino made the
framework for his exploration of the fantastic in urban life, stands as a
useful parable for the nature of the interaction of West and East in the
period between 1200 and 1700, when myriads of Europeans produced
journals and accounts of their journeys into the rest of the world.
Representations of Europeans in Asian works during the same period are
few and episodic. The literature produced by Europeans who ventured
into the rest of the world in that period was once viewed by many
Western academics as documenting objective "discovery." In the past
decade or so, the European production of knowledge about the Other has
been portrayed in quite a different manner as, at base, shot through with
self-interest, in thrall to powerful organizing institutions such as the
colonial state, the trading companies, the imperial universities. In this
version, popularized by Edward Said's *Orientalism*, the Europeans created
in their minds a static, stagnant, chaotic, effeminate Orient, a realm crying
out to be ordered and rendered dynamic by the virile touch of European
proconsuls and investors.[1] This revisionist view often suffers from being
too monolithic in approach to allow an analytical understanding of
cultural interaction, and too inattentive to the nuances of difference in the
views of diplomats, travellers, merchants and academics. Nevertheless,
Said's vision, powerfully informed by Gramsci's idea of culture as a form
of subtle domination (hegemony) by the ruling classes and by Foucault's

insistence on finding a genealogy for knowledge in institutional contexts contains important insights. It also, of course, presents only one side of the equation. Here, I will play turnabout by inquiring into some eighteenth-century depictions of the West written in Persian by Shi`ite notables. Although my main concerns are thematic, I will also attempt to set them in the context of social interests. On the face of it, we might expect to find in these texts, written at a time of unprecedented European encroachment on the Muslim lands, a mirror-image of Orientalism, a systematic critique of Western colonialism and Western culture. But do we?

Muslims were, of course, in contact with Europeans, especially in the Mediterranean, throughout their history. Nevertheless, the public culture in most Muslim lands little acknowledged Europeans or European culture in the early modern period. The Renaissance, the Copernican revolution, the advent of moveable type printing, the Reformation, and the Enlightenment all might as well not have occurred for all the cognizance most Muslim intellectuals took of them.[2]   Although the European expansion and the trading companies made an impact upon Muslims right from the beginning of the Iberian transoceanic voyages, relatively few indigenous accounts concerning developments in Western civilization survive before the eighteenth century.

In the course of the eighteenth century, the British emerged as the predominant European power in the Persian Gulf (succeeding the Portuguese and the Dutch). They gradually crafted a new political order.[3] In India, of course, the British defeated in turn the army of the Shi`ite-ruled Bengal province in 1757 and the Mughal forces led by the Shi`ite governor of Awadh, Shuja` al-Dawla, at Baksar in 1764. Despite the numerical predominance of Hindus in the population and of Sunnis among the Muslims, the post-Mughal era had witnessed the emergence of important Iran-linked Shi`ite elites in northern India, particularly in Bengal and Awadh, though these were gradually displaced from power by the British.[4]   Although only occasionally do the Shi`ite leanings of these authors emerge in the accounts under discussion, it does so happen that all the authors covered adhered to that branch of Islam.

The Westerners loomed too large after 1750 for Persian-speaking writers in Iran and India to ignore them any longer. Natives of Lucknow, or of Shushtar and Kermanshah, began making extensive Persian notes on Europe and the Europeans in the late eighteenth century, several of which were published in manuscript form or lithographed early in the nineteeth. What were the institutional and technological contexts for this writing? We know that the advent of moveable-type printing and the age of European expansionism, along with the literature of travel and description the latter spawned, coincided with one another in the late fifteenth century. Did the rise of printing and lithography in the Persian-speaking world in the late eighteenth century have a similar relationship with the literature describing Europe to Iranians, Central Asians and Indians in Persian? Other social practices are also important here. The literate class of Muslim courtiers, landlords, garrison commanders, and clergymen were called locally in Arabic, Persian and Turkish the *a`yan*, or notables, and Albert Hourani in a classic essay discovered in their interests and activities the essence of pre-modern Middle Eastern politics.[5] They often held land or engaged in court service, or both. The authors discussed below universally derived from this class. In this period the notables became divided between those who opposed the expansion of European power in the Muslim world and those willing to ally themselves or collaborate with the foreigners.[6] Sometimes the career of one leader, such as Shuja` al-Dawlah (r. 1754-1775) of Awadh, demonstrated both leanings, with early opposition to the foreigners followed by a collaborationist phase in the wake of a decisive defeat at British hands. The advent of new transportation and communication technologies brought these elites into closer contact with one another and also established a context for new sorts of cultural production in the Indo-Iranian culture area.

The forces of the British East India Company either subdued recalcitrant Muslim elites, as in Bengal or in the south in the war against Tippoo Sultan, or surrounded and neutralized remaining princely states, such as Awadh and Hyderabad. As a result, most Indian notables who wrote about Europe had either taken employment with the British or dwelt in circumscribed polities that had become `subsidiary allies' of John Company.  Thus, Shi`ite writers in Awadh, not excluding the clergy, tended to look favorably upon the British as patrons (from the late 1760s) of their nawab. In a bizarre victory for Orientalism, notables often received patronage from European consuls or agents to write Persian chronicles about the local political events of the day, from a point of view that flattered the British. Iranians, who retained at least a nominal independence, were often more ambivalent about the foreigners, but those most likely to know anything serious about Great Britain were immigrants to India or students studying in London, and so they gravitated toward the circle of collaborating elites or subsidiary allies. Underlying much of the Persian writing about Europe lay the question of what benefit the notable class might derive from the new encounter with the West. In the absence of notions like nation-state or citizenship in Asia, exclusive national or even communal loyalty had no resonance. Many Iranians, after all had emigrated to join the Mughal army and bureaucracy in India. There, Muslim notables frequently served in the courts of Hindu potentates, and Shi`ite courtiers routinely served Sunni rulers.  In keeping with this tradition of cosmopolitanism, Shi`ites felt that there was nothing wrong with taking service in the British East India Company as long as they did nothing contradictory to their religious principles.

Although the Persian texts purport to discuss "Europeans" (*Farang*), the authors mostly concentrate on high culture and on high politics, in short, on the European equivalent of the notable class. I will focus here on their views of the British, and will discuss three major positive themes in these portrayals: Egalitarianism and parliamentary government, science and technology, and gender. I will then turn to a consideration of their criticisms of European society. The value of these texts lay in their being some of the first widely-available accounts of Europe to reach literate Persian-speakers early in the nineteenth century, much before "Westernization" began in these societies in any meaningful sense. The texts have their flaws and idiosyncrasies, but none of these detracts from their value for our immediate purpose. The authors appear to have depended on interviews with Persian-speaking Europeans, rather than upon reading printed texts, for their information, and this caused them sometimes to garble facts and details (one writer confidently asserts that British monarchs are permitted legal polygamy, and that the hair of all Native Americans is white).[7] The question arises, moreover, of to what extent the picture they derived of Europeans reflected the self-image of their informants; but this problem exists in all `ethnography.'

Abd al-Latif Khan of Shushtar in southwestern Iran, born in 1760, emigrated to Hyderabad around 1790 and during that decade took the notes on which his *Gift to the World* (*Tuhfat al-`Alam*), written in 1800-1801, was based. He had the book printed in Hyderabad in 1805.[8] Another writer, Mirza Abu Talib Khan, was from an Iranian family that fled to India from the tribal turbulence of eighteenth century Iran. He was born in 1752 in Lucknow, in the post-Mughal, Shi`ite-ruled state of Awadh. After a mixed career as a local revenue official, he set out for England from Calcutta in 1799, and wrote up his observations in 1803-1805, as *The Travels of Talib in the Lands of the Franks* on his return to Bengal. The Persian text was published in Calcutta in 1812, after a two-volume English translation had already appeared in London, in 1810.[9] Aqa Ahmad Bihbahani, an Iranian clergyman brought up in Kermanshah, escaped his debts by emigrating to India, where he ultimately settled as a leader of Friday prayers in British-ruled Patna, writing his travelogue, *The World-Revealing Mirror* around 1810; he had access, apparently to a manuscript of Abu Talib Khan's work.[10] Of these three authors only one, Abu Talib, had a direct experience of late eighteenth-century Britain, but all three had ample opportunity to associate with Britishers and derive information from them. I choose these three accounts among others because of the relatively similar backgrounds of the authors, all Indo-Persian Shi`ites of the notable class.

These authors saw Great Britain as a more egalitarian, less hierarchical society than Muslim Iran or South Asia, though Shushtari stresses this aspect of Britain rather more than does Abu Talib, who moved in aristocratic circles and who had an opportunity to observe the practice as well as the theory of British parliamentarism. Shushtari writes that "another of the laws of these people is that no one may dominate another. If the king or nobles make unreasonable demands on their subordinates, these latter may lodge a complaint in the courts."[11] Abu Talib concurs that masters could not directly punish their servants, but rather had to take them before a magistrate, and is awed that even the heir apparent could be sued by an ordinary person.[12] Abu Talib thinks that this equality before the law made the ordinary folk impudent, and tells the story of how a lord, when he sullied his gloves on a newly-painted, unmarked door, upbraided the painter - who saucily asked whether the nobleman had eyes in his head, or not. He says that "their lawmakers are however of the opinion that this freedom tends to make them brave."[13] On the other hand, Abu Talib points out the severe limits to this equality under the law, and suggests that wealth stratification was even greater in England than in India.

The writers here considered derived from countries where royal absolutism predominated, and where elective office was virtually unknown, except perhaps among the guilds or merchant and artisan craft organizations. Shushtari's detailed description of parliamentary government is one of the first to appear in Persian, and it raises questions to be considered below. He concentrates on the political system and its principles, and gives an idealized and somewhat collapsed account of the decline of absolutism in England:

The philosophers, after having implemented most of the above-mentioned laws, began thinking about how to organize power (*saltanat*). For until that time government was absolutist and autocratic. Every day, one ruler was deposed and another achieved dominion through conquest. The turmoil and bloodshed attendant upon changing regimes became apparent. The king at that time was himself a learned man and shared the prevailing opinion among the philosophers. They thought for many years on this issue. In the end, all arrived at the opinion that the king should be deprived of his power, and that they should appoint for him an agreed-upon amount, equivalent to one crore rupees or 500,000 silver tumans, which he would devote to the expenses of the monarchy, excluding the expenditures of the princes and their dependents, for each of whom a separate stipend was appointed. The king, in addition, was willing to become powerless, though in the degree of respect and courtesy everyone offers him, each is free to choose. As noted, he may not kill or harm anyone, or even beat one of his own servants.[14]

He says that the English system based itself on three pillars, the king, the aristocracy, and the subjects, and no great affair could be undertaken without the consent of all three estates. He describes how the British built a great edifice in the capital, which they called Parliament (*shura*, literally consultation) or the House of Consultation (*khanih-'i mashvirat*). "They informed the inhabitants of every village and town that it should choose a suitable representative, so that he should come to the capital and affairs might be accomplished by means of consultation with all." He describes formal balloting, and says the terms of MPs were limited to seven years. "In matters of war, peace, aiding others, the military, etc., the ministers present a brief to the king. The king reserves particular days for going to parliament to meet with ministers and MPs. The great ones are called by the king and they write out their views. In the end, majority rules. If there is a tie, the king breaks it."[15] He depicts the British in the terms of Muslim neoplatonism, as being ruled by a philosopher-king, who took advice from the great philosophers of the realm. A Platonic emphasis on innate knowledge and reasoning as a potential basis for society had fascinated many Muslim philosophers working in the Greek tradition, as an alternative to a literalist dependence on the detailed, almost Talmudic code of revealed Islamic law. The influence of Plato's *Republic* on eighteenth-century Muslim thinkers was third-hand, since the text of the Arabic translation was lost in the medieval period and only a summary survived. Some of its premises, however, had been incorporated strongly into Greco-Islamic thought, and I would argue that this intellectual tradition provided Shushtari with the framework whereby he could understand the rise of constitutional monarchy.

Although Abu Talib also saw the British system as a union of the monarchical, aristocratic, and democratic forms of government, and approved of the mixture, he neglects to give any such detailed picture of how MPs were elected, and he stresses the king's power to approve laws, to command the army, to pardon criminals and to dismiss cabinets. He does admit that, in appointing judges for life, the king gives up control over the judiciary. He depicts Parliament's powers as primarily over taxes and public contractors and agents, and as a check on the power of cabinet ministers.[16]

Aqa Ahmad, from a clerical background, puts a unique twist on his description of the British form of government. He says that, in response to the wars of succession, the philosophers and the learned made the affairs of state dependent on the consent of three entities, the king, the ministers, and the members of Parliament.   He describes Parliament, however, as an assemblage of nobles (*umara'*) who are well-wishers of the king and his subjects, and so he appears to have known only of the House of Lords and not of Commons. He believes that the king is chosen by the nobles, and that he must be learned, a sort of *mujtahid* or accomplished jurist.[17]   Here George III is not the philosopher-king of Muslim Neoplatonism as described in its medieval literature, but is rather a precursor of Khomeini, an expert in Christian legal reasoning elevated to rulership because of his learning. In Shi`ite Islam of the eighteenth century, the victorious Usuli school asserted that all laypersons must emulate and obey the most learned of the Muslim jurists, or mujtahids. The laity was to choose the most learned on their own, so that in Iran and Iraq two or three top mujtahids became "exemplars" (*marja`-i taqlid*) for very large numbers of believers. As we have seen, theoretically, Usulism admitted of the possibility that there might be a single most learned jurist at the top of the hierarchy, but the informal and fluid nature of clerical charisma in fact militated against the emergence of a single Shi`ite "pope."  In this period monarchy was accepted as natural to Islam, and no one advocated that the Shi`ite mujtahid actually rule. But Aqa Ahmad appears to have seen in the British system a sort of rationalization and fulfillment of Usuli ideals. Aqa Ahmad, although he played down the democratic elements in British government, did see the kings and ministers as constrained by Parliament, which he defines as the "place of consultation" (*mahall-i mashvirat*). But he depicts the MPs as pawns in the hand of the prime minister, who could use them to thwart royal policies with which he disagreed.[18]   Of the three authors, Bihbahani stresses British juridical egalitarianism least, and has a tendency to see the aristocracy and the cabinet as the predominant forces in society.

Muslim rulers from the Ottomans in Istanbul to Muhammad `Ali in Cairo took a dim view of the French revolution and its principles, and it would have been strange if the Indian nawabs were less sensitive to the implicit critique of their basis for authority carried in parliamentary democracy. Yet our authors appear to have felt they could depict the British system quite openly, even though Shushtari continued to reside off and on in Hyderabad and Abu Talib could well have returned to Lucknow. Perhaps that this parliamentary system operated in a foreign, exotic land made it seem less seditious than if the writers had been proposing it for India and Iran.   Aqa Ahmad, living under British protection in Patna, was at greater liberty to say what he pleased, but his clericalist Shi`ite ideology apparently made it difficult for him to grasp some of the egalitarian implications of parliamentary governance. As noted, Abu Talib's stress on the remaining power of the king may have derived in part, not only from circumspection, but also from the elevated social circle in which he moved while in London. Shushtari's account clearly exaggerates British democracy as practiced in the late eighteenth century, and depicts the king as having been reduced to a figurehead and pensioned off. His informants presumably were Whig East India Company officials who strongly believed in the achievements of the Glorious Revolution.

Shushtari sees the Westerners' egalitarian, rationalized governmental system as a product of the same sort of ratiocination that led to their mechanical sophistication. "After organizing the state and laws," he writes, "the philosophers then turned their attention to investigating the reality of things on sea and land."[19] He gives an account of the magnetic compass and of the voyages of Columbus, though he, bizarrely enough, depicts Columbus as an Arabic-speaking native of the Arabian peninsula. (It is true that Columbus brought along an Arabic-speaking interpreter, since he expected to be conversing with Asian Muslim potentates). Shushtari is fascinated by clocks, orreries, telescopes, and other technical achievements of the Europeans. He sees that the mechanization of life had far-reaching effects, and depicts all Europeans as subject to a peculiar work-time discipline, such that they carry clocks about on their persons and "organize all their activities, writing, riding, eating, sleeping - and all time - by means of clocks."[20] Likewise, they show inventiveness in weaponry and rationally order their military, unlike Asian commanders whose armies often resembled unorganized crowds. "As long," he writes, as the British "maintain their formations, which they call a `line,' they are like an unmovable volcano spewing artillery and rifle fire like unrelenting hail on the enemy, and they are seldom defeated."[21] He therefore shows an awareness of not just the mechanical inventiveness of the Europeans, but of the synergy between technology and rationalized social organization.

He sees three reasons for this Western excellence in all fields. First, he says, their kings and rulers "strive to see that each person receives an education appropriate to his station." Second, every individual works full-time in his own specialization, and performs no other work. "They say that life is short, and if one learns to excel in one thing during one's seventy years, that is enough." Third, new ideas are protected by patent. If even artisans and craftsmen invent something, the patent is purchased by the crown and its inventors teach it to others. No invention, he says, may be manufactured until its inventor is protected by a patent. He also thinks that the gulf which existed in Iran, between theoretical or philosophical knowledge, and practical mechanics, had been bridged in the West, so that even humble blacksmiths knew how to use levers and pulleys.[22] Aqa Ahmad agrees that "The great philosophers of the West are exceedingly abundant, to the extent that even the character of the common people is philosophical and inclined to investigate mathematics and nature."[23]

Abu Talib sees the English as highly individualistic, and speculates that the climate and soil are responsible not only for a vast variety of crops grown, but also for "such a difference in the tempers and manners of its inhabitants, that no two of them appear to think or act alike."[24] He appreciates the mechanical inventiveness of the West, including the printing press, whereby any book "may be circulated among the people in a very short time; and by it, the works of celebrated authors are handed down to posterity, free from the errors and imperfections of a manuscript."[25] He comments on British shipbuilding technology, on the casting of cannon, the use of the steam engine in manufacturing, and attributed to this mechanization of industry a sharp drop in commodity prices and an improvement in the lot of the common people. He thinks the British more persevering in their determination to set up machinery for any extensive works than, say, the French.[26]

The achievements of Western science and technology had not only made the Europeans formidable, it had also refigured cosmology. Shushtari discovered from his encounters with the British in Hyderabad and Bombay the Copernican model of the solar system. Most Muslims had remained oblivious to the Copernican revolution, and continued to adhere to Ptolemaic astronomy into the nineteenth century. Moreover, as in sixteenth-century Europe, the Ptolemaic system had been adopted into theology and the pious saw heliocentrism as an affront to Islamic cosmology. Discussing the issue was as fraught with dangers as was the delineation of constitutional monarchy in politics. He announces that he had been convinced by the Copernican view, and he argues for the roundness of the earth, as well. He points out that the traditional Muslim view of the cosmos as a series of stacked heavens is incompatible with the circular image of the solar system among Western scientists, and he goes on to discuss Newton and the laws of planetary motion.[27]

Shushtari attempts in two ways to defuse the potentially explosive religious implications of this discussion. First, he points out that earlier Muslim notions about cosmology and astronomy were largely derived from the Greeks. In this way, he seeks to set up a choice between ancient European ideas or modern ones, rather than between Islamic orthodoxy and Western science. Second, he employs a mystical, Sufi discourse about the inadequacy of the intellect to understand God's mysteries. Here, a fundamentalist rejection of eighteenth-century science in favor of medieval theology becomes a sort of hubris inappropriate to a pious believer.[28] The reminder to the audience of the fallibility of human reason had also been a feature of Galileo's writings. Abu Talib was also convinced of the truth of the Copernican theory, especially once he had seen an orrery, or mechanical model of the heliocentric solar system.[29] Aqa Ahmad reported eighteenth-century European cosmology without much comment, interspersing his discussion with numerous pious phrases such as "and God grants success."[30] Aqa Ahmad's status as a leading Shi`ite clergyman may have made it less necessary for him to defend his orthodoxy than it was for a layman such as Shushtari.

Shushtari ends the discussion of European science by saying that the wonders of the modern Europeans are "innumerable," and explains them by pointing out that European civilization was three thousand years old, after all. He remains convinced, however, that even the Western Europeans and the Chinese had not yet succeeded in producing a thousandth of the wonders of ancient Greece, and had not their books been destroyed by the Caliph `Umar in Andalusia and Alexandria, the world would have been much better off.[31]  The story that the Caliph `Umar, the second vicar of the Prophet according to Sunni Islam, was responsible for burning the library at Alexandria, is, of course, quite apocryphal. Here the Shi`ite rationalist manages to blame Sunni know-nothingism for the destruction of the Hellenistic heritage, which by its richness might have made the Muslims - its most vigorous heirs in the early medieval period - great. Modern wonders are offset with a wistful appeal to the myth of a squandered golden age.

One of the major differences between Asian and European societies according to our authors lay in gender relations. Shushtari noted that Europeans in India did not impose veiling or seclusion on their wives, even when these were local Hindu or Muslim women, and he remarked on the prohibition against English men taking their Indian wives back to Britain for fear of tainting the homeland with miscegenation.[32] Abu Talib hugely enjoyed the greater openness of Europe, and was apparently an incorrigible flirt. He explained the lack of seclusion and veiling among British women in four ways. First, the gender-divided household in Muslim lands, with separate sets of servants for husband and wife, he says, would have been too expensive in a country like England, with its high labor costs. Second, the cold weather inclined the husband to live and sleep with his wife. Third, the homegeneity of the population was greater in Britain; in India, Muslims and Hindus secluded their women from each other. Fourth, Europeans expected their wives to take part in the husband's business, which militated against gender segregation.[33]

Abu Talib defends the treatment of women in Muslim lands, and insists that Muslim women have some advantages over Western ones. Indian Muslim men let their women control the family finances, choose the sect of Islam to which the children would belong, and exercise great authority over the servants. Muslim women could separate easily without divorce, and in case of divorce were awarded custody of the daughters - in

contrast to Europe where fathers got custody of all children.[34]   Abu
Talib's construction of gender roles is based, not on equality, but on
control over domestic resources, and he thinks Asian women excercised
greater power in this sphere than did Western women. The system of
gender segregation itself, however, ensured that we heard from no
Muslim women travelers to England in this period, who might have
disagreed with Abu Talib.

It should not be thought that these authors had no criticisms of the
Europeans, though it appears to me that their discussion of positive
aspects of Europe differs radically in nature from their critical comments.
Shushtari, for instance, thought that British dependence on strategic and
technological advances in warfare accounted for their victories, whereas
they "have none of the delight in bravery and courage possessed by other
peoples."[35] In short, they lacked manliness but made up for it artificially.
Abu Talib in particular was quite forthright about devoting a chapter to
their faults. Although he speaks of the "English" as a whole, in fact he
directs his twelve major criticisms at the aristocrats among whom he
moved.   This procedure reinforces the point made earlier, about the
degree to which Shi'ite views of the Europeans were actually views of the
European upper classes. He faults the ethics and morals of the British,
their lack of religious belief, and their inclination to secular philosophy,
which he thought bred dishonesty among the lower classes. He also finds
them wanting in chastity, and exclaims that hardly a street in London
lacked a brothel. They were often selfish, irritable and inconsiderate, he
says, and consumed with acquiring material things. He faults the upper
classes for living extravagantly, keeping more carriages than they needed,
as well as over-furnishing their homes, and says they wasted enormous
amounts of time on eating and dressing.   These habits he contrasts
unfavorably to the ascetic warrior code of Muslim Arabs and Turks.

One of the reasons he thought that the English aristocracy badly erred
in allowing irreligion to spread among commoners was that it led to their
coveting the property of the rich and made them rebellious. He thought
the high officials astonishingly complacent toward working-class riots
and strikes, and believed this insouciance to be an effect of a half-century
of British progress and triumphs; he considered this feeling of
invulnerability highly unwise, in view of the French Revolution.[36]

Finally, some of his criticisms bear upon the issue of colonialism.
Although Abu Talib, as a guest of the aristocracy and a member of the
collaborating notable class back in India, does not cavil at the colonial
enterprise in and of itself, even he is hurt by some British attitudes. He
attributes to them a vanity and arrogance about their attainments in
science and their knowledge of foreign languages. In particular, he thinks
that the British official class knew Asian languages like Persian much less

well than they believed themselves to. One hears at this point echoes of professional disappointment, since Abu Talib had originally thought he would set up an institute for teaching Persian to colonial officials in London, but had for most of his stay there found no encouragement. Finally, he decries their "contempt for the customs of other nations."[37] A slightly discordant note, then, creeps into the generally flattering estimate Abu Talib made of the British when the question of colonial hegemony arises. On another issue, that of the law courts, he displays his pique at colonial abuse. He praises the judicial system in Britain, insofar as it operated in that country, but he excoriates the British courts in India, which he thought laid local Indians open to abuse at the hands of expatriate carpetbaggers.[38] Even this early in its career, the collaborating Asian elite felt some discomfort at the manner in which European arrogance manifested itself, and the way in which European institutions were thoughtlessly grafted onto local ones. Needless to say, for the members of this class, this discomfort was not nearly a sufficient cause for abandoning the collaboration.

It strikes me that whereas these authors focus on systemic features when they discuss European society positively, their criticisms tend rather to concentrate on flaws in what might be called national (or really, I would argue, class) character. The European notables, despite their philosophical and technological prowess, are puffed up with pride or overly concerned with material accumulation or insufficiently courageous or rather too convinced of their mastery of foreign languages. The closest thing to a systemic critique offered appears to be Abu Talib's comments on how British justice went awry when the procedures of London were transplanted in Bengal. There, it is the way the system works that has proven objectionable, rather than simply character flaws in colonial judges. Different conceptions of class also color Abu Talib's cavils. His criticism of opulence of British aristocratic life comes across as a protest against the embourgeoisement of the aristocracy in England. The contrasting image he had in his mind was the steppe or desert warriors of the Arabs or Turks, who in lore at least were depicted as having ascetic values. His friends, the lords and ladies of London, were acting more as he would expect a Muslim long-distance merchant to behave, than as a feudal warlord of Iran or India. Shushtari's depiction of the British officers as lacking in martial spirit echoes this perception that the ruling classes in the Indo-Iranian world held vastly different values than did those in Britain. It is clear that whereas these authors were much impressed by the governmental and technological advances of the Europeans, they had difficulty admiring an aristocracy they felt lacked spartan valor.

As hinted in the introduction, an important context for the new writing about the Europeans lies in the greater impact of printing in the Persian-speaking world from around 1800. The British example in Calcutta and Bombay appears to have proved especially important. Thus, two of the works here discussed were lithographed in the early nineteenth century. The non-adoption of printing by Persian-speaking peoples for three and a half centuries after this technology became widespread in Western Europe reflected, as in Russia, not ignorance of technique, but the hostility of absolutist regimes, low rates of literacy and the smallness of the indigenous middle classes. The old ways had definite drawbacks. Manuscripts were expensive, and hand copying was an inefficient and frequently inaccurate means of transmitting maps and diagrams, which helps to explain the generally low levels of knowledge about world geography and about technology among the Persian-speaking notable class.[39] The new, late-eighteenth-century accounts treating the Europeans could hope for a much wider audience, because of lithography, and could include, for instance, diagrams of the solar system as envisaged by Copernicus and Newton, at a time when most Muslim thinkers remained wedded to Ptolemaic ideas. Printing formed an incentive, a technique, and a medium for the new depictions of Europe, just as it had grown up earlier in Europe in tandem with the travelogues of the age of exploration.

These Shi'ite authors depict the British as philosophers of the highest order, and as having found a way of bridging the gap between elite ratiocination and practical wisdom. They had by giving thought banished the turmoil of wars of succession, had combined the three forms of government delineated in Aristotle's *Politics* into a happy medley, had created stability and order while enlarging the scope of public consultation. Not only did they possess Newtons but their common artisans understood basic physics and mechanical principles, made inventions, and had them patented. This largely positive view of the Europeans comes as a surprise to anyone who came of age during twentieth-century decolonization, when anti-imperial discourse was common in Africa and Asia. But it must be remembered that two of these authors had little means to check independently what their sources told them, and that they therefore frequently were reporting, in their own terms, what they understood as the British self-image. Moreover, the collaborating notables who for the most part wrote about the West had an interest in flattering their potential patrons or allies. A notable class produced these texts at a particular historical moment, when it was without strong national loyalties. They thus often favored the British. Occidentalism was not the mirror image of Orientalism, but rather an extension of the Western power to shape images. Westerners often fashioned a representation of the Orient, which they then substituted for the actual Orient, so that they created a representation of themselves over against the Orient. What is interesting here is that by reporting it to Orientals whom they were wooing as clients, they managed to have their portrayal written up in Persian and widely disseminated. In a colonial version of Gramscian hegemony, by the late eighteenth century, the might of coercive Western institutions such as the trading companies and the colonial army extended right into Asia, allowing Westerners to begin asserting a subtle cultural dominance even there, even in works in Asian languages. I do not wish to deny independent agency and perception to the writers here discussed. It does seem clear to me, however, that their depictions of the West in very large part reflect the Western self-understanding, that the Indo-Persian writers at that point possessed little in the way of an institutional base for the elaboration of an independent, critical examination of the occident. What, then, of the occasional criticisms found in these books? First of all, the genre of "mirrors for princes," with which these works sometimes have affinities, required such blame and praise.[40] Still, I perceive a substantive rather than merely formal pattern in the criticisms. It seems to me that the reproaches are most vehement where the British seemed to be denying that they required the collaborating notables. Abu Talib was miffed at not being immediately acclaimed in London as a greatly needed Persian teacher, and he cavilled at the British judgeships in Calcutta as inappropriate. Posts as Persian teachers and in the judiciary had been the monopoly of the Muslim notable class in the pre-colonial era. At the dawn of modern colonialism, many of the notables did not mind being adopted by a new suzerain, especially one that struck them as powerful and clever. They did want to be assured that the new authorities would want their services, and not sweep them and their existing perquisites away.

We have little idea of how these texts were read by their Persian-speaking audience. We must not assume they were read in a straightforward manner, since the accounts lacked a great deal of essential context, and must have presented many puzzles, not to mention indecipherable names, to their audience. Toward the end of Calvino's *Invisible Cities*, Kublai Khan inquires from Marco Polo, "When you return to the West, will you repeat to your people the same tales you tell me?" The intrepid traveller replies, "I speak and speak . . . but the listener retains only the words he is expecting. The description of the world to which you lend a benevolent ear is one thing; the description that will go the rounds of the groups of stevedores and gondoliers on the street outside my house the day of my return is another." From the eighteenth century to the present, human beings in the various world cultures have continued to rediscover one another in each generation, often forgetting what their forebears had earlier known. Each culture, and each generation, perhaps, retained only the words they were expecting.

8

Women and the Making of Shi`ism

Was there anything distinctive about the Shi`ite beliefs and practices of women of varying social classes, as opposed to those of males? Were women able to influence the terms of discourse or ritual life? Shi`ism was, after all, a scriptural, patriarchal religion, with a powerful corps of clergy who claimed a monopoly on spiritual authority. Farah Azari, among others, has argued that Iranian Shi`ism serves as a mechanism for the suppression of female sexuality.[1] From a Reichian perspective often women, as the subordinate gender, could easily be supposed to have contributed little of importance to Shi`ite devotions, and to have been dependent on the tutelage of their men for religious instruction. For the majority who were illiterate, would it not have been impossible for them to understand the abstract Arabic philosophical terminology which male believers embedded in their Urdu god-talk? On the other hand, in contemporary Iran, Shi`ite feminists such as Zahra Rahnavard have managed to inscribe their own concerns on Khomeinist discourse, and this should make us suspicious of a patriarchal essentialism when studying historical Muslim communities.[2] There was no question of any sort of feminism in nineteenth-century Lucknow, of course. But it is reasonable to ask whether Shi`ite women there succeeded in elaborating a religious discursive practice that had feminine elements.

If one were looking for a social or political phenomenon that evoked the strongest images for contemporary readers of patriarchal authority and repression of women, surely Shi`ite Islam would present itself as a primary candidate. The image is so powerful, in fact, that it almost precludes the posing of questions about the ways in which women might be empowered by Shi`ite Islam, or the ways in which they themselves have helped shape this religion. I do not wish to challenge the idea that the Shi`ite Islam of the ayatollahs is patriarchal, but simply to ask what sorts of cultural agency women can attain under Shi`ite rule. I want, especially, to ask about the devotional lives of pre-modern Shi`ite women. On this stage, of the religion said to oppress them, any feminine agency will surely stand out all the more starkly and ironically. The discovery that Shi`ite women might have had some forms of empowerment even within their patriarchal religion would not, of course, in any way deny their oppression, any more than James Scott's work on the subtle protests of peasants denies that they are exploited and relatively powerless.[3]

Although the study of Middle Eastern and South Asian women has become a larger and more sophisticated field in the last decade, most work has focused on contemporary women, with relatively little writing on medieval and early modern women. It might help us, however, to get some distance from our subject if we look at Shi`ite women living under a Shi`ite state, not in contemporary Iran, but in the past.[4]

Awadh is a promising venue for such a study, since a number of relevant documents about women there survive. As I said above, I want here to offer a thematic focus, on the contribution of these women to the rich religious life of Awadh in the nineteenth century. This theme will best be developed by looking at the different practices of various classes of women. First, we have *responsa* or legal rulings and other material from the Shi`ite ulama or clergy of Awadh, which often deal with women, gender, and sexuality, and which give an idealist view of women in Shi`ite society. Second, there are the "begams," the wives and mothers of the nawabs and then shahs of Awadh, who often played important political roles. Some of these involved themselves, as well, in anti-colonial struggles, and they show up in the chronicles and even in the British consular reports as "warrior-queens." Third, we are fortunate in having an account of Shi`ite life in Lucknow by a British woman who resided there during the decade of the 1820s, Mrs. Meer Hassan Ali, which has quite a lot to say about women of the middling sort. Finally, some material is available on the lives of Shi`ite courtesans in nineteenth-century Awadh, including an early Urdu novel, *Umrao Jan Ada*. Several disparate images of Shi`ite women in Awadh emerge from these sources, which depict the ideal position of Shi`ite women in law, as envisaged by the male hierocracy, the "warrior-queens," or begams, the middling sort, and, finally, the courtesans.

Women in the View of Awadh's Shi`ite Ulama

Rulings directly related to women in the legal writings of the Awadh Shi`ite ulama generally took up issues related to the authority in various social spheres of males over women. In a few instances, the clergy upheld the right of Shi`ite women to make their own choices, especially in regard to marriage and property. Most of their rulings, however, reinforced male authority, requiring veiling, upholding patriarchal control, allowing wife-killing in instances of infidelity, and delineating various sorts of unequal male-female relationships, as with temporary marriage and slavery.

The ulama had fewer means of socialization and social control of women than they did of men. For instance, they could use sermons at communal Friday prayers to teach the community the values they supported, and could use the threat of ostracism from this weekly gathering to discipline those they thought were falling into heresy. But not only were women not required to perform the Friday prayers communally, they were the only group of believers absolutely forbidden from doing so. (Slaves, the blind, the old and infirm, and other marginal groups were also excused, but these could attend if they so desired.)[5]

The ulama recognized the right of women to dispose of their own property. When asked if a wife could give her trousseau and dowry, which is her own property, to someone without his permission, Lucknow's Chief Mujtahid Sayyid Muhammad Nasirabadi replied that an owner may dispose of her property as she pleased. He added a caution that some sin may occur if she disobeys her husband, but God knows best. Here two values of the ulama, belief in the sanctity of private property, and belief in patriarchal authority, clashed. Sayyid Muhammad's fatwa comes down, in the end, on the side of property, since the right to dispose of it is unequivocal, whereas there is only a possibility of sin should a woman do so in a manner of which her husband disapproves. Elsewhere he forbade a husband to repossess something given away by his wife.[6] Moreover, should a man give a woman a present before either a temporary or permanent marriage, it became her property and could not be counted by him as part of the dowry.[7] As will be seen below, among the nobility and the propertied classes this attitude of Shi`ite law to the autonomy of women's property could become extremely important in giving women a base for influencing wider society.

The jurists also recognized a certain freedom of choice for a mature young woman in deciding on her marriage partner, though she was more free to differ with her mother on this issue than with her father. In one instance, when a small girl was sick, her mother vowed that if she recovered, she would marry her to a Sayyid. Then, when she grew up, she wanted to marry someone other than a Sayyid, and Lucknow's chief Shi`ite jurisprudent (*mujtahid*) agreed that "an upright young woman can choose for herself whom she wants to marry."[8] In case of a conflict with the mother, then, the girl's choice takes precedent. The importance of the young woman's freedom to choose her mate, however, came into conflict at times with patriarchal authority. If a mature virgin who has come of age wants to marry someone, but her father wants to marry her off elsewhere, one Lucknow Shi'ite asked, what would the jurisprudent rule? The chief mujtahid was apparently put in a quandary by the conflict of principles, and merely replied that "The answer is not free of doubt."[9]

Most issues in the patriarchal shape of society presented themselves as much less problematic to the ulama. A believer wanted to know whether it was a major sin to appear without a veil in front of persons other than intimates, and what the punishment for this would be. The clergyman replied that to go without a veil in front of persons other than intimates is forbidden, and how great the sin and how it would be punished depended on the Islamic judge and the specific situation.[10] Some women in Awadh apparently attempted to widen their networks of male contacts beyond close relatives by "adopting" unrelated men as brothers, an Indian custom known as *rakhi*. A suspicious husband appears to have inquired about the practice, asking if a woman could adopt a man as her brother or father and then appear before him. Could, he wanted to know, her husband prevent her from doing so? After divorce could she marry this "brother?" The clergy found no support for *rakhi* in their Arabic law-books, ruling that a non-intimate is a non-intimate, and she may not appear before him unveiled. Her husband may prevent her from doing so, and any such "relative" may be married.[11]

The ulama, in other situations as well, steadfastly upheld patriarchal values. A prince put a hypothetical case to the chief mujtahid. Say a father made a request of his son which might injure the honor of the household, but which was legally permissible. Say the mother opposed this request. Could the son obey his mother and disobey his father? The mujtahid replied that he may not obey his mother in preference to his father. But if the request might cause worldly damage to the son or someone else, he was permitted to refuse it. This way of stating matters took the mother out of the picture, making the issue the son, the father, and the law. At another point the mujtahid admitted that although a child owes obedience to both parents, since a wife must obey her husband, obedience to the father took precedence.[12]

Men had many prerogatives of unilateral decision-making, according to the clergy. A man could divorce his wife at will, and it was not even necessary that she be present at the court hearing that granted the divorce. Lucknow's chief mujtahid also upheld the vigilante right of a husband to kill his wife and her lover if he caught them in the act of adultery.[13] If a husband had many rights over his wife, he had even more over a temporary wife. The Shi'ite ulama felt that temporary marriage could serve as a form of worship and charity. Chief Mujtahid Sayyid Muhammad Nasirabadi affirmed that if one contracted a temporary marriage with the right intentions, it could be an act of worship, and should a man make a second contract with the same woman in order to

help her out materially, this good deed would be rewarded.[14]   A
questioner asked Lucknow's mujtahids in the 1830s concerning a woman
who hears of the excellence and rewards of temporary marriage, who is
permanently married.   May she arrange a divorce and remarry her
husband as a temporary wife?   The ulama replied that it was perfectly
permissible to do so.   When asked if a special formula existed that would
allow a woman to cancel the temporary marriage contract before the end
of the specified period, the chief mujtahid virtually ignored the female
subject of the question.   He replied that a man may cancel the contract
whenever he pleases, and that no special formula existed.[15] The way in
which the clergy raised the status of temporary marriage to an act of
religious piety and charity, and even allowed a permanent wife to opt for
temporary status, clearly reinforced the dependency of women on men.

Women who had a living father or guardian always had to obtain
approval to contract a temporary marriage, whether they were virgins or
not.   For them to contract a temporary marriage without such approval
was disapproved, though not penalized.   Chief Mujtahid Sayyid
Muhammad Nasirababdi said women who were of age and without any
guardian could contract either temporary or ordinary marriage without
any restriction.[16] A contract of temporary marriage for a virgin, of course,
ruined her chances for a good match and virtually doomed her to a series
of temporary marriages, if not to becoming a courtesan.   Sayyid
Muhammad's brother Sayyid Husayn had a kinder heart toward such
young women, and said he disapproved of the contraction of a temporary
marriage with a virgin for only one or two months.[17]

In the hierarchy of male and female, the patriarchal superiority of men
worked only within the free Muslim community.   A Muslim man could
not enslave a Muslim woman, for instance.   Nor could a free woman be
married to a male slave without her permission.[18] On the other hand, a
slave owner could marry his female slave against her will, and could even
simply "get close" to her without the formality of a marriage.[19]

The combination of female status and of the status of property in a
slave-girl created some legal anomalies.   A believer put a case, probably
based on reality, to the jurisprudent: If Zayd's male slave commits
adultery with `Amr's female slave, and a child is born, to whom does it
belong?   The jurisprudent replied that it belongs to `Amr, that is, to the
slave-girl's master.[20] This is a sort of maternal custody, and is unlike the
Shi`ite law governing custody among free believers, which gives custody
to the man.   It seems likely that this maternal custody law for slaves was
modeled on issues in livestock property, where a man would own the
calves to which his cattle gave birth.   Note that if a Sayyid forces himself
on his female slave, and a baby is born, it belongs to the Sayyid.[21] The
free man's child is his own, but the slave's child with a slave belongs to

the mother's master. Surely the owning of female slaves, and the arbitrariness with which male masters could treat them in Shi`ite law, contributed to a diminution of women's status in general.

As will be seen below, however, this brief survey of some rulings pertaining to women idealizes the actual situation a good deal. Except in the area of property, and perhaps somewhat in marital choice, the ulama favored strict patriarchal values. Wives and children were to obey their patriarch implicitly. Temporary marriage, which put the woman in an even more dependent situation, was encouraged by the clergy and even considered a form of worship and charity. Men also kept female slaves, reinforcing their image of the female as compliant. Let us turn now, however, to another set of images, drawn from chronicles and travel accounts, which give a bit different impression.

Warrior-Queens

The begams were in a position to influence Shi`ite devotion in Awadh because of their vast wealth and their visible political roles.  These women were often literate, and knew a great deal about Shi`ite law and ritual. They also had the leisure to pursue those devotions In a majority-Hindu region where Sunnism predominated even among the thirteen percent of the population that adhered to Islam, the Shi`ite nobility, both male and female, appears to have embraced an ostentatious display of their Shi`ism, which had the effect of accentuating their elite status. The begams' ability to leave religious endowments and bequests of large property, and their influence on the public commemoration of Shi`ite holy days, lent them an important religious influence in the kingdom.

The extent of the property and control over resources that some begams exercised can hardly be exaggerated. Bahu Begam, from an Iranian family close to the Mughal court, employed her own private fortune to help her husband, the Nawab Shuja' al-Dawla, pay off his war debt after the British defeated him in 1764. In return, he decided to give into her hands all the cash offerings and surplus treasury receipts he received thenceforward. She accumulated a fortune estimated at £2 million, which gave her the ability to play power broker. She and another Begam were involved in a revolt against increasing British rapaciousness in Banaras and southern Awash in the early 1780s, and although it was defeated she and her co-conspirator could not be touched, though they did lose control of some property.[22] Bahu Begam left much of the fortune that remained to her in her old age to the British East India Company, but stipulated that Rs. 90,000 be granted to Shi`ite clergy at the holy city of Karbala in Iraq, and she named the specific clergymen among whom it should be divided.[23] These were leaders of the Usuli school, and, as we saw above, such large gifts helped reinforce their position of leadership at Karbala, making substantial patronage available to them.

The male nawabs and kings themselves donated even vaster sums, of course, but the religious gifts from Awadh's noblewomen may have made a difference to some clerical careers. An unexpected, substantial bequest from Vilayati Begam, widow of the Shi`ite nawab of Farrukhabad near Awadh, helped make a rich man of Sayyid Muhammad Nasirabadi, the chief mujtahid or Shi`ite jurisprudent in Awadh's capital of Lucknow from 1820 to 1867.[24] The begams of the royal family ran household establishments that included positions for Shi`ite clergy as chaplains, another manner in which noblewomen could have an influence on the clergy and on religious culture.[25] Some princesses also maintained imambarahs, buildings on the grounds of their residences especially devoted to commemorating the lives of the Imams, especially the martyrdom of Imam Husayn.[26]

Some begams stand out for the influence they exerted over religious practices. In particular, Badshah Begam, a wife of Ghazi al-Din Haydar Shah (r. 1814-1827) and daughter of the royal astronomer, introduced many new usages into Awadh Shi`ism. In Awadh custom, on the sixth day after the birth of a child, both mother and child took a bath. On this day the family threw a party, inviting relatives and friends to a rich repast, and the mother and child were dressed in their best clothes. The celebration was called Chhati, "the sixth." Badshah Begam began celebrating the Chhati of the Twelfth Imam, Muhammad al-Mahdi, six days after the anniversary of his birth, spending great sums of money on meticulously planned festivities every year in the month of Sha`-ban.[27]

Badshah Begam also brought eleven pretty Sayyid girls to the palace and kept them there as symbolic brides of all the Imams save `Ali, paying their families handsomely for their custody. Each bore the name of one of the historical wives of the Imams, and were called achhuti, Hindi for something too pure to be touched. Fatima was considered too holy a personage to be personified in this manner, so only eleven of the imams' wives were represented. They had female attendants, and Badshah Begam attempted to arrange for one of their faces to be the first thing she saw each morning. She tried to keep the achhutis from marrying, though one got out of this bind by saying she had a dream in which the imam divorced her.

On the birthday of each of the Imams, Badshah Begam richly decorated and illumined a special room at the palace in his honor. She gave expensive clothing and jewelry to the achhuti who was the wife of that imam. Later, she distributed the furnishings of the room to the maid-servants in charity. She also built an imitation tomb for each of the imams, with a small mosque attached, on the palace grounds. These were

known as the *Rawzih-'i davazdah imam*, the graveyard of the twelve
Imams. The Begam spent much of every day in prayer and participated in
the mourning ceremonies at the death anniversaries of each of the Imams.
Badshah Begam believed that, occasionally, she was possessed by the
king of the jinn. At such times she dressed up in finery and sat on her
throne, listening as female musicians played for her, and moving her head
in a trance. "While in such a mood, she would give answers to the queries
about the past and the future made by those who were present there." [28]

In 1827, when her son (some say adopted son) Nasir al-Din Haydar
became shah of Awadh, Badshah Begam arranged for a proclamation that
mourning rites for the Imam Husayn would continue until the fortieth day
(*chihilum*) after his death, that is, the 20th of Safar. Only then would the
replicas of the Imam's tomb that Awadh Shi`ites annually set up in homes
or paraded in the streets be buried or thrown into the river. Previously,
the cenotaphs had been buried on the anniversary of Imam Husayn's death
itself, the 10th of Muharram or `Ashura'. No marriages or amusement
were allowed during this extended mourning period. Hindu and Sunni
pressure led the British resident to intervene against this imposition of
prolonged sobriety, and the shah finally revoked his decree requiring it,
but pledged to observe the forty day mourning period in his own royal
household. [29]

The feminine religious imagination demonstrated by Badshah Begam
greatly influenced her son, Nasir al-Din Haydar Shah (r. 1827-1837). On
his accession he continued the custom of keeping achhutis as symbolic
wives of the Imams, and even added some further innovations.
Interestingly enough, it seemed necessary for him to adopt a female
gender model in order to continue the process of inventing new rituals in
imitation of his mother. `Abd al-Ahad wrote,

On the day of the birth of each of the Imams he would behave like a
woman in childbed and pretend that he was suffering from the pains of
childbirth. A doll studded with jewels was kept lying in the King's lap to
represent the false child. The selected attendants prepared dishes used by
women in childbed and served them to the king. [30]

Other men followed the king in acting out female roles so as to make
present sacred time, especially those from families where Shi`ite women
began claiming to be achhutis. These men "had given up manly habits,
talked and behaved like women and had adopted female costumes." [31]
The elaboration of new rituals by Badshah Begam had involved the
application of ordinary female life-cycle rituals in India to the
commemoration of the lives and deaths of the twelve Shi`ite Imams.
Nasir al-Din Haydar and many other Awadh men, in order to appropriate

this discourse of charismatic religious innovation, found it necessary also to resort to transvestitism and other adoptions of a female gender role.

Aristocratic women in the harem constituted throughout Awadh history one pole of potential power, through their influence on male rulers and nobles. Women's greater knowledge of the full range of religious discourse, both Hindu and Shi`ite, allowed them sometimes to manipulate superstitious males. In September of 1850, Vajid `Ali Shah, the newly installed ruler of the kingdom, fell in love with one of his mother's waiting-maids. His mother, however, was attached to the girl, and when her son demanded her, the old begam proved reluctant to let her go. The shah's mother found a pretext in a birthmark on the nape of the girl's neck, which the Begam interpreted as a sampan or snake-mark, and she gravely informed her royal son that it was a sign of very bad luck. The Begam kept possession of her waiting-maid by this device, but it had further, unforeseen, repercussions. Vajid `Ali Shah began to worry that his huge harem, filled with temporary wives and concubines, might contain other bearers of bad luck. He had his eunuchs examine them all, and the latter found eight who appeared to be marked with the sampan. The shah called his chief mujtahid, Sayyid Muhammad Nasirabadi, and had him preside over the divorce of all eight. Someone with the king's ear, however, then suggested that Brahmins knew more about snake-marks than did Shi`ite clergymen on the whole, and that a solution to the problem less drastic than divorce might be found. The Brahmins, when called, concluded that the sampans could be safely burned off, and two of the wives agreed to undergo the procedure so as to remain in the monarch's harem.[32]

This rich little anecdote illustrates the manner in which religious authority remained profoundly contested even at the most triumphalist period of Shi`ite ascendancy. In focusing on the manner in which the Brahmins were able to overturn a decision of the Shi`ite chief mujtahid, however, we would be forgetting that the initiator of the crisis was the shah's mother. She first hit upon the coding of a birthmark as an ill-fated snake-mark, manipulating conventions of Hindu folk culture in order to keep a favorite servant in her own household and away from the clutches of her much-married son. Vajid `Ali Shah could have, after all, dismissed this objection as nonsense, and insisted that his mother turn over the waiting-maid. Rather, the Begam was able to lend her construction of the supernatural significance of the birthmark such authority that it threw the entire harem into turmoil, led to a symbolic contest between mujtahid and Brahmin, and finally to several divorces and brandings of royal wives. Ironically, an attempt at feminine solidarity in the Begam's mansion rebounded with unpleasant consequences for the palace harem. Women could initiate religious and supernatural discourse with a powerful effect on men, but could not control the manner in which men then appropriated it to their purposes.

The way in which men feared the power of the harem is further illustrated in the story of Mubarak Mahall's attempt to learn the Shi`ite principles of jurisprudence. This queen, one of Vajid `Ali Shah's more important wives, was literate and wished to pursue seminary-type study, through tutorials, in Shi`ite law. She had her physician hire Mawlavi `Ali Hasan Bilgrami, with whom she pursued these studies. Her co-wife, Sultan-`Aliya Begam, also began taking lessons from him from behind a veil. Bilgrami grew wealthy, and, one chronicler sniffed, "superficially eminent" by virtue of the gifts and honors these queens bestowed on him. He also apparently employed his warm relations with several noblewomen in the harem to begin exercising political influence, not only among the king's wives, but indirectly on Vajid `Ali Shah himself. The Shah's minister, Mumtaz al-Dawla, grew to profoundly resent Bilgrami's increasing influence, gained by the instrumentality of his access to the harem. He had to proceed against this new rival cautiously, however. He intrigued with the shah and with the British Resident, and on 1 June 1851 at the time of afternoon prayers, Bilgrami was banished and walked out of town in public view with an escort of royal troops, his property confiscated. Apparently the shah's men isolated him when he was in public, away from the palace, so that the queens could not intervene. The case, according to the chronicler, went all the way to Governor-General Dalhousie, who disapproved of his Resident's having been involved in the mulcting of a local notable, and ordered that the Resident return the mawlavi's goods as far as possible. Mubarak Mahall also managed to compensate him for some of his losses, and the tutor to queens retired to the hill-station of Simla in British India. [33]

The literacy and legitimate quest for religious knowledge of the shah's wives in this instance enmeshed them in a set of male intrigues, as the male chronicler tells the story. Shi`ite clergy in Awadh had a great deal of influence on politics, and were often very close to secular rulers. The shah's first minister would have favorite clergymen, who could act through the minister to influence the shah on religious and legal policy. By inserting themselves into the midst of this political network linking secular nobles and the Shi`ite clergy, the queens offered Bilgrami a new avenue to court influence. The anecdote illustrates that learning Shi`ite law was by virtue of the position of the hierocracy in Awadh an intrinsically political act, and one available to upper-class women as well as to male nobles and notables. The teller of the tale may have underestimated the positive contribution made to policy by the queens, who may, after all, have often simply buttressed the authority of their views by taking Bilgrami's name in order to bestow on them a mujtahid's cache. (In this canny reading of the story, removing Bilgrami was an attempt to deny the begams the ability to increase the authority of their ideas by taking the name of a male religious leader, rather than simply to banish a pernicious male influence on the harem and thence the king.) Even our chronicler admits, however, that Mumtaz al-Dawla was for long stymied in his desire to remove Bilgrami and the rising harem influence over the shah. It is clear that only by achieving a unanimity among the male power elite in Lucknow, the shah, his ministers, and the British Resident, was he able to act against the queens' favorite. Moreover, he was able to do so only in the public, male, sphere, outside the spatial reach of the queens' own authority and power. Royal gender segregation sometimes dictated the geography of gender politics.

Women, then, mattered religiously. The embededness of the feminine in the aristocratic ritual inventiveness of the 1820s and 1830s attests, not only to the religious genius of Badshah Begam as an individual, but to that of Shi`ite women in general. The endowment of religious offices and edifices by the noblewomen may not have been much different in form and effect than those endowments offered by men. But these ladies' contribution to ritual change was more gender-specific. Badshah Begam's championing of a forty-day mourning period for commemorating the Imam Husayn's martyrdom may have reflected the greater leisure available to aristocratic feminine networks for concentration on ritual activities and meetings. Certainly, the manner in which she melded elements of the local Indian female and family life-cycle rites with her celebration of events related to the lives of the Imams showed a specifically feminine imagination at work. Women may also have been more willing to innovate in the area of ritual than men, because they were often illiterate or in any case not bound by a seminary-type reading of key Shi`ite texts. Some Shi`ite men, who for one reason or another had also escaped the influence of the Shi`ite clergy, also took an interest in the devotions introduced by women like Badshah Begam. Just as male poets attempted to appropriate female discourse in the *rekhti* style of Urdu poetry, cast in a feminine voice, so male religious virtuosi attempted to imitate Badshah Begam's religious style by dressing in female clothing and symbolically acting out female life-cycle rituals on the plane of Shi`ite sacred history. The authority of aristocratic feminine constructions of the supernatural is further demonstrated by the stories of Vajid `Ali's mother and the snake-mark, and of Mubarak Mahall's mujtahid.

The Middling Sort of Women and Shi`ite Devotion

The aristocracy, especially the Awadh royal household, would be an inappropriate venue for making generalizations about female devotion, but the wide influence of noblewomen made it necessary at least to discuss them. In looking at a less exalted stratum of the propertied classes we can begin to get a more rounded picture of the religious life of Shi`ite women. This is so, especially because the Shi`ite community of Awadh was disproportionately well off. Very few Shi`ites were peasants, and the vast majority were urban. Though most must have been artisans, a high proportion of Shi`ite men were medium landholders or other rentiers, scribes in the bureaucracy, merchants, and clerics. Our question here centers on how the gender roles ascribed to women from such families affected their religious practice.

Travelers from Iran to Awadh were often struck by the comparative independence Indian Muslim women had from their husbands, and, if true, this independence would have had implications for their ability to worship in their own ways. One Middle Eastern man who traveled in India, including Awadh, early in the nineteenth century, thought gender relations among Indian Muslims very different from those prevailing in Iraq and Iran. Aqa Ahmad Bihbahani, from a prominent Shi`ite clerical family of Isfahan and Karbala, thought Indian Muslim men horribly henpecked. He said the reason that "women in this country are dominant (*musallit*) over men" was that the dowries owed them were so high. Men would agree on paper to pay women dowries of Rs. 50,000 to 100,000, sometimes even accepting sums in the millions of rupees. As long as the couple was married, the wife was unlikely actually to demand payment, but the sum became immediately due upon divorce. Aqa Ahmad thought only a very few good wives were obedient to their husbands, implying that they had no fear of divorce. He also thought men had relatively little intimacy in India with their women, since they resented them as creditors. He condemned the practice he found there of allowing the wife to inherit all the husband's property on his death, which could have the effect of depriving his children, especially those of another wife, of any substantial share in the inheritance. (For the wife to inherit everything also contravenes Shi`ite law.) [34]

In some ways, moreover, Shi`ite law benefited women more than did the Hanafi rite, especially in matters of inheritance. Indeed, concern for the property of daughters seems to have led some households to adopt Shi`ism. When a family produced only daughters in any one line, many Indian Muslims felt that it was much preferable for the Shi`ite law to be applied, which allowed much of the wealth to stay in the immediate family. Mawlavi Sami', an Iranian Shi`ite Sufi resident in India in the late eighteenth and early nineteenth century thought that the willingness of some Sunni families to embrace Shi`ism or at least Shi`ite law derived precisely from the practical benefits they saw for themselves in it, and worried that such a motive for adopting this branch of Islam might produce hypocrisy and blurred borders.[35]

The image of Indian Muslim women as empowered over their husbands in some ways was also reported by the Lucknow notable Abu Talib Isfahani "Landani" (1752-1805) in an essay on Muslim women written during his visit to London in 1800. He noted that Indian Muslim women often controlled the household's purse strings, as well as the upbringing of children. His depiction of the religious influence of women is of particular interest to us here:

It often happens where the wife is a Shya, and the husband a Soony, the children, having been Shyas from their own natural disposition and the instructions of the mother, speak disrespectfully of the chiefs of the Soony Sect in their father's presence, and he, who all his life never bore such language from any person, but was even ready to put the speaker of it to death, has no redress, but patiently submitting to hear it from them, as, on account of their want of understanding, they are excusable; and thus, by frequent repetition, his attachment to his faith is shaken, and, in the course of time, he either entirely forsakes it, or remains but lukewarm in it.[36]

One should, of course, take such depictions of Indian Muslim women with a large grain of salt. Both Aqa Ahmad and Mirza Abu Talib were speaking of a very narrow sort of empowerment, and they did so from a male point of view. Mirza Abu Talib also had an apologetic intent in writing his essay. Still, it would be foolish entirely to disregard these male accounts of some forms of social and religious empowerment among women. They point to a feminine influence over household expenditure, savings, and the training and religious socialization of children, and a feminine claim on inherited property, which, if not universally as powerful as here depicted, are not exactly what one might have expected. South Asian Muslim women had certain sorts of power, and could indeed have an effect on religious and other discursive practice. Aqa Ahmad's impression that Indian Muslim women showed less deference to their husbands in daily life than did their Iranian and Iraqi sisters, if true, seems a valuable insight, and deserves further investigation. It helps save us from a determinist and essentialist use of the idea of "Shi`ite Islam" as a cultural influence.

The relative independence of Awadh Muslim women, the space created for their property by Shi`ite law, and the practice of gender segregation, all contributed to the development of a specifically feminine

Shi`ite religious discourse that was, as in the instance of Badshah Begam
above, more syncretic and innovative than the scripturalism of literate
males. Women, according to the clergy, were often neither orthoprax nor
orthodox. The Iranian Sufi, Mawlavi Sami', said that most Muslim
women (and even men) neglected their ritual daily prayers in the normal
course of affairs, except occasionally on holy days, and wondered, as a
result, whether they could be considered ritually pure. [37]   He thought
"most women" among the Muslims, including upper-caste ladies,
associated with Hindus more than did men and therefore "follow the
Hindu way in most matters."[38]

These Muslim women believed in astrology and worshipped Hindu
idols. The learned observer lamented that it was useless to forbid them
from such beliefs and practices, since they occured in secret, and women
were particularly prone to resort to the Hindu deities when their children
or other loved ones suffered an illness. Here we see the manner in which
the gender segregation advocated by the male ulama worked against their
ability to control laywomen. The Shi`ite women possessed a sphere of
feminine privacy impenetrable to the ulama, where they could believe and
practice in ways the male clergy considered quite heretical. Women also
appear as less communally-minded, associating freely with women of
other religious persuasions, and showing themselves willing to adopt each
others' spiritual practices in a way that males apparently tended to avoid.

On the other hand, it must not be thought that women of the middling
sort were all ignorant or lax in their Islamic observances. Many Shi`ite
women, as we will see below, were quite strict in their observances of
mourning rites for the martyred grandson of the Prophet, Husayn.
Moreover, women were often enough in the society of their male relatives
to appropriate much of their discursive practice for their own ends. Mrs.
Meer Hassan Ali noted that "The ladies' society is by no means insipid or
without interest; they are naturally gifted with good sense and politeness,
fond of conversation, shrewd in their remarks, and their language is both
correct and refined."[39] Eloquent use of Urdu required the knowledge of
many abstract nouns in Arabic and Persian, and Mrs. Ali found the diction
of these women surprisingly high-flown given their low level of
education. She concluded that they learned from conversing with father,
husband and brother, and whenever they heard a word they did not know
they immediately inquired its meaning "which having once ascertained is
never forgotten." Although women lived in a primarily oral world, they
developed the strong memories typical of oral cultures, and made use of
the men around them as walking dictionaries. In the same passage, Mrs.
Ali noticed that even servant women who worked in the female quarters
of Muslim households developed a more sophisticated Urdu idiom than
women of the same class who served Europeans. Sharar, too, observed

that with the emergence in the nineteenth century of Lucknow as a center of Urdu polite letters, "women also started to discuss poetry and language and even in the speech of the uneducated one could find poetically inspired thoughts, similes and metaphors." [40]

The Muslim women whom Mrs. Ali observed were "devout in their prayers and strict in their observance of ordinances." [41] She thought a good Muslim would instruct the females under his "control" in the doctrines of Islam. Awadh's Shi`ite women looked to the life of Fatima, Muhammad's daughter, as their exemplar. Women in their female quarters observed the fast of Ramadan with "zealous rigidness." Some read or had their husbands read religious works to them during the long days of the fast, whereas other illiterate women whiled away their time with embroidery, cooking, or listening to the tales recounted by their female servants. [42] Girls sometimes began fasting at the age of nine or ten, and would celebrate the successful completion of a fast with a special feast to which older women would be invited.[43] Although one often gets the feeling that Mrs. Ali idealizes a bit, or generalizes too much on the basis of her experience with her rather pious and well-educated in-laws, her depiction of the religious observances of the women's quarters rings true. The importance for women of religious narrative during the boring days of the fast seems an accurate detail. It is interesting that two alternatives presented themselves. Either women got access to written religious narratives, by learning to read themselves or by having a male read to them - or they listened to the folk tales of their female working-class servants. The two sorts of religious discourse echoing in the zananah or female half of the house were no doubt very different, and the twin pull that women of the middling sort felt toward both literate male discourse and female oral culture of the working strata helps explain some of the distrust in which the orthodox male clergy held them.

Women celebrated the breaking of the fast, or `Id al-Fitr, with evening gatherings. Women of the Domni caste entertained on such festive occasions in the female quarters. These maintained a reputation for good character, and sang chaste Urdu songs while playing sitar and drum. [44] The Domni dance troupe gesticulated and engaged in mimicry, and "although the free nature of the domnis' performance creates a general atmosphere of laxity, good etiquette on the part of the assembly is preserved throughout." [45] Not only on the holy day, but also at other festive celebrations, such as the Chhati or sixth day after a child's birth, women gathered and kept a vigil all night, as a form of worship. The Domnis' singing and dancing served to keep the group awake, and although they represented these pyjama parties as an act of piety, men like Sharar suspected that a good deal of fun and frolic were involved. At dawn the group went to the mosque, where they made offerings of special sweet dishes they had cooked up. Women of the aristocracy and of the middling sort were the most likely to be kept in some form of seclusion, and one suspects that such festive all-night gatherings, which they represented as acts of worship, served as a means of escape. Again, gender segregation made it difficult for men to challenge the womens' interpretation of these vigils as pious in nature (and therefore necessary). The women also developed a different use of female dance and song, for feminine purposes of worship and entertainment, whereas the men debased these performers into courtesans. Gender segregation made female dancing and singing before a male audience inherently improper, and the Shi`ite practice of temporary marriage made it easy for men to form technically licit unions with such women. Thus, a dancing-girl (*natchni*) and a Domni, despite both being female entertainers, played quite different cultural roles. The Domnis managed to articulate an artistic idiom appropriate to female Muslim piety.

One of the more important religious observances in Awadh was the mourning rituals of Muharram, commemorating the killing of Imam Husayn in A.D. 680. In the Nishapuri Awadh of the early nineteenth century, women of the middling sort could not afford to build their own imambarahs for mourning the Imams, but instead they set aside the nicest room in the zananah or female part of the house for the rituals, to which women invited their acquaintances. Although normally closely related men could enter the zananah without prior notice, during the Shi`ite mourning month of Muharram, the men were wholly excluded except when the female guests had left. "The ladies assemble, in the evening, round the Tazia they have set up in their purdahed privacy - female friends, slaves, and servants, surrounding the mistress of the house in solemn gravity." [46] Mrs. Meer Hassan Ali thought women mourned the martyred Imam Husayn even more seriously than did men, and says they went so far as to put aside their own bereavement. She seems to be saying that, where a woman's husband or child died before or during Muharram, she often considered it "selfish" to publicly grieve, and put her mourning energies rather into commemorating the death of the Imam. Women refused to wear jewelry during the first ten days of Muharram, a very great sacrifice in the Indian context, and they went about unkempt, their hair loose, in drab unadorned clothing, often black or grey in color. Often women did not bathe or wash their clothes during the mourning period. Mrs. Ali's nursemaid refused to drink any liquids all day long during this time. Families kept bamboo replicas of the tombs of the Imams in their homes during these rites, and women often placed wax candles in front of these cenotaphs as they prayed for the Imam's intervention to grant them a boon. [47]

It appears that most Shi`ite women did not participate in the other major form of ritual mourning for the Imam Husayn, the street processions in which men carried the bamboo cenotaphs to a burial ground, a symbolic "Karbala," where they were interred. On the other hand, at least some evidence survives that women occasionally did venture out with the cenotaphs, but perhaps primarily at night, to places where they would not be observed. The memorialist of Lucknow, `Abd al-Halim Sharar wrote of a night he spent with some friends camped out at a shrine on the fortieth day after `Ashura', the anniversary of Imam Husayn's martyrdom:

I awoke suddenly at about two in the morning and the most entrancing melody greeted my ear. This sound had also aroused my friends and made them restless. We left the tent and saw in the still and silent night in the light of the moon a procession of women approaching carrying tazias [paper models of the shrines of Husain]. All were bare-headed and their hair hung loose. In the centre was a woman carrying a candle. By its light a beautiful, delicately formed girl was reading from some sheets of paper and chanting a dirge and several other women were singing with her. I cannot describe the emotions that were aroused by the stillness, the moonlight, these bare-headed beauties and the soul-rending notes of their sad melody. [48]

Sharar also notes that the women of Lucknow especially loved the mourning chants recited for the Imams by Awadh's school of *suz-khvan*s or "cantors," and that they sang lamentations at home, so that the streets reverberated with their voices during Muharram. From a male point of view, there is a shadow quality to much of this female participation in Muharram; it can be caught at an isolated shrine late at night, can be heard anonymously echoing in the lanes. For most Shi`ite women, the public sphere, outside the house, remained a male domain. Some of them nevertheless made forays outside the womens' quarters, and they sent their voices into the public even when they remained secluded. Yet clearly within the zananah itself, Shi`ite women elaborated their own practices and beliefs with some independence.

Although men dominated the formal religious establishment, the exigencies of gender segregation did throw up women "mullas" or religious virtuosi, who offered religious leadership in the female quarters. In Awadh these women often came of poor Sayyid families, whose combination of high status (as descendants of the Prophet Muhammad) and poverty created a bar to marriage. Their families could not offer the sort of trousseau (*jahez*) that would attract a groom from a well-off Sayyid clan. Yet Sayyids often felt that they should not intermarry with non-Sayyids, for fear of losing status. The Sayyid women prevented by their families and circumstances from marrying sometimes gained a religious education, and taught Qur`an to the girls of the aristocracy. During the mourning rites of the holy month of Muharram, these women mullas read the prose stories of the Imams' suffering from Persian sermon manuals to the women's gatherings. The hostess retained these literate women for the ten days of the mourning rites, after which they were released to their families burdened with gifts in remuneration for their services.[49]

These Shi`ite women of the middling sort apparently developed wide-ranging feminine networks that included much association with Hindus, and they seem to have been open to occasional adoption of Hindu ritual and belief. They also listened avidly to the tales purveyed by working-class Muslim and Hindu women whom they employed as servants and attendants. On the other pole, they were attracted by the literate religious discourse of their male Shi`ite relatives, and even the illiterate among them demonstrated an ability to appropriate the heavily Arabized register of Urdu employed in that discourse. Many Shi`ite women of the middling sort zealously said their five daily prayers at home, fasted, and performed the Muharram rituals in a sober and puritan spirit. An informal female Shi`ite clergy even emerged among Sayyid women, who purveyed Arabic and Persian textual sources to other women in ritual and educational contexts.

The images seem contradictory, and so they are. Shi`ite women with children deathly ill of smallpox secretly worshipped Kali Durga when the ministrations of the Muslim physician, clergyman and mystic had proven ineffective. They listened to the stories of Krishna and the cowgirls, of Ram and Sita, and they followed astrology with intense interest. Yet they listened to the stories of the prophets and the Imams from the Qur`an and the hadith, they also said their daily prayers and fasted Ramadan. Indeed, some appear to have listened to Indian folk stories while fasting Ramadan, a nice image that evokes the coexistence of various sorts of religious discourse and practice in their lives.

Courtesans

Courtesans played an important cultural role in Awadh, with its droves of idle, wealthy nobles, and they often plied their trade in Shi`ite society under the pretext of practicing a series of temporary marriages, allowed in Shi`ite law. Courtesans in Awadh came from certain castes, but they tended to become Shi`ite, the same religion as many of their patrons, especially since temporary marriage as an institution did on occasion give them legal benefits. Their cultivation of Urdu poetry and the art of singing gave them an ability to render elegies for the martyred Imam during the mourning month of Muharram, and courtesans often outdid themselves in commemorating Husayn. Given their fallen status, they looked to him for intercession for their sins, and it seems likely that they, as an oppressed and exploited group, identified with the suffering of the Imam and his family during the battle with Yazid's army on the plains of Iraq.

The British census of 1891 returned 28,128 courtesans (*tawa'if*) in the North-Western Provinces and Oudh, of whom 21,958, or 85 percent, were Muslim. Many of these women were recruited from particular castes, such as Mirasi, Kabutari (women who flirted like a pigeon), Hurukiya (dancers to a drum), and Kashmiri. Some significant proportion of the courtesans were Hindu widows, many of whom apparently converted to Islam when they took up the trade. Scripturalist Hinduism prescribed sati or self-immolation for widows, and even when reformists and the British abolished the practice, widows faced difficult circumstances. In their community's ideology, often, they simply were not supposed to be there. Others came from castes that generation after generation specialized in prostitution. They often had an arrangement wherein the men of the caste purchased women from outside, who remained faithful, whereas their sisters became dancing girls. Parents sent the girls to begin their training in singing and dancing at age 8, offering sweetmeats to the poor at the local mosque on this occasion. As note, many of Lucknow's courtesans in the nineteenth century were or became Shi`ites, the religion of the ruling class until 1856.[50]

The chief religious authorities in Lucknow gave rulings concerning the fine line between temporary marriage and prostitution, which even in their condemnation reveal the widespread confusion between the two. Contracting a temporary marriage with a prostitute, Sayyid Husayn Nasirabadi said, was disapproved (but not, apparently, absolutely forbidden or haram) Only the most fastidious would be deterred by this sort of ruling.[51] Chief Mujtahid Sayyid Muhammad Nasirabadi, asked whether it was permissible to marry a prostitute temporarily or permanently, replied that if one has certain knowledge that a woman is an adulteress, marrying her is forbidden.[52] Another questioner threw it up in a later clergyman's face that in point of fact many Shi`ite ulama have allowed temporary marriage with prostitutes. He replied that most ulama have allowed it but grudgingly.[53]

Mirza Rusva's novel, *Umarao Jan Ada*, depicts the lives of courtesans in nineteenth-century Lucknow. Although it was written by a male early in the twentieth century, the book is related in the first person by the female protagonist, and Mirza Rusva has clearly depended for many biographical details and historical insights on conversations with real courtesans in the Chowk district of Lucknow. Umarao Jan Ada may be a construct, but Mirza Rusva himself admitted that he always based his main characters on actual acquaintances.

The courtesans on whom he focused received extensive training in dance and music, and even in the polite letters. He has Umarao Jan describe her many years of study with a Shi`ite clergyman hired by the Madame of her establishment to teach her Persian and Urdu verse, as well as more arcane subjects such as Arabic logic. [54] The more accomplished of these women, then, were highly literate, rivaling noblewomen in the sophistication of their education, even though they often came from poor or middling backgrounds and even though they associated with a wide range of Lucknow society. Sharar noted that "throughout India, including Lucknow, some courtesans have achieved such status that they participate more or less as equals in the gatherings of refined and polished people." He adds, "the houses of Chaudhrayan Haidar Jan and some other courtesans of high status were the 'clubs' of genteel people." [55]

Interspersed among the picaresque details of her biography, we find glimpses into the courtesans' religious roles. Umarao Jan describes how her Madame, known simply as "Khanum (Madame)," mounted impressive commemorations of Muharram:

Khanum's Mohurram observances were organized on a more elaborate scale than that of any other courtesan in the city. The place of mourning was decorated with banners, buntings, chandeliers, globes, etc. And whatever there was, was of the very best. During Mohurram, there were daily gatherings for the first ten days. On the tenth day, the faithful who had been on fast and beggars were fed in hundreds. Later there were gatherings every Thursday right up to the fortieth day of mourning. [56]

The wealth and social prominence of the Madames, then, allowed them to mount the sort of Muharram commemorations that had a wide impact on the city's civic life. Mirza Rusva has Umarao Jan say that she was famous for her own songs of lament for the martyred Imam, and was even invited to perform at the palace by an Awadh queen. [57] While this may have been a piece of fiction, we already know from Sharar the great popularity of heart-rending songs about the tragedy of Karbala among women, and it makes perfect sense that professional singers would have contributed creatively to this aspect of Awadh culture.

The prominence of the courtesans, with their bazaar connections, in Muharram commemorations was a Lucknow innovation, according to Sharar. He evokes the change of mood when the Delhi dilettante class made its way to the Awadh capital, recounting a conversation recorded between a courtesan named Nuran and an old client:

The nobleman and courtesan were both from Delhi but the conversation took place in Lucknow. Nuran said, 'Welcome Mir Sahib! You are like the Eid Moon, which shows up only once a year. In Delhi you used to come and stay with me until late at night. What has happened to you in Lucknow that you never show your face? How I searched for you recently in Kerbala without finding a trace of you! Do not forget to go there on the eighth day of Muharram. For Ali's sake I implore you to go there on the eighth day of mourning.' . . . even courtesans were continuously coming to settle in Lucknow and those who once found delight in the Delhi flower shows now found enjoyment in Kerbala and the celebrations of the eighth day of Muharram. [58]

The morally marginal position of the courtesans, along with the social prominence, appears to have driven some of their interest in religion. Mirza Rusva depicts Umarao Jan as having gone on pilgrimage to the Shi`ite shrine city of Karbala in Iraq, and has her express a desire to retire there eventually. Late in her life she began saying her five daily prayers. He implies that she hoped that, because her sins were victimless ones, her acts of Shi`ite devotion might lead to divine forgiveness. [59]

For the scripturalist ulama, a conundrum arose concerning participation in the mourning observances mounted by Shi`ite courtesans. Were these fallen women, who fasted during Muharram and spent energy and wealth on commemorating the martyrdom of Imam Husayn (the grandson of the Prophet killed in A.D. 680) - were they Shi`ites or not? The Lucknow religious authorities, although they condemned prostitution and debauchery, were not actually very hard on the courtesans. The jurists replied that a born Muslim was a Muslim unless departure from Islam could be proved. Shi`ite jurists also permitted believers to pray in a mosque built by a courtesan if the money employed in its construction came from her remuneration as a temporary wife rather than from simple prostitution. [60]

The courtesans were integrated into the commemoration of other religious festivals, as well. Although the 'Id al-Fitr, the day on which the Ramadan fast was broken, was a holy day, it was observed in Lucknow primarily as a day for secular celebration. Although Mrs. Ali thought "respectable" Muslim families would not allow a dancing-girl in their homes, she admits that on the `Id al-Fitr dancing-girls were much in the demand "in the apartments of the gentlemen."

This survey of women's impact on the practice of Shi`ite Islam in nineteenth-century India suggests that, although the religion's juridical doctrine as elaborated by the clergy was highly patriarchal and restrictive, women nevertheless powerfully shaped ritual life. They took over the rituals of Shi`ism for their own purposes, localizing them by adding touches from their own female life-cycle rituals. Their practices had an impact on how men observed the rituals, as well. At every social level, from the warrior-queens, to the middling sort, to courtesans, women intervened powerfully in everyday religious discourse and practices.

The noblewomen made a gender-specific contribution to ritual change in Awadh Shi`ism. Badshah Begam's championing of a forty-day mourning period for commemorating the Imam Husayn's martyrdom may have reflected the greater leisure available to aristocratic feminine networks for concentration on ritual activities and meetings. Certainly, the manner in which she melded elements of the local Indian female and family life-cycle rites with her celebration of events related to the lives of the Imams showed a specifically feminine imagination at work. Women may also have been more willing to innovate in the area of ritual than men, because they were often illiterate or in any case not bound by a strict seminary-type reading of key Shi`ite texts. Some Shi`ite men also took an interest in the devotions introduced by women like Badshah Begam. They attempted to imitate Badshah Begam's religious style by dressing in female clothing and symbolically acting out female life-cycle rituals on the plane of Shi`ite sacred history. The authority of aristocratic feminine constructions of the supernatural is further demonstrated by the stories of Vajid `Ali's mother and the snake-mark, and of Mubarak Mahall's mujtahid. Women, then, mattered religiously. The embeddedness of the feminine in the aristocratic ritual inventiveness of the 1820s and 1830s attests, not only to the religious genius of Badshah Begam as an individual, but to that of Shi`ite women in general.

Women of the middling sort did not have the same power to shape religious practice and institutions as did the aristocratic begams, and though some were literate, these constituted a minority. Yet these women developed their own distinctive set of religious practices and discourse. They carved out for themselves arenas of relative independence from their men, a process aided in many ways by the practice of gender segregation. In part because of their general illiteracy, and in part because of their unique exposure both to upper-class Muslim males and to working-class Hindu women, the religious culture of Shi`ite women from the middling strata appears to have been "hot" rather than "cold," to have been open to some manipulation and mixture of motifs from several traditions. Of course, the working-strata Muslims in South Asia were notorious for their syncretism. What distinguishes Shi`ite women of the middling sort is their intimate knowledge of literate Islamic norms as well as of Hindu folk culture. One receives the impression from the available sources, not of oppressed and powerless women isolated in the harem and ignorantly parroting male religious orthodoxy, but of women powerful in their own spheres actively appropriating religious discourse from other genders or classes, and putting it to their own purposes. The women sound as though they may have been, in addition, more cosmopolitan and realistic about the true shape of Awadh culture, than were many of the men.

9

Sacred Space and Holy War: The Issue of Jihad

The Arabic word *jihad* simply means to struggle for the faith, and does not necessarily imply holy war. This distinction is especially important for Shi`ites, most of whom until fairly recently held that only defensive holy war could be fought in the absence of the Imam. (We saw calls for defensive jihad in Ottoman Karbala, above). In the following chapter, we shall see the Shi`ites taking a quietist position in support of the civil state. It is militant Sunnis who wished to launch a holy war in the mid-nineteenth century, as a means of contesting with Hindus over possession of a holy building some thought had been a mosque, but which Hindus had dedicated to the worship of the god Hanuman. The motif of the usurped place of worship has formed an important element of South Asian popular culture and communal conflict. In the late twentieth century, Hindu communalist groups charged that the Baburi Mosque at Ayodhya, near Faizabad in the northern province of Uttar Pradesh, stood on the site of the birthplace of the holy figure Ram, and that medieval Muslim rulers demolished the temple that used to commemorate that sacred spot. The ultimately successful campaign by Hindu fundamentalists to see the mosque razed has proved an explosive element in Indian politics, and has signalled a new assertiveness by the Hindu majority in the post-colonial era.[1] In the 1850s a similar controversy agitated North India, but at that time the shoe was on the other foot. Ayodhya, then a town of about 7,000, was ruled by the Shi`ite king of Awadh and the small town was the site of a Hindu temple to Hanuman, the monkey-god of the *Ramayana* who aided Ram. Sunni Muslim activists of the time became convinced that the Hanumangarhi had been built atop the site of an old mosque, and they determined to tear it down and restore the mosque. This Sunni-Hindu conflict of over a century ago posed a profound difficulty for the chief mujtahid or Shi`ite jurisprudent of Awadh, Sayyid Muhammad Nasirabadi (1785-1867), since both Sunni and Shi`ite groups beseeched him for a *fatwa* giving his ruling about whether Muslims had a right to act independently of the state to redress the insult to Islam that they felt the Hanumangarhi to represent.[2]

Sayyid Muhammad eventually delivered more than one juridical opinion (fatwa) on the issue, one of which survives in the original Persian. Many such fatwas were issued by Shi`ite clerics in nineteenth-century Awadh, and some were even collected and published in manuscript or lithograph form.[3] The form and social meaning of these opinions appears not to have differed in Shi`ism and Sunnism. They were pieces of extended, formal legal reasoning applied to a concrete case and typically elicited by the question of a believer or litigant. They differed from the rulings of court judges (*qadi*s) in having primarily moral, rather than legal, force, though they could become the basis for court judgments if adopted by a qadi. Muftis, the jurisprudents who issued the fatwas, derived their status from reputation for great learning, though some were appointed by the state to issue official opinions, which then had greater legal force. In India, most often the state had been in Sunni hands, so that official muftis tended to be Sunnis, whereas Shi`ite fatwas were more informal and internal to the community. In Shi`ite-ruled Awadh, however, the state appointed muftis from both branches of Islam, and the prestige of Lucknow's Shi`ite mujtahids or jurisprudents was very great. Throughout the nineteenth century, North Indian fatwas were written in Persian, a language that was still widely cultivated by educated Indians, not excluding Hindus. They would have had to be translated into Urdu for the non-elite Muslims, but that would have been an easy task, given the grammatical similarities of Persian and Hindustani (the Hindi-Urdu of the time) and the large shared vocabulary between the two. Some of the official fatwas appear to survive only in the British Government of India Archives, in the form of translations made for the British Resident (envoy) to Lucknow and for imperial officials in Calcutta. My translation of the text of Sayyid Muhammad's Persian fatwa is as follows:

Q. What is your guidance concerning those who go to Faizabad to fight the Hindus? For they desire to take revenge on them for their uncivilized behavior with the mosque and the Qur'an. According to the Law, is it permissible for them to go there and fight, and will this be rewarded? Or is it forbidden?

A. Without the participation and aid of the customary-law ruler or the Islamic-law ruler, such actions are in no wise permissible. God knows best.[4]

The ruling appears to be a simple Weberian statement of the monopoly on the use of force enjoyed by the state. In the context of nineteenth-century

Islam, and more particularly the Usuli school of Shi`ite Islam, the fatwa serves to define the relationship of the Shi`ite jurisprudents to lay Muslims and to the Shi`ite-ruled state. It came at the end of a long process whereby the Shi`ite clergy in Awadh had managed to take control of the judiciary and to establish the dominance of the Usuli school, with its clericalist, elitist theory of jurisprudence.

Power and demography were at odds in Awadh, a country of some ten million inhabitants in 1855, with its capital in the metropolis of Lucknow, one of the four largest Indian cities of the day. A vast Hindu majority of 88 percent consisted largely of rural peasants, and only their rajas and a few great merchants and government officials had much political influence. Most of the 12 percent who were Muslims belonged to the Sunni branch of the faith, and these dominated the small towns (*qasabah*s) and provided a disproportionate number of urban residents. They were prominent in skilled and unskilled trades, as butchers and tailors, but also supplied many petty clerks and middle managers for the bureaucracy, as well as troops and officers in the army.[5] Yet Sunnis labored under some disabilities under the Shi`ite government of Awadh. Of Muslims, only 3 to 10 percent were Shi`ite, but as coreligionists of the shah, they dominated high government office and had taken control of the judiciary. As for the Hanumangarhi, a Western observer in the 1830s described it as a large, well-maintained building about a mile from the river, supported by annual revenues of Rs. 50,000 from an endowment in land created by Awadh ruler Nawab Shuja` al-Dawla (1754-1775). "No Musulman is permitted to enter its walls, and the revenues are absorbed by about 500 resident and itinerant bairagis, and Hindu mendicants of all descriptions."[6]

The trouble over the Hanumangarhi became serious enough, in February of 1855, to be noticed by Maj.-Gen. Outram, Calcutta's Resident in Lucknow, when he wrote to the reigning king, Vajid `Ali Shah (r. 1847-1856) that an activist in Faizabad named Shah Ghulam Husayn was bent on destroying the Hindu temple in nearby Ayodhya. He added that this man was being supported by a perhaps even more formidable ("diabolical" was the word he used) lieutenant known as "Mawlavi Sahib," the cleric. Shah Ghulam Husayn led a group from Faizabad that February to begin the work of building a mosque at the site of the shrine to the monkey god, but he was checked by the local government of Agha `Ali Khan. The British believed the two should be arrested for their agitations, in order to prevent a conflict in which blood surely would be spilled.[7] As despicable as advocating preventive detention may have been, the Resident's note demonstrated a sibylline foresight. The heat of summer came, and with it trouble. On 28 July 1855, 500 Muslims clashed at Ayodhya with some 8,000 Hindus (many of them holy men or

vairagis) and at least 80 persons were killed on each side, according to
Alexander Orr, the representative in Faizabad of the British Frontier
Police.

Shah Ghulam Husayn had announced his intention to lead an attack on
the vairagis at the Hanumangarhi after the noon prayers. Orr and the local
Fayzabad government attempted to convince him to take his followers
instead to Lucknow, where they could present their complaints to the
Muslim king. When Shah Ghulam Husayn refused, Orr requested that
they wait five days so that he could get them a response from the nearby
capital, hoping that he could bring in more police reinforcements in the
meantime. At the time, the police only had 150 men of all ranks in place.
The fiery preacher refused to wait, and around one o'clock the crowd of
Muslims met the Hindu holy men. Orr later reported that it was difficult
to know who began the violence, though his investigations indicated that
a Muslim fired the first shot. Once the shooting began the outnumbered
Muslims quickly were routed. Having led his followers into the
confrontation, Shah Ghulam Husayn escaped, abandoning his people.
Some of the Muslims ran to a mosque in the neighborhood, taking refuge
in it. The enraged Hindus, however, refused to recognize this sanctuary.
The vairagis surrounded the place of worship, broke in and cut the
Muslims to pieces. Thereafter Hindus rioted and ransacked the town until
around 6 pm when the violence subsided. Orr thought the Muslims
involved to have been men of low caste "and bad character," from both
Ayodhya and Fayzabad. Their Hindu opponents included not only the
holy men and supplicants at the temple, but also peasants from the estates
of Hindu magnates such as Raja Man Singh and Rajkumar. Two days
later, on 30 July, a local government official, Mirza A`la `Ali, and his
men attempted to arrest the ringleaders of the Muslim rioters in Fayzabad,
suggesting that Shi`ite authorities and their clients had grown alarmed that
the largely Sunni movement against the Hindus was endangering the
stability of the Shi`ite-ruled state. The confrontation turned ugly, and Orr
and the local police chief intervened to disperse the crowd.[8]

Vajid `Ali Shah's response to the crisis was to vacillate and avoid
strong action, in the hope that it would subside. He did dispatch the
governor of Sultanpur and Faizabad, Agha `Ali Khan, back to the
provinces from the court. Although he claimed to have sought the arrest
of Shah Ghulam Husayn, he declined to offer a reward for his
apprehension, lest it be perceived publicly that the activist had been
convicted without a trial. This indecisiveness pointed, not to a flaw in the
king's character, but to a political dilemma. He depended desperately
upon the Sunni-dominated army and Sunni great landholders in the
countryside, and could not afford to be seen taking the side of the
subordinate and despised Hindus against them. As a Muslim ruler, he

himself had a certain amount of sympathy for the Sunni activists' grievance. Early in his reign he had provoked a major demonstration by Hindu merchants and their followers when he ordered the demolition of several temples on the ground that members of the Mahajan jewelers' caste had practiced child sacrifice there. The shah seemed unaware that these groups were extreme pacifists, perhaps even Jains, and that the rumors of human sacrifice were quite incredible in the circumstances. Six years later, he had not developed a sudden sympathy for, or understanding of, the Hindus, and, indeed, he blamed the vairagis for the Ayodhya violence. Yet he needed the support of Hindus, as well, because they formed the majority of his subjects and because their rajas, merchants and holy men were not without power. Moreover, the British worried a great deal about a Hindu uprising against a minority Muslim king, and they put pressure on him to mollify the followers of Ram and Hanuman.[9] In the end he appointed a commission to investigate whether a mosque had indeed once stood on the site of the Hanumangarhi.

Many Muslims interpreted the clash of 28 July as a horrific massacre of Muslims in a mosque, a profanation by unlawful bloodshed of both a place of prayer and of the holy Qur'an which had been reposited there. According to Islamic law as interpreted in India at that time, the Hindus were at best a protected minority (provided they submitted to the political authority of the Muslims), and at worst idolaters who deserved only a choice between death and conversion. For them to kill Muslims in a mosque in the midst of a Muslim-ruled realm proved too much to bear for many adherents of Islam, whatever the provocation. Vajid `Ali's refusal to act decisively convinced many Sunni townspeople that they would have to take matters into their own hands. Muslim volunteers began departing the capital, Lucknow, for Faizabad in small groups. Two small-town preachers, Mawlavi Amir `Ali of Amethi and Mawlavi Ramazan `Ali began grassroots organizing, collecting men from Bijnor and Malihabad, places with significant Sunni populations to Awadh's northwest, and gathering them in the small town of Amethi in preparation for a march on Faizabad. In Fayzabad itself Muslim clerics preached a jihad against the Hindus, and hundreds gathered under the standard of Islam about seven miles from the town. Thousands more were ready to march from Fayzabad itself, but the local governor had the bridge leading to Ayodhya from Faizabad blocked off.[10]

Less than a month later, on 24 August, while passions over the Ayodhya events were still running high, the Festival of Sacrifice (`Id al-Adha) was celebrated. At the holy day prayers held that morning at the Shi`ite mosque in the complex of the Great Imambarah near old Lucknow, the chief mujtahid delivered a sermon to the hundreds of assembled worshippers, who included the great nobles and courtiers, in which he openly cursed Agha `Ali Khan, the governor of Fayzabad and Sultanpur, for having taken bribes from wealthy Hindus to decide the dispute in their favor.[11]

The chief mujtahid, having taken a strong stance in opposition to the equivocation of the shah and his chief minister, briefly became the cynosure of the Muslim activists, who beseeched him for fatwas. Two such exchanges are preserved in the British archives, and I reproduce them with all the idiosyncrasies of their original orthography and punctuation: [12]

The Soonees asked the High Priest [i.e. chief mujtahid] for his opinions on the following matter: Are those who were slain fighting against the infidels martyrs? Ought not Mussulmans to avenge their deaths? If any one attempts to prevent Mussulmans from so acting - what is your judgment on such conduct?

Reply. - Princes of the Faith, who are believers and Mussulmans are bound to put an end to the wickedness of accursed kaffirs (infidels). God he knows. - Signed the High Priest.

Shi`ites sympathetic to the Sunni activists also sought a ruling:

Question put to the High Priest by the Shiahs - Suppose a number of Mussulmans had taken up their abode in a Musjid [mosque] - and suppose they were unprepared - say sleeping, or praying - and suddenly a band of infidels were to attack, and slaughter them; so that the Musjid should be inundated with blood - and suppose the infidels were to make water in the Musjid, to tear a Koran to pieces - and to trample it underfoot - and were to subject the Koran to other indignities - and suppose an immense number of them (infidels) had assembled to slay any Mahomedans [who] from fear of their lives were to run away - then, in that case would it not be obligatory on all Mahomedans of these and other parts to fight with the aforesaid infidels?

Reply. - God be our protector from the wickedness of Infidels! Upon the Rulers of the Moslems it is obligatory to repress the enormities of accursed kafirs. Signed by the High Priest.

In late August, the investigative commission came back with the explosive conclusion that no mosque had existed on the site of the Hanumangarhi for at least a generation, and most likely none had ever been there. The chief minister, `Ali Naqi Khan, wished to break up the alliance developing between the chief mujtahid and the activists by treating the commission's findings as mere preliminaries and giving it a new charge, designating Sayyid Muhammad Nasirabadi as its chairman. Outram, the Resident, insisted that the commission continue to report directly to the shah, but accepted the idea of adding the prominent Shi`ite cleric to it. When Outram pointedly questioned the chief minister about Nasirabadi's sermon and fatwas, `Ali Naqi Khan replied that he had been sitting too far away to hear the sermon of 24 August; and that the formulation of the questions left no room for any other answer. Whereas the British saw these rulings as inflammatory, insofar as they demanded government action against the Hindus, the Awadh government probably already perceived a crucial difference between the chief mujtahid's stance and that of the small-town Sunni preachers - the Shi`ite fatwas authorized state action rather than enjoining individuals to act on their own.[13]

Vajid `Ali Shah attempted to reach a compromise with Amir `Ali of Amethi, proposing to build a mosque resting on one wall of the Hindu temple, with a door on the opposite side. In this manner the interior of the Hanumangarhi would retain its sanctity. Amir `Ali, at Amethi with his followers, gave the government a one-month deadline by which such building would have to be initiated or he would take action. When they heard of this plan in mid-September, the vairagis in Ayodhya rejected it forcefully, convincing the British that any attempt to implement it would result in more bloodshed.[14]

In late September, the sacred month of Muharram arrived, with its potential for further communal violence. Shi`ites particularly honor this month, during which they commemorate with weeping and flagellation the martyrdom of the Prophet's grandson, Imam Husayn, sometimes cursing early Muslim figures revered by Sunnis. In Awadh, on the tenth of Muharram (`Ashura') both Shi`ites and Sunnis (and often Hindus) carried colorful bamboo and paper replicas of the Imam's tomb in the holy city of Karbala, and at the end of day-long processions buried them in sacred burial grounds. As a sign of protest against the Hanumangarhi, Amir `Ali called upon Muslims that Muharram not to bury their tomb-replicas, called ta`ziyahs. In Kheri, in the Khayrabad province, Muslims deliberately neglected to bury fifteen ta`ziyahs on 25 September, the Tenth of Muharram, whereas in Zaydpur, where a local elite of Shi`ite descendants of the Prophet held great power, the Shi`ites insisted on burying their tomb-replicas, refusing to play politics with this sacred ritual, and therefore clashing with Sunni adherents of Amir `Ali. Communal rioting spread. On 26 September 2,000 Muslims rioted in Kheri, attacking a vairagi and his disciple, slashing a cow with swords to show their contempt for an animal held holy by their opponents; in the subsequent week, fifty men were killed on both sides, Hindu temples were defiled and cow's blood spilled. Followers of Amir `Ali in the *qasabah* town of Suhali also fought Hindus, attacking temples and destroying idols.[15]

The alarmed sovereign submitted a request to his chief mujtahid for a ruling on the Hanumangarhi dispute, formulated so as to stress the interests of the state:

Suppose that some of the Faithful imagined that in former times, a mosque had been built in certain lands, possessed by Infidels and that they therefore laid claim to the said lands; that the claim had lain dormant for centuries in fact had never been advanced; either in the memory of man, or in the traditions of the Country; that the Infidels expressed their willingness and desire, to refer the claim to the arbitration and decision of the sovereign of the Country, himself a Mahomedan; that the Faithful rejecting these terms, sought by force of arms, to dispossess the Infidels and with that object assaulted them; but were beaten back, followed up, and in the heat of pursuit, slain wherever found. Are you of the opinion, under these circumstances, that any one of the subjects of the aforesaid Mohamedan is empowered by Law; to call the Faithful to arms, and to conduct a Holy war; When the Sovereign himself has not thought fit to proclaim the Jehad or to lead the religious movement, or to countenance it by any public act?

Reply. - Under these circumstances the order for the waging of the Jehad does not apply; but the sovereign has the right to build the Musjid; and the Hindu Ryots ought not to disobey.

-Sealed Syud Mahomed, High Priest[16]

Sunni supporters of Amir `Ali alleged that the shah had summoned Sayyid Muhammad Nasirabadi with his brother, Sayyid Husayn, and forcefully pointed out to them that the efflorescence of Shi`ism in Awadh depended heavily on the Nishapuri dynasty, and that the high station enjoyed by the Shi`ite clergy was a result of the favors of the nawabs and shahs. These supporters further alleged that Vajid `Ali Shah argued that the Hindus were a protected minority, dhimmis, and that it was not lawful for Muslims to attack them, and that in any case Shi`ite law maintained that holy war no longer was permissible during the Occultation of the Imam. [17] Even if this report of the shah's views is accurate (which is not certain), it is it seems unlikely that the chief mujtahid agreed in viewing the Hindus as dhimmis.

In the subsequent meeting between Outram and Vajid `Ali Shah, the Resident conceded that Sayyid Muhammad Nasirabadi's prohibition of holy war was helpful, but objected that the last phrase authorizing government action against the Hindus was inflammatory. In reply, Vajid

`Ali blamed the trouble on the audacity of the Hindus. He said they were claiming more land for the Hanumangarhi than their official land-grant warranted, that in fact they claimed all land trod by their monkey-god, and that they had provoked a riot in the north of the realm (apparently referring to events in Kheri). The Resident did not let the remark pass, insisting that the shah reread the Shankar Dyal report, after which the sovereign admitted that Muslims did seem at fault.[18]

By the beginnings of October, Vajid `Ali, under strong British pressure, was denying he had ever pledged to build a mosque adjacent to the Hindu temple, though Amir `Ali and the Sunni activists insisted that he had. On 2 October, the Officiating Resident handed the shah a note warning that he would be held personally responsible if he should attempt to build the mosque or if Muslims attacked Hindus. The shaken monarch agreed to do his duty. British officials suspected that Vajid `Ali had counted on being able to employ British troops to quell the Hindus in the last instance, and his government had already broached the possibility of using them to put down Amir `Ali's forces.[19] The British had now put him in the position of having to take the Hindu side against the Sunni activists, and of having to find a way to put them down militarily without provoking his largely Sunni army to split or rebel. On 13 October, the shah issued a decree (*hukm-namah*) offering amnesty to the activists, but sentencing to death anyone who did not desist from the so-called holy war.[20]

In mid-October, Amir `Ali his followers began a procession through the small towns of Awadh toward Faizabad, having despaired of government intervention against the Hindus. The 1800 men, 200 of them Sufi murids of Amir `Ali, camped at Daryabad. This area was garrisoned by 5,000 Shi`ite troops loyal to Vajid `Ali Shah. The government dispatched a contingent of Sunni muftis to debate the activists publicly there. By late October, these muftis, high-powered clerics from the capital and from such respected Hanafi institutions as the Farangi Mahall seminary, managed to convince substantial numbers of Mawlavi Amir `Ali's supporters to desert him.[21] Those men who had sold their shops or given up their employment in order to join the movement remained the most hard-line. They were urged on by supporters outside Awadh such as the Begam of Bhopal (central India), who sent an elephant and funds for three hundred men to Amir `Ali at Daryabad. On 7 November, Amir `Ali and his forces attempted to advance toward Faizabad, but were met and defeated by Shi`ite army troops along with soldiers supplied by Shi`ite great landlords such as Mahmudabad. Some 400 activists died, among them Amir `Ali, against 12 dead and 70 wounded among government troops.[22]

Although many Sunnis came to revere Amir `Ali as a martyr and a holy man, the Shi`ite clergy did not accept such claims. Someone asked Sayyid Husayn Nasirabadi, brother of the chief mujtahid, whether Amir `Ali and his followers were saved and martyrs. He replied, "Only Twelver Shi`ites are saved, and no others can be, whether they are killed or die naturally." [23]

The conflict over the Hanumangarhi in Ayodhya provides a fascinating set of insights into the workings of communalism in mid-nineteenth-century India. Militant leaders of the three religious communities attempted to mobilize their adherents behind them by wielding religious symbols, often in a crude manner, focusing on what divided Indians rather than what united them. Urinating in a mosque, carving up a cow with a sword, refusing to bury *ta`ziyah*s - all these acts were intended to distinguish friends and enemies, and to push the wavering off their fence. It is important to note that these events occurred against the background of a joint civic culture characterized by a high degree of eclecticism (for example, Sunnis, Shi`ites and Hindus often joined together in Awadh to commemorate the martyrdom of Imam Husayn). In this crisis, members of the three communities turned such cooperation on its head. Instead of jointly burying *ta`ziyah*s, some Muslims refused to bury theirs at all. Yet agreement on such shifts was elusive, so that Sunnis and Shi`ites clashed over the propriety of leaving *ta`ziyah*s unburied, and a gesture meant by Sunnis to unite Muslims against Hindus served instead to divide the two branches of Islam, showing the ad hoc and tentative nature of the symbol-reversals.

Perhaps the most striking aspect of the conflict is the vague allegation - lacking any convincing material or documentary proof - that the sacred space of one community had been usurped from that of another. Why should such an assertion be found credible? Surely at least one reason for its believability lay in a (perhaps unarticulated) conviction that the dominant, ruling community ought to control the disposition of sacred space. The large, well kept-up, and wealthy Hanumangarhi stood as an affront to some Muslims, those beset by status anxiety in particular. Especially prey to such anxieties were the lower middle class Sunnis, squeezed between the Shi`ite nobility and the Hindu merchants and rajas who supported the Ayodhya vairagis. It is common in North India for groups that see themselves as rightfully dominant but somehow denied their full privileges to express their resentments in the form of competition over sacred space. If this interpretation is correct, then it is no accident that Sunni Muslim shopkeepers and artisans living under a Shi`ite Muslim government took the offensive in attempting to reassert rights over a Hindu holy place in 1855, whereas in the Hindu-majority,

Congress-dominated India of the late twentieth century it was a predominantly lower middle class Hindu movement that tore down the Baburi Mosque on 6 December 1992, seeking to replace it with a temple to Ram.

What of the import of the fatwa for our understanding of Shi`ism? Sayyid Muhammad Nasirabadi was put in an extremely delicate position by the Ayodhya temple conflict. He clearly believed that the grievance of the Sunni activists was legitimate, and that a righteous Muslim government would in fact build a mosque on the site of the Hanumangarhi and would punish the Hindus who clashed with the Muslims on 28 July. The moral dilemma arose when the British intervened to prevent the Muslim government from acting as it otherwise would have, for surely if left to their own devices Vajid `Ali Shah and his minister, `Ali Naqi Khan, would have built the mosque and penalized the vairagis. The question then became, what do you do if the duly constituted Muslim authorities neglect to carry out their duties?

Amir `Ali and other Sunni activists believed the answer to that question lay in taking the law into their own hands. Sunni jurisprudence often does allow individual activism on moral issues, and there has frequently been an activist interpretation of the commandment to "enjoin the good and prohibit evil," as can be seen among the "volunteers" (*mutawwa`un*) who enforce the command to pray and who police morals in Wahhabi Saudi Arabia. In Awadh, as in Iran, during the course of the nineteenth century the clericalist Usuli school of jurisprudence won out among Shi`ites. Usulis believe that outside major ritual and legal obligations (such as the five pillars of witness to faith, prayer, fasting, alms-giving, pilgrimage) law becomes too complex and subtle for lay believers to determine by themselves. They have an obligation, on these murkier issues, to ask the opinion of an upright, trained, and knowledgeable Shi`ite clergyman. The Usuli tradition therefore militates against independent lay activism, though a major clergyman can by his ruling authorize laypersons to take action.

The kind of lay and Sufi grassroots activism represented by the holy warriors in the *qasabah* towns was anathema to the chief mujtahid. Moreover, it certainly is true that most nineteenth-century Shi`ites believed that holy war could no longer be fought in the absence of an Imam (a divinely inspired descendant of the Prophet), and Twelvers believed the last Imam to have gone into occultation in the ninth century A.D. Only in an instance in which the lands of Islam were attacked would most Shi`ite clerics authorize a "defensive jihad." From an Usuli Shi`ite point of view, then, only the duly constituted Shi`ite authorities could act in the Ayodhya dispute, which was not a suitable grounds for holy war. Sayyid Muhammad Nasirabadi, who did his part by authorizing

government action against the vairagis, could go no further except by
endangering the stability of the minority, Shi`ite kingdom. Interestingly
enough, he recognized that although the Shi`ite state in Awadh was a
"common-law" (`urfi) government, not having the divine sanction that
would underpin the government of an Imam, it nevertheless had the
authority to punish the vairagis and build the mosque. When it did not do
so, the chief mujtahid was left with no choice, doctrinally or politically,
except to acquiesce in this inaction, however wrong he might have
thought it. The Shi`ite minority chose to stand with their shah, and to
disallow the claims by Amir `Ali's followers that he was a holy warrior
and, later, a martyr. The fatwas of the chief mujtahid serve to underscore
the falsity of the idea that the Shi`ite clergy have throughout history been
opposed to the civil state.

10

Shi`ites as National Minorities

Among the key struggles of the Twelver Shi`ite communities in the twentieth century was the problem of coming to terms with being minorities in a nation-state. For the most part they were numerical minorities, as in what became Lebanon, Saudi Arabia, India, Pakistan and Afghanistan. Elsewhere they were functional minorities, as in Bahrain, Iraq and the Soviet Socialist Republic of Azerbaijan, all three of which had a numerical preponderance of Shi`ites who were altogether deprived of political power. Bahrain and Iraq were ruled by powerful Sunni Muslim elites, and Azerbaijan was under Russian and then Soviet rule until 1989. Only Iran had a Shi`ite government, by the terms of the 1906 Constitution, though the more militantly secular policies of the Pahlevi dynasty (1925-1979) were felt by some Shi`ite activists to disenfranchise them. Because of their minority status, the process of nation-building that took place in the Middle East and South Asia was often more problematic for Shi`ites than for majority communities. Their success over the century in finding a place at the table has been extremely mixed. There is a sense in which Imam Ruhollah Khomeini in Iran initially rejected the nation-state as a model altogether, preferring a populist theocracy without borders instead. Nevertheless, the nation-state model reasserted itself in Iran over time. The Shi`ites outside Iran, despite the rhetoric of some radicals in Lebanon, have never had the luxury of even thinking about opting out of the nation-state model. It is my thesis here that outside Iran, Shi`ite politics has been a politics of finding ways to assert Shi`ite interests in developing nation-states that had non-Shi`ite elites at their helm. Indeed, I would argue that much of what the outside world has understood as activism and militancy among Shi`ites after about 1975 has been a manifestation of attempts to find political representation in their various nations as an ethnic and religious community, as they moved from being peasant subjects to being urban citizens. In some instances, radical Shi`ites have resorted to terrorism, a rejectionist tool. Terrorism, whatever its practical successes, has retarded the integration of the community into the nation-state system, and had negative effects on their political and economic standing.

The formation of new nation-states in Iraq and Lebanon gave impetus to the development of localistic Shi`ite identities. The Arab Shi`ite communities began the century as peasants or pastoral nomads living under an agrarian bureaucracy staffed by Sunni, Ottoman Turkish-speaking officials. Twelver Shi`ites have in the twentieth century been greatly affected by and often involved in the making of new national states that broke away or were detached from the Ottoman empire. Yet their sectarian distinctiveness has made their integration into a national ethos based on Arab nationalism difficult, and offered little hope of a better deal for the poverty-stricken Shi`ites. The Shi`ites' characteristic position at the bottom of the economic scale has tended to impede escape from their rural, and more lately urban, ghettoes. This marginal status in the new Arab states made Shi`ites particularly susceptible to the pan-Islamic or pan-Shi`ite ideology promulgated by Iran's clerics during and after the Islamic Revolution of 1978-79.

The breakup of the Ottoman Empire in World War I and the rise of independent Arab states changed the framework within which Twelvers competed for resources. Not only did the modern national state differ from the empire in the way it governed and redistributed resources, but opportunities arose for minorities to redefine their identities. Secular Arabism and socialism provided, at least potentially, alternative ways of seeing themselves. Many hoped that it would matter little whether the Arabs of Iraq were Twelver or Sunni if all were Arabs or all were socialists. The Comtean shock of the twentieth century, however, has been precisely the continuing importance of religiously based group identities, and thus of religious influences from Shi`ite Iran.

The British invasion of Iraq during WW I was seen by some Twelvers (especially Sayyids) as an opportunity to escape Ottoman Sunni rule. At first some Twelver leaders seemed amenable to the idea of British rule replacing that of Istanbul, but events following the British occupation of the shrine cities in 1917 caused the estrangement of their inhabitants from the Europeans. In the three subsequent years many Shi`ite ulama and notables made common cause with local Sunni nationalists in hopes of seeing an Arab, Muslim state emerge. The 1920 declararation of a British mandate, however, disappointed nationalist hopes in Iraq and Twelver ulama, notables and tribal leaders joined in the country's revolt against British rule. The chief mujtahid in the shrine cities declared all service with the British illicit, and other ulama and nationalist leaders cooperated in urging rebellion.[1] Of all the new Arab states, the Twelvers participated most actively in the formation of Iraq, even though its subsequent mandate status and Sunni domination disappointed them.

In April of 1922 a major conference of Imami ulama from both Iraq and Iran met at Karbala to denounce any treaty with the British. Some also wanted half of government posts, including the cabinet, reserved for Twelvers, and a declaration of holy war against the Wahhabis of Saudi Arabia. The following year the leading mujtahids of Kazimayn, Karbala and Najaf issued rulings requiring a boycott of forthcoming elections under Faisal's cabinet. This rejectionist policy set them against, not only the British, but King Faisal, who wanted a treaty with London. His cabinet expelled the most uncompromising mujtahid from the country, and other major ulama left for Iran in protest, remaining there about a year. A reconciliation of sorts was effected with the distribution of finance and education portfolios to Twelver ministers, and the ulama ultimately acquiesced in the elections.[2] In the Iraq that emerged, Twelvers formed about 55 percent of the population, with Sunni Arabs at 22 percent and Kurds at 14 percent, according to rough British censuses of the early 1920s. Despite the Imami majority the community subsisted as a functional minority.[3] The 1920s witnessed the sharp decline of Iranian influence. Iranian residents in Iraq had their privileges removed and were forced to become citizens of the new state if they wished to continue to reside there. For its part, the new nationalist, secular government of Reza Shah Pahlevi attempted to limit Iranian Shi'ites' pilgrimages to the Iraqi shrine cities and drastically reduced links between them and Iran.[4]

The new Iraqi state made some efforts to placate Arab Shi'is, as in the early decision that civil status cases among Imami parties would be tried by Imami jurists, in contrast to the Ottoman practice.[5] Although the Iraqi bureaucracy and educational system discriminated heavily against Twelver Arabs, the Shi'ites over time clearly adopted a specifically Iraqi identity. Their linguistic and ethnic identity was as important to them as the religious, and the pull of Iran was spiritual rather than separatist. For many Iraqi Shi'ite intellectuals, it was more important to be an Iraqi and an Arab than to be a Shi'ite. Twelvers in Lebanon, which the French carved out of Syria for their Maronite clients, showed more evidence of mixed feelings about their new country. The religion's adherents in Jabal 'Amil had felt longstanding grievances against the Ottomans, resenting their conscription into the army and imperial trade policies in regard to the already important crop of tobacco. The outbreak of WW I raised the same questions for the Levantine Twelvers as for the Iraqi, the appeals of Ottomanism competing with those of incipient Arab nationalism. In 1915 a group of Arab nationalists in Sidon were denounced to the authorities by rival notables, and tried for treason. Among both denouncers and accused were prominent Imamis. The Shi'ites' grievances were not only political: the region's agriculture suffered greatly from extensive conscription and a locust plague during the war, leading to near-famine conditions.[6]

The post-war Arab kingdom in Damascus made every effort to draw Jabal `Amil into its orbit, and may have briefly succeeded, despite local rivalries among notables. The threats of French annexation and of the partition of Greater Syria brought into being several major armed groups among the Twelvers determined to resist the French, as well as smaller Maronite groups supporting the idea of greater Lebanon. Tensions reached the point where, in April 1920, Twelvers attacked the Christian village of `Ayn Ibl. In response, the French sent 4,000 troops south the following month. The French crushed the Shi`ite resistance and imposed the payment of huge indemnities to the Christians. Thereafter, as in Sunni-dominated Iraq, the Twelvers of Maronite-dominated Lebanon found themselves poor peasants in a backwater, relatively deprived of government posts as well as of state services. Although they made up some 16% of the country's inhabitants (including refugees and the foreign-born) in 1932, Twelvers shared in considerably less than that percentage of the country's wealth and power.[7]

The political and economic development of Lebanon continued to favor Beirut and Mt. Lebanon, excluding most Twelver peasants from the country's growing prosperity. The new mandate agreements, giving the British Palestine, left Imamis in a different country than their traditional markets to the south. The French recognized the Twelvers in 1926 as a religious group with its own legal system and allowed them openly to commemorate Muharram, something the Ottomans had refused to do. In 1936 many fewer Shi`ites rioted in favor of union with Syria than did their Sunni counterparts. Of course, the colonial dependence on collaborating large landholders left most Imamis with little real franchise, and they formed the only religious community underrepresented in both the executive and the legislature under the French.[8] A small stratum of literate Twelver intellectuals flourished in southern cities like Sidon, and published an important journal, al-`Irfan, which was an important vehicle for disseminating information about the Shi`ite tradition, including the Iranian heritage. The establishment of Israel in 1948 finally cut off the Shi`ites in southern Lebanon entirely from their traditional markets, as well as from their landholdings in Palestine. Moreover, about 100,000 of the Palestinians who fled from war or were expelled by the Zionists in Palestine in 1948-49 immigrated into South Lebanon and put another burden on the limited resources of this area.

Later, under the independent Lebanese state from 1946, Twelvers' control of the office of president of the Chamber of Deputies provided them with virtually their only important entree to government service, in the Chamber's staff. Political parties remained weak in Twelver areas, though for long the Arab nationalist parties and the communists had some success in attracting their votes. Despite the clout of its landlord politicians, the South remained deprived of resources for infrastructural development such as electricity, roads, hospitals and schools in the 1940s ad 1950s.[9] Only in the 1960s did the extension of roads, increased literacy, and other developmental programs begin strongly to affect Jabal 'Amil.

Although Twelvers in Iraq and Lebanon remained at best junior partners in the process of state formation, their condition contrasted favorably with that of their coreligionists in al-Hasa, which the Saudis conquered from the Ottomans in 1913. The Ottomans had granted the Shi'ites of this region relative freedom to worship in their own mosques and follow their own local religious leaders. In contrast, the fiercely monotheistic partisans of Ibn 'Abd al-Wahhab excoriated Imamis as the worst sort of polytheists. The Saudis, imbued with this puritan conscience, placed severe restrictions on Twelver religious observances, and in general deprived them of religious liberty. A minority of activist local Shi'ite leaders, especially Hasan 'Ali al-Badr, called for armed resistance to the Wahhabi invaders in Qatif, but more quietist figures won the day. The more militant Shi'ites then emigrated to Bahrain or Iraq. The new ruler, Ibn Sa'ud, imposed harsh taxes on the Shi'ites of al-Hasa. A vigilante-like group of Wahhabis called the Ikhwan, adherents of an ultra-strict interpretation of Sunni Islam, forbade Shi'ite mourning processions for the Imams and other public manifestations of Shi'ism in the 1920s, either at the ruler Ibn Sa'ud's behest or with his complaisance. Judgeships were increasingly held by radical anti-Shi'ites. In 1927 the Ikhwan pressured Ibn Sa'ud into staging formal ceremonies in al-Hasa where Shi'ite notables were forced to convert to "Islam" (i.e. Sunnism) and renounce their former "polytheism." Many Shi'ites emigrated or were forced out. Wahhabis began selecting some Shi'ite mosques and houses of mourning to be destroyed, and Wahhabi prayer leaders were installed in others. In 1928 Ibn Sa'ud broke with the Ikhwan and subdued them by force, and thereafter he lessened pressure on the Shi'ites of al-Hasa to conform to Wahhabi norms. He did not, however, relent on the issue of over-taxation, and his policies are said to have driven many Shi'ite landowners from the kingdom, allowing Sunni carpetbaggers to buy up their estates at a pittance. Most Shi'ite communities suffered these abuses silently, but in 1929 a brief revolt broke out in Qatif, which was put down. Even after the decline in the influence of the Wahhabi clerics after 1930, Imamis could practice their religion only in private, and the one attempt to re-establish a local seminary in Qatif resulted in the imprisonment of its main supporter. The local Shi'ites were further hurt economically by the collapse of the natural pearl industry in the face of the rise of cultured pearls. Until 1945, Twelvers tended to be craftsmen working for Sunni merchants or laborers in the gardens of the predominantly Sunni big landowners of al-Hasa. The Twelvers of al-Hasa dwelt above the rich oil deposits discovered in 1936, and later on naturally supplied much of the labor needed to exploit them. Attempts were made to restrict them to relatively unskilled positions, but it was impossible to prevent them from benefiting from the economic windfall of petroleum altogether. Ironically, of all the Imami Arab communities, that of Saudi Arabia's Eastern Province possessed fewest religious rights but were the most integrated (albeit as proletarians) into the structures of a modern economy. They were not dirt farmers, marsh Arabs or slum dwellers, but rather came to constitute a third of the workers on the oil rigs. Since their region did not, however, profit from its petroleum to the same extent as, say, The Saudi capital of Riyadh, al-Hasa's Twelvers were doubly exploited. [10]

The fall of the Qajars in 1925 and the rise of the new Pahlevi dynasty, along with the gradual emergence of Iranian nationalism, much reduced Iranian Shi`ite influence abroad. The Pahlevi shahs, committed to a secular ideal, were not much interested in including support for Shi`ism abroad in their foreign policy goals. The networks of Shi`ite ulama in Qum, Isfahan, Mashhad and elsewhere continued to run seminaries and to attract students from abroad, and this was probably Iran's main influence on neighboring Shi`ite communities in the middle third of the twentieth century.

For some Arab Twelvers of the elite or the intelligentsia, the ideologies of nationalism and ethnic Arabism proved increasingly attractive ways of integrating their communities with those of the dominant Sunnis. But among the masses many retained a religious ideology of the righteousness of the oppressed Imams and the sacredness of Imam Husayn's martyrdom at the hands of a tyrannical government, which continued to harmonize with their political reality. Of course, even such specifically Shi`ite cultural symbols need not be incompatible with loyalty to Iraq or Lebanon (Saudi Arabia is another matter).

The Shi`ites of South Asia in the period before 1947 continued to be under British rule and so the question of their relationship to postcolonial nation-states was deferred. They did organize on a communal basis, and some Shi`ites supported the Muslim League's call for Pakistan in the 1930s-1940s. Others, especially the All-India Shia Conference in Lucknow, backed the Congress Party, which they felt was more relevant to those Muslims whose provinces had no hope of being included in Pakistan and who intended to remain in India. After Partition in 1947-48, Shi`ites emigrated to Karachi from the Indian United Provinces (the old Awadh or Oudh of which we have spoken so much in previous chapters) in substantial numbers, though most, of course, remained in India and continued to ally with Congress. Thus, before Partition their community politics was most often subsumed under broader forces such as the Muslim League and the Congress Party.

The last three decades of the twentieth century witnessed great changes in the situation of the Twelvers, though it is clearly too early to draw a balance sheet or to come to any real conclusion about where these changes will take West and South Asia. So far, the governmental structures and private commitments that promoted discrimination against the Shi`ites in Iraq and Saudi Arabia's Eastern Province have not been much altered. But they have been stretched and challenged. Their position in Lebanon has, however, altered dramatically. The organizing of a significant Shi`ite community in Pakistan after 1947 has so far not dramatically altered their status as a minority, but the Pakistani state has in any case been relatively tolerant of them, moreso than any government in the Arab world with the exception of early twenty-first century Lebanon. In the Arab world, the Shi`ites have often moved from peasant villages to city slums, which while it has not helped national integration in the way some theorists predicted, has made them available for political mobilization on ethnic grounds in new ways. What has been the impact of the Islamic Revolution in Iran on that country's neighbors?

Although in the late 1950s a significant proportion of the members of the Arab nationalist Baath party were Twelvers, after 1963 Sunnis began to predominate and to monopolize its upper echelons. The Baath-military coup of 1968 brought an elite of Sunnis to power. Although the Baath espoused a secular ideology of nationalism and "socialism," it became one more vehicle for relatively small Sunni Arab power elite to dominate Twelver Arabs and Kurds. The secularism of the Sunni elite brought them into conflict with committed Twelvers clergy and intellectuals, who, like their coreligionists in Iran, increasingly sought solutions to their social problems in a resurgent Islam. That Imamis were largely excluded from power and the country's burgeoning oil wealth in the 1970s made things even worse. From early in their rule, the Baathists closed Twelver Muslim institutions, enforced strict censorship on religious publications, authorized the sale of alcohol in the shrine cities, persecuted activist Imami ulama, and quelled subsequent demonstrations by force. In the early 1970s some 60,000 Iraqis of "Iranian extraction" were expelled from the country into Iran; most of them did not even know Persian. The state was clearly attempting to deprive the Iraqi Shi`ite community of the resources of its urban merchant class, from which many of those expelled derived.

The Twelver reaction to de facto discriminatory policies was various. On the one hand, some activists began setting up, from the late 1950s, underground movements such as ad-Da`wa and al-Mujahidun which worked toward an Islamic state. A more dramatic reaction came in 1977, when tens of thousands of Twelvers rioted in the provinces of Najaf and Karbala, and in the slum of al-Thawra township in Baghdad, demanding the end of the infidel Baath regime. By the late 1970s, as well, Da`wa had become increasingly militant and even had decided that the only way to fight the Baath's increasingly repressive and totalitarian turn was violence. Saddam Hussein and the party elite resisted both pressure to institute an Islamization program and to admit more Twelvers into the highest government offices with real power. He harshly responded by arresting Twelver leaders and executing some of the more prominent or militant. But the regime did spend more money on Imami areas, and in so doing avoided further major unrest in the succeeding decade. Saddam Husein's increasing cult of personality, and his commitment to battling Islamism with an Arab nationalist ideology, led him into the misstep of attempting to forestall a Twelver uprising at home (as called for by Khomeini in 1979) by launching an attack on revolutionary Iran in 1980. Although the largely Twelver Iraqi troops performed listlessly, and 10,000 or so are said to have defected to Iran, most clearly chose to be Iraqi Arabs rather than Persian-dominated Imamis - despite the strong Islamist leanings of many Iraqi Twelvers in the 1970s. More militant Shi`ites of a Da`wa cell attempted to assassinate Saddam in 1987, but failed.

Saddam's 1990-1991 attack on and occupation of Kuwait, which provoked the Gulf War, seemed to give an opening to Shi`tes chafing under Baathist repression. Although some important number of them continued to support and be involved with the Ba`th party, the leaders of the oppositionally-minded among them attempted to coordinate with the Kurds and other dissidents with a view toward planning a post-Ba`thist Iraq. Probably a majority of Shi`ites joined the ranks of the opposition in the fateful spring of 1991 when, in the wake of the defeat inflicted on the regime by the U.S. and its allies, Shi`ites in Najaf, Karbala, Basra and elsewhere rose up against the Ba`th. The regime's retaliation was brutal and effective, leaving countless casualties (rumors of 40,000 dead in Karbala alone have reached me from Iraqi expatriates). More recently, the Iraqi government has waged ecological war on the marsh Shi`ites of the south, draining their swamps and forcing tens of thousands of them to flee to Iran. The situation in Iraq in the late 1990s through the present is difficult to know about in detail, and the world economic blockade against it has produced a highly abnormal political economy, so that generalizations about the place of Shi`ites in contemporary Iraq are parlous. It is safe to say, however, that a very large proportion of the community is extremely alienated from the regime and that there is a real question as to whether it can ever truly gain their loyalty.[11]

In Lebanon the social position of the Twelvers changed drastically in the postwar period, even before the country plunged into a period of prolonged political instability from 1975.[12] In 1956 Twelvers constituted around 18% of the population and subsisted largely in the south or around Baalbek as poor, illiterate sharecroppers and dirt farmers. Thereafter they suffered because of high indebtedness and agricultural mechanization, being forced off the land into the cities or abroad to West Africa and the Gulf. Some Twelvers accumulated enough capital to go into commerce or banking, and many increased their literacy and access to other media such as radio and television, though most became concentrated in the grimy bidonvilles of Beirut. But their forced urbanization and greater access to media did make them easier to organize. The insecurity of life for Twelvers in these decades also spurred a demographic spurt at a time when middle-class Maronites were reducing their family size and emigrating abroad in large numbers. By 1975 Twelvers were about 22 percent of Lebanon's population. Given the huge Maronite emigration since that date, and the continued large families of the Twelvers, some have suggested they constituted by the mid-1980s over 30 percent of the country's population.

In the civil war in the mid-70s, national order broke down and coalition militias based in neighborhoods emerged as the most important unit of government, each organized on the basis of religious or ethnic community. The Syrians, who invaded in 1976, chose not to pacify the country, but rather to play local militias and communities off against one another. Willy-nilly, some Twelvers had to join militias, including one of their own, AMAL, in order to survive. Many poor Twelver youth joined Communist and other leftist organizations, and fought in their militias, as well. Developing out of the Iranian cleric al-Sayyid Musa al-Sadr's Movement of the Deprived, Amal, like other militias, forms the security wing of a political party. Amal had to compete with other political currents among Shi`ites. As noted, the appeal of the Left for many ethnic Shi`ites cannot be discounted.

In the wake of the Israeli invasion of Lebanon of 1982, and the truck-bombing of the U.S. Marine barracks in October, 1983 by radical Shi`ites, Amal in coalition with Druze fighters in 1984 took over West Beirut - formerly a Sunni power base. Amal leader Nabih Berri, a French-trained lawyer with an American green card, gained the cabinet portfolio of minister for the south, and has played an important governmental role ever since, whether in the cabinet or the parliament. For some years, he has served as Speaker of Lebanon's reconstituted parliament. Although Amal had a paramilitary wing that was for a while in the 1980s involved in airplane hijackings, kidnappings and other terrorist actions, it gradually evolved into a fairly mainstream political party representing the interests of the new Shi`ite middle class. Amal's basic political demands, the end of confessional representation and greater political weight for Twelvers in view of their new plurality, demonstrate conclusively that it aims at national integration for Shi`ites. Amal so far forms part of a remaining stream of specifically Lebanese nationalism, having largely resisted the appeals of pan-Islam or Shi`ite irredentism. As the largest religious and ethnic minority in Lebanon, which has thrown up an important bourgoisie and professional class, the Shi`ites had a great deal to gain from the restoration of some stability to Lebanon in the 1990s. Whether Amal leaders from the middle strata can offer a stake in the system to the poor Shi`ites in the bargain, and retain their loyalty, remains a crucial question. Amal has run politically savvy political campaigns against its main competitor, Hizbullah, in the late 1990s, dealing the latter substantial defeats in parliamentary and some municipal elections.

The other major political grouping among Lebanese Shi`ites is the Hizbullah, notable for its decade and a half guerilla war against the Israeli occupation of a swath of land in the far south of the country. Hizbullah emerged into prominence first in 1983, when more radical Islamists broke with the Amal party. They carried out bombings of the U.S. embassy and a Marine barracks in October of 1983, and attacked a U.S. embassy annex a year later. Its fighters were also involved in kidnappings of Americans and airplane hijackings in the 1980s. Its major focus from 1985 was fighting Israeli forces and their proxies in South Lebanon. It is said that in the beginning this party was predominantly controlled by Iran, and Revolutionary Guards have been stationed in training camps near the city of Baalbek. Hizbullah has developed more local leadership in recent years. It has received, and continues to receive, major funding from Iran estimated in the late 1990s at $7-20 million per month. Only a portion of it is probably put to the military purposes of its armed wing, the 5,000-man Islamic Resistance, however. Much of the money goes to social welfare institutions run by the party.

In the 1990s, the Hizbullah has emerged as a political party of some sophistication. It has attracted middle class members. In 1996 a militant faction, headed by Shaykh Subhi Tufayli, split from the party mainstream over its softening political line. At the dawn of the twenty-first century, the Hizbullah holds nine seats in the 128-member Lebanese parliament (down from 12 in the early 1990s), along with members in forty municipalities. It has established 3 hospitals, 9 schools, 13 dental clinics, and other social service institutions, including the provision of clean drinking water to slum dwellers in Beirut. Its leaders say they are dedicated to making Lebanon into a Shi`ite Islamic republic (an unlikely development in a country with powerful Christian, Sunni and Druze minorities and a strong secularist position, where Shi`ites are at most a plurality). They have announced their unswerving allegiance to Iranian spiritual leader `Ali Khamenei and they are suspicious of liberalizing reforms in Iran. The Hizbullah won a major victory when Israeli troops withdrew from South Lebanon in 2000 and their proxy Lebanese forces disbanded. The militia refused to disarm even in the wake of winning its main goal, however, and Israeli newspapers complain that it has continued to lob mortars over into Israeli-held territory and to encourage Palestinian terrorism against Israel. Some sources charge Hizbullah in fund-raising and Islamist extremist actions in Latin America and in Europe in the 1990s. The American War on Terror from September 11, 2001, had severe implications for continued paramilitary or terrorist operations of Hizbullah. The party was named by President George W. Bush a terrorist organization, the financial accounts of which must be frozen. Lebanese Prime Minister Rafik Hariri angrily rejected this demand, insisting that Hizbullah is a bona fide Lebanese political party and that its paramilitary activities against Israel's occupation of the Shebaa Farms area claimed by both Syria and Lebanon were legitimate anti-imperialist warfare. The scene was therefore set for a potentially violent confrontation between an America dedicated to reducing the use of transnational violence by non-state actors as a political weapon, and a radical Shi`ite party committed to its continued use against Israel.[13]

In al-Hasa, the Saudi authorities, after a number of missteps, appear for the moment to have achieved something like a detente with its Shi`ites. In 1979, following the revolution in Iran, Twelvers in Saudi Arabia's Eastern Province mobilized to express their grievances.[14] They spread pamphlets, and in November of 1979 insisted on holding public `Ashura' processions to mourn the martyrdom of Imam Husayn. The processions became the flashpoint for riots and demonstrations throughout the area's major towns, including the oil towns. Further demonstrations and clashes occurred in February of 1980. After harshly suppressing these manifestations of social discontent, the Saudi government went on to promise Twelvers a better lot in life. Monies were slated for electrification, roadwork, and housing loans in Twelver areas. In February 1986 King Fahd visited the Eastern Province and pledged still more spending on public projects and an equal treatment of Shi`ites. In order to keep in closer touch with the area's Twelvers, he had appointed his son Prince Muhammad as governor of the province. This carrot appears to have been proffered with some success, given the general lack of subsequent turmoil in the province, marred only by the 1996 bombing of a U.S. barracks at al-Khobar, which many in the U.S. lay at the feet of Iran. Others have blamed radical Saudi Shi`ites of Eastern Arabia, who were said to have organized in a small clandestine cell of less than a hundred members in the mid-1990s, leading to a 1996 crackdown. In spring of

2000, violence erupted between the Saudi state and a small Ismaili Shi`ite community near the Yemeni border over Wahhabi restrictions on their worship practices, and intolerance toward Shi`ites continues to be strong in the kingdom. [15]

Shi`ites have witnessed repression and then acceptance in Bahrain, a Sunni-ruled island, the population of which is two-thirds Shi`ite.[16] There, the ruling family prorogued parliament in 1975.   When a coalition of Sunni and Shi`ite reformers campaigned in 1991 for its restoration, they were harshly suppressed.   In the 1990s Bahrain was the scene of a concerted struggle by local Shi`ites for greater rights and a say in their own governance, in which dozens of persons died in various acts of violence. Some of the more radical Bahraini Shi`ites appear to have had close connections to Iran, but most clerics in Bahrain are from a different and far more conservative school of jurisprudence (the Akhbari) than that which prevails in Iran. Many of the issues were social rather than religious, however. There are resentments about guest workers taking jobs that Shi`ites could fill.   In 2001, a newly powerful member of the royal family finally instituted certain reforms and lifted somewhat the severe persecution of Shi`ite and democratic activists, leaving the door open to more optimism about how Bahraini religion-state relations will develop in the future.

In South Asia, the Shi`ite community of Pakistan emerged as the most numerous in the world after Iran.   The precise percentage of Pakistan's 130 million people who are Shi`ites is a matter of dispute, but the imprecise range of 6 to 12 percent is often suggested.   The majority of Pakistani Twelvers consists of rural Punjabis, probably the peasant followers of the Suhravardi and other mystical Sufi leaders who converted to Twelver Shi`ism, mainly in the course of the nineteenth century. Karachi's well-organized Shi`ite community consists of Urdu-speaking "Muhajirs" or immigrants from India at Partition. There are also Shi`ites in the far north of the country, in Hunza and Gilgit, as well as among the Sindhis.   Pakistani Shi`ites split in the years after 1947 into two main organizations, one committed to the equal status of all Pakistanis, and the other more communally oriented and dedicated to preserving a specific Shi`ite identity.   As Pakistan moved toward having a written constitution in 1956 and toward greater implementation of Islamic law, Shi`ites were concerned that the Sunni interpretation of Islam not become hegemonic such that they were governed by it themselves.   They succeeded in gaining protections for Shi`ism in the constitution, though it has been alleged that in actual practice they have been discriminated against in the law.   Sunni activists pressed for restrictions on Shi`ite mourning processions, hoping to ban them or at least ensure they did not go through Sunni neighborhoods, and sometimes they succeeded in the latter.   Sunni-

Shi'ite riots during such processions in the month of Muharram have been endemic, and particularly bad violence broke out between the two in the mid-1960s in the Punjab and in the 1980s in Karachi. The violence had the effect of encouraging government restrictions on the processions. In the late 1960s Shi'ites successfully mobilized to ensure that the government, which was taking over Muslim pious endowments (*awqaf*) would not put them under the control of Sunni clerics, and in this they succeeded.[17]

In the 1970s, Prime Minister Zulfikar Ali Bhutto's socialist policies hurt many Shi'ite great landlords and inspired fear of secular hegemony among many clerics. Shi'ite ulama were among those who preached against Bhutto in the mid-1970s, and who helped provoke the military coup of General Zia ul-Haqq in 1977. General Zia was committed to "Islamization," the replacing of secular or British-derived law with statutes drawn from medieval Sunni jurisprudence. Since Islamic law recognizes few grounds for depriving persons of private property, this tack had the political advantage of attracting the support of wealthy Pakistanis hurt by Bhutto's nationalization policies. The implementation of Islamic law as Sunni law, however, threatened the interests of Shi'ites. Among the new policies was the involuntary collection of alms (zakat) from Pakistani bank accounts, through the deduction of 2.5 percent per annum of the principal. Zia envisaged the Sunni ulama as the body that would distribute the money to the poor, provoking howls of protest from the Shi'ite community, sure that they would end up being taxed for the benefit of Sunnis. In July of 1980 some one hundred thousand angry Shi'ites descended on the capital of Islamabad to protest. Later the same month, a demonstration by 25,000 Shi'ites turned violent. Zia ul-Haqq then backed down and allowed Shi'ites to exempt themselves from payment of the tax. Khomeini-style Shi'ism gained adherents in Lahore. In the 1980s, the Karachi Shi'ite community was roiled with Sunni-Shi'ite violence that had an ethnic tinge (often their adversaries were immigrant Pushtuns, militant Sunnis, who had settled in the city because of the Afghan wars). In the 1990s the epicenter of Sunni-Shi'ite violence switched to the Punjab, where a shadowy ultra-Sunni group called the Army of the Companions [of the Prophet], dedicated to violence against Shi'ites for their alleged insults to the Sunni caliphs, conducted numerous militia-style raids on Shi'ite communities. Shi'ites in Pakistan have gained de jure protections as a minority, and the presence among them of big landlords and other wealthy gives their community political weight. They have demonstrated an ability to sustain civil-society organizations and to mobilize for the attainment of political goals. The example of their co-religionists in Iran has probably encouraged them to be more activist and sometimes militant. Still, they are a small minority in a large Sunni country and are open to de facto discrimination and sometimes even campaigns of violence. The Sipah-i Sahaba or Army of the Companions allied with the Afghan Taliban, which received monetary and other support from Saudi Arabia assassinated Shi`ites. Rivalries between Shi`ite Iran and Sunni powers like Saudi Arabia, Iraq and Afghanistan are sometimes played out among Pakistani Shi`ite and Sunni communities.

The Islamic Revolution and the war with Iraq in the 1980s also challenged the relatively quietist Shi`ites left back in India, who had largely supported the Congress Party, and it exacerbated Shi`ite-Sunni tensions in centers like Lucknow. (Sunnis tended to support Iraq in the war). Khomeinism became an ideology that competed with the more politically subdued versions of Shi`ism popular in Lucknow and other old Shi`ite centers, but it is my impression that it remained a minority taste. The greatest impact of the rise of revolutionary Iran on South Asia was probably in Afghanistan, where the beleaguered minority of Hazara Shi`ites found themselves forced to develop their own militia and party (Hizb-i Vahdat) and to make a shifting series of alliances in order to survive during that country's long civil war. Ultimately the ultra-Sunni Taliban conquered their main territory, with much bloodshed. At one point in the late 1990s Iran appeared to be mobilizing for war with the Taliban over its treatment of Afghan Shi`ites and of Iranian personnel in the country.[18] The threat passed, but the incident no doubt influenced Iran to side quietly with the U.S. in its battle against the Taliban in 2001. American special operations forces fought side by side with and gave key tactical support to the Shi`ite Hazara fighters and the other members of the Northern Alliance who battled and defeated the Taliban.

The spiritual and political impact of the Islamic Revolution in Iran has often spurred the Shi`ites in the countries around Iran to greater activism and made them a force the civil state had to reckon with. Nabih Berri's position as a non-feudal part of the mainstream of Lebanese politics was new, even if having a Shi`ite speaker of parliament is not. At the same time, the various communities' new militancy has sometimes been extremely costly in lives and property damage, as in the disaster visited on rebelling Shi`ites by Saddam Hussein in 1991 and after. One might also instance the constant fighting between Israel and its Christian allies in South Lebanon and the AMAL and Hizbullah militias, which has often harmed Shi`ite and other civilians. Continued commitment to violent tactics by Hizbullah could well bring it into a fateful confrontation with the United States.

On closer examination, however, it seems obvious that Shi`ite activism in the late twentieth century had the practical effect of integrating Shi`ites more closely into the post-colonial nations in which they found themselves. This integration has been an often brutal and costly struggle.

Although the Baath Party in Iraq has conducted major pogroms against Shi`ites in the south of the country, it has also been open to substantial Shi`ite talent within its own civilian ranks. Amal gradually evolved from a community militia that sometimes resorted to terror into a mainstream political party dedicated to maintaining the integrity of a Lebanon characterized by a civil government and parliamentary rule. Hizbullah has not made that transition, but with the Israeli withdrawal from the south of the country in 2000, it may well be unable to sustain a paramilitary mission. Severe American pressure to abandon transnational violence as a tactic could also play a role in such a transformation. The necessity of trading horses for political campaigns and parliamentary maneuvering seems unlikely to leave in place its somewhat quixotic attachment to old-style Khomeinist rhetoric about an Islamic republic ruled by Shi`ite clerics.

Shi`ites in Pakistan had suffered systematic persecution and assassinations at the hands of hyper-Sunni groups such as the Sipah-i Sahaba, which had strong links to, and fought alongside the Taliban and al-Qaida in Afghanistan. Although they were careful not to be too vocal about it, they must have rejoiced at the destruction of the Taliban in the joint U.S./Northern Alliance military actions of fall, 2001. After all, the Afghan Shi`ite Hazaras, with their Hizb-i Vahdat militia, played a central role in the Northern Alliance forces that liberated Hazara regions like Bamiyan and then the country's capital, Kabul in November of that year. Both Afghan and Pakistani Shi`ites, despite their small proportion of the total population, were well placed in the aftermath of the War on Terror to seek integration into the political establishment of their countries. Pakistani President Pervez Musharraf, who had come to power in a 1999 coup, will need the Shi`ites if he is to complete his turn against the militant Sunni Deobandis and their seminaries, which had graduated the Taliban. (Deobandism was a revivalist movement among Indian Muslims beginning in the colonial period, but under Saudi influence and in reaction to the Soviet occupation of Kabul, it became radicalized in northern Pakistan and Afghanistan).

Of all these communities, the Saudi Shi`ites have been least successful in gaining their demands or finding a means to national integration. Saudi Arabia has a less significant civil society than most of the rest of the Middle East, and no party organization, and is ruled by fiat on the part of a twenty-first century absolute monarchy. Its power structures are therefore narrow and exclusionary, leaving little opportunity for Shi`ites to make an impact. Their struggles, however, have played a significant role in Saudi Arabia, and even moreso in recent years in Bahrain. The Shi`ite Arab minorities may often lack much political power   in conventional terms, but they continue to be significant actors in state-making in the Middle East.

11

*The Modernity of Theocracy**

The government of Iran is a theocracy, and guaranteed to be so by the Iranian constitution. It gives enormous powers into the hands of the Supreme Jurisprudent, the cleric who stands at the head of the system of Islamic law and administration, as well as into the hands of the clerically dominated supreme court and Guardianship Council. In so identifying the Iranian state, it is not my intention to posit Islam or theocracy as essentialist and unchanging cultural formations. Rather, as I will attempt to show, the very process of institutionalizing a Shi`ite theocracy in a modern state has radically changed the Twelver Shi`ite tradition. As Talal Asad has argued convincingly, a religious tradition is in any case a set of arguments over time rather than a static object of transmission.[1] Taking religion seriously does not ipso facto imply a commitment to an essentialist view of it or of social causation. I want here, however, to go rather beyond a consideration of a religious tradition as a bounded set of internal arguments to an assertion that "tradition" is always a social construct, and that what is "traditional" in a modern setting is in reality a core of earlier texts or doctrines wrapped in an unacknowledged set of innovations. Certainly, in important sectors of society, Islamic law has made a large impact on revolutionary Iran. Law has been "Islamized." In 1982 the Supreme Court abolished remaining legal institutions surviving from the Pahlevi period as well as laws still on the books that contravened its understanding of Islamic law. In 1983, it established "Islamic" punishments, decreeing 109 capital offenses, including adultery, drinking alcohol, and homosexuality. Hands were to be severed for theft, and fornication or violation of the dress code resulting in flogging. Most justice was administered summarily, and executions took place almost immediately after sentencing. The touchstone for many of these laws is medieval Muslim jurisprudence (which is not exactly the same thing as Islamic law, though often the two are confused).

As a result of this sort of legislation, the question of whether Iran's theocratic republicanism represents a form of medieval romanticism or a form of modern populism has been a theme of the literature on Iran since 1979. The "medievalist" argument has often inflected the writing of journalists and of Iran's theocratic republicanism's opponents. Ervand Abrahamian has made the strongest case against medieval romanticism and for Iran's theocratic republicanism as akin to Latin American populism, juxtaposing the ayatollah to Peron.[2] I concur in the value of this comparison, but my concerns here are different from those of Abrahamian. It is the argument of this paper that Iran's theocratic republicanism as a state project is a distinctive form of high modernism, which is influenced by the demands of Shi`ite nativism. That is, medievalism is a motif in Iran's current version of modernism, but it is like the medievalism of Dali's surrealist paintings, like Walter Benjamin's use of the kabbalah, like neo-Thomism in twentieth century Catholic theology. The medieval is encapsulated by and employed for the construction of an anti-liberal modernism, thus becoming something quite un-medieval.

I would like to begin by examining the premises underlying the medievalist thesis. Among its proponents was the shah himself. While in power (1941-1979) he frequently characterized the Shi`ite clergy as "black reactionaries," and, perhaps under the influence of his Swiss education, saw many social institutions in Iran, including the bazaars, as medieval holdovers that were better swept away by modernity. Already in the summer of 1979, from his exile in Mexico, the shah described the revolutionary government as "under the influence of medieval leadership" and "crumbling of its own ineptitude.'[3] A year and a half later Steven V. Roberts of the New York Times wrote that "A year ago at this time, Americans were already in a funk. Iran, one of our strongest allies in the Middle East, had fallen to the forces of a medieval religious fanatic who was turning back the clock with both hands."[4] In 1986 Gary Sick, formerly of the Carter National Security Council, wrote of Khomeini in France that "During his four-month sojourn at Neauphle-le-Chateau outside Paris, he gave hundreds of personal interviews to those who flocked to his door, curious to meet this medieval prophet turned revolutionary."[5] Imam Khomeini's 1989 jurisprudential ruling (fatwa) condemning Salman Rushdie's book *The Satanic Verses* as a capital offense created a virtual flood of newsprint coupling the words "Iran" with "medieval." As late as 1995, Thomas Friedman could write, "In my next life I want to be a European statesman. I want to be able to turn up my nose at the United States when it puts principle before profit and naively imposes an embargo on Iran to prevent this medieval theocracy from acquiring nuclear arms."[6] Iranian secularists tend not to use the diction "medieval," which has connotations in Persian of Western historical periodization, preferring to call the regime "reactionary" (*irtija`i*), though they also speak of it taking Iran "back to the stone ages." Moreover, of course, Khomeini and other Islamist activists often had a sharply critical view of the Muslim medieval period, which was dominated by Sunni caliphates and by monarchies, so that the terminology was not by any means indigenous.[7]

Whether its adherents recognize it or not, the idea that a contemporary state can be a throwback to medieval times rests upon Auguste Comte's "law of the three stages" of human intellectual development. Comte (1798-1857) believed that there had been a progression from a theological stage (that of belief in gods) to a metaphysical stage (that of medieval theology and sometimes theocracy with its belief in abstractions such as essences), and finally that of positive, empirical knowledge typical of scientific rationalism. From this point of view, what Iranians have done since 1979 appears to have been to displace the high modern technocracy of the shah in favor of an imposition on Iran of medieval-religious governmental and social forms of the "second stage." They have gone "backward" and so violated Comte's law. The shah's wholly unwarranted conviction that the 1979 Khomeinist government was "crumbling" was probably tied up with this idea of the unnatural nature of a regression to the metaphysical stage of medieval theocracy, which seemed unlikely to those in the Comtean tradition to persist.

The trope of medievalism is actually quite peculiar. It maps the globe in four dimensions rather than only three. That is, Khomeinist Iran is not only over 600,000 square miles in its dimensions, but it lies 800 years in the past. Perhaps, in good science-fictional fashion, journalists who speak in this manner see parts of the U.S., e.g. Silicon Valley or Cape Canaveral, as in the future. By slicing time up into static, linear blocs and then locating each geographical region on this temporal grid, a Comtean moral hierarchy is established, wherein a humane and advanced West is in the future compared to barbaric "medieval" countries. These considerations aside, it is not at all clear that the authors who appeal to the pervasive trope of the medieval understand what the medieval period was really like, so that what is being invoked is a modernist set of myths about the medieval in any case.

Those who find the medievalist argument unconvincing frequently have a dialectical rather than a linear view of history. From a dialectical point of view, no medieval template could simply be lifted from past history and misplaced onto the present. Rather, any social movement or form of government now existing has come into being by dialectical interaction with modernity and so itself partakes of modernity. The oaths that Catholic clergy had to swear in the early twentieth century to oppose modernism were modern oaths. The Bharatiya Janata Party in India, which some would see as devoted to restoring a medieval vision of Hindu rule in India, is a quite modern and sophisticated political party. The Hinduism of the BJP has evolved in dialectic with modernity and the heritage of both colonial utilitarianism and Nehruvian secularism. Likewise, the Christian Coalition of the late twentieth century U.S. is, despite the biblical literalism of many of its members, a most modern political movement.

Sociologist Anthony Giddens has been among the more thoughtful commentators on modernity as a dialectical rather than a static social form.[8] It is fluid and changing and full of contradictory forces. The modernist impulse that overthrew royal absolutism in the eighteenth and nineteenth centuries could also give rise to amoral republics and national security states, which in turn gave rise to "utopian realist" movements for greater civil liberties within the modernist republic. Modernism cannot be placed in a simplistic way under the sign of secularism and scientism. Rather it is itself a field of contention on which religious and secular ways of viewing the world battle with one another and influence one another. Twentieth century religion has been transformed by modernity, with regard to everything from bureaucratization to doctrine. Modernity in turn has been shaped in important respects by religious institutions and concerns, whether negatively or positively. I will argue that republican Iran has been such a field of contention, in which theocratic forces have battled secularizing ones, proponents of state socialism have struggled with capitalists, militarists have contended with forces favoring a small military, and those seeking greater religious censorship have grappled with those advocating greater intellectual freedom. The balance sheet of these various struggles about the shape of Iranian modernity has to be drawn differently in the 1980s (when the first term in each of these binary oppositions prevailed) than in the 1990s (when, despite the continued strength of the theocrats, the ground began to shift against them). An Iranian observer, `Ali Asghar Kazimi, has characterized the entire past two decades as a "crisis of modernity."[9]

Medieval and Modern Shi`ism

One response to the argument for medievalism is that despite the rhetoric appealing to Shi`ite tradition, the Islamic Republic of Iran does not resemble the functioning or even ideals of medieval Shi`ism. As we have seen above in this book, Twelver Shi`ism was initially premised on the notion that after the death of the Prophet Muhammad he should have been succeeded by his cousin and son-in-law, `Ali, and then by `Ali's lineal descendants through Fatimah, his wife and the daughter of the

Prophet. When the eleventh of the Shi`ite Imams, Hasan al-`Askari, died, some alleged that he had had an infant son in hiding, who had gone into Occultation in a supernatural, subterranean realm, from which he would return someday to restore justice to the world. The absence of an Imam in this world threw the Twelvers into severe crisis. Some took the Akhbari literalist line, holding to the sayings and doings of the Prophet and the Imams as guides to how life should be lived now that the Imam was not present. They came to hold that the sayings of the Imams had to be taken on faith, and they collected enormous volumes of putative sayings, which they sought to put off-limits for reasoned examination. They even came to argue that the Qur'an itself could not be understood in a common-sense manner without taking into account the sayings and interpretations of the Imams.

Note that even for the rationalist Usulis, the law was never standardized. Apparently contradictory sayings of various Imams all co-existed in enormous folio volumes that entirely lacked indexes. The consensus of past jurisprudents was an unscientific instrument, since scholars often picked and chose among the jurisprudents they considered "great." Usulis maintained that in the absence of the Imam, the Shi`ite learned men were his general deputies. They could thus authorize religious taxes, Friday prayers, and at least defensive holy war (most medieval jurisprudents disallowed offensive holy war in the absence of the Imam, since only he would have the authority to launch one). This Usuli school of scholastic rationalists in jurisprudence tended to garner greater support from and to give greater support to the civil states erected by Shi`ites. Some great Akhbaris did also come to support, e.g., the Safavid state, however, so the distinction is not an absolute one.

Some Usuli jurisprudents were recognized as having only partial expertise, able to rule on some issues but not others. Only a handful were seen as absolute jurisprudents. Some Usuli writers asserted that ideally there should be a single, most learned jurisprudent, to whom all would turn. In practice, however, each city tended to have several senior jurisprudents, and at any one time there were usually five or six major contenders in Iran and (from the late eighteenth century) the Iraqi shrine cities for the position of supreme jurisprudent. That is, Usuli ideals sound like Roman Catholicism, whereas Usuli practice was much more like that of Greek Orthodoxy, with its polycephaly or several equal archbishops rather than a single pope.

Occasionally, beginning in the mid-nineteenth century, a scholar would locate to the shrine cities in Iraq and attain such great prestige by virtue of having trained an entire generation of ulama that he would be given the right to disburse the donations and religious taxes coming into Iraq, a prerogative referred to as *riyasa* or leadership. Such a scholar might be very widely emulated, as well. But it was seldom the case that other senior mujtahids in Iran's major cities saw themselves as subordinate to him or bound by his rulings (indeed, classical Usuli teachings held that no trained jurisprudent was allowed to simply emulate another jurisprudent, but rather always had to reach his conclusions about the law independently).

Usulis strongly held that it was illegitimate to continue to cling to the ruling of a jurisprudent once he had died. Jurisprudence was seen as a continual, dynamic activity of the jurisprudent's mind. Should he, by reasoning upon the relevant texts, ever reach a conclusion that reversed his previous ruling, he was bound to declare it, and the new ruling stood. Commercial litigants complained endlessly of the arbitrary and unstable character of Muslim law, where in a sense no case was ever finally closed until the presiding judge was dead. Since a dead mujtahid cannot engage in this dynamic process of continual reconsideration, and since we cannot know if his great legal mind would have continued to maintain his positions had he lived longer, his rulings cannot form the basis for lay emulation once he is dead. The laity must rather choose a new, living mujtahid to rule on difficult and abstruse matters for them. The previous jurisprudent's rulings might be influential, but they were hardly binding, and only constituted a consideration with regard to any sort of "precedent" insofar as that scholar might be entered among the ranks of the great legal thinkers and so become part of the tradition's consensus (*ijma'*).

Both Akhbaris and Usulis tended to hold that in the absence of the Imam, civil governmental authority could only derive from common law (*'urf*) rather than from Islamic law. In Shi'ite law, after all, the state should be a theocracy ruled by the Imam. In the Imam's absence, governmental authority was not illegitimate, but it was not divinely bestowed, either. It welled up out of customary practice and was therefore mundane or in some sense "secular." To the extent that the Qajar civil state, for instance, did incorporate the ulama into itself with regard to the judiciary, it could be recognized as having some religious charisma, but never very much. Since the state officials and notables were often rapacious and lived by imposing uncanonical taxes on the little people, some of the more radical ulama saw them as holding power illegitimately, though this was a minority view among them.

In contrast to this medieval hodgepodge of unrationalized authority claims and welter of conflicting texts, the Islamic Republic of Iran radically reconfigured Shi'ite institutions via its constitution and legal system. Instead of being an unattainable idea, the Supreme Jurisprudent becomes the holder of a political, institutionalized post, as Iran's head of state. Instead of being a personalized jurisprudent for particular clients and followers, whose rulings lose their force upon his death, he is an institution whose fatwas, as with Khomeini's death decree against Salman Rushdie, are felt by most Iranian Shi'ites to be irrevocable. Instead of being able to pick and choose among thousands of sayings attributed to the Imams (with all of their potential contradictions), law is now made by state jurisprudents in accordance with a fixed constitution, a codified legal system, and parliamentary legislation.

The ability of rival jurisprudents to strike a stance of independence from the supreme jurisprudent, guaranteed in premodern Iran by the informal, personalistic structure of authority in Shi'ism and by poor transportation and communications technologies, has been substantially eroded. Too severely questioning or critiquing Supreme Jurisprudent 'Ali Khamenei can impose threats of imprisonment or even actual jailings on the critics, even if they are themselves high-ranking clergymen. The shotgun marriage between the old Shi'ite ideal of a "source for emulation" (*marja'-i taqlid*) and the Khomeinist institution of the Supreme Jurisprudent (*Faqih*) has produced a far more modern, rationalized structure of authority in Iranian Shi'ism. Nothing like the office of the Faqih existed in medieval Shi'ite Islam, nothing even approaching it.

Medieval Shi'ite learned men were wary of the civil state and saw it as lacking direct divine sanction in the absence of the Imam. Khomeini promulgated the new and quite innovative idea that the clerically-ruled state is not just the general deputy of the Twelfth Imam, but something closer to his specific representative. Whereas medieval Shi'ites fought over whether Friday prayers could even be said, religious taxes paid, and defensive holy war fought, on behalf of a common-law civil state in the absence of the Twelfth Imam, Khomeinism asserted divine sanction for an entire state, with its various branches and extensive bureaucracy, despite the Occultation of the Imam. In his famous pronouncement toward the end of his life, Khomeini affirmed that the Islamic Republic, as the representative of the Hidden Iman, had the authority temporarily to suspend pilgrimage to Mecca and to make other, similar demands on believers.[10] In Islamic law, a distinction was made between basic Islamic law (*usul*) and subsidiary legal issues (*furu'*). Most jurisprudence concentrated on the subsidiary issues, and the demand that the laity emulate the jurisprudents related only to these. A layman was to say his five daily prayers or go on pilgrimage in a straightforward way with reference to the basic Qur'anic texts. Khomeini demolished this fine distinction, projecting the Islamic State's power even into the area of basic, common-sense Islamic obligations like pilgrimage. He further extended its powers by appealing the to Sunni jurisprudential principle of *maslaha* or state action on behalf of the public good, a principle not recognized by medieval Shi`ite jurisprudents but which was taken up from Hanafi thought and foregrounded by Sunni modernists like Muhammad `Abduh. In essence, the "public good" principle allowed the new state to do virtually anything and declare it in accordance with Islamic law, assuming it could be argued it was benefited Muslims. The Khomeinist state is not only not medieval, and it is full of features that would have been branded heretical and unthinkable by the major Shi`ite thinkers of that time. [11] They are so because they are modern.

Let us turn, then, to the question of theocratic Iran as a project of high modernism. James Scott argues that the "most tragic episodes of state-initiated social engineering" occur when four conditions are present. The first is a commitment on the part of the ruling elite to an administrative ordering of nature and society. The second is a high modernist ideology that consists in an aggressive program of scientific and technical progress, the expansion of production, and mastery of nature and of human life. The third is an authoritarian state that unreservedly backs and seeks to implement the high modernist project. Such a state often comes to power through war and revolution, headed by those who repudiate the past and wish radically to reshape society. Finally, Scott believes that such a thoroughgoing state intervention can only be accomplished where civil society is prostrate, such that the populace lacks the means to resist the enterprise. [12]

Scott explicitly names Muhammad Reza Pahlevi as among the purveyors of a high modernist project in the twentieth century, and no one who knows modern Iran can read his description of the phenomenon without immediately thinking of this dynasty. Reza Shah (1925-1941) had initiated the high modernist period in Iran. He demanded that all Iranians take last names so as to establish social "legibility" of the society by the state. He standardized law and thrust aside premodern practices, reducing the power of the clergy, expanding the capital of Tehran, establishing a national school system and the first university. He renegotiated in a small way the royalties on Iranian petroleum, and built the first extensive railroad links throughout the country. The coercive character of this project is symbolized by the forced unveiling campaign of the 1930s, by the banning of trade unions, the jailing and assassination of some political opponents, the banning of socialist movements, and attacks on writers. His successor, Muhammad Reza Pahlevi (r. 1941-1979), established if anything a more complete dictatorship, pursuing industrialization, favoring large businesses, promoting literacy, and vastly expanding the school and university system. Iran was to become "modern" and "like France" by the year 2000, overcoming its "medieval" heritage and institutions, with the clergy and the covered bazaars serving as the shah's bêtes noires.

The high modernist projects of many states have foundered. Some were conquered by outside powers (the Axis). Some ran out of steam, and were supplanted by parliamentary processes, free markets, and civil society in the second or third generation (Kemalist Turkey, the Soviets). Some were overthrown by revolution at the hands of the enraged objects of their social engineering (British India, French Algeria, the Pahlevis in Iran). When high modernist regimes are overthrown, they are often supplanted by Liberal ones. For a society that felt hobbled and impoverished by a large public sector, it is tempting to deliver the economy into private hands and renounce micromanaging it, as the Poles did in the 1990s. For a society that resented the high-handed fiat of dictators, apparatchiks, or politburos, it is appealing to turn to multiparty elections instead. For a society that had experienced severe constraints on public organization, it is often felt desirable that a plethora of civil society organizations be allowed to form.

Yet an authoritarian high modernist regime is not always replaced by a Liberal state. The paradoxes of Iran derive from dialectic. The Islamic revolution represented a severe critique and rejection of prominent features of Pahlevi high modernism. The rhetoric of inclusion, of populism, and of religious authenticity with all its "medieval" referents, was intended to offer an alternative to the shah's vision, which was coded as elitist, exclusionary, foreign, secular and inauthentic. The Khomeinist project is not high modernism (characterized by a scientistic ideology) but nativist modernism, in which the tropes of Western scientism have been subordinated in public to those of indigenous authenticity, here Shi`ite Islam. That the project is now carried out in the name of Islam rather than of science and progress should not deceive us, however. For one thing, the constitution of the Islamic Republic mandates "the utilization of science and technology."[13] There is a real sense in which theocratic Iran continues the Pahlevi project and even exceeds the former in its "high modernism." This is easy to see if we examine the basic initiatives of social engineering since 1979. Khomeinist Islam is not anti-modern, but rather anti-liberal.[14] But as the twentieth century relentlessly showed us, there have been many forms of anti-liberal modernism.

Nativist Modernism in the Economy

Let us consider the economy. One of Scott's indices of high modernism is extensive state intervention in the economy. Fred Halliday famously argued that the regime of Mohammad Reza Pahlevi was properly seen not as a fascist one but as a capitalist dictatorship.[15] Although plagued by cronyism, maldistribution of wealth, and a severe bias toward big business and modern urban enterprises in its loan policies, the Pahlevi state was in fact capitalist. True, the state-owned petroleum industry played a central role in the economy, and the Soviet-built steel mill at Isfahan was a state enterprise. Nevertheless, Iran in the 1960s and 1970s also had a significant private sector. Akhavi has characterized this system not as private enterprise but as exclusionary corporatism, wherein the state intervenes both to bargain with social groups about the scope of their action and to curtail moves toward independence from the state. That is, both "capitalism" and "private sector" meant something different in the shah's Iran than they do in the global north.[16] Nevertheless, unlike many of Scott's examples, the Iranian state was hardly socialist.

In contrast, the Khomeinist state carried out massive nationalization of banks and industries.[17] As economist Jahangir Amuzegar has pointed out, the radical faction around Khomeini chose the Soviet-inspired "Indian model" for the Iranian economy.[18] At the height of Nehruvian economic policies, the Indian public sector constituted about 25 percent of the economy. It is difficult to compare this situation with Khomeinist Iran because the state-owned oil sector distorts the statistics (thus, in almost all oil states large proportions of the economy are in state hands, even rightwing Saudi Arabia). Still, in the Islamic Republic something close to 70 percent of the gross domestic product came to be controlled by the state or state foundations, and even if one subtracted the oil sector some 30 to 50 percent would remain in the public sector, depending on the price of petroleum and currency exchange rates at any one time. This outcome puts Iran somewhere between India and the old Soviet bloc countries such as Hungary (50 percent) or Nasserist Egypt (also 50 percent). Rashidi notes,

Today [1993], the public sector, including the government, public organisations (*nahad, boniyad*) and institutions considered to be part of the government, directly or indirectly control some 70 percent of the GDP, and spend 75-80% of foreign exchange earned by the country. Even though the ratio of the general budget to GDP in 1991 (1370) was 17.3%, the "government" employed about half of the labour force in cities, and 31.8% of the total manpower of the country (4.166 million out of 13.00 million).[19]

The nationalized industries were either placed under direct governmental control or under that of government philanthropies. Between the Revolution and March, 1993 some 580 industrial units were nationalized by the state. Even after the beginnings of privatization in the late 1980s, in 1990 state industries still produced all washing machines and spools, most light bulbs, and about half of the auto tires, refrigerators and freezers, paper, vegetable oil and pharmaceuticals manufactured in the country. By March, 1982, 637 businesses had been placed under the jurisdiction of the Foundation for the Oppressed (*Bunyad-i Mustaz`afin*). Among the holdings of such state institutions are Alborz Silica, Avand Plastic, Ilam Cement, Indamin Shock Absorber, Iran Tire, Radio Electric Iran, Quds Cellulose Manufacturing, and other industries notably lacking in any medieval overtones. Banks and credit institutions were also nationalized, as were the some 600 engineering consultant and construction companies. Very large numbers of businesses and pieces of real estate belonging to pro-Shah political refugees who fled the country were absorbed into the public sector.[20] And, of course, the petroleum industries, which had already been in the public sector under the shah, continued to be a prime source of income to the state. Media such as television and radio are also state-owned and controlled.

Although factory workers participated in the Revolution and then organized themselves into independent Consultative Unions (*shuras*) in the first year after the revolution, attempting to assert workers' control over the shop floor, they were gradually subordinated to the state, as Assef Bayat has shown. In 1979-1981, first Prime Minister Mehdi Bazargan and then President Abolhassan Bani Sadr, promoted a liberal, technocratic management strategy that accommodated some greater worker input but insisted on a technically qualified management making the key decisions in the factory. This strategy was opposed not only by the Consultative Unions themselves, who struck and agitated for worker control, but by the proponents (known as *maktabi*) of Islamic Ideology. Bayat explains that Islamic Ideology as a managerial strategy:

is management by those whose position derives not from certain relevant skills (education or experience) but is based mainly on character and personal, or more importantly, ideological connections with the ruling clergy, especially the IRP (This does not imply that all managers lacked managerial skills.) They were in authority to preserve the presence of the ruling party in the factories, these being the most vulnerable parts of Iranian society . . . In essence, their major policy was repressive one-man management . . .The implication of this approach is that, in practice, there is a tendency to create and support ideological gangs—informal workers' organizations which aret he functionaries of different external organizations of factional powers, such as [the] Islamic Association of the IRP, *Pasdaran* (Revolutionary Guards) and *Basij* (mobilization organization), etc.[21]

Bayat concurs with Akhavi that the labor policy of the Islamic Republic has been corporatist, in which an attempt has been made organically to unite labor, capital and state interest. Although in the first two years after the Revolution Khomeini made numerous statements in favor of the "barefoot" or "oppressed," by which he meant Iran's masses of slum dwellers, he gradually backed off supporting them, throwing his authority behind capital and property instead. By 1992 the Rafsanjani government was engaging in "urban renewal," as Abrahamian has pointed out, which involved the bulldozing of shantytowns, provoking major riots in five cities.[22]

The state has a large role in economic planning and the building of infrastructure. Much more infrastructure, from schools to roads, has been built in the rural areas than was the case under the shah (many of the more powerful members of parliament are from the countryside). But, as Patrick Clawson has noted, the appeal of big industry has not entirely faded:

Iran is also pouring billions of dollars into creating heavy industries that do not seem particularly appropriate from an economic standpoint. Iran's experience with heavy industries, such as the Sar Cheshmeh copper refinery or the Mubarakeh steel mill, should show that such projects can consume billions of dollars for dubious results . . . Perhaps the decision to put so much emphasis on heavy industry in the National Priority Projects reflects the same attitude that led to the investment of billions in the Mubarakeh steel mill. But outside observers can only note that the emphasis on heavy industry gives Iran the capacity to produce a wide range of military goods.[23]

In 1976-1986 the average number of workers employed by each large firm owned by the state or para-state organizations increased from 294 to 407, at a time when employment and output in privately-owned medium firms was plummeting.[24] If state intervention in the economy on a large scale is a sign of high modernism, then Iran's theocratic republicanism has been far more interventionist than the Pahlevis.

The Military

Because of the large number of irregular "revolutionary guards" thrown up by the 1978-79 Revolution, and because of the outbreak of the Iran-Iraq war in 1980, Iranian society became significantly militarized in the 1980s. The number of soldiers in the shah's army, air force and navy in 1977 was 342,000, with military expenditures (in 1992 dollars) of $15 billion. By some estimates, the Islamic Republic in 1986 had 705,000 men under arms, including the revolutionary guards. Military expenditures were $29 billion in 1984 and $20 billion in 1985, falling precipitously thereafter to \$7-\$10 billion until 1991, when the total was halved.[25]

Given the drastic fall in petroleum prices, and the decline in GDP in the course of the 1980s, the increase in military spending was even steeper in proportional terms than it appears. The revolutionary guards were often poorly integrated into the military, sometimes actually competing with regular army troops in the fighting in southwestern Iran against Iraqi invaders. In addition to their battlefield role, they often acted as vigilantes in urban areas, policing morality and the appearance of women, and attacking those they viewed as enemies of the state, not only Mujahidin and Baha'is, but also supporters of elected officials such as President Abolhassan Bani Sadr.

The militarization of Iranian society and a preference for violent means of settling disputes led to tragedies such as the attacks on Kurds seeking greater autonomy in Sanandaj in the early 1980s.[26]   It also resulted in the decision to prolong the Iran-Iraq war even after Saddam Hussein began suing for peace in 1984. Just as Nixon and Kissinger had needlessly prolonged the Vietnam War out of domestic political considerations, so Khomeini prosecuted the war with Iraq for four years longer than he had needed to. Iraq, admittedly the naked aggressor in 1980, was already in 1984 offering substantial concessions and even reparations. Khomeini sought to take Baghdad and to add to Iran's territory a country that was majority-Shi'ite, wherein lay the holiest Shi'ite shrines (Najaf and Karbala), and which was among the richest oil states in the world. His greed and stubbornness cost the country tens of thousands of additional lives and hundreds of thousands of casualties. It is probably not the case that the failing economy was significantly affected by the war, but continuing it incurred many opportunity costs.

The most grotesque manifestation of the high-modern militarism of the 1980s was the tactic of human wave attacks. Foolhardy frontal assaults on heavily fortified Iraqi positions had succeeded in pushing them out of Iranian territory earlier in the war. But after 1982, the Iraqis were dug in, defending their own country rather than attempting to occupy someone else's and their morale appears to have improved. They were, moreover, far better armed than the Iranians and had control of the air. Controversy swirled around the human wave tactic inside Iran, with Khomeini beginning to back away from it in 1985 and Rafsanjani, then speaker of the parliament, openly condemning it in 1988. Still, as late as January 16, 1987, the *Washington Post* quoted U.S. Defense Department reports that 40,000 Iranian troops, many as young as 14, had been killed since the previous December 24 in human wave attacks on Iraqi positions around Basra.[27]

The vigilante cadres of the revolutionary guards, the cultural revolution of 1980 (which was coopted by the Khomeinist state), and the human wave attacks were all consistent with the monumentality and single-mindedness of a high modernist approach to reordering society. No premodern state in the Middle East maintained the demographic equivalent of a 700,000-man standing army. Professional soldiers' lives were valued in the early modern period. It was a Napoleonic innovation to draft hundreds of thousands of peasants and throw them at well-trained, well-armed opponents, using them up at dreadful rates in order to batter down the enemy. Khomeini was not a Richard the Lion-Hearted in his military tactics, but rather a Napoleon Bonaparte, a modern military leader of grandiose ambition and complete lack of respect for individual human lives (though to be fair, Khomeini only came to want Iraq, not the whole of his continent).

The Nuclear Program

Another area where the Iranian state has pursued a program reminiscent of the worst features of high modernism is its nuclear reactor program. Such an energy source makes a certain amount of sense for countries such as France, which can afford big science and which lack petroleum reserves of their own.[28] Even there, the problems of the storage of nuclear waste have never been satisfactorily resolved, creating a very long-term and dangerous potential pollution problem (and a security issue with regard to the potential for terrorists to use nuclear waste to create "dirty" conventional bombs). Iran is virtually floating on petroleum and natural gas, and does not need to risk Chernobyl-style disasters nor face the problems of nuclear waste disposal. It is, moreover, prone to earthquakes. Finally, the unfinished Bushehr nuclear facility was in fact attacked by the Iraqis during the Iran-Iraq war, and should another war break out in the Persian Gulf, an active reactor would pose a tempting target, with terrible consequences should it be hit.

The shah had developed extensive nuclear ambitions in the 1960s, and had acquired from the U.S. a small nuclear research reactor of the Triga type, installed at Amirabad, which became the center for subsequent Iranian nuclear research. The shah hoped to build twelve nuclear power plants and almost certainly had ambitions of developing nuclear weaponry. He actually contracted for and began building two nuclear reactors in the Persian Gulf port of Bushehr, with French, German, Belgian, Italian and Japanese partners, investing $3 billion in the project.

Khomeini cancelled work on these reactors projects on coming to power, seeing nuclear energy as satanic. In 1982, Reza Amrollahi, a relative of then speaker of parliament Ali Akbar Hashimi Rafsanjani, was appointed to the Iranian Atomic Energy Organization and became an advocate for reviving it. He mapped out in public a plan for a civilian power program that would provide about 20 percent of Iran's energy needs. There have been allegations, however, that he also spent a great deal of time lobbying Khomeini and Rafsanjani during the 1980s for the nuclear program, attempting to convince them that Iran could hope to build an atomic bomb. In the end, he was appointed one of four vice presidents and given a budget to restart the nuclear program. In 1985 Iran began seeking agreements with foreign countries, and made plans to site nuclear-related facilities throughout the country in order to make them less vulnerable to attack (taking a lesson, no doubt, from the successful Israeli preemptive strike on Iraq's nuclear facility in Baghdad in 1981). At the height of the Iran-Iraq war and only a few years after the winding down of the cultural revolution and the Great Terror, Iran then lacked the highly-trained scientists and engineers to pursue the program effectively, and needed to rebuild its scientific infrastructure. Amrollahi sought and received permission from the International Atomic Energy Agency, given that Iran had signed the non-proliferation pact, to buy 20 percent enriched uranium for their old American research reactor, and the IAEA authorized Argentina to supply it. Iran further sought another research reactor from the Argentinians, which had the potential to produce weapons-grade plutonium, but this purchase was blocked by the U.S.[29]

President Ali Akbar Hashimi Rafsanjani revived Iran's nuclear ambitions upon becoming president in 1989, however. Initially, he sought to convince Iran's earlier partners to resume work, but these had been alienated by the Iranian role in the terrorist tactic of taking Western hostages in Lebanon, and refused. Rafsanjani then sought a contract for the reactors with China or India. He signed a contract with the Chinese to import a small nuclear research reactor in 1991, which nuclear engineers saw as ominous, since this technology could eventually be used, as it had been by Iraq, to produce atomic bombs. Iran's vice president, Ayatollah Ata'u'llah Muhajirani, did nothing to allay such fears when he said in 1991 in an interview in *Abrar* that all Muslim countries should attempt to acquire nuclear weaponry.[30]

Further momentum toward the Bushehr plan was blocked by the first Bush administration, which also convinced the Kraftwerk Union division of the German Siemens Corporation not to go forward, on the grounds that the project might have military applications. Rafsanjani insisted that Iran only wanted to develop its nuclear research facilities for peaceful purposes. Finally, after four years of seeking another partner, President Rafsanjani prevailed upon a cash-strapped Russia to do the work. In 1995, Iran granted Russia an $800 million contract to build its first nuclear power plant, a VVER-1000 water-cooled, water-moderated reactor, at the Persian Gulf port of Bushehr. Despite enormous pressure applied by Washington to prevent the deal from going forward, the project appears to be quite alive. In April, 1999, a St. Petersburg-based company began producing equipment for the planned nuclear power plant, with delivery set for 2001.[31] The Iranians subsequently sought from the Russians a deal to install three more reactors at Bushehr, even though some high Russian officials have spoken against the wisdom of building further such plants. In spring of 2001, Russian President Vladimir Putin reaffirmed a Russian commitment to helping Iran build nuclear reactors for energy production, despite the sanctions the United States had placed on the Russian firms contracting for this project.[32] Despite Iran's having signed the Nuclear Non-Proliferation Treaty, and despite the lack of firm evidence that it seeks to acquire nuclear weaponry, Washington continues to be convinced that Iran aims at doing so. The reactor at Bushehr would probably not in fact be much help in any weapons program, and it is open to international inspections. It has, however, been alleged by some American journalists and officials that the real nuclear weapons program is far more clandestine, scattered around at secret facilities in Iran not open to inspection. [33] Given that such neighbors as Russia, Pakistan, India and Israel all now have nuclear weapons, and Iraq has in the past been close to developing them, it would not be far-fetched that the Iranian state is seeking this capacity itself. Even a purely civilian nuclear program, however, seems foolish in its risks and monumentality for an oil-rich, income-poor nation. A high modernist project has been refurbished as a nativist-modernist one. Note, too, the obvious contradiction between all the talk of Iran as a "medieval" society in Washington and among the Western journalists, and their simultaneous anxiety about Iran's high-technology capabilities (this startling oxymoron is visible in the quote from Friedman cited earlier).

Political Repression

Although the grounds for censorship and the jailing of dissidents for thought crimes have shifted enormously, the specific state technologies of social control show continuities, as well. While Muhammad Reza Pahlevi led a repressive police state with extensive censorship and jailing of dissidents, the average number of prisoners in the shah's jails held for thought crimes in any one year in the 1970s was about 1,000. This number compares to about 300 in the Soviet Union under Brezhnev. Relatively few dissidents were actually executed, though that any at all were is, of course, monstrous.

Under Khomeini literally tens of thousands of Iranians were serially jailed. Some 10,000 members of or sympathizers with the "Islamic

Marxist" Mujahidin party were killed, most through execution after arrest.[35] Political parties other than the loose Islamic Republican grouping were gradually banned and destroyed, including the revived National Front that had opposed the shah in the early 1950s and which had a significant religious wing. In 1986 there were 600 members of the Baha'i religion in jail simply for adhering to the wrong religion, almost as many as the total number of the Shah's prisoners of conscience in any one year, and in the 1980s nearly 200 Baha'is were executed for their faith. Although the numbers of killings declined dramatically after Khomeini's death in 1989, as did the number of prisoners of conscience, theocratic Iran has for most of its history been far more repressive than the shah's regime.[35]

Religious persecution and struggles over the Mujahidin version of liberation theology have tended to be depicted as a form of "medievalism." But in fact, the various technologies of social control implied by the huge numbers of jailed and killed indicate clearly that we are in the presence of a bureaucratized process, of Hannah Arendt's banality of evil. The gendarmeries, revolutionary guards, holding cells, prisons, execution squads, burial grounds, dunning of families of the executed to pay the costs—all of these institutions and repertoires are those of the high modernist state, not the ramshackle and inefficient methods of medieval baronies. In the mid-1990s, the prison system of Iran according to official government sources held 160,000 prisoners, or 266 per 100,000 population.[36] For comparison, in Europe Romania at 200, Poland at 170, and Portugal at 140 per 100,000 population are considered among those with "relatively high" numbers of inmates. These numbers are, of course, much smaller than those of the former Cold War superpowers, the U.S. and Russia. But they are sufficiently large for a country of Iran's size to indicate a substantial penal bureaucracy that compares ably with the high end of European states. As for the theological dimension, the large-scale jailing and even execution of persons for holding the wrong views has been a persistent feature of high modernism. In a state like Iran characterized by nativist modernism, with a theocratic politics, religious views are at once a form of theology and a form of political ideology.

Theocratic republicanism in Iran has entailed extensive pre-publication censorship by the state. Articles have been vetted. Liberal Islamist writers like `Abd al-Karim Soroush have been denied visas to speak abroad on occasion. Periodicals and newspapers have frequently been closed. In 1998 a number of writers were assassinated by agents of the Ministry of Intelligence, later branded "rogues" by the supporters of President Khatami, who condemned the killings. Still, nothing has been done to the so-called rogues. Informal mechanisms of censorship also operate, often with tacit state support. Soroush, for instance, has sometimes been prevented from speaking on campuses by hordes of radical Islamists opposed to his brand of Islamic liberalism. In 2001 the campaign against the press and suppression of other human rights by hardline clerics intensified.

Literacy and Schooling the Nation

Among the big social engineering projects adopted by the shah was vastly increasing literacy. The Middle East had relatively low rates of literacy in world terms for most of the nineteenth and twentieth centuries. Around 1900 only 7 percent of Egyptians were literate according to British colonial statistics, and the percentage was likely to have been rather smaller in Iran, with its rugged landscape, low population density, and extremely low levels of governmental investment in areas such as national education. Despite the shah's Literacy Corps program that began in 1963 as part of the White Revolution, which involved the drafting of urban youth to teach reading and writing in villages, by the late 1970s the national literacy rate was still less than 50 percent. Women were only 35 percent literate. In Khomeinist Iran, 1980 witnessed the cultural revolution, which was coopted by the state with its Supreme Council for Cultural Revolution. This body groups the heads of the judiciary, legislature and executive with the "ministers of education, culture and higher education and health and medical education, as well as several cultural experts." The ministry of education under the Islamic Republic receives about a fifth of all governmental expenditures, and employs 41 percent of the country's civil servants, more than any other ministry. Thus, a modernist commitment to universal literacy, along with a concomitant desire to socialize all students to state values, characterizes the Khomeinist state just as much as it had the Pahlevi, if not more. By 1994 over 17 million students were enrolled in about 96,000 schools. There are now over one million students enrolled in 44 universities in Iran, compared to 16 in the late 1970s. In the 1990s, the number of women entering the universities tripled.[37]

The highly ideological and theocratic nature of Iran's nativist modernism, indeed, encourages a special concentration on education and indoctrination. Ironically, even though an Islamic revolution brought Arabic words flooding back into newspaper Persian, the populist character of the revolution, with its emphasis on reaching out to the poor, led to a Persianization of grade school textbooks so as to enhance the facility with which children could become literate (Arabic words pose special orthographic and lexical problems).[38] The daughter of the former president, Fatemeh Hashimi Rafsanjani, alleged that by 1996 the literacy rate had climbed 72 percent over-all, with women at about 68 percent, representing nearly a doubling of literacy rates among women since the Revolution. Other sources were more conservative, estimating over-all literacy at 68 percent in 1995. By 2000, the deputy head of Iran's Literacy Movement estimated that only 10 million out of 65 million Iranians were illiterate, or 15 percent. Of these, 6 million were women (and most were rural), suggesting that women's literacy had nearly pulled equal to that of men at over 80 percent. [39] Whatever the exact statistics, it certainly is the case the both literacy and female literacy has improved enormously under the Islamic republic. Ironically, given the highly patriarchal rhetoric of the theocracy, the education of women has been among its greatest successes the education. Many of these newly literate women, moreover, have become active in politics, and they were among the major constituents who helped elect Mohammad Khatami president in 1997.

Society Responds to Nativist Modernism

The dialectical, fluid and changing character of republican Iran has allowed for the emergence of forces that moderated the excesses of the Khomeini years during the subsequent decade. Nativist modernism has been a battleground over which various social and cultural forces have fought, from Khomeini's theocratic radicalism to Soroush's Islamic liberalism and even to a defiant Iranian secularism, though proponents of the latter have been so far out of the mainstream of political discourse that their battles tend to end in martyrdom.

The prolongation of the Iran-Iraq war from the early 1980s, when the Iraqis first signaled an eagerness to settle, until 1988, produced extensive disaffection with the Khomeinist regime in Iran. The evidence is that Iranians simply did not put their hearts and souls into the war effort, especially in the second act of the drama when it was clear that the Iraqis wanted peace and that the reason for the continuation of the war was Khomeini's ambition to take Baghdad. Less than two percent of the population was enlisted in the military, and only about 3 percent of gross domestic product was spent on the war effort in the mid-to-late 1980s. The expenditures on the military declined dramatically from $20 billion (in 1994 prices) in 1984 to $13 billion in 1985 and only about $6 billion in 1986, even though the war itself continued to rage throughout this period.[40] After the end of the war, and with the death of Khomeini, military expenditures declined further, to only a little over 2 percent of GDP. Iran has continued to maintain a relatively large military force, especially if one counts the paramilitary revolutionary guards, but as Clawson notes, it is used for road-building, revolutionary indoctrination, and other non-military purposes. Iran's military spending in the late 1990s has been much lower per capita than neighbors such as Turkey or Saudi Arabia.

The massive state control of the economy has been, of course, a huge economic disaster for the country and poses a long-term threat to Iran's future, to the extent that many observers have spoken of the "de-industrialization" of the economy. The state has faced a number of economic constraints, including low oil price troughs in the mid to late 1980s and again in the mid to late 1990s. The initial disruptive effects of the revolution were dramatic. In 1979-1982, Iran lost fully a third of its gross domestic product. Given the near doubling of the population since the revolution, the lackluster performance of the public-sector industries, and that petroleum and gas income is the major source of foreign exchange, the sometimes low oil prices have largely kept Iranians from attaining again, much less surpassing, the real per capita income levels they saw under the shah in the 1970s. Per capita income in Iran, despite the significant petroleum wealth, is far less than that of a non-oil neighbor like Turkey, with its more vibrant private sector.

The government control of so much of the economy resulted in lack of significant investment in key areas like machinery or construction and the retardation of the process of capital accumulation, as Sohrab Behdad has shown. He argues for economic involution, such that institutions of the market have been disrupted and the workforce has been deproletarianized, forced into petty bourgeois status in small self-owned workshops. He has demonstrated that in 1977-1990, investment in machinery and construction declined an average of 6 percent per year, so that by 1990 investments by the government and the private sector in machinery were a third what they had been under the shah in 1977. The private sector, mainly smaller workshops, has occasionally attempted to take up the slack, though he notes that medium-sized firms were much weakened at the expense of small workshops employing one or two persons, and large state-owned factories with hundreds of employees. The sector of medium firms, he believes, is key to capitalist development, and it was failing. In contrast, in 1987 the small workshops produced 30 percent of manufacturing output (up from 16 percent in 1976) and employed fully 50 percent of manufacturing workers (up from 29 percent in 1976). Self-employed workers, who predominated in the small workshops, increased 1976-1986 from 2.8 million to 4.4 million, or by a factor of 57 percent. Medium-sized firms correspondingly declined. Wage workers in the private sector declined from about 3 million in 1976 to 1.9 million in 1986, a reduction of 39 percent. Along with the expansion in the number of smaller workshops, there was a proliferation of service activities, most of them of a make-work nature, and government workers increased in the same period by 1.9 million (though about half of this number is accounted for by larger military and paramilitary forces.[41]

That Khomeini's policies had made Iran a pariah made it unable to receive international credit in the 1980s, and divorced it from the Bretton Woods institutions, such as the International Monetary Fund and the World Bank. In the 1990s Rafsanjani and Khamenei attempted to repair Iran's reputation internationally sufficiently to again receive a World Bank loan. Opening Iran to such global influences inevitably brought scoldings from economists about Iran's bloated and stagnant public sector. Rafsanjani was convinced by the dismal economic statistics that the massive nationalizations of the 1980s has been a tragic error, and decided in 1991-92 to pursue privatization. In the subsequent five years, the Industrial Development and Renovation Organization (IDRO), which holds the majority of the country's heavy industries, raised $467 million from the sale of public companies to the private market. This process accelerated in the late 1990s, though only a small proportion of the heavy industries have actually been sold off. "Government policy calls for IDRO to sell up to 57 per cent of its holdings in firms, with the rest being distributed among the employees of privatised companies."[42] Sales in the late 1990s included one-quarter of the main automobile manufacturer. Plans have been put forward to privatize the tourist industry, as well. Steps are now also being taken to allow private non-bank credit organizations in Iran, giving the state banking sector some private competition, with hopes of increasing the amount of credit available to the economy. After 1997, the dialectic between the communitarian and egalitarian impulses of the nationalizers and the desires for economic progress and efficiency of the privatizers began to swing toward the latter. The conservative clerics, however, continued to throw up roadblocks to legislative reforms. [43]

Political repression and censorship, and even occasionally assassination, continue to be features of the Iranian political scene, though there are periods, as with the late 1990s, when a wider range of political speech and opinion was permissible—a window the hardliners tried hard to close in 2000-2001. The more liberal provisions of the Iranian constitution, which although it allows the vetting of candidates does insist on elected, representative officials, have been employed by forces in Iranian society to mitigate the most authoritarian aspects of nativist modernism. More recently, the authoritarians have struck back by more intensively vetting candidates to exclude liberals. In the five elections for parliament, there has been a decided retreat in the hegemony of radical or hardline clerics, and an increasing number of non-clerical representatives elected. The emergence of seminary-trained, unabashed Muslim theologians advocating a sort of Lockian liberalism, such as `Abd al-

Karim Soroush, was an unexpected development of the 1990s. The way in which Rafsanjani and Khamenei backed off the large-scale killing of those they saw as enemies of the regime, whether Mujahidin sympathizers or the apolitical Baha'is, demonstrated that state actors' determination to employ the authoritarian state as a blunt instrument for the forcible reordering of society was waning. In the 2001 elections liberals associated with President Muhammad Khatami, first elected in 1997, swept the parliamentary elections as Khatami received a second term. [44]

Conclusion

Theocratic republican Iran meets many of the criteria for James C. Scott's vision of High Modernism gone bad. The ruling elite certainly had a commitment to an administrative ordering of nature and society. They asserted that they were conducting this reordering in the name of Islam. But the "Islam" of the Islamist technocrats around Khomeini, including Mehdi Bazargan (an engineer and factory owner), Abolhassan Bani Sadr (a French-trained economist), and many members of subsequent cabinets, was seen as entirely compatible both with science and with high modernist forms of social engineering. The human wave attacks on entrenched Iraqi army positions, the nationalization of much of the economy and the imposition of ideological control on workers, the instances of urban renewal requiring the expulsion of slum dwellers, the pursuit of nuclear and other high-technology weaponry, are all consistent with high modernism, despite being pursued under the rubric of theocratic republicanism. Nativist modernism allows the ideological assertion of localist authenticity as an over-all framework for the working out of a High Modernist project.

The authoritarian Khomeinist state came to power through revolution and immediately was plunged into war by Saddam Hussein, responding by amassing an enormous 700,000-man military. It arose in a society where civil society or intermediary institutions between the state and the people had been largely suppressed by the Pahlevi state or incorporated into state organs. The top quintile of the country in terms of wealth was chased into exile, killed, or expropriated, such that the old power elite was decapitated. There were very few checks on the new state's power, despite the flailing guerrilla actions of the Mujahidin or the futile minor revolts of the Kurds and Turkmen.

Still, the marriage of high modernism to Islamist anti-liberalism produced severe contradictions that ultimately posed challenges to Khomeinism of the 1980s variety. The alignment of discontents among large social groups has shifted over time. A new bourgeoisie emerged from the bazaar and government contracting in the course of the 1980s, replacing the old Pahlevi elite and restoring the wealth stratification to a shape very similar to that of 1977.[45] This new bourgeoisie found a political ally in Rafsanjani. Some clerics are rumored to have desired to abolish women's suffrage on coming to power, but had not done so, perhaps because women had been among the groups that mobilized for the revolution and they felt they needed their support. Despite restrictions on women, the labor needs created by the expansion of the army led to greater women's participation in the work force, and the massive schooling and literacy campaigns created millions of newly educated women. The voting age in Iran was also set relatively low, allowing youth to have an impact on elections.

When the Guardianship Council allowed a former minister of culture named Mohammad Khatami, who had been sacked for being too liberal, to run for president in 1997 against the right wing clerical favorite, `Ali Akbar Natiq Nuri, they unwittingly admitted into the race a Trojan horse for disgruntled women and youth, who voted for Khatami decisively and helped ensure that he received 70 percent of the vote. Khatami has been constrained by the relative lack of power the president enjoys under the Iranian constitution, and by his de facto lack of control over the army, the police, and a number of important ministries, including Intelligence. He has moved behind the scenes, however, in an attempt to put his men into power in the bureaucracy, and his hand was strengthened by subsequent municipal elections, in which candidates identified with his political party or with his program did exceedingly well. During most of his first term, many members of parliament remained to his right, however, which allowed the representatives to block some of his appointments. The judiciary and Guardianship Council are solidly under the control of clerical hard liners, so that even his more recent supportive parliament can make little headway on reform. Nevertheless, these developments of the late 1990s and early 2000s demonstrate that Iran's long-supine civil society is reviving. The resulting polarization has created greater political tension, and raised question marks about the future. Whatever Iran has looked like in the past two decades and will look like in the succeeding two, it has not looked anything like a medieval state or society. Indeed, if anything the more admirable virtues of medieval Iran, its love of poetry and life, its reasoning approach to religion, its relative tolerance of other creeds (certainly compared to much of Europe at the time)—have all been damaged by the excesses of nativist modernism.

Notes

1 Introduction

1. Prasenjit Duara, *Rescuing History from the Nation: Questioning Narratives of Modern China* (Chicago: University of Chicago Press, 1995).
2. Chibli Mallat, *The Renewal of Islamic Law: Muhammad Baqer al-Sadr, Najaf and the Shi`I International* (Cambridge: Cambridge University Press, 1993).

2 The Shi`ites as an Ottoman Minority

1. Anthony Smith, *Ethnic Origins of Nations* (Oxford: Basil Blackwell, 1987), p. 74.
2. George E. Simpson and J. Milton Yinger, *Racial and Cultural Minorities: An Analysis of Prejudice and Discrimination,* 3rd ed. (New York: Harper and Row, 1965), pp. 20-25.
3. Ibid., chapter 10.
4. The Arabic text of the *fatwa* is given in Adel Allouche, *The Origins and Development of the Ottoman-Safavid Conflict (906-962/ 1500-1555)* (Berlin: Klaus Schwarz Verlag, 1983), pp. 170-73; for discussion, see Mario Grignaschi, "La Condanna dell'apostasia (irtidad) Sciita nella "Risalah" di Ibn Kemal a Selim I," *Oriente Moderno* 64 (1984): 57-64; for the general intellectual context see Elke Eberhard, *Osmanische Polemik gegen die Safawiden im 16 Jahrhundert nach arabischen Handschriften* (Freiburg im Breisgau: Klaus Schwarz Verlag, 1970); for Mufti Ebussuud's distinction between Qizilbash and Shi`i, see C. H. Imber, "The Persecution of the Ottoman Shi`ites according to the Muhimme Defterleri, 1565-1585," *Der Islam* 56 (1979), p. 245 (the same source gives further information on persecution of Anatolian Shi`ites in pp. 250-63). See also Jean-Louis Bacqué-Grammon, "Les Ottomans et les Safavides dan la première moitié du xvi$^e$ siècle," in *Convegno sul tema la Shi`a nell'impero ottomano* (Rome: Accademia Nazionale dei Lincei, Fondazione Leone Caetani, 1993), pp. 7-24.
5. Eberhard, *Osmanische Polemik,* pp. 164-65; Allouche, *Origins,* pp. 85, 112. For the general political context see H. Sohrweide, "Der Sieg der Safawiden in Persien

und seine Ruckwirkung auf die Schiiten Anatolians im 16. Jahrhundert," *Der Islam* 41 (1965): 95-223.

6. Yusuf al-Bahrani, *Lu'lu'at al-Bahrayn fi al-ijazat wa tarajim rijal al-hadith*, ed. Sayyid Muhammad Sadiq Bahr al-'Ulum (Najaf: Matba'at an-Nu'man, 1966), p. 153.

7. Imber, "The Persecution of the Ottoman Shi`ites," p. 246.

8. Ibid., pp. 246-250.

9. Stephen H. Longrigg, *Four Centuries of Modern Iraq* (Beirut: Librairie du Liban, 1968 repr. ed.), pp. 72-73.

10. Jon E. Mandaville, "The Ottoman Province of al-Hasa in the Sixteenth and Seventeenth Centuries," *Journal of the American Oriental Society* 90 (1970): 488-96; Salih Ozbaran, "A Note on the Ottoman Administration in Arabia in the Sixteenth Century," *International Journal of Turkish Studies* 3,1 (1985): 93-95. Even Arab Twelvers who dwelt outside Ottoman borders did not escape Sunni sanctions in the sixteenth century. Although the Portuguese took Twelver Bahrain in 1521, they ruled it by proxy through Sunni Hurmuz until the Safavids conquered it in 1602. The Sunni Hurmuzi governors persecuted Shi`ism, and the Ottoman-Portuguese naval rivalry hurt trade. Bahrainis lost land they owned in al-Hasa when it became part of a foreign empire. In the seventeenth century the Muslim land powers managed to expel the Portuguese from the Persian Gulf. The succeeding Dutch maritime empire had a mainly economic impact on the Shi`ites of the Gulf and on Twelver kingdoms of South India. These encounters with foreign mercantile powers marked a long-term shift in relative trading advantages between Twelver merchants and craftsmen and the Europeans, and may be seen in retrospect as harbingers of a fateful encounter with the West in later centuries. See J. Cole, "Rival Empires of Trade and Imami Shi`ism in Eastern Arabia, 1300-1800," *International Journal of Middle East Studies,* 19, 2 (1987), now Chapter Three below.

11. Abdul-Rahim Abu-Husayn, *Provincial Leaderships in Syria, 1575-1650* (Beirut: American University of Beirut Press, 1985, pp. 129-152; and the same author's "The Shi`ites in Lebanon and the Ottomans in the 16$^{th}$ and 17$^{th}$ Centuries, in *Convegno sul tema la Shi`a nell'impero ottomano*, pp. 107-119; and Marco Salati, "Toleration, Persecution and Local Realities: Observations on Shiism in the Holy Places and the Bilad al-Sham (16th-17th Centuries)," in *Convegno*, pp. 121-148..

12. Muhammad Adnan Bakhit, *The Ottoman Province of Damascus in the Sixteenth Century* (Beirut: Librairie du Liban, 1982), pp. 28, 55, 175-78, 185-86, 207-208; Moojan Momen, *An Introduction to Shi`ite Islam* (New Haven: Yale University Press, 1985), pp. 119-120.

13. Muhammad Baqir Khvansari, *Rawdat al-jannat fi ahwal al-'ulama' wa al-sadat,* 8 vols. (Qumm: Isma`iliyan, 1970), 3:352-87.

14. Stephen H. Longrigg, *Syria and Lebanon under French Mandate* (London: Oxford University Press, 1958), p. 9.

15. Khvansari, *Rawdat al-jannat*, 2:298-99; for other Lebanon-Iraq links in the seventeenth century see ibid., 4:15-16. See for intellectual life in this period see Muhammad Kazim Makki, *al-Haraka al-fikriyya wa al-adabiyya fi Jabal `Amil* (Beirut: Dar al-Andalus, 1963), ch. 4; and `Ali Muruwwa, *Ta'rikh Juba': Madiha wa hadiriha* (Beirut: Dar al-Andalus, 1967), ch. 1.

16. Albert Hourani, "From Jabal `Amil to Persia," *Bulletin of the School of Oriental and African Studies* 49, 1 (1986): 133-40; Said Amir Arjomand, *The Shadow of God and the Hidden Imam* (Chicago: University of Chicago Press, 1984); for the India connection see Makki, *al-Haraka al-fikriyya*, pp. 27-28.

17. Michel M. Mazzaoui, "Shi`ism and Ashura in South Lebanon," in *Ta`ziyah: Ritual and Drama in Iran*, ed. Peter J. Chelkowski (New York: New York University Press, 1979):228-237.

18. "A'inah-'i haqq-numa," Rijal Shi`a, Persian MS 1, fol. 20b, Nasiriyyah Library, Lucknow, India. Cf. Etan Kohlberg, "Some Imami-Shi`ite Views on Taqiyya," *Journal of the American Oriental Society* 95 (1975): 395-402 and Egbert Meyer, "Anlass und Anwendungsbereich der taqiyya," *Der Islam* 57 (1980): 246-80.

19. Sayyid Dildar `Ali Nasirabadi, "Najat al-sa'ilin," Fiqh Shi`a, Persian MS 256, fol. 6a, Nasiriyya Library; Sayyid Muhammad Quli Kinturi, *Tathir al-mu'minin 'an najasat al-mushrikin* (Lucknow: Matba'-i Haydar, 1260/1844).

20. Cf. Smith, *Ethnic Origins*, pp. 111-114.

21. Albert Hourani, "Ottoman Reform and the Politics of the Notables," in W. Polk and R. Chambers, eds, *Beginnings of Modernization in the Middle East*, (Chicago: University of Chicago Press, 1968), pp. 41-68. Karl Barbir has advanced the argument that this vastly increased importance of local magnates as semi-independent surrogates for the Ottomans cannot legitimately be seen before 1760, and that the first half of the eighteenth century actually had witnessed an Ottoman resurgence - see Karl K. Barbir, *Ottoman Rule in Damascus, 1708-1758* (Princeton, N. J.: Princeton University Press, 1980), chapter 2.

22. For Twelvers in the shrine cities in the eighteenth century, see J. Cole, "Shi`ite Clerics in Iraq and Iran, 1722-1780: The Akhbari-Usuli Conflict Reconsidered," *Iranian Studies*, 18, 1 (1985): 1-33 (now Chapter Four of this book); for negative Ottoman attitudes to Shi`ites in the Iraqi shrine cities, see Abu Talib Isfahani, *Masir-i Talibi*, ed. Husayn Khadivjam (Tehran: Kitabha-yi Jaybi, 1352 s./1974), pp.406-07, 418; for Iran-Iraq relations in the eighteenth century see A. M. K. Nawras, *al-'Iraq fi al-'ahd al-'Uthmani: Dirasa fi al-`alaqat al-siyasiyya 1700-1800 m.* (Baghdad: Dar al-Hurriyya, 1979).

23. J. Cole, "'Indian Money and the Shi`ite Shrine Cities of Iraq, 1786-1850," *Middle Eastern Studies* 22,4 (1986): 461-81 (now Chapter Five below); J. Cole and M. Momen, "Mafia, Mob and Shi`ism in Iraq: the Rebellion of Ottoman Karbala, 1824-1843," *Past and Present* 112 (August 1986): 112-43 (now Chapter Six below).

24. Abdul-Karim Rafeq, *The Province of Damascus, 1723-1783*, (Beirut: Khayats, 1966), pp. 246-47; Amnon Cohen, *Palestine in the 18th Century* (Jerusalem: Magnes Press, 1973), pp. 13-14, 83-84.

25. `Ali al-Zayn, *Fusul min ta'rikh ash-Shi`a fi Lubnan* (Beirut: Dar al-Kalima li'n-Nashr, 1979), pp. 43-91, 131-139. This source is especially valuable for extended quotations of primary sources and tough-minded historical sense, which allows it to supersede older, less professional works in Arabic. See also Cohen, *Palestine in the 18th Century*, pp. 123-25, 200-201, 288.

26. Al-Zayn, *Fusul min Ta'rikh ash-Shi`a*, pp. 140-65.

27. Ibid., pp. 170-191; Makki, *al-Haraka al-fikriyya*, ch. 5.

28. Hasan Nasr Allah, *Ta'rikh Ba'labakk*, 2 vols. (Beirut: Mu'assasat al-Wafa', 1984), 1:311-324; Moshe Ma'oz, *Ottoman Reform in Syria and Palestine 1840-1861: The Impact of the Tanzimat on Politics and Society* (Oxford at the Clarendon Press, 1968), pp. 111-113.

29. Cf. Smith, *Ethnic Origins*, pp. 94-96.

30. Meir Litvak, *Shi`ite Scholars of Nineteenth Century Iraq: The `Ulama of Najaf and Karbala'* (Cambridge: Cambridge University Press, 1998), chs. 6, 9.

31. Yitzhak Nakash, *The Shi`ites of Iraq* (Princeton: Princeton University Press, 1994), pp. 22-23.

32. Cole and Momen, "Mafia, Mob and Shi`ism."

33. Tom Nieuwenhuis, *Politics and Society in Early Modern Iraq: Mamluk Pashas, Tribal Shayks and Local Rule Between 1802 and 1831* (The Hague: Martinus Nijhoff, 1982), pp. 133 ff.; `Abd al-`Aziz S. Nawwar, *Ta'rikh al-'Iraq al-hadith: Min nihayat hukm Da'ud Basha ila nihayat hukm Midhat Basha* (Cairo: Dar al-Kitab al-`Arabi, 1968), chapters 4 and 8.

34. Hanna Batatu, *The Old Social Classes and Revolutionary Movements in Iraq* (Princeton, N. J.: Princeton University Press, 1978), pp. 73-78; Marion Farouk-Sluglett and Peter Sluglett, "The Transformation of Land Tenure and Rural Social Structure in Central and Southern Iraq 1870-1958," *International Journal of Middle East Studies* 15 (1983): 491-505; Roger Owen, *The Middle East in the World Economy, 1800-1914* (New York: Methuen, 1981), ch. 7.

35. Ali Haydar Midhat Bey, *The Life of Midhat Pasha* (London: John Murray, 1903), p. 53; see pp. 47-62; Nawwar, *Ta'rikh al-'Iraq al-hadith*, chapters 9, 10; Selim Deringil, "The Struggle against Shiism in Hamidian Iraq: A Study in Ottoman Counter-Propaganda." *Die Welt des Islams* vol. 30 (1990):45-62.

36. A.K.S. Lambton, "Secret societies and the Persian Revolution of 1905-6", St. Antony's Papers, no. 4, Middle Eastern Affairs, no. 1 (London, 1958) pp. 43-60; Abdul-Hadi Hairi, *Shi`ism and Constitutionalism in Iran* (Leiden: E. J. Brill, 1977), pp. 88-108; `Abd al-Halim ar-Rahimi, *Ta'rikh al-haraka al-islamiyya fi al-'iraq: al-judhur al-fikriyya wa al-waqi' al-ta'rikhi (1900-1924),* (Beirut: ad-Dar al-`Alamiya, 1985), pp. 144-151.

37. Al-Zayn, *Fusul*, pp. 192-214; Nasr Allah, *Ta'rikh Ba`labakk*, 1:324 ff.; Ma'oz, *Ottoman Reform in Syria and Palestine*, p. 113; Engin Akarli, *The Long Peace: Ottoman Lebanon, 1861-1920* (Berkeley and Los Angeles: University of California Press, 1993), pp. 82, 136. For Ottoman Lebanon in this period see also Leila Fawaz, *An Occasion for War* (London: I.B. Tauris, 1994); Ussama Makdisi, *The Culture of Sectarianism: Community, History and Violence in Nineteenth-Century Ottoman Lebanon* (Berkeley and Los Angeles: University of California Press, 2000).

38. Jacob Goldberg, "The Shi`ite Minority in Saudi Arabia," in Juan R. I. Cole and Nikki R. Keddie, eds., *Shi`ism and Social Protest* (New Haven: Yale University Press, 1986), pp. 232-33; Muhammad A. Nakhla, *Ta'rikh al-Ahsa' al-siyasi 1818-1913* (Kuwait: Manshurat Dhat al-Salasil, 1980).

39. `Ali Hasan al-Biladi al-Bahrani, *Anwar al-badrayn fi tarajim 'ulama al-Qatif wa al-Ahsa' wa al-Bahrayn* (Najaf: Matba'at an-Nu'man, 1960), pp. 241-42. For the Shi`ites of al-Hasa in the nineteenth century, see the valuable informatiion and analysis in Hala Fatta, *The Politics of Regional Trade in Iraq, Arabia, and the*

Gulf, 1745-1900 (Albany: State University of New York Press, 1997), especially pp. 51-56, 63-68, 119-122 For the deteriorating position of Twelvers in nineteenth century Bahrain, see Momen, *An Introduction to Shi`ite Islam,* p. 145.

3 Rival Empires of Trade and Shi`ism in Eastern Arabia

1. Micheal Jenner, Bahrain: *Gulf Heritage in Transition* (London: Longman, 1984); Fuad I. Khuri, *Tribe and State in Bahrain* (Chicago: University of Chicago Press, 1980); Roger M. Savory, "A.D. 600-1800," in Alvin J. Cottrell, ed., *The Persian Gulf States: A General Survey* (Baltimore: The Johns Hopkins Press, 1980), pp. 14-40; James H. D. Belgrave, "A Brief Survey of the History of the Bahrain Islands," *Journal of the Royal Central Asian Society,* 39 (1952), 57-68; Abbas Faroughy, *The Bahrein Islands (750-1951)* (New York: Verry, Fisher & Co., 195 1); G. Rentz and W. E. Mulligan, "al-Bahrayn," *Encyclopaedia of Islam,* 2nd ed., 5 vols.-Suppl.-(Leiden: E. J. Brill, 1954-) [hereafter E12]; Muhammad al-Nabhan, *al- Tuhfa al-nabhaniyya imara al-jazira al-`arabiyya, 1, Bahrayn* (Baghdad: al-Adab, 1332/1914); and sources cited below.

2. G. Rentz, "Qatif,"" *EI²;* F. S. Vidal, *The Oasis of al-Hasa,* Arabian American Oil Company, 1955, pp. 35-39, 96, 137; F. S. Vidal, "al-Hufuf," *EI²;* Muhammad A. Nakhla, *Tarikh al-Ahsa' al-Siyasi, 1818-1913* (Kuwait: Manshurat Dhat al-Salasil), 1980; for contemporary developments, see the articles by R. Ramazani and J. Goldberg in Juan R. I. Cole and Nikki R. Keddie, eds., *Shi`ism and Social Protest* (New Haven: Yale University Press, 1986).

3. W. Madelung, "Karmati," *EI²*

4. Jean Aubin, "Le Royaume d'Ormuz au début du XVIe siècle," *Mare Luso-Indicum,* 2 (1972), 77-179.

5. Momen, *An Introduction to Shi`ite Islam,* pp. 90-91.

6. Maytham b. `Ali al-Bahrani, "Kitab al-Qawa'id," British Library Arabic MS Or. 6265.

7. Shihab al-Din Ahmad Ibn Hajar al-`Asqalani, *al-Durar al-kamina fi a`yan al-mi'a al-thamina,* 4 vols. (Hyderabad: Da'ira al-Ma`arif al-`Uthmaniyya, 1930), 1:73-74; Faroughy, *The Bahrein Islands,* pp. 60-61; G. Rentz and W. E. Mulligan, "Bahrayn," and J. Lassner, "Kays," E12; Muhammad b. `Abd al-Rahman al-Sakhawi, *al-Daw' al-Lami` li ahl al-qarn al-tasi`* 12 vols. (Beirut: Dar Maktaba al-Haya, 1966), vol. 1, p. 190.

8. Ibn Battuta, *Rihla Ibn Battuta* (Beirut: Dar Sadir, 1964), pp. 279-80.

9. Yusuf b. Ahmad al-Bahrani, *Lulu'at al-Bahrayn fi al-ijazat wa tarajim rijal al-hadith,* Sayyid Muhammad Sadiq Bahr al-`Ulum, ed. (Najaf- Matba`a al-Nu`man, 1966), pp. 177-85; `Ali b. Hasan al-Bahrani, *Anwar al-Badrayn fi tarajim `ulama' al-Qatif wa'l-Ahsa' wa'l-Bahrayn* (Najaf: Matba`a al-Nu`man, 1960), pp. 70-72. The latter source is especially useful for the 18th and 19th centuries.

10. al-Bahrani, *Anwar al-badrayn*, p. 400.

11. Ibid.

12. Eliyahu Ashtor, *Levant Trade in the Later Middle Ages* (Princeton, N.J.: Princeton University Press, 1983), pp. 323-24 and notes.

13. Nur Allah Shushtari, *Majalis al-mu'minin*, 2 vols. (Tehran: Chapkhanih-i Islamiyyih, 1955), vol. 2, pp. 143-48; Said Amir Arjomand, *The Shadow of God and the Hidden Imam* (Chicago: University of Chicago Press, 1984), pp. 74-76.

14. al-Bahrani, *Anwar al-badrayn*, p. 74.

15. These included Shaykh Ahmad b. Fahd b. Idris al-Ahsa'i (fl. 1403) and Shaykh Ahmad b. Muhammad al-Saba`i al-Ahsa'i (fl. 1432): Yusuf al-Bahrani, *Lulu'at al-Bahrayn*, p. 168; A. al-Bahrani, *Anwar al-badrayn*, pp. 396-98.

16. al-Sakhawi, *al-Daw' al-lami`*, 1:190.

17. Aubin, "Le Royaume d'Ormuz au début du XVIe siècle," 123-27.

18. al-Sakhawi, *al-Daw' al-lam`'*, 1:190; G. Rentz, "Djabrids," *EI²*.

19. al-Bahrani, *Anwar al-badrayn*, pp. 76-77.

20. Yusuf al-Bahrani, *Lu'lu'at al-Bahrayn*, pp. 166-68; A. al-Bahrani, *Anwar al-badrayn*, pp. 398-99; W. Madelung, "Ibn Abi Jumhur al-Ahsa'i," *EI²*; W. Madelung, "Ibn Abi Jumhur al-Ahsa'is Synthesis of *kalam*, Philosophy and Sufism," in *La significance du bas moyen age dans l'histoire el la culture du monde musulman.* Actes du 8e Congrès de l'Union Euro-péenne des Arabisants et Islamisants (Aix-en-Provence, 1978), pp. 147-58; Sabine Schmidtke, *Theologie, Philosophie und Mystik im zwölferši`itischen Islam des 9./15. Jahrhunderts: Die Gedankenwelten des Ibn Abi Ğumhur al-Ahsa'i* (Leiden: E.J. Brill, 2000).

21. Sayyid Haydar Amoli, *Jami` al-asrar wa manba` al-anwar*, Henry Corbin and Osman Yahya, eds. (Tehran: Institut Franco-Iranien de Recherche, 1969); Peter Antes, *Zur Theologie der Schi`a* (Freiburg im Breisgau: Klaus Schwarz Verlag, 1971); E. Kohlberg, "Amoli, Sayyed Baha' al-Din Haydar," *Encyclopaedia Iranica*, Ehsan Yarshater, ed. (Boston: Routledge and Kegan Paul, 1982).

22. Bras de Albuquerque, *The Commentaries of the Great Afonso Dalboquerque, Second Viceroy of India*, Walter de Gray Birch, ed., 4 vols. (London: Hakluyt Society, 1875-1884), vol. 1, pp. 84, 99-256, vol. 4, pp. 113-50; Duarte Barbosa, *The Book of Duarte Barbosa*, Mansel Longworth Dames, ed., 2 vols. (London: The Hakluyt Society, 1918), vol. 1, pp. 80-82, 101-5; Jaoa de Barros, *Asia. Dos feitos os portugueses fizeram no descobrimento e conquista dos mares e terras do Oriente*, Hernani Cidade, ed., 4 vols. (Lisbon: Agencia Geral das Colonias, 1945-46), vol. 3, pp. 318-22; Jean Aubin, "Cojeatar et Albuquerque," *Mare Luso-Indicum, 1* (1971), 99-134.

23. Bras de Albuquerque, *Commentaries*, vol. 4, pp. 153-54, 176-77, 181-84; Seydi Ali Reis, *Mir'atül-memalik*, Necdet Akyildiz, ed. (Istanbul: Kervan Kitapqilik, n.d.), pp. 31'-47; Jon E. Mandaville, "The Ottoman Province of al-Hasa in the Sixteenth and Seventeenth Centuries," *Journal of the American Oriental Society,* 90 (1970), 488-96; Salih Özbaran, "The Ottoman Turks and the Portuguese in the Persian Gulf, 1534-1581," *Journal of Asian History,* 6 (1972), 50-68; S. Özbaran, "A Note on the Ottoman Administration in Arabia in the Sixteenth Century," *International Journal of Turkish Studies, 3,* 1 (1985), 93-99; Fernand Braudel, *The Mediterranean and the Mediterranean World in the Age of Philip 11,* Sian Reynolds, ed., 2 vols. (London: Collins, 197273), vol. 1, p. 546. For general

issues in this period see Andrew C. Hess, *The Forgotten Frontier* (Chicago:Univ. of Chicago Press, 1978).

24. Gaspar Correa, *The Three Voyages of Vasco da Gama to India* (London: Hakluyt Society, 1869; 1964 ed.), p. 408; Bras de Albuquerque, *Commentaries,* vol. 4, p. 187; Aubin, "Le Royaume d'Hormuz," p. 143n, 152.

25. Mandaville, "The Ottoman Province of al-Hasa," pp. 496-99.

26. Braudel, *The Mediterranean*, vol. 1, pp. 543-70; for the spice route across Iraq to the Levant in the late 1500s, see John Huyghen van Linschoten, *The Voyage of John Huyghen van Linscholen to the East Indies,* A. C. Burnell and P. A. Tiele, eds., 2 vols. (London: Hakluyt Society, 1885), vol. 1, pp. 46-54. For analysis of this route based on a British traveler in 1580 see Niels Steensgaard, *The Asian Trade Revolution of the Seventeenth Century: The East India Companies and the Decline of the Caravan Trade* (Chicago: University of Chicago Press, 1974), pp. 37-39.

27. Muhammad al-Hurr al-`Amili, *Amal al-amil,* Sayyid Ahmad al-Husayni, ed., 2 vols. (Baghdad: Maktaba al-Andalus, 1966), vol. 1, pp. 121-22; Yusuf al-Bahrani, *Lulu'at al-Bahrayn,* pp. 151-54; Arjomand, *The Shadow of God and the Hidden Imam,* pp. 133-37.

28. Arjomand, *The Shadow of God,* ch. 5.

29. Y. al-Bahrani, *Lu'lu'at al-Bahrayn,* p. 153.

30. Ibid., pp. 159-66; A. al-Bahrani, *Anwar al-badrayn,* pp. 282-88.

31. Muhammad Baqir Khvansari, *Rawdat al-jannat,* 8 vols. (Tehran: Maktabat-i Isma`iliyan, 1970), vol. 1, pp, 25-29.

32. al-Hurr al-`Amili, *Amal al-amil,* 2:246; Khvansari, *Rawdat al-jannat,* 7: 120-39.

33. Arjomand, *The Shadow of God,* ch. 5.

34. Quoted from the *Bihar al-anwar* by `Ali Zarrin-Qalam, *Sarzamin-i Bahrayn az dawran-i bastan ta imruz* (Tehran: Sirus, 1337 s.), p. 83.

35. al-Bahrani, *Anwar al-badrayn,* pp. 112-13, 81-84.

36. For al-`Amili see al-Hurr al-`Amili, *Amal al-amil,* vol. 1, pp. 74-77; Shaykh Husayn was on his way to a pilgrimage in Mecca. For Shaykh Da'ud see A. al-Bahrani, *Anwar al-badrayn,* pp. 80-81.

37. al-Bahrani, *Anwar al-badrayn,* p. 78.

38. Iskandar Bey Munshi, *Tarikh-i 'alam-ara-yi `Abbasi,* Iraj Afshar, ed., 2 vols. (Tehran: Musavi, 1335), vol. 2, pp. 614-16; English trans. Roger Savory as *History of Shah `Abbas the Great,* 2 vols. (Boulder, Col.: Westview Press, 1978), vol. 2, pp. 803-5.

39. Pedro Teixeira, *The Travels of Pedro Teixeira,* William F. Sinclair, ed.,(London: Hakluyt Society, 1902), pp. 174-76; al-Nabhan, *al-Tuhfa,* vol. 1, pp. 63-64, gives a list of Safavid governors of Bahrain as follows: Sundak Sultan, with one tenure before 1633, when he was recalled, and another tenure thereafter when his gifts to the shah won him reinstatement; Baba Khan, to 1666 when the people complained of his oppression; Sultan b. Qizil Khan, from 1666; Mihdi Quli Khan to 1701; Qazagh Khan, from 1701. (Bahrain was lost to the Safavids in 1717.)

40. Iskandar Bey, *`Alam-ara-yi `Abbasi,* vol. 2, pp. 979-82; Eng. trans., vol. 2, pp. 1200-1204; Paulo Craesbeck, *Commentaries of Ruy Freyre de Andrada,* C. R. Boxer, ed. and trans. (New York: Robert M. McBride & Co., 1930), pp. 14-173, 198; an extended analysis of the global economic implications of the fall of

Hormuz is Steensgaard, *The Asian Trade Revolution of the Seventeenth Century,* especially pp. 154-343; on Dutch-Portuguese rivalry see also Dietmar Rothermund, Asian *Trade and European Expansion in the Age of Mercantilism* (Delhi: Manohar, 1981), ch. 5.

41. For the importance of Congoun in marketing Bahrain pearls under the Safavids see Alexander Hamilton, *A New Account of the East Indies,* W. Foster, ed., 2 vols. (London: The Argonaut Press, 1930), vol. 1, p. 59. For the Safavid administration of Bahrain, see V. Minorsky, *Tadhkirat al-Muluk: A Manual of Safavid Administration (circa 1137/1725)* (London: Luzac & Co., 1943), pp. 122, 129 of the Persian text, 104, 109 of the English translation; see Minorsky's comments and quote from Chardin on Bahrain's relative independence of the Kuhgilu chief, p. 172.

42. For the economic situation after the fall of Hurmuz see Steensgaard, *The Asian Trade Revolution, ch.* 10, and Rothermund, *Asian Trade and European Expansion,* ch. 7. For trade patterns in the Persian Gulf, see Holden Furber, *Rival Empires of Trade in the Orient 1600-1800* (Minneapolis: University of Minnesota Press, 1976) and K. N. Chaudhuri, *The Trading World of Asia and the English East India Company 1660-1760* (Cambridge University Press, 1978), ch. 9, esp. pp. 207-8.

43. Yusuf al-Bahrani, *Lu'lu'at al-Bahrayn,* pp. 135-38; A. al-Bahrani, *Anwar al-badrayn,* pp. 85-90; Imam Quli Khan was the son of Allahvirdi Khan, the governor of Fars who annexed Bahrain. Imam Quli Khan became governor of Fars on his father's death in 1613; Iskandar Bey, `Alam-ara-yi `Abbasi, Eng. trans., 2:1084.

44. A. al-Bahrani, *Anwar al-badrayn,* p. 131.

45. Y. al-Bahrani, *Lu'lu'at al-Bahrayn,* pp. 68-69; A. al-Bahrani, *Anwar al-badrayn,* pp. 127-28.

46. Y. al-Bahrani, *Lu'lu'at al-Bahrayn,* pp. 70-71; A. al-Bahrani, *Anwar al-badrayn,* pp. 128-31.

47. A. al-Bahrani, *Anwar al-badrayn,* pp. 288-94.

48. Arjomand, *The Shadow of God,* p. 129, cf. pp. 130-31..

49. Y. al-Bahrani, *Lu'lu'at al-Bahrayn,* p. 138; A. al-Bahrani, *Anwar al-badrayn,* pp. 117-19.

50. A. al-Bahrani, *Anwar al-badrayn,* pp. 103-5.

51. Jean de Thévenot, *Suite du voyage de Mr de Thévenot au Levant,* 5 vols. (Amsterdam: Michael Charles le Cene, 3rd ed., 1727), vol. 4, pp. 576-77.

52. See A. Sachedina, "Al-Khums: The Fifth in the Imami Shi`ite Legal System," *Journal of Near East Studies,* 39 (1980), 276-89; Norman Calder, "Khums in Imami Shi`ite Jurisprudence from the Tenth to the Sixteenth Century A.D.," *Bulletin of the School of Oriental and African Studies,* 45 (1982), 39-47; and N. Calder, "Zakat in Imami Shi`ite Jurisprudence from the Tenth to the Sixteenth Century A.D.," *Bulletin of the School of Oriental and African Studies,* 44 (1981), 468-80.

53. Amin Banani, "Reflections on the Social and Economic Structure of Safavid Persia at Its Zenith," *Iranian Studies,* 11 (1978), 95-97.

54. Y. al-Bahrani, *Lu'lu'at al-Bahrayn,* pp. 87-89; A. al-Bahrani, *Anwar al-badrayn,* pp. 125-27, 160-61.

55. Y. al-Bahrani, *Lu'lu'at al-Bahrayn*, pp. 86-87.
56. Ibid., p. 15.
57. Y. al-Bahrani, *Lu'lu'at al-Bahrayn*, pp. 61-63; A. a]-Bahrani, *Anwar al-badrayn*, pp. 136-40.
58. Y. al-Bahrani, *Lu'lu'at al-Bahrayn*, p. 14; A. al-Bahrani, *Anwar al-badrayn*, pp. 119-20.
59. Y. al-Bahrani *Lu'lu'at al-Bahrayn*, pp. 7-12; A. al-Bahrani, *Anwar al-badrayn*, pp. 136-40, pp. 165-68.
60. Y. al-Bahrani, *Lu'lu'at al-Bahrayn*, pp. 63 -66; A. al-Bahrani, *Anwar al-bodrayn*, pp. 136-40.
61. Y. al-Bahrani, *Lu'lu'at al-Bahrayn*, pp. 13-14; A. al-Bahrani, *Anwar al-badrayn*, pp. 148-50.
62. Y. al-Bahrani, *Lu'lu'at al-Bahrayn*, pp. 138-39; A. al-Bahrani, *Anwar al-badrayn*, pp. 123-25.
63. Hamilton, *A New Account of the East Indies, vol.* 1, p. 50; Niebuhr, quoted in Jenner, *Bahrain*, p. 19; Salil ibn Raziq, *History of the Imams and Seyyids of 'Oman*, George Percy Badger, trans. (New York: Burt Franklin, repr. 1963), pp. 226-27; Shadravan Ahmad Faramarzi, *Karim Khan Zand va Khalij-i Fars* (Tehran: Davar Panah, 1346 s.); John R. Perry, *Karim Khan Zand: A History of Iran, 1747-1779* (Chicago: University of Chicago Press, 1979), ch. 10; Ahmad Mustafa Abu Hakima, *History of Eastern Arabia 1750-1800* (Beirut: Khayats, 1965).
64. Y. al-Bahrani, *Lu'lu'a*, pp. 96-103; A. al-Bahrani, *Anwar al-badrayn*, pp. 170-75; an early, still unstudied MS by Shaykh `Abd Allah is "Jawabat al-masa'il al-thalath," Arabic MS 87, Library of the Institute of lsma'ili Studies, London, copied in 1710.
65. Y. al-Bahrani, *Lu'lu'a*, pp. 92-93; A. al-Bahrani, *Anwar al-badrayn*, pp. 175-76. Sayyid `Abdullah was no doubt the Akhbari nemesis against whom the Usuli revivalist Muhammad Baqir Isfahani "Bihbahani" fought in the 1740s and 1750s in Bihbahan.
66. For the significance of Shaykh Yusuf see Juan Cole, "Shi`ite Clerics in Iraq and Iran, 1722-1780: The Akhbari-Usuli Conflict Reconsidered," *Iranian Studies*, 18, 1 (1985), 3-34; sources for Yusuf al-Bahrani's life include his autobiography, in *Lu'lu'a*, pp. 442-51; Khvansari, *Rawdat al-jannat*, 8:203-8; and A. al-Bahrani, *Anwar al-badrayn*, pp. 193-202.
67. Yusuf al-Bahrani, *al-Hada`iq al-nadira li ahkam al-`itra al-tahira*, Muhammad Taqi al-Irani, ed., 12 vols. (Najaf: Dar al-Kutub al-Islamiyya., 1966), vol. 1, pp. 27 ff.; vol. 1, p. 39; vol. 1, pp. 41-65; vol. 1, pp. 125-33; Yusuf al-Bahrani, *al-Kashkul*, 3 vols. (Karbala: Mu'assasa al-A`lami li'l-Matbu`at al-Haditha, 1961), vol. 3, pp. 50-55; vol. 3, pp. 148-50.
68. A. al-Bahrani, *Anwar al-badrayn*, pp. 189-91.
69. Ibid., pp. 228-29, 207-11.
70. For the early Shaykhis see Henry Corbin, *En Islam iranien*, 4 vols. (Paris: Gallimard, 1972) vol. 4; *idem.*, *Spiritual Body and Celestial Earth: From Mazdean Iran to Shi`ite Iran*, Nancy Pearson, ed. (Princeton, N.J.: Princeton University Press, 1977); Denis MacEoin, "Ahsa'i, Shaikh Ahmad b. Zayn-al-Din," *Encyclopaedia Iranica;* "From Shaykhism to Babism," (Ph.D. Diss.: Cambridge

University, 1979), ch. 2; Vahid Rafati, "The Development of Shaykhi Thought in Shi`ite Islam" (Ph.D. Diss.: University of California, Los Angeles, 1979); Abbas Amanat, *Resurrection and Renewal: The Making of the Babi Movement in Iran, 1844-1850* (Ithaca, N.Y.: Cornell University Press, 1989), pp. 48-69; Mangol Bayat, *Mysticism and Dissent: Socioreligious Thought in Qajar Iran* (Syracuse University Press. 1982); and three articles by Juan R. I. Cole: "The World as Text: Cosmologies of Shaykh Ahmad al-Ahsa'i," *Studia Islamica* 80 (1994): 1-23; "Shaykh Ahmad al-Ahsa'i on the Sources of Religious Authority," in Walbridge, ed., *The Most Learned of the Shi`a*, pp. 82-93; and "Casting Away the Self: The Mysticism of Shaykh Ahmad al-Ahsa'i," in Rainer Brunner and Werner Ende, eds., *The Twelver Shia in Modern Times: Religious Culture and Political History* (Leiden: E. J. Brill, 2001), pp. 25-27; see also in this latter volume Muhammad Ali Amir-Moezzi, "An Absence Filled with Presences: Shaykhiyya Hermeneutics of the Occultation," pp. 38-57.

71. Shaykh Ahmad al-Ahsa'i, "`Ayn al-yaqin," Shaykhi Coll., 1053/C, University of California, Los Angeles; "Risala fi al-ijma`," Arabic MS 164, Library of Institute of Ismalili Studies, London; *Sirat al-Shaykh Ahmad al-Ahsa'i,* Husayn `Ali Mahfuz, ed. (Baghdad: Matba`a al-Ma`arif, 1957); Sayyid Kazim Rashti, "Dalil al-mutahayyirin," Persian trans., Curzon Collection Asiatic Society Library, Calcutta, MS 46.

72. A. al-Bahrani, *Anwar al-badrayn,* 191-93, 207-11, 231-32; MacEoin, "Ahsa'i."

73. A. al-Bahrani, *Anwar al-badrayn,* pp. 136-40, 400-405; Murtada Mudarris Chahardihi, *Shaykh Ahmad-i Ahsa'i* (Tehran: `Ali Akbar `Ilmi, 1334 s.), p. 45; for Ibn Abi Jumhur's influence, see Amanat, *Resurrection and Renewal.*

74. William Gifford Palgrave, *Narrative of a Year's Journey Through Central and Eastern Arabia (1862-1863),* 2 vols. (London: Macmillan Co., 1865; repr. Hants.: Gregg, 1969), vol. 2, pp. 201-15.

4 Jurisprudence: The Akhbari-Usuli Struggle

1. See Hamid Algar, *Religion and State in Iran 1785-1906: The Role of the Ulama in the Qajar Period* (Berkeley and Los Angeles: University of California Press, 1969), pp. 33-41.

2. These events have been studied in Laurence Lockhart, *The Fall of the Safavi Dynasty and the Afghan Occupation of Persia* (Cambridge: Cambridge University Press, 1958); idem., *Nadir Shah* (Lahore: al-Irfan, repr. 1976); John R. Perry, *Karim Khan Zand: A History of Iran, 1747-1779* (Chicago: University of Chicago Press, 1979); A. K. S. Lambton, "The Tribal Resurgence and the Decline of the Bureaucracy in the Eighteenth Century," in T. Naff and R. Owen, eds., *Studies in Eighteenth Century Islamic History* (Carbondale: Southern Illinois University Press, 1977), pp. 109-29; Clement Huart, *Histoire de Baghdad dans les temps*

modernes (Paris: Ernest Leroux, 1901); A. M. K. Nawras, *Hukm al-mamalik fi al-`Iraq, 1750-1831* (Baghdad: Wizarat al-A' lam, 1975); S. Longrigg, *Four Centuries of Modern Iraq* (Oxford: at the Clarendon Press, 1925); and Thomas M. Ricks, "Politics and Trade in Southern Iran and the Gulf, 1745-1765" (Ph.D dissertation: Indiana University, 1974).

3. See Hamid Algar, "Shi`ism and Iran in the Eighteenth Century," in Naff and Owen, *Studies*, pp. 288-302.

4. Said Amir Arjomand, "The Office of Mulla-Bashi in Shi`ite Iran," *Studia Islamica* 57 (1983), 135-146.

5. John Chardin, *Voyages de monsieur le chevalier Chardin en Perse et autres lieux de l'orient*, 3 vols. (Amsterdam: Jean Louis de Lorme, 1709), 3: 82.

6. Ibid., 2: 206-08. See the discussion in A. K. S. Lambton, *State and Government in Medieval Islam: An Introduction to the Study of Islamic Political Theory: The Jurists* (Oxford: Oxford University Press, 1981), Chap. XV.

7. Chardin, *Voyages*, 3: 208.

8. Lambton, *State and Government*, p. 285.

9. The following analysis is based on Aqa Ahmad Bihbahani, "Mir'at al-ahwal-i jahan-numa," Persian MS add. 24,~52, foll. 17b-43b, British Library, London.

10. Muhammad Baqir Khvansari, *Rawdat al-jannat fi ahwal al-`ulama' wa's-sadat*, 8 vols. (Tehran: Maktabah-'i Isma`iliyan, 1970), 2: 118-23; for his social context see Said Amir Arjomand, "Religious Extremism (Ghuluww), Sufism and Sunnism in Safavid Iran: 15()1-1722," *Journal of Asian History* 15 (1981): 24-28.

11. Chardin, *Voyages*, 3: 82.

12. Ibid., 3: 310.

13. Khvansari, *Rawdat al-jannat*, 2: 78-93; Arjomand, "Religious Extremism," pp. 28-29.

14. Bihbahani, "Mir'at al-ahwal," foll. 33b-34a. For Mazandarani see Khvansari, *Rawdat al-jannat*, 4: 118-20.

15. Khvansari, *Rawdat al-jannat*, 2: 360-65.

16. Ricks, "Politics and Trade," pp. 55-60.

17. See Ghulam `Ali Azad Bilgrami, *Ma'athir al-Kiram*, Vol. 2 (Lahore: Matba`-i Dukhani-yi Rifah-i `Amm, 1913): 116-19.

18. Bihbahani, "Mir'at al-ahwal," fol. 20b.

19. For Shi`ism in Awadh see Juan R. I. Cole, *Roots of North Indian Shi`ism in Iran and Iraq: Religion and State in Awadh, 1722-1859* (Berkeley and Los Angeles: University of California Press, 1989); for Murshidabad in Bengal see K. M. Mohsin, "Murshidabad in the Eighteenth Century," in K. Ballhatchet and J. Harrison, eds., *The City in South Asia, Pre-modern and Modern* (London: Curzon Press, 1980), pp. 71-84; G. Bhadra, "Social Groups and Relations in the Town of Murshidabad 1765-1793," *Indian Historical Review* 2 (1975): 312-338; Philip B. Calkins, "The Formation of a Regionally Oriented Ruling Group in Bengal 1700-1740," *Journal of Asian Studies* 29 (1970): 799-806.

20. Sushil Chaudhry, "The Rise and Decline of Hughli - a Port in Medieval Bengal," *Bengal Past and Present* 86, 1 (1967): 33-67; Holden Furber, "Glimpses of Life and Trade on the Hugli 1720-1770," *Bengal Past and Present* 86, 2 (1967): 13-23; Ashin Das Gupta, "Trade and Politics in 18th Century India," D. S. Richards, ed., *Islam and the Trade of Asia* (Oxford: Bruno Cassirer, 1970), p. 199. For Shi`ite

institutions in Hughli see Syud Hassein, "Haji Mahomed Muhsin and the Hughli Imambarah," *Bengal Past and Present* 2 (1908): 62-73 and S. M. Hasan, "The Hooghly Imambarah, Its Madrasah and the Library," *Bengal Past and Present* 87 (1968): 217-33.

21. Cf. Nikki R. Keddie, "The Roots of the Ulama's Power in Modern Iran," *Scholars, Saints and Sufis: Muslim Religious Institutions in the Middle East since 1500*, idem., ed., 2nd ed. (Berkeley and Los Angeles: University of California Press, 1978), pp. 211-229.

22. Bihbahani, "Mir'at al-ahwal," foll. 36a, 44a-45b; Ricks, "Politics and Trade," p. 316.

23. Bihbahani, "Mir'at al-ahwal," fol. 38; for this viceroy see K. Datta, "Alivardi Khan," in Jadunath Sarkar, ed., *The History of Bengal: Muslim Period 1200-1757* (Patna: Academia Asiatica, 1973).

24. Ricks, "Politics and Trade," pp. 388-405.

25. Mohsin, "Murshidabad," pp. 80-81; Bihbahani, "Mir'at al-ahwal," fol. 137b.

26. Cf. Purnendu Basu, *Oudh and the East India Company, 1785-1801* (Lucknow: Maxwell Co., 1943), pp. 20ff..

27. See G. Scarcia, "Intorno alle controversie tra Abbari e Usuli presso gli Imamiti di Persia," *Rivista degli Studi Orientali* 33 (1958): 211-250. The account of Algar, *Religion and State in Iran*, pp. 33-41 contains errors and is dated. Aqa Muhammad Baqir did not study with his father in Karbala, but in Isfahan; he lived thirty years in Bihbahan, rather than briefly passing through; he died in 1790, not 1803, and the Usuli revival he led was a feature of the Zand period rather than coinciding with the rise of the Qajars.

28. Khvansari, *Rawdat al-jannat*, 4: 143-46. Andrew Newman, in a personal communication, first pointed out the continuing appeal of Akhbarism in the provinces.

29. Khvansari, *Rawdat al-jannat*, 7: 96-105; Sayyid I`jaz Husayn Kinturi, *Kashf al-hujub wa'l-astar `an al-kutub wa'l-asfar*, ed. Muhammad Hidayat Husayn (Calcutta: Asiatic Society, 1330/1912), p. 289.

30. For Ni`mat Allah see Khvansari, *Rawdat al-jannat*, 8: 150-59; for his son `Abd Allah see ibid., 4: 257-61.

31. For a brief autobiography written in 1768 a few years before his death, see Yusuf al-Bahrani, *Lu'lu'at al-Bahrayn*, ed. S. Mahmud Sadiq (Najaf: Matba`at al-Nu`man, n.d.), pp. 442-51; see also Khvansari, *Rawdat al-jannat*, 8: 203-08.

32. Lockhart, *The Fall of the Safavi Dynasty*, pp. 115-16; J. G. Lorimer, *Gazeteer of the Persian Gulf, 'Oman, and Central Arabia*, 2 vols. (Calcutta: Superintendent Government Printing, India, 1908-15, repr. 1970), 1: 836; Ricks, "Politics and Trade," pp. 77-78.

33. al-Bahrani, *Lu'lu'at al-Bahrayn*, pp. 442-43; Khvansari, *Rawdat al-jannat*, 8: 205.

34. For Tabataba'i, see ibid., 7: 203-09; for Niraqi, 7: 200-03 and Muhammad `Ali Mu`allim Habibabadi, *Makarim al-athar dar ahval-i rijal-i dawrah-'i Qajar*, 2 vols. (Isfahan: Matba`-i Muhammadi, 1958), 2: 360-64.

35. For Qummi see Khvansari, *Rawdat al-jannat*, 4: 122-25.

36. Bihbahani, "Mir'at al-ahwal," fol. 45a.

37. Muhammad Shafi` Varid Tihrani, *Tarikh-i Nadir-Shahi*, ed. Riza Sha'bani (Tehran: Chapkhanahha-yi Zar, 1349 s.), p. 31; Mirza Muhammad Mihdi Kawkab

Astarabadi, *Tarikh-i Nadiri*, trans. William Jones as The History of the Life of Nadir Shah (London: J. Richardson, 1773), pp. 46-63; Lockhart, *Nadir Shah*, pp. 67-77.

38. `Ali Davvani, *Ustad-i kull Aqa Muhammad Baqir b. Muhammad Akmal ma`ruf bih Vahid-i Bihbahani* (Qumm: Chapkhanah-'i Dar al-`Ilm, 1958), p. 130.
39. Lockhart, *Nadir Shah*, pp. 77-78.
40. Ricks, "Politics and Trade," pp. 68-69.
41. Davvani, *Ustad-i kull*, pp. 129-30.
42. Bihbahani, "Mir'at al-ahwal," fol. 46b.
43. Ibid., fol. 45b, mentions only the marriage into the merchant family. See Mu`allim Habibabadi, *Makarim*, 1: 223-24 for the other alliance. Cf. Davvani, *Ustad-i kull*, pp. 140-42.
44. Lockhart, *Nadir Shah*, p. 99.
45. Mu`allim Habibabadi, *Makarim*, 1: 235-37.
46. Astarabadi, *Tarikh-i Nadiri*, Jones trans., pp. 66-67; Sayyid `Abd Allah al-Suwaydi, *Mu'tamar an-Najaf* (Cairo: al-Matba`a al-Salafiyya, 1393/1973), pp. 16-17; Algar, "Shi`ism and Iran," pp. 291ff.
47. `Abd Allah al-Suwaydi, *Mu'tamar an-Najaf*, pp. 39ff.; Astarabadi, *Tarikh-i Nadiri*, Jones trans., pp. 105-06; Lockhart, *Nadir Shah*, pp. 99-102.
48. Mu`allim Habibabadi, *Makarim*, 1: 127-29.
49. Lockhart, *Nadir Shah*, p. 255; Astarabadi, *Tarikh-i Nadiri*, Jones trans., p. 111.
50. J. B. Kelly, *Britain and the Persian Gulf 1795-1880* (Oxford: at the Clarendon Press, 1968), pp. 35-36.
51. Muhammad Sadiq Musavi Nami Isfahani, *Tarikh-i gitigusha dar tarikh-i khandan-i Zand*, ed. Sa'id Nafisi (Tehran: Iqbal, 1317 s.), pp. 137-39; Perry, *Karim Khan Zand*, pp. 113-16; Ricks, "Politics and Trade," p. 266.
52. Mirza Muhammad Tunikabuni, *Qisas al-`ulama'* (Tehran: Kitabfurushi-yi 'Ilmiyyah-'i Islamiyya, n.d.), p. 201.
53. Khvansari, *Rawdat al-jannat*, 2: 95.
54. Bihbahani, "Mir'at al-ahwal," fol. 47a.
55. Sayyid Muhammad Mihdi's father, Murtada, had been the prayer leader in Yazdigird: Sayyid `Abbas Ardistani, "al-Hisn al-matin fi ahwal al-wuzara' wa's-salatin," 2 vols., Arabic MSS 235a-b, 1: 17, National Archives of India, New Delhi.
56. The ethnic dimension of the Usuli-Akhbari struggle has been pointed out by `Abbas Amanat, *Resurrection and Renewal* (Ithaca, N.Y.: Cornell University Press, 1989).
57. See Ricks, "Politics and Trade," p. 268.
58. For Niraqi see Khvansari, *Rawdat al-jannat*, 7: 200-03 and for Shahristani, Mu`allim Habibabadi, *Makarim*, 2: 611-14. The two Arab figures will be treated below.
59. Nami Isfahani, *Tarikh-i giti-gusha*, pp. 180-81; Perry, *Karim Khan*, p. 171.
60. `Abd al-Rahman al-Suwaydi, *Ta'rikh hawadith Baghdad wa'l-Basra min 1186 ila 1192 A.H./1772-1778 M.*, ed. `Imad A. Ra'uf (Baghdad: Wizarat ath-Thaqafa wa'l-Funun, 1978), pp. 41ff.; Perry, *Karim Khan*, p. 170.
61. For the corpse traffic, see Yitzak Nakash, *The Shi`is of Iraq* (Princeton: Princeton University Press, 1994), chapter 7; cf. William El. McNeill, *Plagues and Peoples*

(Garden City, N.Y.: Anchor Books, 1976), p. 232 for the similar effect of Hindu pilgrimage in India on the spread of disease.

62. `Abd al-Rahman al-Suwaydi, *Ta'rikh*, p. 43.

63. Bihbahani, "Mir'at al-ahwal," foll. 47b-48a.

64. "A'inah-'i haqq-numa," Rijal Shi`a, Persian MS 1, fol. 25b, Nasiriyya Library, Lucknow. This anonymous biography of Sayyid Dildar `Ali Nasirabadi, written in Lucknow around 1815, represents an important and hitherto untapped source for the history of Shi`ism in the eighteenth and nineteenth centuries.

65. Mu`allim Habibabadi, *Makarim*, 2: 316; Khvansari, *Rawdat*, 2: 105-06.

66. `Abd al-Rahman al-Suwaydi, *Ta'rikh*, p. 48; Nami Isfahani, *Tarikh-i giti-gusha*, p. 181.

67. Mu`allim Habibabadi, *Makarim*, 2: 360-64.

68. William Francklin, *Observations Made on a Tour from Bengal to Persia in the Years 1786-7* (London: T. Cadell, 1790), pp. 62-63; Muhammad Hashim Asaf Rustam al-Hukama', *Rustam at-tawarikh*, ed. M. Mushiri (Tehran: n.p., 1969), pp. 404-405; and Bihbahani, "Mir'at al-ahwal," fol. 49a. But cf. Perry, *Karim Khan*, pp. 220-21.

69. Mu`allim Habibabadi, *Makarim*, 2: 343-46.

70. Bihbahani, "Mir'at al-ahwal," foll. 48a-49b.

71. Khvansari, *Rawdat*, 2: 200.

72. For a similar journey a few years earlier see Carsten Niehbur, *Reisebeschreibung nach Arabien und den umliegenden Landern*, 2 vols. (Graz: Akademische Druck-u. Verlagsanstalt, repr. 1968), 2: 240-42.

73. This and succeeding paragraphs are based on "A'inah-'i haqq-numa," foll. 48a-49b and Sayyid I`jaz Husayn Kinturi, "Shudhur al-`iqyan fi tarajim al-a`yan," 2 vols. Buhar Collection, Arabic MSS 278-279, 1: 136-37, National Library, Calcutta. For the issue of consensus (ijma') see Harald Loeschner, *Die dogmatischen Grundlagen des Si`itischen Rechts* (Cologne: Karl Heymans Verlag, 1971), pp. 111-147.

74. Khvansari, *Rawdat al-jannat*, 6: 104-05. Originally a student of the Akhbari Sayyid Sadr al-Din Qummi, he went over to Bihbahani's Usulism.

75. For this issue see Löschner, *Grundlagen*, pp. 101-09.

76. "A'inah-'i haqq-numa," fol. 49b.

77. Ibid., foll. 20b-24a.

5 `Indian Money' and the Shi`ite Shrine Cities

1. When a version of this chapter was first published as a journal article in 1986, there was very little academic literature on the finances of the Shi`ite clergy in the eighteenth and nineteenth centuries. Important work along these lines has appeared since then, notably: Litvak, "The Finances of the `Ulama' Communities

of Najaf and Karbala, 1796-1904," *Die Welt des Islams* 40, 1 (1999):41-66; *idem, Shi`i Scholars of Nineteenth-Century Iraq*, passim; and Willem Floor, "The Economic Role of the Ulama in Qajar Persia," in Linda Walbridge, ed., *The Most Learned of the Shi`a: The Institution of the Marja` Taqlid* (Oxford: Oxford University Press, 2001), pp. 53-81.

2.   E. Honigman, "Karbala", in *Encyclopedia of Islam*, 2nd edn.; Yitzhak Nakash, *The Shi`is of Iraq*, pp. 18-22,

3.   For the slave-soldiers in eighteenth-century Iraq see `Abd al-Rahman al-Suwaydi, in `Imad A. Ra'uf (ed.). *Tarikh hawadith Baghdad wa 'l-Basra min 1186 ila 1192 H. 1772-1778 M.*, (Baghdad: Wizarat ath-Thaqafa wa'l-Funun, 1978); A.M. K. Nawras, *Hukm al-mamalik fi al-Iraq, 1750-1831* (Baghdad: Wizarat al-I`lam, 1975); 5. Longrigg, *Four Centuries of Modern Iraq* (Oxford: Clarendon Press, 1925).

4.   Gavin R. G. Hambly, chapters 2-3 of Peter Avery, Gavin Hambly and Charles Melville, eds. *The Cambridge History of Iran Volume 7* (Cambridge: Cambridge University Press, 1991), pp. 104-173.

5.   For the political history of North India in this period see especially Muzaffar Alam, *The Crisis of Empire in Mughal North India: Awadh and the Punjab, 1707-48* (Delhi ; New York : Oxford University Press, 1986); Richard B. Barnett, *North India between Empires* (Berkeley: University of California Press, 1980); Michael H. Fisher, *A Clash of Cultures : Avadh, the British and the Mughals* (London : Sangam, 1988); and Cole, *Roots of North Indian Shi`ism.*

6.   Cole, *Roots of North Indian Shi`ism*, pp. 127-139.

7.   For Sayyid Dildar `Ali Nasirabadi see Cole, *Roots of North Indian Shi`ism.*

8.   Muhammad Muhtashim Khan, "Tarikh-i Muhtashim Khani," Persian MS H.L. 156, foll. 129b-130a. Khodabakhsh Oriental Public Library, Patna; Kamal al-Din Haydar Mashadi, *Savanihat-i salatin-i Avadh* (Lucknow: Naval Kishor. 1897), p. 113; Sayyid `Abbas Ardistani, "al-Hisn al-matin fi ahwal al-wuzara' wa's-salatin," 2 vols., New Delhi, National Archives of India. Arabic MSS 235a. 235b, I: 70; Ja`far Al-Mahbuba al-Najafi, *Madi an-Najaf wa hadiruha* (Sidon: Matba`at al-`Irfan. 1353/ 1934), p. 131 and note; Nakash, *The Shi`is of Iraq*, pp. 19-20.

9.   Aqa Ahmad Bihbahani, "Mir'at al-Ahwal-i jahan-numa," foll. 58a-59b.

10. Hasan Riza Khan to Hajji Karbala'i Muhammad, 26 Rabi` I, 1213, enclosure no. 55 in Resident to Vazir, 22 November 1806, For. Dept. Pol. Cons., 22 November 1806, no. 53, National Archives of India (NAI), New Delhi.

11. King of Iran to Vazir of Oudh, n.d.. enclosure in Persian Secretary to the Government of India to the Resident, Lucknow. 14 October 1806. For. Dept. Pol. Cons., 16 October 1806, no. 25.

12. See Rahman `Ali, *Tazkirah-'i `ulama-i Hind* (Lucknow: Naval Kishor, 1914). pp.99-100; Qiyam al-Din Muhammad `Abd al-Bari Farangi-Mahalli, *Athar al-awwal min `ulama' Faranji Mahall* (Lucknow: Matba'-i Mujtaba'i. 1321:1903), p. 16.

13. Decision of the Mufti of the Adawlut, enclosure no. 54 in Resident to the Vazir, 22 November 1806.

14. On Iranian merchants and trade in this period, see A. K. S. Lambton, "The Case of Haji `Abd al-Karim: A Study in the Role of the Merchants in Mid-Nineteenth Century Persia," in C.F. Bosworth (ed.) *Iran and Islam. in Memory of the late*

Vladimir Minorsky (Edinburgh: University of Edinburgh Press. 1971); and her "Persian Trade under the Early Qajars," in D.S. Richards (ed.). *Islam and the Trade of Asia*, (Oxford: Bruno Cassirer, 1970).

15. Resident to Secretary to the Government in the Political Department. 14 August 1802, For. Dept. Pol. Cons.. 2 September 1802, no. 15.

16. Vazir to Resident, 7 September 1811. For. Dept. Pol. Cons.,20 September 1811, no. 27; Deputy Persian Secretary to the Government to Resident, 12 August 1816, For. Dept. Pol. Cons.. 4 January 1817.

17. Tom Nieuwenhuis, *Politics and Society in Early Modern Iraq: Mamluk Pashas, Tribal Sharks and Local Rule between 1802 and 1831* (The Hague: Martinius Nijhoff, 1982), p. 130.

18. Vazir to Resident, 11 September 1816. For. Dept. Pol. Cons., 20 February 1818, no. .47; Political Agent. Baghdad, to Chief Secretary to the Government, Bombay, 10 September 1817, For. Dept. Pol. Cons., 20 February 1818, no. 53. For Iraqi political leadership in this period see Nieuwenhuis, *Early Modern Iraq* and `Abd al-`Aziz S. Nawwar, *Daud Basha Wali Baghdad* (Cairo: al-Maktaba al-`Arabiyya, 1968).

19. Secretary to the Government of India to Resident, 30 December 1815, For. Dept. Pol. Cons.. 30 December 1815, no. 32. For growing European influence in Awadh in the first half of the nineteenth century see John Pemble, *The Raj, the Indian Mutiny and the kingdom of Oudh 1801-1859* (London: Harvester Press, 1977)

20. Resident to Secretary to the Government of India in the Political Department, For. Dept. Pol. Cons., 9 November 1816, no. 17. Far Mirza Muhammad Husayn Shahristani (d. 1840) see Muhammad `Ali Mu'allim Habibabadi, *Makarim al-athar dar ahval- i rijal-i dai'rah- 'i Qajar*, 2 vols. (Isfahan: Matba'-i Muhammadi, 1958), 2:613, where he is described as Mirza Muhammad Mihdi's grandson through a daughter. By Sayyid Muhammad, Bahu Begam almost certainly meant the son of Sayyid `Ali Tabataba'i, who inherited his father's position of leadership in Karbala, who died in 1826-27 while accompanying Fath-`Ali Shah's expedition against the Russians: see Muhammad Baqir Khvansari, *Rawdat al-jannat fi ahwal al-`ulama' wa's-sadat*, 8 vols. (Tehran: Maktabat-i Isma`iliyan 1390/1970), 7: 145-7. For the political significance of Bahu Begam's will, see Barnett, *North India*, pp.237-8.

21. Resident to Secretary to the Government, 21 November 1814, For. Dept. Pol. Dept., 13 December 1814, no. 10; Resident to Secretary to the Government in the Secret Department, 18 April 1815, For. Dept. Pol. Cons., 18 April 1815, no. 58; Resident to Secretary to the Government in the Political Department, 12 August 1825, For. Dept. Pol. Cons., 16 September 1835. Nas.35-7.

22. Governor-General to Resident, Lucknow, 6 May 1826, For. Dept. Pol. Cons., 23 June 1826, no. 6; Resident to Governor-General, 18 and 20 May 1826, For. Dept. Pol. Cons., 23 June 1826. Nos. 7-8.

23. Resident to Secretary to the Government in the Political Department, 25 July 1826, For. Dept. Pol. Cons. 18 August 1826, no. 8.

24. Nasirabadi, "Najat al-sa'ilin," Fiqh Shi`a, Persian MS 256, fol. 23b, Nasiriyya Library, Lucknow.

25. Musharraf `Ali Khan Lakhnavi (ed.). *Bayaz-i masa'il*, 3 vols. (Lucknow: n.p., 1251/1835-36), 3:26; the fatwa is signed by Sayyid Muhammad.

26. Cf. Max Weber, *The Protestant Ethic and the Spirit of Capitalism*, trans. Talcott Parsons (New York: Charles Schribner's Sans, 1958) and R.H. Tawney, *Religion and the Rise of Capitalism* (New York: Penguin Books, repr. 1947), esp. pp.91-1 15. For ideological accommodation to merchant capitalism in Muslim countries see S.D. Goitein, "The Rise of the Middle Eastern Bourgeoisie in Early Islamic Times," in idem., *Studies in Islamic History and Institutions* (Leiden: E.J. Brill, 1968), pp.217-41; Maxime Rodinson, *Islam and Capitalism*, trans. Brian Pearce (Austin: University of Texas Press, 1978); and Peter Gran, *The Islamic Roots of Capitalism* (Austin: University of Texas Press, 1979).

27. "Proposed Deed between King and Company," 17 August 1825, For. Dept. Pol. Cons. 16 September 1825. no. 37; other deeds have similar clauses.

28. See Sayyid Kazim Rashti, "Dalil al-mutahayyirin," Kerman Shaykhi Library, Microfilm MS, Reel 5, Book 25, University of Michigan Hatcher Research Library; and Muhammad `Ali Kashmiri, *Nujum al-sama' fi tarajim al-`ulama'* (Lucknow: Matba'-i Ja`fari. 1302/1884-85). pp. 367, 397. For published scholarship on early Shaykhism, see footnote 71 of Chapter 3 in this book, above.

29. For the way in which Usulis viewed `Azimabadi and his teachings see Muhammad Mihdi Lakhnavi Kashmiri, *Nujum al-sama': takmila*, 2 vols. (Qumm: Maktabat-i Basirati, 1397, 1977) 1:42-3; Sayyid Muhammad `Abbas Shushtari, "al-Ma`adin adh-dhahabiyya," Adab `Arabi, MS 4446, pp.76-77, Raza Library, Rampur; and Sayyid Husayn Nasirabadi, "Al-Fawa'id al-Husayniyya," `Aqa'id Shi`a, Arabic MS 101, Nasiriyya Library, Lucknow.

30. Murtaza Mudarrisi Chahardihi. *Shaykhigari va Babigari: az nazar-i, falsafih, tarikh, ijtima`* (Tehran: Kitabfurushi-yi Furughi 1966), p. 177; see Denis M. MacEoin, "From Shaykhism to Babism" (Ph.D. dissertation, Cambridge University. 1979), p. 111.

31. Sayyid Muhammad `Abbas Shushtari, ed., "al-Zill al-mamdud," Arabic MS in the Library of the Raja of Mahmudabad, Lucknow, pp. 274-9 (an important collection of letters between the ulama in Najaf and Karbala and those in Awadh, compiled in 1849). For the policies of the Awadh government in the 1840s see Safi Ahmad, *Two kings of Awadh: Muhammad Ali Shah and Amjad Ali Shah (1837-47)* (Aligarh: P.C. Dwadash Shreni & Co.. 1971).

32. Acting Resident to Secretary to the Government of India, 15 June 1839, For. Dept. Pol. Cons.. 26 June 1839. Nos. 41-3; Acting Resident to Officiating Political Secretary to the Government of India. 13 August 1841, For. Dept. For. Cons., 24 August 1840, no. 65; Resident to Secretary to the Government of India, 30 November 1841. For. Dept. For. Cons., 13 December 1841, no. 69, NAI.

33. Political Department. Ft. William, to the Resident, Lucknow, 23 October 1841, For. Dept. For. Cons., 25 October 1841, Nos. 25-6. For the British in Iraq see M.G.I. Khan. "British Policy in Iraq 1828-43," *Journal of the Asiatic Society of Bangladesh* 18 (1973): 173-94.

34. Sayyid Ibrahim al-Musawi al-Ha'iri [Qazvini] to Muhammad `Ali Shah, Rabi' II 1257 June-July, 1841. Persian MS 271, Regional Archives, Allahabad.

35. Political Agent in Turkish Arabia to Secret Committee, 27 January 1842, For. Dept. Secret Cons., 30 March 1842, Nos. 34-5.

36. Sayyid Ibrahim al- Musawi al-Ha'iri [Qazvini] to Amjad `Ali Shah, Persian MS 272, Regional Archives. Allahabad.

37. Muhammad Hasan al-Najafi (d. 1850), the author of *Jawahir al-kalam*, was widely recognized toward the end of his life as the preeminent leader of the Imami community; see Khvansari. *Rawdat al-Jannat*, 2: 304-6 and M.M. Kashmiri, *Nujum al-sama: takmila.* 1: 71-84.

38. Shushtari (ed.), "al-Zill al-mamdud," pp. 145-6.

39. J .G. Lorimer, *Gazeteer of the Persian Gulf, Oman and Central Arabia,* 2 vols. (Calcutta: Superintendent of Government Printing, India, 1908-1915, reproduced, London, 1970), 1: 1348-58: for further sources an this rebellion and analysis see Chapter Six.

40. Shushtari (ed.). "al-Zill al-mamdud," pp. 126-37.

41. Ibid., pp.139-44.

42. Ibid., pp.316-27.

43. Ibid., pp.328-34.

44. Ibid., pp.398-422.

45. Officiating Secretary to Chief Commissioner, Oudh, to Sec. to the Government of India, 27 April 1874, with enclosed note dated 30 August 1861, Board of Revenue, Lucknow File 6, Uttar Pradesh State Archives, Lucknow.

46. Secretary to the Government of India in the Foreign Department to Political Agent in Turkish Arabia, 8 October 1852, For. Dept. For. Cons.. 22 December 1852, no. 5.

47. Shushtari (ed.), "al-Zill al-mamdud," pp.74-7.

48. Note by Secretary to the Government in the Political Department. 11 April 1839, For. Dept. Pol. Cons., 8 May 1839, Nos. 13-14.

49. Political agent in Turkish Arabia to Secretary to the Government of India, 21 March 1844, For. Dept. For. Cons., 8 June 1844, Nos.28-9.

50. India Political Dispatches from the Court of Directors, no. 11 of 1845, 19 March, National Archives of India, New Delhi; Political Agent in Turkish Arabia to Officiating Resident, Lucknow. 26 June 1846, For. Dept. For. Cons., 17 April, no. 97.

51. Note dated 30.8.61 enclosure with Off. Secretary to Chief Commissioner, Oudh, to Secretary to the Government of India, 27 April 1874; Lorimer, *Gazetteer of the Persian Gulf*, 1:264-5.

52. Shushtari (ed.). "al-Zill al-mamdud, pp. 199-203.

53. For Sayyid Ibrahim Qazvini's very large classrooms, partially a function of the resources at his disposal, see Muhamad Tunikabuni, *Qisas al-`ulama* (Tehran: Kitabfurushi-yi `Ilmiyyah-'i Islamiyya, n.d.), pp.4 ff.

54. See Shushtari (ed.), "al-Zill al-mamdud," pp.200, 489.

55. Ibid., p.492.

56. In Shushtari (ed.), "al-Zill al-mamdud," pp. 105-10; for Sayyid `Ali Naqi see Sayyid Muhammad Hadi al-Kazimi, *Ahsan al-wadi`a fi tarajim mashahir mujtahidi ash-Shi`a,* 2 vols. (Najaf: al-Matba`a al-Haydariyya, 1968), 2: 223-6.

57. In Shushtari (ed.), "al-Zill al-mamdud," pp. 111-14.

58. In ibid., p.487.

59. The letter is in Shushtari (ed.), "al-Zill al-mamdud," pp.87-101. For a brief biographical notice of Astarabadi see M. M. Kashmiri, *Nujum al-sama takmila,* 1: 395; he later became a student of the great Shi`ite leader Murtada Ansari in Najaf.

60. Shushtari, "al-Ma`adin adh-dhahabiyya," p. 14.

61. Khvansari, *Rawdat al-jannat*, 2: 305.
62. Murtada al-Ansari Al-Shaykh, *Zindigani va shakhsiyyat-i Shaykh Ansari*, (Ahwaz?: n.p., 1380/1960-61). pp. 72-4; see Abbas Amanat, "In Between the Madrasa and the Marketplace: The Designation of Clerical Leadership in Modern Shi`ism," in Said Amir Arjomand, ed., *Authority and Political Culture in Shi`ism* (Albany: State University of New York Press, 1988), pp. 98-134; Juan R. Cole, "Imami Jurisprudence and the Role of the Ulama: Mortaza Ansari on Emulating the Supreme Exemplar," in Nikki R. Keddie, ed., *Religion and Politics in Iran: Shi`ism from Quietism to Revolution* (New Haven: Yale University Press, 1983), pp. 33-46.
63. M.M. Kashmiri, *Nujum al-sama': takmila*, 1: 123.
64. In Shushtari (ed.), "al-Zill al-mamdud," p. 408.
65. In ibid., pp.67-8.
66. Imam-Jum`a of Tehran to Lord Palmerston and to the Governor-General of India, enclosure from E. Farrant. near Tehran, 15 May 1849, For. Dept. Secret Cons., 25 August 1849, Nos. 23-4.
67. Meir Litvak, "A Failed Manipulation: The British, the Oudh Bequest and the Shi`i `Ulama' of Najaf and Karbala," *British Journal of Middle Eastern Studies* 27, no. 1 (2000):69-89; *idem.* "Money, Religion and Politics: The Oudh Bequest in Najaf and Karbala', 1850-1903," *International Journal of Middle East Studies* 33, no. 1 (2000):1-21; Nakash, *The Shi`is of Iraq*, 211-213.
68. Nakash, *The Shi`is of Iraq*, 214; Litvak, "Money, Religion and Politics," pp. 7-12.
69. Floor, "The Economic Role of the Ulama in Qajar Persia," pp. 67-68.

6 Mafia, Mob and Shi`ism in Iraq

* The authors are grateful for comments on earlier drafts of this chapter from Hanna Batatu, Geoff Eley and Hala Fattah (none of whom is in any way responsible for what follows). This chapter is reprinted in this book with the kind permission of its co-author, Dr. Moojan Momen.

1. The role of the Shi`ite religious scholars in the rebellion is discussed briefly by Hamid Algar in his *Religion and State in Iran 1785-1906: The Role of the `Ulama' in the Qajar Period* (Berkeley and Los Angeles, 1969), pp. 114-16. See also Mangol Bayat, *Mysticism and Dissent: Socioreligious Thought in Qajar Iran* (Syracuse, 1982), p. 42; and Denis MacEoin, "From Shaykhism to Babism: A Study of Charismatic Renewal in Shi`ite Islam" (Univ. of Cambridge Ph.D. thesis, 1979), pp. 112-13.

2. Hanna Batatu, *The Old Social Classes and the Revolutionary Movements of Iraq* (Princeton, 1978), pp. 37-9. 3.

3.   Tom Nieuwenhuis, *Politics and Society in Early Modern Iraq: Mamluk Pashas, Tribal Shayks and Local Rule between 1802 and* 1831 (The Hague, 1982), p. 10.

4.   Batatu, *Old Social Classes,* pp. 44-50.

5.   Primary sources for early modern Iraq include Sayyid `Abd al-Rahman al-Suwaydi, *Ta'rikh hawadith Baghdad wa'l-Basra* 1186-1192/1772-1780[A Chronicle of the Events in Baghdad and Basra 1772-17801, ed. 'Imad A. Ra'uf (Baghdad, 1978); Shaykh Rasul al-Kirkukli, *Dawhat al-wuzara' fi ta'rikh waqa'i' Baghdad al-zawra'* [(Family?) Trees of the Ministers in the History of Occurrences in Baghdad], Arabic trans. M. K. Nawras (Baghdad, n.d.); and Sulayman Fa'iq Bey, *Ta'rikh Baghdad* [History of Baghdad], Arabic trans. M. K. Nawras (Baghdad, 1962). For recent analytical studies, see Nieuwenhuis, *Politics and Society in Early Modem Iraq;* and M. K. Nawras, *Hukm al-mamalik fi al-Iraq, 1750-1831* [The Rule of the Mamluks in Iraq, 1750-1831] (Baghdad, 1975). Still useful are Clement Huart, *Histoire de Bagdad dans les temps modernes* (Paris, 1901); and Stephen H. Longrigg, *Four Centuries of Modem Iraq* (Oxford, 1925).

6.   E. Honigman, "Karbala", in *Encyclopaedia of Islam,* 2nd edn.

7.   Public Record Office, London, Foreign Office (hereafter P.R.O., F.O.) 195/204, "Translation of a Persian Account of Karbala", spring 1843.

8.   See Mohammad Reza Afshari, "The *Pishivaran* and Merchants in Precapitalist Iranian Society", *International. Jl. Middle East Studies,* xv (1983), pp. 133-55; for the historical note of this group in Iran, see also Ervand Abrahamian, "The Crowd in the Persian Revolution", *Iranian Studies,* ii (1969), pp. 129-50. Cf. E. J. Hobsbawrn, *Primtitive Rebels- Studies in Archaic Forms of Social Movement in the 19th and 20th Centuries* (New York, 1965 edn.), p. 11 5; and George Rude, *Paris and London in the Eighteenth Century: Studies in Popular Protest* (New York, 1973), 1 pp, 11-34. Robert J. Holton, "The Crowd in History: Some Problems of Theory and Method", *Social Hist.,* iii (1978), pp. 219-33, points out that crowds gather on a continual basis, and for purposes other than protest, such as carnival and religious events.

9.   For the huge sums that flowed into the Shi`ite shrine cities of Iraq from the Shi`ite-ruled north Indian kingdom of Awadh or Oudh see Cole *Roots of North Indian Shi`ism*; and Chapter Five above.

10. Cf. Hobsbawm, *Primitive Rebels,* pp. 118-19.

11. See Roy P. Mottahedeh, *Loyalty and Leadership in an Early Islamic Society* (Princeton, 1980), pp. 157-8; for overviews of the phenomenon outside Iraq, see Claude Cahen, *Mouvements populaires et autonomisme urbain dans l'asie musulmane du moyen age* (Leiden, 1959), and C. E. Bosworth, *The Mediaeval Islamic Underworld: The Banu Sasan in Arabic Society and Literature,* 2 vols. (Leiden, 1976); Ira Lapidus notes in discussing such groups in medieval Syria that "fundamentally intra-urban organization was not in their hands": see his *Muslim Cities in the Later Middle Ages* (Cambridge, Mass., 1967), pp. 105-7.

12. Hobsbawm, *Primitive Rebels,* pp. 30-40; see also Henner Hess, *Mafia and Mafiosi.- The Structure of Power,* trans. Ewald Osers (Lexington, 1973); Anton Blok, *The Mafia of a Sicilian Village, 1860-1960: A Study of Violent Peasant Entrepreneurs* (New York, 1975); and Pino Arlacchi, *Mafia, Peasants and Great Estates: Society in Traditional Calabria,* trans. J. Steinberg (Cambridge, 1983). (We are grateful to Geoff Eley for drawing our attention to the last-named work.)

Ironically, as Hess notes, the word "mafia" may derive from the Arabic "Ma`afir", the name of the Arabic tribe that ruled Palermo in medieval times.

13. The word luti has connotations of homosexuality, among the deviant behaviors attributed to this group. See Willem Floor, "The Political Role of the Lutis in Iran", in Michael F. Bonine and Nikki R. Keddie (eds.), *Modem Iran: The Dialectics of e La Continuity and Change* (Albany, 1981), pp. 83-95; Willem Floor, "Lutis – A Social Phenomenon in Qajar Persia: A Reappraisal", *Die Welt des Islams,* xiii (1971), PP - 103-20; Reza Arasteh, "The Character, Organization and Social Role of the Lutis (javanmardan) in the Traditional Iranian Society of the Nineteenth Century", 11. *Econ. and Social Hist. of the Orient,* iv (1961), pp. 47-52; H. G. Migeod, "Die Lutis: Ein Ferment des shiitischen Lebens in Persien", *Jl. Econ. and Social Hist. of the Orient,* ii (1959), pp. 82-91. Floor has demonstrated the distinction between sporting neighborhood organizations of the popular classes, which he calls lutigar, and the gangs or *awbash;* both are commonly referred to as *lutis.* The Ottomans in Iraq referred to the lutis as *yaramaz* or good-for-nothings, and as *girami.*

14. Information in this and succeeding paragraphs is based on P.R.O., F.O. 195/ 204, "Translation of a Persian Account"; and on F.O. 248/108, Lt.-Col. Farrant to Sir Stratford Canning, dated Baghdad, 15 May 1843. The Farrant letter is a detailed report, based on extensive interviews, prepared by the British after the Ottoman siege of Karbala.

15. Nieuwenhuis, *Politics and Society in Early Modem Iraq,* p. 86.

16. P.R.O. F.O. 248/108, Farrant to Canning, 15 May 1843. There were 3,400 houses in Karbala and the population fluctuated between 20,000 normally and 80,000 at pilgrimage times. Estimates as high as 10,000 for the *lutis* are given, but this probably results from confusing the gangs with the lower classes in general: see `Abbas al'-Azzawi, *Ta'rikh al-`Iraq bayn Ihtilalayn* [History of Iraq between Two Occupations], 8 vols. (Baghdad, 1955), vii, p. 65.

17. See Said Amir Arjomand, "The Shi`ite Hierocracy and the State in Pre-Modern Iran: 1785-1890", *Archives europeenes de sociologie, XX* (1981) pp. 45-60; and Momen, *Introduction to Shi`ite Islam,* pp. 191-6.

18. In 1803 Sunni officials had been in control of many Shi`ite shrines: see Abu Talib Khan Isfahani, *Masir-i Talibi* [Talibi Travels], ed. Husayn Khadivju (Tehran, A.H. 1352), pp. 406-7, 418; trans. Charles Stewart as *Travels of Mirza Abu Taleb Khan,* 2nd edn., 3 vols. (London, 1814), iii, pp. 190-1.

19. On Shaykhism, see footnote 71 of Chapter Three above. The movement developed a millenarian wing, discussed below, that led to the messianic Babi movement that shook mid-nineteenth century Iraq and Iran.

20. P.R.O., F.O. 248/108, Farrant to Canning, 15 May 1843. For Mirza Salih as Qazvini's student, see Muhammad Tunikabuni, *Qisas al-'ulama'* [Stories of the Religious Scholars] (Tehran, n.d.), p. 4, where an "Aqa Mirza Salih `Arab" is listed.

21. Bernard Lewis, *The Emergence of Modern* Turkey, 2nd edn. (Oxford, 1975), pp. 37-9; A. G. Gould, "Lords or Bandits? The Derebeys of Cilicia", *Internat. Jl. Middle East Studies,* vii (1976), pp. 485-506.

22. For details, see Isfahani, *Masir-i Talibi,* pp. 407-9 (trans. Stewart, *Travels of Mirza Abu Taleb Khan,* iii, pp. 162-7); and for the reaction in neighboring Najaf,

see Ja`far Al-Mahbuba al-Najafi, *Madi an-Najaf wa hadiruha* [The Past and Present of Najaf (Sidon, 1934), pp. 234-6.

23. `Abd al-`Aziz S. Nawwar, *Da'ud Basha Wali Baghdad* [Da'ud Pasha, Governor of Baghdad] (Baghdad, 1967), p. 114 and n. 2.

24. Isfahani, *Masir-i Talibi*, p. 401 (trans. Stewart, *Travels of Mirza Abu Taleb Khan,* iii, pp. 144-5).

25. Al-Kirkukli, Dawhat *al-wuzara' fi Ta'rikh waqa'i` Baghdad al-zawra',* pp. 298-301; Longrigg, *Four Centuries of Modem Iraq,* pp. 242-7; Murtada al-Ansari Al-Shaykh, *Zindigani va Shakhsiyyat-i Shaykh Ansari* [The Life and Personality of Shaykh Ansari (Ahwaz, 1960-1), p. 64. Reports from Karbala in 1843 repeatedly insist that Da'ud Pasha did not actually enter the city in the 1820s, but only besieged it for eleven months before accepting a large bribe as a compromise: see P.R.O., F.O. 195/204, "Translation of a Persian Account".

26. Fa'iq Bey, *Ta'rikh Baghdad,* pp. 82-116; Nawras, *Hukm al-mamalik,* ch. 5; Nawwar, *Da'ud Basha,* ch. 7; and Muhammad Golam Idris Khan, "British Policy in Iraq, 1828-43", *Jl. Asiatic Soc. Bangladesh,* xviii (1973), pp. 173-94.

27. Ibrahim al-Haidari, *Zur Soziologie der schiitischen Chiliasmus: Ein Beitrag Zur Erforschung des irakischen Passionspiels* (Freiburg im Breisgau, 1975), p. 24.

28. P.R.O., F.O. 248/108, Farrant to Canning, 15 May 1843; al-`Azzawi, *Ta'rikh al-`Iraq,* vii, p. 65.

29. National Archives of India, New Delhi, Foreign Department Proceedings (hereafter N.A.I., For. Dept. Proc.), Political Consultations, 5 Oct. 1835, file nos. 16-26, political agent in Turkish Arabia to secretary to the government of India, 27 July 1835.

30. P.R.O., F.O. 195/204, "Translation of a Persian Account".

31. P.R.O., F.O. 248/108, Farrant to Canning, 15 May 1843. See E. J. Hobsbawm, *Bandits* (New York, 1969), pp. 73-4: bandits, social or otherwise, need urban middlemen to dispose of their goods - a role into which Sayyid `Abd al-Wahhab slipped.

32. For bazaar strikes, see Sir John Malcolm, *The History of Persia, 2* vols. (London, 1829 edn.), i, pp. 443-4.

33. Cf. Hobsbawm, *Primitive Rebels,* pp. 110-13.

34. Rude, *Paris and London in the Eighteenth Century,* pp. 18-23.

35. R. Y. Ebied and M. J. L. Young, "An Unpublished Letter from `Ali Pasha, Ottoman Governor of Iraq, to the Sharif of Mecca", *Die Welt des Islams,* new ser., xviii (1976-7), pp. 58-71.

36. H. Inalcik, "Application of the Tanzimat and its Social Effects", *Archivum ottomanicum,* v (1973), pp. 97-127.

37. C. E. Farah, "Necip Pasa and the British in Syria 1841-1842", *Archivum ottomanicum,* ii (1970), pp. 115-53.

38. P.R.O., F.O. 249/108, Najib Pasha to political agent in Turkish Arabia (n.d.) [autumn 1842).

39. Ibid., Farrant to Canning, 15 May 1843.

40. Ibid.

41. Ibid.

42. Ibid., Najib Pasha to political agent (n.d.).

43. P.R.O., F.O. 60/96, Najib Pasha to Lt.-Col. Sheil (n.d.).

44. P R 0 , F.0. 249/108, Najib Pasha to political agent (n.d-)
45. P.R.O., F.O. 60/96, Najib Pasha to French consul (n.d.).
46. Ibid., Farrant to Canning, 22 Apr. 1843; F. 0. 248/108, Farrant to Canning, 15 May 1843.
47. P.R.O., F.O. 248/108, Farrant to Canning, 15 May 1843; F.O. 60/95, Persian agent at Baghdad to Hajji Mirza Aqasi (n.d.) [Jan. 1843].
48. The autumn negotiations are reported in detail in P.R.O., F.O. 248/106, Farrant to Canning, 15 May 1843.
49. P.R.O., F.O. 60/97, Najib Pasha [to Zill al-Sultan or Sayyid Kazim Rashti], 11 Dec. 1842. Cf. Muhammad "Nabil" Zarandi, *The Dawnbreakers [Matali`-i anvar]*, partial trans. Shoghi Effendi Rabbani (Wilmette, 1974), p. 36.
50. N.A.I., For. Dept. Proc., Secret Consultations, 10 May 1843, file nos. 5-10, Persian consul-general, Baghdad, to Mirza `Abd al-Husayn Khan, Dec. 1842; P.R.O., F.O. 248/10, Farrant to Canning, 15 May 1843; F.O. 195/204, "Translation of a Persian Account"; Zarandi, *Dawnbreakers,* p. 35.
51. P.R.O., F.O. 248/108, Farrant to Canning, 15 May 1843.
52. Muhammad Karim Khan Kirmani, *Hidayat al-talibin* [Guide to the Seekers] (Kirman, A.H. 1380), p. 153.
53. Zarandi, Dawnbreakers, pp. 35-6.
54. N.A.I., For. Dept. Proc., Secret Consultations, 10 May 1843, file nos. 5-10, Zill al-Sultan to Aqa Sayyid Ibrahim, Dh al-Qa`da 1253/Decernber 1842; P.R.O., F.O. 248/108, Farrant to Canning, 15 May 1843.
55. P.R.O., F.O. 60/95, Persian agent at Baghdad to Hajji Mirza Aqasi (n.d,) [Jan, 1843); F.O. 248/108, Farrant to Canning, 15 May 1843.
56. P.R.O., F.O. 248/108, Farrant to Canning, 15 May 1843.
57. Ibid.*;* see Norman Calder, "The Structures of Authority in Imami Shi`ite Jurisprudence" (School of Oriental and African Studies, Univ. of London Ph.D. thesis, 1980), pp. 147-51. This is a different question from whether it was permissible to wage defensive holy war against non-Muslims in the time of the Occultation of the Imam. In the first quarter of the nineteenth century, militant Usuli ulama repeatedly argued that it was permissible, with reference to Russia. See A. K. S. Lambton, "A Nineteenth Century View of *Jihad", Studia Islamica,* xxxii (1970), pp. 179-92; Algar, *Religion and State,* pp. 79-80; Arjomand, "Shi`ite Hierocracy", pp. 52 ff.
58. P.R.O., F.O. 248/108, Farrant to Canning, 15 May 1843.
59. Al-Qatil ibn al-Karbala'i, "Risalah", printed in Asad Allah Fadil Mazandarani, *Ta'rikh-i zuhur al-haqq* (History of the Manifestation of Truth), iii (Tehran, n.d., c. 1944), pp. 506-7; Abbas Amanat, "The Early Years of the 135131 Movement: Background and Development" (Univ. of Oxford D.Phil. thesis, 1981), pp. 44-5.
60. See, for example, Mrs. Meer Hassan Ali, *Observations on the Mussulmauns of India,* first publ. 1832 (Karachi, 1978 edn.), p. 76; Amanat, "Early Years of the Babi Movement", pp. 78 ff.
61. P.R.O., F.O. 195/204, "Translation of a Persian Account"; F.O. 248/108, Farrant to Canning, 15 May 1843.
62. P.R.O., F.O. 248/109, Farrant to Canning, 15 May 1843; F.O. 60/97, Dr. John Ross to Lt.-Col. Taylor, 22 Jan. 1843.

63. P.R.O., F.O. 248/108, Farrant to Canning, 15 May 1843; F.O. 195/201, "Translation of a Persian Account".

64. The substantive sources for the account that follows of the occupation include P.R.O., F.O. 248/108, Farrant to Canning, 15 May 1843; F.O. 1951201, "Translation of a Persian Account"; F. 0. 60/97, Ross to Taylor, 22 Jan. 1843; N.A.I., For. Dept. Proc., Secret Consultations, 22 July 1843, no. 41, deposition made by Mulla Aqa of Darband (March 1843); and Yusuf Astarabadi to Sayyid Husayn Nasirabadi, Safar 1259/Mar. 1843, in Sayyid Muhammad `Abbas Shushtari (ed.), "al-Zill al-mamdud" [The Outspread Shadow], Lucknow Arabic MS. in the library of the Raja of Mahmudabad, fos. 44a-51a (a collection of letters between the ulama in Iraq and in north India compiled in 1848). Secondary sources that provide important material or insights include J. G. Lorimer, *Gazetteer of the Persian Gulf, 'Oman, and Central Arabia, 2* vols. (Calcutta, 1908-15, reproduced London, 1970), i, pp. 1348-58; al-`Azzawi, *Ta'rikh al-'Iraq,* vii, pp. 66-8; and `Ali al-Wardi, *Lamahat ijtima`iyya min Ta'rikh al-`Iraq al-hadith* [Social Glimpses from the History of Modern Iraq], 2 vols. (Baghdad, 1969), ii, pp. 116-24.

65. For the last point, see P.R.O., F.O., 248/111, Taylor to Sheil, 16 Feb. 1843; and F.O. 248/111, letter of Ross to Baghdad, 17 Feb. 1843.

66. Astarabadi to Nasirabadi, Safar 1259/Mar. 1843, in Shushtari (ed.), "al-Zill al-mamdud".

67. P.R.O., F,O. 248/111, letter of Ross to Baghdad, 17 Feb. 1843; F.O. 248/108, Farrant to Canning, 15 May 1843. Cf. al-`Azzawi, *Ta'rikh al-`Iraq,* vii, pp. 66-7, who gives 4,000. Iranians floated figures as high as 22,000. According to Farrant, Sayyid `Abd al-Wahhab estimated the city's population at the time of the siege at about 20,000, including 8,000 tribesmen and 6,000 ethnic Iranians.

68. P.R.O., F.O. 60/96, Najib Pasha to Persian consul, 22 Jan. 1843.

69. P.R.O., F.O. 195/201, "Translation of a Persian Account"; F.O. 60/95, Persian agent at Baghdad to Hajji Mirza Aqasi, 20 Dh al-Hiijah/22 Jan.1843.

70. P.R. O., F. O. 60/70, Farrant to Canning, Baghdad, 22 Apr. 1843.

71. N.A,I., For. Dept. Proc., Secret Consultations, 28 Nov. 1846, file nos. 87-96, H. C. Rawlinson to Canning, 29 Apr. 1846.

72. Astarabadi went on to become a student of the leading jurisprudent Murtada al-Ansari in Najaf. For a brief biographical notice, see Muhammad Mihdi Lakhnavi Kashmiri, *Nujum al-sama'- takmila* [Supplement to "Stars of the Heavens"], 2 vols. (Qumm, c. 1977), i, p. 395.

73. Astarabadi to Nasirabadi, Safar 1259/March 1843, in Shushtari (ed.), "al-Zill al-mamdud", fo. 49b.

74. But see J. Chardin, *Vovages de monsieur le chevalier Chardin en Perse et autres lieux de l'orient,* 3 vols. (Amsterdam, 1709), ii, pp. 207-8, 337; and A. K. S. Lambton, *State and Government in Medieval Islam: An Introduction to the Study of Islamic Political Theory: The Jurists* (Oxford, 198 1), ch. 15.

75. Al-Qatil ibn al-Karbala'i, "Risalah", p. 507. Astarabadi likewise referred to the apocalyptic nature of the occupation, writing, "Great God, what a momentous calamity! We saw the reality of the Day on which a man will flee from his brother, his friend, his son and the very clan that gives him shelter": Astarabadi to Nasirabadi, Safar 1259/Mar. 1843; cf. Qur'an 80:34-36. Later Shaykhis like Karim

Khan Kirmani pointed out that Sayyid Kazim's house was respected as a sanctuary even when the shrine of Husayn was desecrated, emphasizing the sanctity of the Shaykhi leader's residence: Kirmani, *Hidayat al-talibin,* pp. 153-4; cf. Zarandi, *Dawnbreakers,* pp. 367; al-ʿAzzawi, *Ta'rikh al-ʿIraq,* vii, p. 68.

76. Alphonse Denis, "Question de Perse: affaire du Kerbela", *Revue de L'Orient, i* (1843), p. 139.

77. The Iranian war chest was depleted as a result of Muhammad Shah's recent unsuccessful campaigns against Herat; the anti-clerical first minister feared the incident would allow a resurgence in the power of the religious scholars; and the British and Russian governments exerted their considerable influence against any hostilities: P.R.O., F.O. 60/95, Sheil to earl of Aberdeen, 14 Feb. 1843; N.A.I., For. Dept. Proc., Secret Consultations, 22 July 1843, no. 41, Justin Sheil to secretary to the government of India, 29 Mar. 1843; R. G. Wilson, A *History of Persia from the Beginning of the Nineteenth Century to the Year 1858* (London, 1866), p. 341.

78. Moojan Momen (ed.), *The Babi and Baha'i Religions, 1844-1944: Some Contemporary Western Accounts* (Oxford, 1981), pp. 87-8.

79. See Moojan Momen, "The Social Bases of the Babi Upheavals in Iran (1849-53): A Preliminary Analysis", *Internat. Jl. Middle East Studies,* xv (1983), pp. 157-83.

80. Longrigg, *Modern Iraq,* p. 288; Nieuwenhuis, *Politics and Society in Early Modern Iraq,* pp. 31-2.

81. Momen, *Babi and Baha'i Religions,* pp. 106-7.

82. For the situation in Shiraz, see Hasan Fasa'i, *History of Persia under Qajar Rule [Farsnamih-'s Nasiri],* trans. Heribert Busse (New York, 1972), pp. 235-8, 262-7, 285-7, 350-1; and Amanat, "Early Years of the Babi Movement", pp. 382-7.

83. Hobsbawm, *Bandits,* pp. 84-5. Hobsbawm deserves full credit for drawing our attention to these phenomena, and this criticism is meant to be constructive. For another critical view of Hobsbawm's approach to rural bandits, see P. O'Malley, "Social Bandits, Modern Capitalism, and the Traditional Peasantry: A Critique of Hobsbawm", *Jl. Peasant Studies,* A (1979), pp. 489-502. For other studies and conceptual refinements of rural banditry, see L. Lewin, "The Oligarchical Limitations of Social Banditry in Brazil", *Past and Present,* no, 82 (Feb. 1979), pp. 116-47; and Henk Driessen, "The 'Noble Bandit' and the Bandits of the Nobles: Brigandage and Local Community in Nineteenth Century Andalusia", *Archives europeenes de sociologie,* xxiv (1993) pp- 96-114.

84. Anton Blok, "The Peasant and the Brigand: Social Banditry Reconsidered", *Comp. Studies in Society and Hist.,* xiv (1972), pp. 494-503.

7   The Shi`ite Discovery of the West

An earlier version of this chapter was read at a conference on the Eighteenth Century held in November, 1991 at the University of California, Berkeley. The author is grateful to James Turner, the organizer, as well as to Barbara Metcalf and Nasir Hussain, the commentators. A revised draft was published in *Iranian Studies*.

1. Muhammad Abu Rayhan al-Biruni, *Kitab fi tahqiq ma li al-Hind*, ed. Edward Sachau (Leipzig: Otto Harrassowitz, 1925); trans. Edward Sachau, *Alberuni's India* (London: K. Paul, Trench, Trübner & Co., Ltd., 1910).
2. Bernard Lewis, *The Muslim Discovery of Europe* (New York: W.W. Norton, 1982); Fatma Müge Göcek, *East Encounters West: France and the Ottoman Empire in the Eighteenth Century* (Oxford: Oxford University Press, 1987). For a strong statement of the thesis of early modern cultural isolation between the northern and southern Mediterranean lands, see Andrew C. Hess, *The Forgotten Frontier* (Chicago: University of Chicago Press, 1978).
3. For eighteenth-century Iran and its relations with the British East India Company in the Persian Gulf, see John R. Perry, *Karim Khan Zand* (Chicago: University of Chicago Press, 1979). For the British view, see J.B. Kelly, *Britain and the Persian Gulf 1795-1880* (Oxford: at the Clarendon Press, 1968).
4. See Philip B. Calkins, "The Formation of a Regionally Oriented Ruling Group in Bengal 1700-1740," *Journal of Asian Studies* 29 (1970):799-806; Richard B. Barnett, *North India between Empires: Awadh, the Mughals, and the British, 1720-1801* (Berkeley and Los Angeles: University of California Press, 1980); and Cole, *Roots of North Indian Shi`ism*.
5. Albert Hourani, "Ottoman Reform and the Politics of the Notables," in W. Polk and R. Chambers, eds. *Beginnings of Modernization in the Middle East: The Ninteenth Century* (Chicago: University of Chicago Press, 1968).
6. The classic statement of this theory is Ronald Robinson, "Non-European Foundations of European Imperialism: Sketch for a Theory of Collaboration," in Roger Owen and Bob Sutcliffe, eds. *Studies in the Theory of Imperialism* (London: Longman, 1972), pp. 117-142.
7. Mir `Abd al-Latif Khan Shushtari, *Tuhfat al-`alam va zayl al-tuhfa,* ed. S. Muvahhid (Tehran: Tahuri, 1984), pp. 277, 329.
8. Ibid.
9. I have used: Mirza Abu Talib Isfahani, *Masir-i talibi fi bilad-i ifrangi*, ed. Husayn Khadivjam (Tehran: Sharikat-i Sihami, 1972); trans. Charles Stewart, *Travels of Mirza Abu Taleb Khan* (New Delhi: Sona, repr. 1972). The accounts of Shushtari and Abu Talib are briefly noticed in Denis Wright, *The Persians amongst the English: Episodes in Anglo-Persian History* (London: I.B. Tauris, 1985), pp. 44-52.
10. Aqa Ahmad Bihbahani, "Mir'at al-ahwal-i jahan-numa," London, British Library, Persian MS, Add. 24,052; the MS circulated very widely in manuscript in India and Iran, and I understand it has recently been published in Iran, but I know of no nineteenth century lithograph edition.
11. Shushtari, *Tuhfat*, p. 275.

12. Abu Talib, *Masir-i Talibi*, pp. 232-233, Eng. trans., pp. 129-30.
13. Abu Talib, *Masir-i Talibi*, p. 232, Eng. trans., p. 130.
14. Shushtari, *Tuhfat*, pp. 275-76.
15. Ibid, p. 276.
16. Abu Talib, *Masir-i Talibi*, pp. 239-242, Eng. trans., pp. 134-39.
17. Bihbahani, *Mir'at*, foll. 270a-b.
18. Bihbahani, *Mir'at*, fol. 273a.
19. Shushtari, *Tuhfat*, p. 284.
20. Ibid., p. 299.
21. Ibid., p. 316.
22. Ibid., pp. 298-99, 312.
23. Bihbahani, *Mir'at*, fol. 227b.
24. Abu Talib, *Masir-i Talibi*, p. 182, Eng. trans., p. 103.
25. Ibid., pp. 195-196, Eng. trans., p. 110.
26. Ibid., pp. 205-214, 263-64, Eng. trans., pp. 114-22, 181-82.
27. Shushtari, *Tuhfat*, pp. 300-303.
28. Ibid., pp. 306-07.
29. Abu Talib, *Masir-i Talibi*, p. 188, Eng. trans., p. 106.
30. Bihbahani, *Mir'at*, foll. 227b ff.
31. Shushtari, *Tuhfat*, p. 315.
32. Ibid., p. 295.
33. Abu Talib, *Travels*, pp. 343-45.
34. Ibid., pp. 348-51.
35. Shushtari, *Tuhfat*, p. 316.
36. Abu Talib, *Masir*, pp. 265-274, Eng. trans., pp. 167-77.
37. Ibid., pp. 270, 272, Eng. trans., pp. 173, 177 (quote).
38. Ibid., pp. 279-281, Eng. trans., pp. 156-60.
39. Elizabeth Eisenstein, *The Printing Press as an Agent of Change*, 2 vols in one (Cambridge: Cambridge University Press, 1985).
40. I am grateful to Barbara Metcalf for this suggestion.

8   Women and the Making of Shi'ism

1. Farah Azari, ed. *Women of Iran: The Conflict with Fundamentalist Islam* (London: Ithaca Press, 1983).
2. For this point I am indebted to Nahid Yeganeh and Nikki R. Keddie, "Sexuality and Shi'ite Social Protest in Iran," in Juan R.I. Cole and Nikki R. Keddie, eds., *Shi'ism and Social Protest* (New Haven: Yale University Press, 1986), pp. 108-136.
3. James Scott, *Weapons of the Weak* (New Haven: Yale University Press, 1985);

4. A major collection of pieces on premodern Muslim women has appeared since these words were originally written: Gavin Hambly, ed., *Women in the Medieval Islamic World: Power, Patronage and Piety* (New York: St. Martin's Press, 1998).Sayyid Muhammad `Abbas Shushtari, *Mi`raj al-mu'minin* (Lucknow: Matba`-i Majma` al-`Ulum, 1293/1876), pp. 316-317.Vajid `Ali Shah, *Bahr-i hidayat* (Lucknow: Matba`-i Sultani, 1267), pp. 5, 51.

5. Sayyid Muhammad 'Abbas Shushtari, *Mi'raj al-mu'minin* (Lucknow: Matba`-I Majma` al-`Ulum, 1293/1876), pp 316-317

6. Vajid 'Ali Shah, *Bahr-i hidayat* (Lucknow: Matba`-I Sultani, 1267), pp. 5, 51.

7. Ibid., p. 8.

8. Sayyid Dildar `Ali Nasirabadi, "Najat al-sa'ilin," Lucknow, Nasiriyya Library, Fiqh Shi`a, MS 256, fol. 18a

9. Nasirabadi, "Najat," 16b-17a.

10. Vajid `Ali Shah, *Bahr-i hidayat* (Lucknow: Matba`-i Sultani, 1267), p. 108.

11. Vajid `Ali Shah, *Bahr*, pp. 109-110.

12. Ibid., pp. 11, 37-38.

13. Sayyid Dildar `Ali Nasirabadi, "Ajwibah-i sa'ilin," ed. Muhammad Aman, Calcutta, Asiatic Society Library, Curzon Collection, MS 1016, fol. 67b; idem., "Najat," fol. 21a-b.

14. Vajid `Ali Shah, *Bahr-i hidayat*, pp. 6-7, 80.

15. Ibid., pp. 21-22; Musharraf `Ali Khan Lakhnavi, ed., *Bayad al-masa'il*, 3 vols. (Lucknow: n.p., 1251/1835-36), 3:48.

16. Vajid `Ali Shah, *Bahr*, pp. 9-10

17. Sayyid Muhammad `Abbas Shushtari, ed., *Murtaziyyat-i Husayniyyih* (Ludhiana: Matba`-i Majma` al-Bahrayn, 1277/1860-61), p. 27.

18. Vajid `Ali Shah, *Bahr*, pp. 22-23.

19. Dildar `Ali Nasirabadi, "Najat," fol. 17a; Vajid `Ali Shah, *Bahr*, p. 50.

20. Vajid `Ali Shah, *Bahr*, p. 62.

21. Ibid, p. 65.

22. Barnett, *North India between Empires*, p. 76; Richard B. Barnett, "Embattled Begams: Women as Power Brokers in Early Modern India," in Hambly, ed., *Women in the Medieval Islamic World*, pp. 521-536; K.S. Santha, *Begums of Awadh* (Benares: Bharati Prakashan, 1980), p. 63;

23. Resident to Sec. Govt. India in the Political Dept., For. Dept. Pol. Cons., 9 November 1816, no. 17, National Archives of India, New Delhi. For the issue of Awadh donations to Iraq, see Juan R.I. Cole, "'Indian Money' and the Shi`ite Shrine Cities of Iraq, 1786-1850," *Middle Eastern Studies* 22, no. 4 (Oct. 1986):461-480. For the political significance of Bahu Begam's will, see Barnett, *North India*, pp. 237-38.

24. Mrs. Meer Hasan Ali, *Observations on the Mussulmans of India* (London: Oxford Univ. Press, repr. 1917), pp. 360-63.

25. For instance, Sayyid Hasan Riza Zangipuri, a mujtahid from Awadh who spent some time in Iran, gained employment on his return to Lucknow in the establishment of Mubarak Mahall, a wife of Ghazi al-Din Haydar Shah (r. 1814-1827): Sayyid Muhammad Husayn Nauganavi, *Tazkirah-'i be-baha fi tarikh al-`ulama'* (Delhi: Jayyid Barqi Press, n.d.), pp. 129-31.

26. Ali, *Observations*, p. 23.

27. This and following paragraphs are based on `Abd al-Ahad Rabit, *Tarikh Badshah Begam*, tr. Muhammad Taqi Ahmad (Delhi: Idarah-'i Adabiyat, repr. 1977), pp. 6-9. See also the discussion in Michael H. Fisher, "Women and the Feminine in the Court and High Culture of Awadh, 1722-1856," in Hambly, ed., *Women in the Medieval Islamic World*, pp. 505-506.

28. `Abd al-Ahad, *Tarikh Badshah Begam*, pp. 9-10.

29. Ibid., p. 14.

30. Ibid., p. 11.

31. Ibid., p. 12.

32. W.H. Sleeman, *A Journey through the Kingdom of Oudh in 1849-1850*, 2 vols. (London: Pelham Richardson, 1850), 1:107-08.

33. Kamal al-Din Haydar Husayni Mashhadi, *Qaysar al-tawarikh* (Lucknow: Naval Kishor, 1896), pp. 87-88.

34. Aqa Ahmad Bihbahani, "Mir`at al-Ahwal-i jahan-numa," British Library, Add. 25,052, fol. 102.

35. Sayyid Dildar `Ali Nasirabadi, "Risalih dar radd-i mazhab-i sufiyyih," Lucknow, Nasiriyya Library, Kalam Shi`a, Persian MS 111, fol. 3b. The views reported are those of Mawlavi Sami`, expressed around 1804 in Lucknow.

36. Abu Talib Isfahani, *Travels of Mirza Abu Taleb Khan*, 2nd ed. 3 vols., tr. Charles Stewart (London: Longman, Hurst, Rees, Orme and Brown, 1814), 3:276. These remarks come, not in the course of the travelogue, but in an essay, "On the Liberties of the Asiatic Women," translated by Captain Richard Davidson and published originally in the *Asiatic Annual Register* for 1801, then appended to the English translation of *Masir-i Talibi*. I do not know if the Persian original of this tract survives, but it is not included in the Persian editions of the travel account.

37. Nasirabadi, "Risalih dar radd-i mazhab-i sufiyyih," fol. 5b.

38. Ibid., fol. 8a.

39. Ali, *Observations*, p. 64.

40. Abdul Halim Sharar, *Lucknow: The Last Phase of an Oriental Culture*, tr. E.S. Harcourt and Fakhir Hussain (Boulder, Co.: Westview Press, 1976), p. 81

41. Ali, *Observations*, pp. 96-97.

42. Ibid., pp. 99-100.

43. Sharar, *Lucknow*, p. 205.

44. `Ali, *Observations*, pp. 106-07.

45. Sharar, *Lucknow*, pp. 202-03.

46. Ali, *Observations*, p. 29.

47. Ibid., pp. 23-27, 51.

48. Sharar, *Lucknow*, p. 149.

49. Ali, *Observations*, p. 29.

50. W. Crooke, *Tribes and Castes of the North-Western Provinces and Oudh*, 4 vols. (Calcutta: Office of the Superintendant of Government Printing, 1896), 4:364-71; *Gazetteer of the Province of Oudh*, 3 vols. (Allahabad: North-Western Provinces and Oudh Government Press, 1877), 2:395-96; see also Fisher, "Women and the Feminine in the Court and High Culture of Awadh," pp. 507-508.

51. Shushtari, ed., *Murtaziyyat*, pp. 20-21

52. Musharraf `Ali Khan Lakhnavi, ed., *Bayad al-masa'il*, 3:112; Vajid `Ali Shah, Bahr, p. 62.

53. Sayyid Muhammad `Abbas Shushtari, `Ashara Kamila (Lucknow: Matba`
    Husayniyya Ithna `Ashari, 1296/1878), pp. 43-45.
54. Mirza Rusva, The Courtesan of Lucknow (Umarao Jan Ada), trans. Khushwant
    Singh and M.A. Husaini, (New Delhi: Hind Pocket Books, 1970), p. 41.
55. Sharar, Lucknow, p. 196.
56. Mirza Rusva, Umarao Jan, p. 84.
57. Ibid., p. 85.
58. Sharar, Lucknow, pp. 80-81.
59. Mirza Rusva, Umarao Jan, pp. 166, 175-77.
60. Vajid `Ali Shah, Bahr-i hidayat (Lucknow: Matba`-i Sultani, 1267), pp. 27-29;
    Dildar `Ali Nasirabadi, "Risalih dar radd," 5b.

9   Sacred Space and Holy War in India

1. See for background Koenraad Elst, Ram Janmabhoomi vs. Babri Masjid: a case
    study in Hindu-Muslim conflict (New Delhi: Voice of India, 1990).
2. I discussed this incident briefly in my Roots of North Indian Shi`ism, pp. 244-49; it
    has also been analyzed, from different points of view, by Gaurishwar Dayal
    Bhatnagar, Lucknow under Wajid `Ali Shah (Varanasi: Bharatiya Vidya Prakashan,
    1968) and by Michael H. Fisher, Clash between Cultures (Riverdale, Md.:
    Riverdale Co., 1987). Here I wish to enlarge on my previous discussion and focus
    on the import of the fatwas issued by the Shi`ite chief mujtahid during the crisis.
3. See, e.g., Sayyid Dildar `Ali Nasirabadi, "Ajwibat al-sa'ilin," Calcutta, Asiatic
    Society Library, Curzon Collection, MS 1016; idem., "Najat al-sa'ilin," Lucknow,
    Nasiriyya Library, Fiqh Shi`a, MS 256; Musharraf `Ali Khan Lakhnavi, ed.,
    Bayaz-i masa'il, 3 vols. (Lucknow: n.p., 1251/1835-36); Sayyid Husayn
    Nasirabadi, Majmu`ah-'i Irshad al-mu'minin (Lucknow: Matba`-i Muhammadi,
    1265/1848-49), idem., Murtaziyyat-i Husayniyya (Ludhiana: Matba`-i Majma` al-
    Bahrayn, 1277/1860-61); Vajid `Ali Shah [and Sayyid Muhammad Nasirabadi],
    Bahr-i hidayat (Lucknow: Matba`-i Sultani, 1267/1850-51).
4. Kamal al-Din Haydar Husayni Mashhadi, Qaysar al-tavarikh (Lucknow: Naval
    Kishore, 1896), p. 109.
5. See C.A. Bayly, Rulers, Townsmen and Bazaars: North Indian Society in the Age
    of British Expansion, 1770-1870 (Cambridge: Cambridge University Press, 1983).
6. Donald Butter, Outlines of the Topography and Statistics of the Southern Districts
    of Oud'h and of the Cantonment of Sultanpur-Oud'h (Calcutta: Bengal Military
    Orphan Press, 1839), p. 163.
7. National Archives of India [NAI], New Delhi, Foreign Department Foreign
    Correspondence [FDFC], 28 Dec. 1855, Resident/King, 8 Feb. 1855, no. 342;
    Mashhadi, Qaysar al-Tavarikh, pp. 110-111.

8. NAI, FDFC, 28 Dec. 1855, Capt. Alexander Orr/Sup't, Frontier Police, 29 July 1855; Orr/Sup't Frontier Police, 31 July, 1855, both in no. 341; Mashhadi, *Qaysar*, pp. 111-112.

9. NAI, FDFC, 28 Dec. 1855, Resident/Off'g. Sec. Govt. India, 24 March 1847, no. 94, 17 April 1847; "Notes on a Conference between the Resident and the King of Oudh," 1 Aug. 1855, no. 342; and King of Oudh/Resident, 12 Aug. 1855, no. 355.

10. NAI, FDFC, 28 Dec. 1855, Resident/King, 10 Aug. 1855, no. 355; Orr/Sup't Police, with Resident/Sec. Govt. India, 16 Aug. 1855, no. 351; Mirza Jan, *Hadiqah-'i shuhada'* (n.p, 1272/1855), pp. 8-16; Mashhadi, *Qaysar*, pp. 121-124.

11. NAI, FDFC, 28 Dec. 1855, "Conduct of the High Priest of Lucknow," encl. 4 with Resident/Sec. Govt. India, 8 September 1855, no. 363.

12. Ibid.

13. NAI, FDFC, 28 Dec. 1855, Conference between Minister and Resident, 30 Aug. 1855, no. 364; Captain G.K. Weston/Resident, 30 Aug. 1855, no. 365.

14. NAI, FDFC, 28 Dec. 1855, 28 Dec. 1855, Resident/Sec. Govt. India, 8, 12, 16, 17 Sept., nos. 360, 370, 379.

15. NAI, FDFC, 28 Dec. 1855, "Report made by Shankar Dyal of Kheree, dated 26 Sept. 1855," appendix B to "Conference between Resident and King, 29 Sept. 1855," no. 389; Off'g Resident/Off'g Sec. Govt. India, 4 Oct. 1855, no. 394; Off'g Resident/Sec. Govt. India, 5 Oct. 1855, no. 396.

16. NAI, FDFC, 28 Dec. 1855, "Enclosure No. 1, Fatwa of High Priest," with Conference Res./King, 29 Sept. 1855, no. 389.

17. Mirza Jan, *Hadiqah-'i shuhada'*, pp. 40-41.

18. NAI, FDFC, 28 Dec. 1855, Conference Res./King, 29 Sept. 1855, no. 389.

19. NAI, FDFC, 28 Dec. 1855, Off'g Resident/Sec. Govt. India, 2 Oct. 1855, no. 388.

20. Mirza Jan, *Hadiqah-'i shuhada*, pp. 52-53.

21. For this institution see F.C.R. Robinson, "The `Ulama' of Farangi Mahall and their *Adab*," in Barbara Daly Metcalf, ed., *Moral Conduct and Authority: The Place of Adab in South Asian Islam* (Berkeley and Los Angeles: University of California Press, 1984), pp. 152-83.

22. NAI, FDFC, 28 Dec. 1855, "Report from Daryabad, 24 Oct. 1855," no. 434; Off'g Resident/Sec. Govt. India, 31 October 1855, no. 440; Off'g Resident/Sec. Govt. India, 8, 9, 10 Nov. 1855, nos. 448, 449, 450; Mashhadi, *Qaysar*, pp. 125-128.

23. Mirza Jan, *Hadiqa*, p. 65.

10   Shi`tes as National Minorities

1. Al-Sayyid Muhammad `Ali Kamal al-Din, *Thawrat al-'ishrin fi dhikraha al-khamsin* (Baghdad: Matba'at al-tadamun, 1971); Elie Kedourie, "The Iraqi Shi`ites

and Their Fate," in Martin Kramer, ed., *Shi`ism, Resistance and Revolution* (Boulder: Westview Press, 1987), pp. 143-151; Pierre-Jean Luizard, *La formation de l'Irak contemporain : le rôle politique des ulémas chiites à la fin de la domination ottomane et au moment de la construction de l'Etat irakien* (Paris: Editions du Centre national de la recherche scientifique, 1991); Nakash, *Shi`ites of Iraq*; Ar-Rahimi, *Ta'rikh al-haraka al-islamiyya fi al-'iraq,* pp. 189-234; ; Peter Sluglett, *Britain in Iraq 1914-1932* (London: Ithaca/St. Antony's, 1976), pp. 300-304; Amal Vinogradov, "The 1920 Revolt in Iraq Reconsidered: The Role of the Tribes in National Politics," *International Journal of Middle Eastern Studies* 3 (1972): 123-39; Sami Zubaida, "The Fragments Imagine the Nation: The Case of Iraq," *International Journal of Middle East Studies* 34 (2002):205-215.

2. Sluglett, *Britain in Iraq,* pp. 39, 78-86, 306; ar-Rahimi, *Ta'rikh al-haraka al-islamiyya fi al-'iraq,* ch. 3 and facsimile letters in appendices.

3. Sluglett, *Britain in Iraq,* pp. 114, 150-54, 300-314; Mohammad A. Tarbush, *The Role of the Military in Politics: A Case Study of Iraq to 1941* (London: Kegan Paul, 1982), pp.91-92.

4. Nakash, *Shi`ites of Iraq,* pp. 100-105, 170-71

5. D. Cobbett, F. Hazelton, P. Sluglett, C. Whittleton and U. Zaher, eds., *Saddam's Iraq: Revolution or Reaction?* (London: Zed, 1986), p. 123.

6. Hasan Muhammad Sa'd, *Jabal `Amil bayn al-atrak wa al-faransiyyin 1914-1920* (Beirut: Dar al-Katib, 1980), pp. 1-49.

7. Ibid., pp. 51-102.

8. Sabrina Mervin, *Un réformisme chiite: Ulémas et lettrés du Ǧabal `Amil* (Paris: Karthala, 2000); Mas'ud Dahir, "Jabal `Amil fi itar al-tajzi`a al-ist`imariyya li'l-mashriq al-`Arabi," in Habib Sadiq, ed., *Safahat min ta'rikh Jabal `Amil* (Beirut: Dar al-Farabi, 1979), pp. 107-130; Abdo I. Baaklini, *Legislative and Political Development: Lebanon, 1842-1972* (Durham, N. C.: Duke University Press, 1976), pp. 99-100; Joseph Olmert, "The Shi`ites and the Lebanese State," in Kramer, *Shi`ism,* pp. 191-93.

9. Baaklini, *Legislative and Political Development,* pp. 142-43, 188-89, 199-203; Olmert, "The Shi`ites and the Lebanese State," pp. 193 ff..

10. Guido Steinberg, "The Shi`ites in al-Ahsa', 1913-1953," in Brunner and Ende, eds., *The Twelver Shia in Modern Times,* pp. 236-254; F. Vidal, *The Oasis of al-Hasa* (Arabian American Oil Company, 1956), pp. 37-38; Goldberg, "The Shi`ite Minority in Saudi Arabia," pp. 233-239.

11. For Iraq see Marion Farouk-Sluglett and Peter Sluglett, "Iraqi Baathism: Nationalism, Socialism and National Socialism," in *Saddam's Iraq,* pp. 89-107; Ofra Bengio, "Shi`ites and Politics in Baathi Iraq," *Middle Eastern Studies* 21, 1 (1985): 1-14; Hanna Batatu, "Shi`ite Organizations in Iraq: al-Da`wah al-Islamiyah and al-Mujahidin," in Cole and Keddie, *Shi`ism and Social Protest,* pp. 179-200; and Joyce N. Wiley, *The Islamic Movement of Iraqi Shi`ites* (Boulder, Co.: Lynne Riener, 1992); Ofra Bengio, "Nation Building in Multiethnic Societies: The Case of Iraq," in

Ofra Bengio and Gabriel Ben-Dor, eds., *Minorities and the State in the Arab World* (Boulder, Co.: Lynn Rienner, 1999), ch. 8.

12. Useful figures on Lebanese Shi`ites are assembled by the journalist Nabil Khalifa in his *ash-Shi`a fi Lubnan: Thawrat ad-dimughrafiyya wa al-hurman* (Beirut: Silsilat al-Fikr al-Siyasi, 1984). Among much scholarly writing on the Shi`ites of contemporary Lebanon, some of the better is the following: Fouad Ajami, *The Vanished Imam: Musa al-Sadr and the Shia of Lebanon* (Ithaca, N.Y.: Cornell University Press, 1986); "Lebanon's Shi`as: Revolt of the Dispossessed," *Middle East Research and Information Project Reports*, vol. 15, no. 5 [# 133] (June 1985), especially the comments of Salim Nasr; Augustus Richard Norton, "Shi`ism and Social Protest in Lebanon," and Helena Cobban, "The Growth of Shi`ite Power in Lebanon and its Implications for the Future," both in Cole and Keddie, *Shi`ism and Social Protest*; and articles by Norton and C. Bailey in Kramer, ed., *Shi`ism*; Augustus Richard Norton, *Amal and the Shi`a: Struggle for the Soul of Lebanon* (Austin: University of Texas Press, 1987); Graham E. Fuller and Rend Rahim Francke, *The Arab Shi`a: The Forgotten Muslims* (New York: St. Martin's, 1999), chapter nine.

13. Nomi Morris, "Hezbollah shows a kinder, gentler face: Political wing gains ground as military arm begins to fade into history," July 03, 1999, Knight Ridder Newspapers, (Lexis-Nexis); Nicholas Blanford, "Hizbullah: Lebanon's heir apparent?" *Jane's Intelligence Review*; Coulsdon; Nov 1, 1999 (Proquest); "Facts and figures on Hezbollah in Lebanon," February 28, 1999, Associated Press (Lexis-Nexis).

14. Goldberg, "The Shi`ite Minority in Saudi Arabia," pp. 239-46.

15. Patrick E. Tyler, "King Fahd Tries to Meet Challenge to Stability," *The Washington Post*, 22 February 1987; Fuller and Francke, *The Arab Shi`a*, ch. 8; Douglas Jehl, "Saudis Crack Down on an Obscure Shiite Militant Group," NYT 21 October 1996; "40 Die as Saudi Troops Clash with Muslim Sect," Associated Press, 25 April 2000; Howard Schneider, "Saudi Skies Seem Brighter; Post-Gulf War Turbulence Has Calmed Down," *International Herald Tribune*, January 10, 2000.

16. Graham E. Fuller, "Another Powder Keg in the Persian Gulf," *Los Angeles Times*, June 3, 1998; Uzi Rabi and Joseph Kostiner, "The Shi`is in Bahrain: Class and Religious Protest," in Bengio and Ben-Dor, *Minorities and the State*, ch. 9.

17. Andreas Rieck, "Shia Communal Organizations in Pakistan (1948-1968)," in Ende and Brunner, *The Twelver Shia in Modern Times*, pp. 268-283. David Busby Edwards, "The Evolution of Shi`i Political Dissent in Afghanistan," in Cole and Keddie, *Shi`ism and Social Protest*, pp. 201-229; Amir Shah, "UN human rights investigator says sorry state in Afghanistan," March 18, 1999, Associated Press, (Lexis-Nexis).

11 The Modernity of Theocracy

*Special thanks to Sohrab Behdad for his comments on this chapter.

1. Talal al-Asad, *Genealogies of Religion* (Baltimore: Johns Hopkins University Press, 1993).
2. Ervand Abrahamian, *Khomeinism* (Berkeley and Los Angeles: University of California Press, 1993).
3. "Shah criticizes Tehran Regime," Washington Post, July 28, 1979.
4. "The Year of the Hostage," *New York Times*, November 2, 1980.
5. Gary Sick, "Khomeini from Exile To Revolution," *Book World, Washington Post*, March 2, 1986.
6. Thomas Friedman, "In My Next Life," *New York Times*, May 7, 1995.
7. Sohrab Behdad, personal communication, December 22, 1999.
8. Anthony Giddens, *The Consequences of Modernity* (Stanford: Stanford University Press, 1990).
9. Ali Asghar Kazimi, *Buhran-i nawgira'i va farhang-i siyasi dar Iran* (Tehran : Qumis, 1997).
10. Shaul Bakhash, *Reign of the Ayatollahs* (New York: Basic Books, 1990 edn.), pp. 250-255.
11. Abrahamian, *Khomeinism*.
12. James C. Scott, *Seeing Like a State: How Certain Schemes to Improve the Human Condition have Failed* (New Haven: Yale University Press, 1998), pp. 4-5.
13. Ali Rashidi, "The Process of De-Privatisation," in Thierry Colville, ed., *The Economy of Islamic Iran* (Tehran: Institut Français de Recherche en Iran, 1994), p. 53.
14. Stephen Holmes, *Anatomy of Anti-Liberalism*, (Cambridge, MA.: Harvard University Press, 1993).
15. F. Halliday, *Iran: Dictatorship and Development* (Harmondsworth: Penguin, 1979); see also Ervand Abrahamian, *Iran Between Two Revolutions* (Princeton: Princeton University Press, 1982); and Nikki R. Keddie, *Roots of Revolution* (New Haven: Yale University Press, 1981).
16. Shahrough Akhavi, "Shi'ism, Corporatism, and Rentierism in the Iranian Revolution," in Juan R. I. Cole, ed. *Comparing Muslim Societies* (Ann Arbor: University of Michigan Press, 1992), pp. 261-293.
17. See useful comments on the ideological underpinnings of the Khomeinist view of property in Sohrab Behdad, "Islam, Revivalism and Public Policy," in Sohrab Behdad and Farhad Nomani, eds., *International Review of Comparative Public*

Policy, Series ed. by Nicholas Mercuro, vol. 9 (Greenwich, Conn.: IAI Press, 1997), pp. 28-32.

18. Jahangir Amuzegar, *Iran's Economy under the Islamic Republic* (London: I.B. Tauris, 1993), pp. 297-298; see also Shaul Bakhash, *The Reign of the Ayatollahs* (New York: Basic Books, 1990); Muhammad 'Ali Khatib, *Iqtisad-i Iran* (Tihran: Intisharat-i Danishgah-i Azad-i Islami, 1374 [1995]) and Ibrahim Razzaqi, *Iqtisad-i Iran* (Tehran: Nashr-i Nay, 1367 [1988]).

19. Rashidi, "The Process of De-Privatisation, p. 54.

20. Rashidi, "The Process of De-Privatisation, pp. 37-68.

21. Assef Bayat, *Workers and Revolution in Iran* (London: Zed, 1987), pp. 175-176.

22. Abrahamian, *Khomeinism*, pp. 139-40.

23. Patrick Clawson, "The Impact of the Military," in Thierry Colville, ed., *The Economy of Islamic Iran* (Tehran: Institut Français de Recherche en Iran, 1994), p. 71.

24. Sohrab Behdad, "Production and Employment in Iran: Involution and the De-Industrialization Thesis," in Colville, pp. 100-101.

25. Clawson, p. 82.

26. Robert W. Olson, *The Kurdish question and Turkish-Iranian relations: from World War I to 1998* (Costa Mesa, Calif.: Mazda Publishers, 1998). For an Iranian perspective see Hamid Riza Jala'i'pur, *Kurdistan : 'ilal-i tadavum-i buhran-i an pas az inqilab-i Islami (1358-1370)* (Tehran : Vizrat-i Umur-i Kharijah, 1993).

27. George C. Wilson, "Iran Losses Put at 40,000 in Weeks," *Washington Post*, January 16, 1987.

28. Gabrielle Hecht, *The Radiance of France: Nuclear Power and National Identity after World War II* (Cambridge, Mass.: MIT Press, 1998).

29. Herbert Krosney, *Deadly Business: Legal Deals and Outlaw Weapons : the Arming of Iran and Iraq, 1975 to the Present*, (New York : Four Walls Eight Windows, 1994).

30. Jim Mann, "Iran Determined to Get A-Bomb, U.S. Believes," *Los Angeles Times*, March 17, 1992; Yossi Melman, "Iran's Lethal Secret; How the Rafsanjani Regime Is Closing in on Atomic Weaponry," *The Washington Post*, October 18, 1992.

31. In Brief: Iran," *Middle East Economic Digest*, April 23, 1999, p. 17; "Moscow Defiant over Reactor," *Nuclear Engineering International*, Feb. 28, 1999 (Lexis-Nexis).

32. "Russian Minister Cautions against Building New Nuclear Reactors in Iran," BBC Monitoring Former Soviet Union - Political, BBC Worldwide Monitoring , March 29, 1999, at Lexis-Nexis; Michael Wines, "Putin to Sell Arms and Nuclear Help to Iran," *New York Times*, March 13, 2001.

33. Bill Samii, "Iran Seeking Fusion Reactor?" Radio Free Europe/Radio Liberty *Iran Report*, Vol. 2, No. 28, 12 July 1999; Seymour Hersh, "The Iran Game: How will Tehran's Nuclear Ambitions Affect our Budding Partnership," *The New Yorker*, December 2, 2001.

34. For the Mujahidin see Ervand Abrahamian, *Radical Islam: The Iranian Mujahidin* (London: I.B. Tauris, 1989).

35. Cf. Ervand Abrahamian, *Tortured Confessions: Prisons and Public Recantations in Modern Iran* (Berkeley and Los Angeles: University of California Press, 1999).

36. "Space in Iran's Prisons Not Meeting Standards," IRNA, 23 November 1998.

37. Iranian government statistics available on the Web at: http://www.salamiran.org/IranInfo/State/Government/Education/index.html; Susan Sachs, "In Iran, More Women Leaving Nest for University," *New York Times*, 22 July 2000.

38. This point is based on a seminar paper written for me by Mani Limbert.

39. Muharyani Othman, "Rapid progress of Iranian women," *New Straits Times* (Malaysia), April 22, 1996; "Six Million Women are Illiterate in Iran," Deutsche-Press Agentur, 21 November 2000.

40. Clawson, "Impact of the Military," in Colville.

41. Sohrab Behdad, "Production and Employment in Iran: Involution and the De-Industrialization Thesis," in Colville, pp. 90-91, 97-102; and personal communication, 22 December, 1999.

42. "IDRO Presses ahead with Privatization," *Middle East Economic Digest*, April 11, 1997.

43. "Iran Banks on Private Sector to Help Credit-Starved Economy,"*Financial Times*, Marcy 26, 1999; Nazila Fathi, "Iran's Reformers set out to Save the Economy," *New York Times*, July 8, 2001.

44. Charles Recknage and Azam Gorgin, "Reformers, Conservatives Prepare for Renewed Struggle," Radio Free Europe/Radio Liberty, *Iran Report*, June 13, 2001.

45. Sohrab Behdad, "Winners and losers of the Iranian revolution: a study in income distribution," *International Journal of Middle East Studies* 21 (August 1989):327-58.

Suggestions for Further Reading

For general coverage of Shi`ite Islam in English that includes or focuses on the period since 1500, the subject of this book, see: Moojan Momen, *An Introduction to Shi`ite Islam* (New Haven, Ct.: Yale University Press, 1985); Heinz Halm, *Shi`a Islam from Religion to Revolution* (Princeton: Markus Wiener, 1997); Juan R. I. Cole and Nikki Keddie, *Shi`ism and Social Protest* (New Haven, Ct.: Yale University Press, 1986); Martin Kramer, ed., *Shi`ism, Resistance and Revolution* (Boulder: Westview Press, 1987); Graham E. Fuller and Rend Rahim Francke, *The Arab Shi`a: The Forgotten Muslims* (New York: St. Martin's, 1999); Rainer Brunner and Werner Ende, eds., *The Twelver Shi`a in Modern Times* (Leiden: E.J. Brill, 2001); and Linda Walbridge, ed., *The Most Learned of the Shi`a* (New York: Oxford University Press, 2001).

For Shi`ism in the Safavid and Ottoman periods, see Roger Savory, *Iran under the Safavids* (Cambridge: Cambridge University Press, 1980); Adel Allouche, *The Origins and Development of the Ottoman-Safavid Conflict (906-962/ 1500-1555)* (Berlin: Klaus Schwarz Verlag, 1983) and Said Amir Arjomand, *The Shadow of God and the Hidden Imam* (Chicago: University of Chicago Press, 1984).

For women, see Gavin Hambly, ed., *Women in the Medieval Islamic World: Power, Patronage and Piety* (New York: St. Martin's Press, 1998); Farah Azari, ed. *Women of Iran: The Conflict with Fundamentalist Islam* (London: Ithaca Press, 1983); Erika Friedl, *The Women of Deh Koh* (Washington: Smithsonian Institution Press, 1989); Haleh Afshar, *Islam and Feminisms: An Iranian Case Study* (New York: St. Martin's, 1998); Ziba Mir-Hossaini, *Islam and Gender: The Religious Debate in Contemporary Iran* (Princeton: Princeton University Press, 1999).

For Indian Shi`ism see Juan R. I. Cole, *Roots of North Indian Shi`ism in Iran and Iraq: Religion and State in Awadh, 1722-1859* (Berkeley and Los Angeles: University of California Press, 1989); Athar Abbas Rizvi, *A Socio-Intellectual History of the Isna `Ashari Shi`is of India*, 2 vols. (New Delhi: Munshiram Manoharlal, 1986); David Pinault, *The Shiites: Ritual and Popular Piety in a Muslim Community* (New York: St. Martin's, 1992); and David Pinault, *Horse of Karbala: Muslim Devotional Life in India* (New York: St. Martin's, 2001);

For Iraq see Tom Nieuwenhuis, *Politics and Society in Early Modern Iraq: Mamluk Pashas, Tribal Shayks and Local Rule Between 1802 and 1831* (The Hague: Martinus Nijhoff, 1982); Hanna Batatu, *The Old Social*

Classes and Revolutionary Movements in Iraq (Princeton, N. J.: Princeton University Press, 1978), Peter Sluglett, *Britain in Iraq 1914-1932* (London: Ithaca/St. Antony's, 1976); Chibli Mallat, *The Renewal of Islamic Law: Muhammad Baqer al-Sadr, Najaf and the Shi`i International* (Cambridge: Cambridge University Press, 1993); Hala Fattah, *The Politics of Regional Trade in Iraq, Arabia, and the Gulf, 1745-1900* (Albany: State University of New York Press, 1997); Meir Litvak, *Shi`ite Scholars of Nineteenth Century Iraq: The `Ulama of Najaf and Karbala'* (Cambridge: Cambridge University Press, 1998); and Yitzhak Nakash, *The Shi`ites of Iraq* (Princeton: Princeton University Press, 1994).

For Lebanon see Fouad Ajami, *The Vanished Imam: Musa al-Sadr and the Shia of Lebanon* (Ithaca, N.Y.: Cornell University Press, 1986); Augustus Richard Norton, *Amal and the Shi`a: Struggle for the Soul of Lebanon* (Austin: University of Texas Press, 1987); Majed Halawi, *A Lebanon Defied: Musa al-Sadr and the Shi`a Community* (Boulder: Westview Press, 1992); and Magnus Ranstorp, *Hizb'allah in Lebanon: The Politics of Western Hostage Crisis* (New York: St. Martin's Press, 1997).

For Shi`ism in ninteenth-century Iran see Hamid Algar, *Religion and State in Iran 1785-1906: The Role of the Ulama in the Qajar Period* (Berkeley and Los Angeles: University of California Press, 1969); Nikki R. Keddie, *The Roots of Revolution* (New Haven, Ct.: Yale University Press, 1981); Mangol Bayat, *Mysticism and Dissent: Socioreligious Thought in Qajar Iran* (Syracuse University Press. 1982); and Nikki R. Keddie, ed., *Religion and Politics in Iran* (New Haven: Yale University Press, 1983); and Abbas Amanat, *Resurrection and Renewal* (Ithaca, NY: Cornell University Press, 1989).

For the twentieth century background to the Islamic Revolution, see Shahrough Akhavi, *Religion and politics in contemporary Iran* (Albany: State University of New York Press, 1980); Michael M. J. Fischer, *Iran: From Religious Dispute to Revolution* (Cambridge, Ma.: Harvard University Press, 1990); Said Amir Arjomand, *The Turban for the Crown* (New York: Oxford University Press, 1988); Roy P. Mottahedeh, *The Mantle of the Prophet: Religion and Politics in Iran* (New York: Simon and Schuster, 1985); Said Amir Arjomand, ed., *Authority and Political Culture in Shi`ism* (Albany: State University of New York Press, 1988); and Hamid Dabashi, *The Theology of Discontent* (New York: New York University Press, 1993) and Mehrzad Boroujerdi, *Iranian Intellectuals and the West: The Tormented Triumph of Nativism (Syracuse, N.Y.: Syracuse University Press, 1996).*

For Iran since 1979, see especially Nikki R. Keddie and Eric Hooglund, eds., *The Iranian Revolution and the Islamic Republic*

(Syracuse, N.Y.: Syracuse University Press, 1986); Reinhold Loeffler, *Islam in Practice: Religious Beliefs in a Persian Village* (Albany: State University of New York Press, 1988); Ervand Abrahamian, *Radical Islam: The Iranian Mojahedin* (London: I.B. Tauris, 1989); Michael M.J. Fischer, *Debating Muslims* (Madison: University of Wisconsin Press, 1990); Ervand Abrahamian, *Khomeinism* (Berkeley and Los Angeles: University of California Press, 1993); Bahman Baktiari, *Parliamentary Politics in Revolutionary Iran* (Gainesville: University of Florida Press, 1996); Ervand Abrahamian, *Tortured Confessions: Prisons and Public Recantations in Modern Iran* (Berkeley: University of California Press, 1999); Vanessa Martin, *Creating an Islamic state : Khomeini and the making of a new Iran* (London ; New York : I.B. Tauris, 2000); Robin Wright, *The Last Great Revolution: Turmoil and Transformation in Iran* (New York: AA Knopf, 2000); Elaine Sciolino, *Persian Mirrors: The Elusive Face of Iran* (New York: Free Press, 2000); and Daniel Brumberg, *Reinventing Khomeini* (Chicago: University of Chicago Press, 2001).

Index

Abdülhamid II, 27, 30
Afghans, 5, 14, 20, 52, 53, 56, 59, 60,
    62, 63, 67, 69 , 70, 101, 185-187
Ahsa, al-. See Hasa, al-.
Ahsa'i, Ahmad al-, 52, 54-55, 57, 85,
    106, 216, 219-220
Ahsa'i, Ibn Abi Jumhur, 36, 55
Ahsa'i, Ibrahim b. Nizar, 34
Akhbaris, 4, 5, 10, 31, 34, 41, 42, 49-57,
    58-77, 79, 84, 96, 184, 192, 193
`Ali b. Abi Talib, 3
Ali, Mrs. Meer Hassan, 139, 151, 152,
    153, 158
`Ali Riza Pasha, 86, 102, 108, 109, 110
AMAL, 181, 182, 187, 243
Amethvi, Amir `Ali, 165, 167-172
`Amili, Baha al-Din, 42, 44, 45, 49
`Amili, al-Hurr, 67
`Amili, Zayn al-Din, 208
Ansari, Sayyid Murtada, 25, 26,
    93, 95
`Askari, Hasan al- 3, 191
As`ad, `Ali Bey, 23, 28
`Ashura', 18, 145, 154, 167, 183
Astarabadi, Muhammad Amin, 41, 53,
    74-76
Astarabadi, Muhammad Yusuf, 92, 117,
    119
Awadh, 6-9, 22, 23, 25, 62, 65, 74, 76-
    77, 78-98, 102, 110, 124-126, 138-
    172, 178, 225
`Ayn Ibl, 176
Ayodhya, 8, 161-172
`Azimabadi, Mirza Hasan, 85, 90
Baalbek, 19, 24, 28, 181, 182
Baath, 179, 180, 187
Babis, 91, 120
Badr, Hasan `Ali al-, 177
Badshah Begam, 144-145, 148, 151, 159
Baghdad, 4, 5, 17, 18, 19, 21, 23, 25, 26,
    27, 30, 102, 70, 72, 73, 75, 79, 82,
    86, 87, 89, 90, 94, 95, 97, 99-122,
    180, 200, 202, 206

Baha'is, 13, 200
Bahrain, 4, 5, 16, 17, 24, 31-57, 59, 67,
    68, 173, 177, 184, 187
Bahrani, Maytham, 33, 36
Bahrani, Sayyid Husayn al-Ghurayfi, 41
Bahrani, Yusuf, 48, 49, 50, 51, 53, 54,
    55, 56, 66-73
Bahu Begam, 82, 143, 226
Baksar, 7, 124
Bani Sadr, Abolhassan, 13, 198, 200,
    209
Banu Jarwan, 33-35
Banu Jabr, 35-37
Bayezid, Sultan, 18
Bazargan, Mehdi, 12, 198, 209
Beirut, 28, 30, 176, 181, 182
Bengal, 6, 43, 62, 63, 64, 65, 72, 124,
    125, 126, 134
Berri, Nabih, 181, 186
Bihbahan, 43, 53, 63, 66, 68, 69, 70, 71,
    72
Bihbahani, Aqa Ahmad, 60, 61, 62, 64,
    65, 123-137, 149
Bihbahani, Muhammad Baqir, 63, 70-75,
    79, 80, 82
Bilad: See Manama
Biladi, `Abd Allah, 47
Biladi, Ahmad, 49
Biladi, Muhammad al-Majid, 49
Bunyad-i Mustaz`afin, 197
Burhan al-Mulk, 6
Bushehr, 63, 201, 202, 203
Carmathians, 4, 32, 33, 56
Comte, Auguste, 174, 190
Damascus, 9, 19, 21, 23, 109, 176
Da`wa, al-, 179, 180
Demography, 3, 11, 59, 100,
    163, 181, 201
Dirazi, Sulayman, 47, 48, 51
Druze, 17, 19, 20, 23, 28, 181, 182
East India Company, British, 53, 82,
    83, 84, 86, 97, 125, 126, 130, 143,
    202
Faisal, King, 175-176
Faizabad: See Ayodhya

Ghazi al-Din Haydar, Shah, 81-84, 94, 144
Ghulam Husayn, Shah, 163-164
Golconda, 6, 20, 45
Guardianship Council, 12, 14, 188, 210
Harfush, 19, 24, 28
Hamd Bey, 23
Hasa, al-, 4, 5, 17, 19, 20, 24, 27, 29, 31-57, 177-178, 183
Hasan Pasha, 19, 59, 79
Hazaras, 14, 186, 109
Hijaz, 18, 19, 21, 38, 154
Hindus, 6, 7, 8, 61, 65, 84, 97, 124, 125, 132, 143, 145, 146, 151, 155, 156, 159, 161-172, 190
Hizbullah, 182-183, 186
Hizb-i Vahdat, 14, 186, 187
Hostage crisis, 13, 14
Hurmuz, 32, 33, 35-39, 43, 44, 45, 56, 212
Husayn, Imam, 16, 18, 21, 26, 79, 81, 86, 87, 92, 101, 102, 108, 110, 112, 113,117, 118, 144, 145, 148, 151, 153, 154, 156, 158, 159, 167, 170, 178, 183
Hussein, Saddam, 13, 180, 186, 200, 209
Hyderabad, 6, 45, 94, 125, 126, 129, 131
India, 5-9, 20, 22, 23, 25, 45, 61, 62, 63, 65, 69, 72, 74-76, 78-98, 123-137, 138-160, 161-172, 178-179, 184, 186, 187, 190-191, 196, 197, 203////
Iran, 2-15, 17-20, 22, 23, 24, 25, 27, 29, 31, 35, 36, 38, 39-52, 55, 56, 58-77, 78, 79, 80, 81, 85, 89, 92, 95-97, 99-121, 124-127, 129, 130, 134, 138, 139, 143, 149, 150, 151, 171, 173, 174, 175, 176, 178-181, 183-186, 188-210
Iraq, 173-176, 179-180, 187, 192, 199, 200, 201, 202, 203, 206, 209 (see also Baghdad)
`Irfan, al-, 176

Isfahan, 20, 25, 40, 41, 42, 44, 48, 49, 50, 53, 59, 60-70, 72, 73, 77, 92, 93, 119, 149, 150, 178, 197
Isfahani, Mirza Abu Talib Khan, 126-129, 131-134, 136, 150
Islamic Revolution, 10-13, 174, 183, 186, 196, 199, 207
Isma`il, Shah, 39,
Ismailis, 4, 6, 24, 44, 45, 47, 51, 58
Jabal `Amil, 6, 17, 19-20, 22-24, 28, 29, 30, 39, 40, 42, 45, 176-177
Jabri, Sayf b. Zamil al-, 35
Jazzar, Ahmad Pasha al-, 23, 24
Jidd-Hafsi, S. Majid al-, 44
Karaki, `Ali al-, 39-42, 67
Karbala, 9, 16, 17, 20, 21, 23, 25, 26, 29, 52, 53, 56, 60, 62-65, 68, 70-74, 75, 78-98, 99-122, 143, 144, 149, 154, 157, 158, 161, 167, 175, 180, 200
Khamenei, Ali, 13, 14, 183, 194, 208
Khatami, Muhammad, 14, 15, 204, 206, 209, 210
Khatunabadi, Muhammad Salih, 61, 62
Khomeini, Ruhollah, 10, 12-14, 129, 138, 173, 180, 185, 186, 189, 190, 193, 194, 198, 200, 201, 202, 203, 204, 206, 209
Kuwait, 73, 180
Lebanon, 173, 174, 175, 176-177, 179, 181-183, 186, 187, 202 (see also Jabal `Amil)
Lucknow, 7-9, 65, 76, 78-98, 124, 126, 129, 138-160, 161-172, 178, 186
Mahdi: See Twelfth Imam
Mahmud II, Sultan, 23, 26, 108
Mahuzi, Muhammad, 47, 49
Mahuzi, Sulayman, 47, 49, 67
Majlisi, Muhammad Baqir, 41, 60-66, 67, 68, 71
Majlisi, Muhammad Taqi, 60, 61, 68, 76
Manama (Bilad al-Qadim), 1, 46, 48, 50, 51, 54, 56, 57
Maqabi, Muhammad, 46, 47-48, 49, 51, 54
Mazandarani, Muhammad Salih, 61, 62, 63
Mazandarani, Amina, 61

Mecca, 19, 21, 36, 38, 40, 41, 71, 85, 194
Medina, 19, 21
Midhat Pasha, 27
Mongols, 33
Mubarak Mahall (1), 84
Mubarak Mahall (2), 147-148, 159
Muflih b. Hasan, 35, 36, 37, 42
Mughals, 6, 7, 8, 61, 62, 83, 124, 125, 143
Muhajirani, Ayatollah Ata'u'llah, 202
Muhammad Reza Shah, 9, 11-13, 195, 196, 199, 201-202, 203, 205
Muhammad Shah, Qajar, 25, 85, 119, 235
Muharram, 118, 145, 153, 154, 155, 156, 157, 158, 167, 176, 185
Mujahidin-i Khalq, 13, 200, 203, 204, 209
Muqrin, 37-38
Murshidabad, 62, 63, 64, 65
Musaddiq, Muhammad, 9, 12
Musawi, S. `Abd al-Ra'uf, 45-46, 47
Musharraf, Pervez, 187
Nabatiya, 21
Nadir Shah, 7, 52, 58, 59, 60, 62, 64, 68, 69-70
Najaf, 1, 17, 20, 25, 26, 27, 36, 52, 62, 63, 64, 65, 67, 68, 70, 71, 73, 75, 78-98, 101, 115, 116, 120, 175, 180, 201
Najafi, Ja`far, 72, 74, 75
Najafi, Muhammad Hasan, 87, 88, 90, 92, 93
Najib Pasha, 26, 87, 109-113, 115, 117-119, 122
Nasirabadi, Sayyid Dildar `Ali, 74-77, 79, 82
Nasirabadi, Sayyid Husayn, 88, 91-93, 142, 156, 168, 170
Nasirabadi, Sayyid Muhammad, 84, 87, 90, 93, 140, 141, 142, 144, 146, 156, 161, 162, 167, 168, 171
Nasir al-Din Haydar, Shah, 82, 145
Nationalism, 9, 16, 27, 174, 175, 178, 179, 182
Nishapuris, 6, 79, 90, 153, 168

Nuclear program, in Iran, 202-204
Oil: See petroleum
Oman, 4, 37, 53
Oudh: See Awadh
Oudh Bequest, 84-89, 90, 94-97
Pahlevi, 2, 9, 10, 12, 173, 175, 178, 196, 197, 204, 206, 210, 211
Pakistan, 14, 173, 178-179, 184-186
Pashazade, Ibn Kamal, 18
Persian, 4, 5-6, 7, 8, 25, 85, 91, 101, 124-127, 133-136, 151, 155, 157, 162, 179, 190, 206
Petroleum, 11, 31, 178, 196, 197, 198, 199, 201, 202, 208
Portuguese, 4, 31, 37-42, 43, 44, 46, 56, 208, 213
Putin, Vladimir, 204
Qadami, `Ali, 46-47, 49, 50
Qadami, Ja`far, 51
Qaida, al-, 14, 187
Qaramita: See Carmathians
Qaramani, Uways al-, 19
Qatif, 31-38, 40, 44, 45, 52, 56, 67, 177
Qatifi, Ibrahim al-, 40-41
Qizilbash, 4, 7, 17-18, 20, 43, 48, 49, 69, 212
Qazvini, Ibrahim, 85-87, 89, 90, 91, 92, 106, 113
Rafsanjani, `Ali Akbar Hashimi, 13, 14, 200, 201, 202, 203, 206, 209, 211
Rashti, Sayyid Kazim, 85, 106, 110-114, 115, 117, 118, 119-120
Reza Shah, 9, 11, 175, 196
Rusva, Mirza Muhammad Hadi, 156-158
Ruwaysi, Sh. Muhammad, 45, 47
Sadr, Muhammad Baqir, 10
Sadr, Musa al-, 10, 181
Safavids, 3-5, 6, 17-20, 29, 38, 39-53, 55, 56, 57, 58, 59, 60, 63, 65-67, 78, 100, 101, 193
Samahiji, `Abd Allah, 53
Saudis, 15, 29, 32, 53, 171,173, 175, 177, 178, 179, 183, 184, 186, 187, 198, 207
Selim I, Sultan, 18
Shafti, Muhammad Baqir, 92,93, 119

Shahristani, Muhammad Mihdi, 68, 72, 82
Shaykhis, 52, 84-85, 90, 91, 96, 106, 110, 111, 113, 114, 115, 119, 120, 220-221
Shiraz, 9, 44, 48, 49, 50, 53, 59, 63, 67, 72, 74, 104, 120, 121
Shushtari, `Abd al-Latif, 123-137
Sidon, 4, 17, 20, 175, 176
Sipah-i Sahaba, 14, 186, 187
Slavery, 140, 142, 143, 153
Soroush, `Abd al-Karim, 205, 207, 209
Sultan Husayn, Shah, 49, 53, 59, 61
Sunnis, 2, 3, 4, 5, 6, 7, 8, 10, 14, 16-30, 31-57, 59, 60, 61, 62 69, 70, 73, 78, 79, 81, 84, 91, 92, 97, 99-122, 124, 125, 132, 143, 145, 150, 161-172, 173-188, 191, 195
Tabataba'i, Sayyid `Ali, 71, 73, 75, 80
Tabataba'i, Sayyid `Ali Naqi, 91, 95
Tabataba'i, Sayyid Mihdi, 21
Tabataba'i, Sayyid Muhammad, 63, 68
Tabataba'i, Sayyid Muhammad Mihdi, 68, 71, 73, 76
Taqiyya, 19, 21, 40, 69, 118
Tahmasp, Shah, 18, 39, 40
Taliban, 14, 15, 186, 187
Tanzimat, 5, 29, 30
Thawra Township, 180
Twelfth Imam, 10, 33, 34, 40, 66, 86, 93, 100, 105, 106, 114, 119, 120, 144, 195
Tyre, 4, 9, 17, 23, 24
Urdu, 1, 7, 8, 9, 138, 139, 148, 151, 152, 155, 157, 162, 184
Usulis, 4, 5, 10, 21, 26, 31, 34, 35, 37, 39, 40-42, 45, 46, 49-54, 55-57, 58-77, 79-82, 84-86, 90, 92, 96, 97, 106, 113, 119, 120, 129, 143, 163, 171, 193-196
Vajid `Ali Shah, 91, 146-148, 159, 163, 164, 165, 167, 168, 169, 171
Wahhabis, 24, 27, 29, 53, 55, 65, 81, 107, 171, 175, 177, 184
Za`farani, Ibrahim, 104, 105, 106, 108, 111, 112, 114, 116, 117, 119
Zia ul-Haqq, 185

Zill al-Sultan, 111, 112, 113, 117